New Zealand Society
A Sociological Introduction

Second Edition

Diane Ferrel
194 Heads Rd
Wanganui.   3447073

The front cover painting, 'Buzzy Bee Over The Beehive' 1984 is reproduced with the kind permission of George Baloghy

New Zealand Society
A Sociological Introduction

Second Edition

Paul Spoonley
David Pearson
Ian Shirley

Dunmore Press

©1994 Paul Spoonley, David Pearson, Ian Shirley
©1994 The Dunmore Press Limited

First edition published in 1990

Second edition published in 1994
by
The Dunmore Press Limited
P.O.Box 5115
Palmertson North
New Zealand

Australian Supplier:
Nyroca Press
P.O. Box 90, Hawksburn
Victoria 3142
Phone & Fax (03) 562 6272

ISBN 0 86469 188 2

Text:Times 9.8/11.5
Page Layout: June Mercer
Printer: The Dunmore Printing Company Ltd,
Palmerston North

Copyright. No part of this book may be reproduced without written permission except in the case of brief quotations embodied in critical articles and reviews.

Contents

Introduction		Paul Spoonley, David Pearson and Ian Shirley	7
1.	Family	David Swain	11
2.	Community	David Pearson	26
3.	Urban	David Thorns	39
4.	Rural	Ian Carter	55
5.	Class	Chris Wilkes	66
6.	Racism and Ethnicity	Paul Spoonley	81
7.	Gender	Rosemary Du Plessis	98
8.	State	Nicola Armstrong	113
9.	Social Policy	Ian Shirley	130
10.	Health	Geoff Fougere	146
11.	Education	Roy Nash	161
12.	Politics	Jack Vowles	177
13.	Mass Media	Brennon Wood and Steve Maharey	193
14.	Crime, Deviance and Punishment	John Pratt	213
15.	Work	Terry Austrin	237
16.	Leisure and Recreation	Bob Gidlow, Harvey Perkins, Grant Cushman and Clare Simpson	253
17.	Art and Ideology	Peter Beatson	271
18.	Religion	Michael Hill	292
19.	Population	Arvind Zodgekar	308
List of Contributors			325
Bibliography			329
Index			377

CONTENTS

Introduction

Paul Spoonley, David Pearson and Ian Shirley

Sociologists seek to identify and explain the social relations which form the basis of every society. Individuals and groups will always bring their own *unique* characteristics to any social situation but they live out their lives within a shared framework of *social* institutions and *cultural* conventions. It is these institutions and conventions which provide the raw material for the sociologist, who must then develop a convincing explanation of how they constitute the basis of a society. It is not an easy task because so few of us think sociologically. Our commonsense explanations of social phenomena tend to be couched in individualistic terms. We see failure or success as the product of a specific background. We also tend to rely on established social myths and beliefs, which is why they are called 'commonsense'. They are accepted and usually unexamined explanations of the social world.

Sociology is an uncomfortable discipline for many because of two aspects. First, its focus is on the social or shared nature of society and it requires new skills or a 'sociological imagination' for those who are used to thinking in terms of individual motivations or behaviour. Sociology poses different questions and answers to those asked by politicians, planners or the apocryphal person in the street. For example, in opposition to those who would argue that economic success or failure is a product of an individual's motives, competitiveness or skills, the sociologist would point to the way in which socially important characteristics and structures, such as gender, ethnicity or class, limit or encourage particular outcomes. Such considerations are not popular in some quarters, but despite this unpopularity, sociological explanations are now much more accepted than in the early 1980s, particularly given the effects of recent economic and social changes.

Second, sociology is by nature a critical discipline. Little is taken at face value, and there is a constant questioning of the way in which societies operate and of existing explanations for social behaviour. Sociology frequently contradicts those things we 'take for granted' and provides an alternative understanding of what is happening. For those comfortable with the status quo, this is an unsettling exercise which requires them to rethink their values, assumptions and cherished beliefs. At the same time, the insights generated by sociology make it an exciting discipline which is capable of providing new skills and understandings. This book combines an introduction to sociological thinking with an analysis of New Zealand society.

Contributors were asked to provide a relatively brief introduction to the area of their expertise and then apply that to New Zealand. The basic approach was derived from an earlier publication, *New Zealand: Sociological Perspectives,* which was published in 1982. This proved to be a successful book. But sociology in New Zealand has developed enormously since the early 1980s and one of the most exciting features has been the attempt to translate theories, concepts and methods from their European or North American origins to a New Zealand context. New Zealand, by virtue of its history and other social considerations, is unique and thus requires a sociology which is sensitive to local issues and debates. Although it has some way to go, sociology is now much better placed to analyse circumstances pertaining in New Zealand. This development has been encouraged by the growth of sociology as a discipline and by the new generations of sociologists who are no longer confined to universities. Sociology is alive and well in polytechnics and secondary schools, in local authorities and government departments, in private enterprise and community organisations. It has to be acknowledged that there are facets of sociology and New Zealand society which have not been included here, but the present book is much more inclusive and New Zealand-oriented than its predecessor.

This does not exempt the previous edition – or this one – from the criticism that more could be done by way of editorial intervention or by opting for a different way of organising the book. Nick Perry (1991) offers a critique of the first edition and highlights the exigencies and limitations of publishing texts in a small society.

> There is at once a paucity of text and a limited space in which they might move. A given text may therefore come to effectively occupy all of its designated site, irrespective of whether that text is good, bad or indifferent. Under such conditions, recourse to the type of criticism which presupposes a plurality of texts would seem to be hopelessly idealist and anachronistic, since what is at issue is not so much what to read as how to read. What unites the critic with other readers is the problem of how to make something coherent out of the *bricolage* which results from the pragmatic collaboration of producers who are not cognitively integrated and whose competence varies markedly (Perry, 1991: 399).

It is to be hoped that the burgeoning although still relatively small community of sociologists – and the market for sociological texts – will encourage a range of books that might then overcome some of the concerns identified by Perry. For the moment, this book has sought to improve on its predecessor.

The earlier book did have some obvious gaps and this book has been able to rectify some of these. It was anomalous that in a publication that claimed to provide a relatively complete introduction to New Zealand society, there should be no chapter which dealt with rural sociology. Ian Carter remedies this, although, as he makes abundantly clear, rural sociology is underdeveloped in this country. Equally anomalous was the absence of a chapter which explored the issues of sport and leisure in New Zealand. A group at Lincoln University provides an exciting and important chapter in this area and indicates where further work needs to be done. Finally, Brennon Wood and Steve Maharey discuss the way in which the media influence social relationships and understandings. Given the importance of the media to a society reliant on communications technology, the sociology of the media is rightly beginning to take its place as a central area of sociological interest.

The first chapters in the book concern themselves with key institutions: the family and community, both urban and rural. They are followed by chapters which deal with the structural inequalities that arise from class, racism and ethnicity, and gender. These are central concerns of sociology and are addressed to some degree in all chapters. The book then turns to the state and matters of social policy and social service delivery in such areas as health and education. Finally, the last section of the book includes chapters which focus on ideology and its reproduction in forums as various as the arts and religion. The last chapter rounds off the book by exploring the issues of population within a New Zealand context.

1 Family

David Swain

Families and family life are too close to home for academic comfort. Family sociologists steer a precarious course between nitpicking and heresy (Swain, 1984). The propinquity theory of mate selection illustrates the former: the finding that one is likely to marry the person next door does seem a touch trivial, at least until we understand the 'social ecology' of our cities and the social (parental) control of mating. The proposition that we are in greatest danger of violence and death when we are at home with our nearest and dearest illustrates the latter. As people living our everyday lives and as family sociologists, we know at once too much (personal experience can colour and even shape our analysis) and not enough (we have yet to build comprehensive explanatory theories of family life) about our subject.

A sound understanding of families and family life requires a knowledge of several disciplines related to sociology, such as social anthropology, demography, social psychology, women's studies and history. This chapter focuses on family sociology (kinship is covered in the previous edition; see James, 1982). The very few family sociologists in Aotearoa/New Zealand share a perspective characterised by Peter Berger (1966: Chapter 2) as the four 'motifs of the sociological consciousness'. These motifs are scepticism or 'debunking', unrespectability, relativisation, and cosmopolitanism, and they all underlie this chapter.

Scepticism or the 'unmasking tendency' has a methodological basis in sociology's 'built-in procedure of looking for levels of reality other than those given in the official interpretations of society' (Berger, 1966: 51). The finding that marriage is good for men but a health hazard for women (Bernard, 1973), which rather contrasts with folk wisdom on the subject, illustrates the power of the debunking motif.

The unrespectability motif is illustrated by the parallels between the stark transactions of prostitution and exchange analyses of marriage (Hamilton, 1909; 1981). Relativisation – the acknowledgement that norms and indeed, all the ways in which we make sense of the social world, vary with time and place – is well-illustrated by cross-cultural variations in the definition of 'normal' marriage (polygamy, polygyny, polyandry, group marriage) with our supposed pattern of monogamy being better understood as serial polygamy.

In the light of this sociological consciousness, we soon recognise that our very definitions of 'the family' are fraught with problems (Cameron, 1985; Gilling, 1988). They are culture-bound, saturated with partisan values. Indeed, the use of 'the' itself implies that there exists some 'normal', 'typical' or 'average' family, either statistically or normatively. The variations from this 'normal' family are then the '[adjectival term] families', such as 'the single parent family', 'the reconstituted [or blended] family', 'the childless family', 'the childfree family' (note the difference between the last two), and so on.

In our everyday usage, 'the family' seems to mean to contemporary middle class Pakeha – the dominant majority – 'the nuclear family' with a male breadwinner, a female caretaker, and (ideally) two children (one of each sex, the boy being firstborn). This kind of family often seems to be regarded as 'normal'. It is not normal – cross-culturally, historically, or even statistically – in our pluralistic society but it suits a variety of political and religious commentators to assume or argue that it is.

Many taken-for-granted assumptions – in social policy as in everyday life – about families and family life are misleading or wrong. Sexual intercourse, conception, pregnancy, childbirth and breastfeeding, and even the nurture of the young, may be 'natural', but their context, regulation and practice are socially and culturally shaped. Indeed, much of our family life has been invented.

Marriage, it has been argued, was a fortuitous invention which improved our ancestors' survival chances at a time when they were threatened by a change in the weather (Reynolds, 1968; Sprey, 1971-2). Children and childhood, as Pakeha know them, were invented in Europe in the late middle ages (Aries, 1960). Grandparenthood was a nineteenth century invention (Laslett, 1965), and teenagers were invented within living memory. These 'natural' family phenomena were and are social and cultural artefacts.

Contrary to popular (and politicians') beliefs, the quality of family life in urban industrial societies (including New Zealand) has been steadily improving for the last century or more, and is still improving. The wretched experience of women and children in the nineteenth century (Eldred-Grigg, 1984) has been forgotten. And yet the home, not the street, is still the most dangerous place there is for women and children. The broadly sociological perspective on families and family life yields some surprises when we focus our attention close to home.

It is not easy to examine families and family life on the basis of these four motifs of the sociological consciousness. Love and marriage, birth and death, passion and pain – the personal relevance of family sociology can be immediate, challenging, difficult. Family sociologists draw upon various theoretical perspectives to help make sense of family life, to guide research, to suggest interpretations of the data. In this chapter I introduce some of the theoretical perspectives which are most helpful and relevant to Aotearoa/New Zealand. I also illustrate the practice of family sociology by describing some of what we think we know about families and family life here. However, you should be warned that the rigorous application of the sociological consciousness to families and family life can be both insightful and disturbing.

Theory and Family Sociology

There is no shortage of material on families and family life. For example, the University of Waikato on-line library catalogue lists over seven hundred books and reports coded with the keywords 'family' and 'families' published in the 1980s. New Zealand Social Research Abstracts listed 49 entries in 1985 and 102 in 1986 under keywords such as 'family' and 'life cycle'.

The problems lie in asking the right research questions and in interpreting the data. What do we know about marriage? How do we break this topic down into more manageable elements such as 'mate selection' and 'conjugal roles' and 'post-parental interaction patterns'? How do we build reliable findings, based on replicating and extending previous research, when family researchers make different assumptions, use different concepts, come to different conclusions? How do we 'make sense' of the data? We begin to do so by paying careful attention to family sociologists' theoretical perspectives and conceptual frameworks.

The term 'theoretical perspectives' is used in this chapter to refer to the various major sets of assumptions, concepts and dispositions which have been identified as underpinning sociologists' perceptions and explanations of families and family life. The term 'conceptual frameworks' is used to refer to the more specific sets of inter-related and inter-defined concepts used within each theoretical perspective to describe, discuss and analyse family data. Much of the literature offers little or no explicit attention to theoretical perspectives or even conceptual frameworks. Nevertheless, they are crucial, and if we are not told what preconceptions a family researcher is using we must work this out for ourselves.

Holman and Burr (1980) also refer to 'middle-range theories' which are explanations of family behaviour in specific substantive areas, such as 'mate selection' or 'conjugal power' (where the theories explaining this behaviour are quite complex and complete), and 'sibling behaviour' or 'intergenerational continuities' (where they are not). Some family sociologists in the 1970s believed that such 'middle-range theories' could be assembled into 'grand theory' or a 'general theory of family'. Holman and Burr (1980) argue that such 'general theory' is impossible and unnecessary. It is impossible because family life is so complex; unnecessary because 'theory construction' will continue to yield 'middle-range theories' which will gradually account for a greater and greater proportion of the family field of study.

As Goethe pointed out many years ago: 'We see what we look for, and we look for what we know' (quoted in Swain, 1984). What 'we know' is theoretical perspectives and conceptual frameworks; our 'looking' is the topics we choose and the research questions we pose; what we 'see' is our findings. Consider the different implications of the terms 'childless' and 'childfree'. Or, in the study of first parenthood (Swain, 1978; 1985), consider how some researchers have used a symbolic interaction conceptual framework (in which they have emphasised 'homeostasis' or equilibrium) and some have used a developmental framework (which emphasises developmental transitions and change). The former researchers found that new parents experienced a crisis, the latter found that they did not!

A structural-functional perspective is fundamentally different from a Marxist perspective – different topics are regarded as important, different assumptions are made, different concepts are used, different conclusions are drawn. Phenomenologists and positivists practise very different kinds of family sociology. And so on.

The considerable family sociology empirical research effort published in the 1950s and 1960s was largely atheoretical. However, efforts to organise a user-friendly bibliography of family studies prompted sociologists to search out ('discover') the implicit theoretical perspectives and conceptual frameworks underlying empirical research. This made it possible to work out what studies could be combined and what studies – although apparently on the same topic – were incompatible. It also made clearer the 'bias' implicit in every researcher's approach to family study.

Once theoretical perspectives and conceptual frameworks had been 'discovered' and researchers had begun to identify the ones they used, it became clear that there are several competing theoretical perspectives in the family field. This is not necessarily undesirable, of course, because it is unlikely that any one perspective has all the answers – or even all the interesting questions! Once these perspectives and frameworks were discovered, sociologists could be aware (beware) of their influence on research, and could also further develop them.

Selected Perspectives

There are quite a variety of theoretical perspectives available to would-be family sociologists, including (in alphabetical order): balance theory, behaviourism, conflict theory, developmental approach, ecosystems approach, exchange theory, feminist perspective, field theory, game theory, institutional approach, learning theories, Marxist analysis, phenomenological approach, psychoanalytical theory, situational approach, structural-functionalism, symbolic interactionism, systems theory and transactional analysis. The following are the more important ones.

Structural-functionalism

The ideas central to the structural-functional perspective date back to Emile Durkheim, have been explicated by Talcott Parsons and Robert Merton, and are thus a strong link with mainstream sociology. Within this perspective, all human societies are understood to have the same basic 'functional prerequisites' which must be met if they are to survive, although there is no general agreement on a definitive formulation of these prerequisites (Merton, 1957).

'The family' is identified as a significant 'structure' within society, performing certain essential 'functions' – such as sexual reproduction and primary socialisation – which contribute to the well-being and continuance of society (Pitts, 1964; McIntyre, 1966). Within this approach, certain structures (e.g. the nuclear family) are seen as consistent with particular macrosociological features of society (e.g. urbanism and industrialism)(Goode, 1963).

The microsociological – the internal dynamics of family life – are often neglected in this approach. There also tends to be an implicit conservative assumption in the use of this approach, that existing structural arrangements (e.g. the structured inequity in the allocation of domestic and employment roles between men and women) are by definition necessary and thus desirable for the well-being and even the survival of society.

This approach was used most extensively in the 1950s and 1960s in theoretical discussions and in macrosociological overviews of families and society. It also underlies some microsociological studies of family members' interactions and intrafamilial processes such as primary socialisation. It has not been so widely used in the late 1980s, but its conservative assumptions linger on in politicians' and commentators' views of families.

Symbolic Interactionism

This perspective is also strongly linked to mainstream sociology and has been used in family sociology since the 1920s. It has underpinned a large number of empirical studies (Burr *et al.*, 1979). In contrast to the structural-functional approach with its focus on the links between families and the wider society, the symbolic interaction perspective centres on the interpersonal dynamics within families, and family members' perceptions and interpretations of these dynamics. A family is, in this view, defined by its 'members' interaction with one another. Roles are learned, re-negotiated, modified; norms are enforced or changed; processes such as socialisation and decision-making are constant and ongoing.

This approach has its limitations too. The major concepts in this approach are not entirely clear, and are difficult to operationalise. Both the wider society outside the family and the psychological processes within the individual receive limited attention. Perhaps most crucially, this approach necessarily deals with short periods of time (Rodgers, 1973). Nevertheless, those researchers and scholars using it have generated some considerable insights into family interactions.

Developmental

This approach has long been used (as in William Shakespeare's 'seven ages of man'), and is the only major approach unique to the family field in sociology, and the only one to have been developed through deliberate concept explication and theory-building – sometimes in advance of empirical inquiry (Holman and Burr, 1980; Swain, 1984). It is also the most 'open' of the theoretical perspectives in family sociology, incorporating other concepts and theory fragments fairly readily (Broderick, 1971).

Individuals and families are seen as having inherent patterns of development which can be conceived and discussed in terms of 'stages' or 'phases' making up a 'family life cycle' or 'family career'. Transitions between phases or stages occur as developmental tasks (which are cumulative) are accomplished. Families are organised in terms of roles and positions underpinned by norms. At developmental transitions, old roles are relinquished and new roles are undertaken. A number of concepts, such as role clarity and role compatibility, are used to account for the ease or otherwise with which role transitions are accomplished. Families' boundaries are seen as 'semi-closed' – there are transactions with other social structures and systems, mediated through 'conjunctive roles' such as employee-breadwinner.

The limitations of this approach are a lack of cross-cultural applicability of its concepts to non-Western societies/cultures, and a limited relevance of its 'typical' family pattern in our increasingly diverse and pluralistic urban industrial societies.

Conflict/Marxist Perspective

This theoretical perspective has both microsocial and macrosocial aspects. The microsocial focuses on conflict and power within families, especially 'normal' conflict at times of transition (LaRossa, 1977) and structured inequities in conjugal power and decision-making (Bernard, 1973). Most theoretical perspectives assume that conflict is 'dysfunctional' or otherwise undesirable. This approach regards conflict as 'normal' in two senses: it occurs frequently and even routinely, and it cannot be avoided in a world in which needs, wants and goals may differ and resources are limited. Conflict, these theorists argue, can also have positive outcomes.

The macrosocial aspect derives from the work of Karl Marx and Friedrich Engels, much reinterpreted and developed, in emphasising that families perpetuate the class structure and hence class conflict, and the social dominance of males over females. Other social institutions are regarded by sociologists of this persuasion as sharing in this role, such as the school system.

Given that most theoretical perspectives in family sociology tend to assume (and some emphasise) peaceful co-operation, this perspective is a valuable alternative. Sociologists using this approach do not condone violence and inequality; they do regard conflict as 'normal' and thus conflict-resolution as interesting and worthwhile for study.

Feminist Perspective

Feminism is a personal value system and practice, a political philosophy and movement, and a theoretical perspective and intellectual challenge. The personal component must be the oldest; the political component dates back at least to the 'first wave' in Europe in the 1840s (although the 'second wave' in the 1960s is more salient for most observers). Feminist sociology has begun to transform family sociology by challenging its theoretical assumptions and concepts (Bart, 1971), its methodology (Oakley, 1981), and its data and analysis (Bernard, 1973). Feminism and feminists vary in some of their assumptions, concepts and analyses of society (Novitz, 1978; Macionis, 1987: 338-9), but the central ideas are shared.

Feminism – like sociology – involves an unconventional view of ourselves and our society. Feminists – like sociologists – link personal experience and social analysis. Feminism – like sociology – is a critical pursuit, challenging conventional assumptions and ideas, including those of the majority of family sociologists of the 1970s and earlier. Families are powerful institutions for sustaining a particular status quo or changing it; families are the arena for much conflict, violence and oppression, and one focus for hope of a transformed future. Thus, feminist family sociology is of considerable importance. But feminism is also a commitment to 'the reintegration of humanity' (French, 1985:443), offering 'a process of resocialisation in which all human beings have the opportunity to develop and express the full range of their human potential' (Macionis, 1987: 337).

Phenomenological Approach

The phenomenological perspective is another one which challenges a shared feature of most of the other approaches, in this case, that they mostly centre on the researcher's chosen 'construction' of the social world (which may be structural-functional, symbolic interactionist, etc.). The phenomenological approach centres on the analysis and description of everyday life, focusing on the meanings attributed by people to everyday life as they 'make sense of' or 'construct' their social world.

In family sociology, phenomenologists place the ordinary individual's own 'construction' of the social world at the centre of attention. People in families make sense of them for their own purposes; they have to reach some sort of precarious and provisional agreement on the nature of their family in order to live in it. In this approach, family sociologists listen to what people say about their families, recording their own words, and strive to understand how it is for them without imposing the sociologists' own assumptions, concepts, categories and sense.

Such an approach has been criticised as dealing with trivial topics, being limited to description, having prompted very little empirical inquiry, and neglecting the idea of social structure (Abercrombie, Hill and Turner, 1984: 158). However, this perspective is part of a broader critique of positivist methods in sociology, and as such serves to remind sociologists that when they impose their theoretical perspectives and conceptual frameworks on families and family life they risk selecting and distorting the phenomena they study.

Theoretical Perspectives for Aotearoa/New Zealand

There are three theoretical perspectives which are particularly relevant for family research and analysis in Aotearoa/New Zealand: developmental, feminist, and phenomenological. Each has its uses; each has its limitations.

Developmental

This perspective and its key concepts (such as the family life cycle or career, role transitions, developmental tasks) has a good 'fit' with the ways in which people working in government departments and many community agencies view families. Research data organised in these terms will 'make sense' to them. Policy recommendations phrased in these terms are more likely to be adopted than those based on (say) Marxist or even feminist perspectives.

The New Zealand Planning Council's Social Monitoring Group used a variant of this approach, the 'life event' framework (New Zealand Planning Council, 1985: 12), to present useful information in their *From Birth To Death* report, and updated this with a more family-oriented 'life cycle' framework in their *From Birth To Death II* (1989). However, they presented separate analyses in terms of gender and ethnicity because these 'significantly affect the lives and opportunities of particular individuals [and] their families (New Zealand Planning Council, 1989:1). A different theoretical perspective – say feminist or Marxist – would probably have been more insightful on this matter, but less influential at senior government levels. Why?

There are some problems with the developmental conceptual framework; these were barely acknowledged in these reports (New Zealand Planning Council, 1985: 12; New Zealand Planning Council, 1989: 1). The phases (or 'stages') are not 'real', they are analytical concepts and thus one should ask whether they are useful, not whether they are true. Their utility will depend on their proposed use, and the emphasis on the firstborn child leads to some difficulties (e.g. the point at which the youngest child starts school is often a significant event, at least in Aotearoa/New Zealand, but is not captured as a transition). There is also the difficulty of including statistically or culturally non-normative families in such schemes, e.g. child-free couples, those who are single by choice, and those who 'leave' the supposedly normative sequence (e.g. due to marital breakdown). Such family types have for some time constituted a substantial proportion of all households in New Zealand (Swain, 1978b). The developmental framework has been developed largely by American family sociologists who mostly research white American middle class families, so there are important questions about the framework's broader applicability to Aotearoa/New Zealand. Finally, there are the various practical problems of research, such as the operationalisation of these concepts.

Feminist Perspectives

It is now 'essential for [a male] ... academic to be aware of the continued feminist critique and research and to make himself aware of the implications of that for his own practices in all aspects of his life' (Morgan, 1985: 2). It may also now be the case that 'it is probably impossible, and certainly impolitic, for a male academic to write about feminism'. However, it is also essential in writing about family sociology in Aotearoa/New Zealand to acknowledge the importance of a feminist theoretical perspective in family sociology, for without it we cannot understand much of the change we are experiencing in family life and in the policy, legislation and practice which impinge on it.

The feminist critique of sociology (and not just family sociology) has not been confined to theory, but has addressed 'the main assumptions that have guided sociological research and theorising, ... the male-dominated institutions within which such work was and continues to be carried out, and ... the relationships of the men in these institutions with their colleagues, with their wives and lovers, and with the secretaries and interviewers who have served male sociologists' (Morgan, 1985:218).

Family sociology, in this critique, has concentrated on an uncritical study of a few types of relationships 'to the exclusion of wider considerations of history and social structure' (Morgan, 1985: 218). The family model most widely used has been relatively benign, and even where less benevolent aspects have been admitted, this has been against a background assumption of 'a more or less universal set of needs which are or should be met by the family' (Morgan, 1985: 218). The patriarchal character of sociology has not only rendered women and their interests invisible in the practice of sociology, it has also sustained and legitimated male domination.

This has important implications. A feminist critique is not simply concerned with details, with specific errors and omissions. It is necessary to consider the assumptions made by patriarchal sociologists about theorising (see Morgan, 1985: 7-13 for a critique) and methodology (see Oakley, 1981 and 1983 for a critique). This feminist critique relates back to the first paragraph of this chapter. It is argued that feminist theory 'is fundamentally experiential' (Keohane *et al.*, 1982: vii) and thus feminist writers on methodology criticise the conventional disdain for personal experience in scholarly/academic writing. For feminists, the personal is not only political, it can also be scholarly.

Phenomenology

The phenomenological approach has yet to be realised in extensive studies of families and family life. It is, rather, 'a set of potentialities and issues rather than fully realised projects' (Morgan, 1985: 183). It has problems. There is a relative lack of attention to social structural and historical factors. Phenomenological methodology is more easily described than conducted. Nevertheless, '[the] ... strengths of the phenomenological orientation have a particular relevance in the study of the family and related matters since it is here that so much is taken for granted and ... it is here where so many taken-for-granted assumptions are carried over into sociological models and applied analysis and practice ...' (Morgan, 1985: 207). A phenomenological disposition and practice is important because it improves the chances that family sociologists will hear the experience of the oppressed, disadvantaged and powerless.

Family Change and Diversity in Aotearoa/New Zealand

Change has always characterised family life. Here and now structures are changing. Families are shrinking. Our average household size has fallen below three for the first time (at the 1991 Census, it was 2.8 – Department of Statistics, 1993: 13), with over half of all households (52.4 per cent) comprising one or two people. Less than half our private households are now families with children (48.9 per cent); a quarter are families without children (25.0 per cent); a quarter are non-family households (26.1 per cent). The Department of Statistics (1989) is the source for statistics unless otherwise indicated, while 'the 1991 Census' refers to the 1991 Census volume *New Zealanders At Home*, unless otherwise indicated.

We are having fewer children. Average family size (number of children born to women aged 15-44) has fallen steadily from around six in the 1870s (Swain, 1978: 69-70) to well below two now. The number of families with preschool children has fallen steadily; at the 1991 Census, a third (34.6 per cent) of families had a youngest child under 5, and more than a quarter (27.9 per cent) had a youngest child aged 15 plus). There are more couples without children (for whatever reason – whether childless, child-free, pre-parental or post-parental), and these constitute a third (34.8 per cent) of families at the 1991 Census; over a third of families (39.0 per cent) have only one child. One in eight households (12.0 per cent), or more than a quarter (26.4 per cent) of all families, is headed by a sole parent. The stereotypical family (breadwinner, caretaker, children) is now statistically one among several family patterns (three in ten of all households): 'The traditional two-child family has been overtaken by the one-child family as the most common type' (Department of Statistics, 1992: 13).

Maori families have been changing in similar ways although their specific rates and patterns vary somewhat from the total pattern. Their total fertility rate is also falling, although it is still a little higher; the proportion of all Maori families which comprise two parents and their dependent children is a little higher than for the total population; they have fewer single-person households, and somewhat more single-parent families (37.7 per cent).

Most dramatically, compared with the general population, a larger proportion (three-quarters or 72.4 per cent) of Maori households are families with children, with smaller proportions of both families without children and non-family households. At the 1991 Census, three-quarters (72.4 per cent) of Maori households were families; a quarter of all households (27.3 per cent) were sole parent; almost half (45.1 per cent) were two-parent households. Pacific Island Polynesian households show some similarities to Maori patterns and some similarities to total population patterns.

Family roles and behaviour are changing. Parents' participation in the labour force continues to increase: nine out of ten fathers in two-parent families, and more than six out of ten mothers in two-parent families are in paid employment. However, women still do most of the housework and childcare. For sole-parent families, six out of ten fathers and four out of ten mothers are in the labour force.

At the same time, women have increasingly been delaying their first nuptial birth: in 1971, the median age was 22.9, while in 1986 it had increased to 26.6 (Maxwell, 1989: 25). The median age at childbearing was 24.8 for women born in 1948; for their 'younger sisters' born in 1958, it rose to 27.1 (Department of Statistics, 1993: 43). People are also marrying later, from a 1971 average age of first marriage for men of 23.7 and for women of 21.2 to average ages of 27.4 and 25.2 respectively in 1991 (Department of Statistics, 1993: 57). This may reflect the growing recognition by young women of educational and occupational alternatives to early marriage.

De jure marriage is our most popular institution: more than nine out of ten people aged 35 plus are or have been married, and de facto marriage accounts for only one in twenty of these marriages (with two-thirds of de facto marriages involving the 20-34 age group). De facto marriage includes both 'pre-marital' cohabitation (with *de jure* marriage probably associated with the transition to parenthood) and 'post-marital' cohabitation where one or both partners are or have been *de jure* married. Data from the 1986 Census (Department of Statistics, 1989) indicated that de facto marriage was more frequent in the North Island, perhaps reflecting Maori and metropolitan values. The subsequent 1991 Census does not provide information on *de facto* marriage. In an increasingly pluralistic society, the official conceptualisation of kinds of marriage is clearly increasingly problematic.

It is generally assumed that family breakdown ('separation' and 'divorce', now legally termed 'dissolution') is increasing. This perception reflects both a lack of historical perspective (Maxwell, 1989: 1) and an omission of remarriage from the picture. The dissolution (divorce) rate no longer accurately reflects the breakdown of heterosexual relationships (if it ever did), just as the *de jure* marriage rate no longer accurately reflects their establishment, but we may note that in 1991, there were 12.3 dissolutions per 1,000 marriages (Department of Statistics, 1993). However, the total pattern of marital and family breakdown in the nineteenth century was more extensive and much more traumatic (Phillips, 1981). The annual number of dissolutions has decreased in recent years (New Zealand Planning Council, 1989: 71), probably because people are less inclined to process their family changes through the courts. The number of children involved in formal dissolutions is dropping.

We now handle family breakdown and change much more humanely and constructively than before (Swain, 1987: 194-196). Patterns of child custody are changing (New Zealand Planning Council, 1989: 71). There is more joint custody (16 per cent in 1986) and paternal custody (12 per cent), but sole parent mothers still predominate (72 per cent).

We have an ageing population, especially at present for Pakeha. As the current debate over retirement income shows, it is now widely recognised that the elderly proportion of our population will increase significantly in the early twenty-first century, especially the oldest age groups. This has significant implications for family caregivers, who in our society are primarily women in their 40s and older. These are the same people who are experiencing the 'post-parental revolution', a new human experience. For the first time, adults expect to live active lives for 20 to 30 years after their children are launched into the adult world. This changes the nature of marriage for older people. Thus, for a while, people in the middle years will have both young adult children still in need of various forms of support (especially as or when they become parents) and increasingly dependent older parents while they struggle to cope with this post-parental revolution.

The impact of women's changing ideas on marriage and family life are widely documented. As young women recognise more educational and employment options than their mothers or even their older sisters did, so other changes will occur, such as a further increase in the age of first marriage for women. As women's labour force participation increases, so will their power in conjugal decision-making, with implications for family expenditure patterns, geographical mobility and the like.

More recently, another oppressed group in our society has begun to articulate a demand for change: te tangata whenua. At present we have a multicultural population in a monocultural society. Much of the present change towards a bicultural society is being experienced in sectors which impinge on families and family life, from the Department of Social Welfare to MG (previously Marriage Guidance), from early childhood services (kohanga reo, childcare, even kindergartens and playcentres) to kainga housing. The monocultural middle class masculine construction of family life is disintegrating. These changes offer the possibility of a greater variety of family options for everybody, even middle class Pakeha males!

Change in our public attitude to sex is slow and fraught. We continue to agonise over moral issues in Aotearoa/New Zealand. All of our social policies and legislation relating to sex – abortion, contraception, sex education, homosexuality, pornography – have been debated and decided in an uproar. Yet we are a morally pluralistic society. There is growing private tolerance of diversity. There is no longer – if there ever was – consensus on broad 'moral' issues. Even the census, not an overly sensitive instrument, demonstrates the diversity of ideas about family life in practice, and there is much which the census does not cover.

The assumptions we take for granted, the concepts we use, the questions we ask, the interpretations we offer – these shape the ways in which we make sense of families and family life, and thus the rules we enforce and the provisions we make. These rules and provisions advantage some and disadvantage others. At the heart of the struggle for the social control of family life is this struggle for advantage. In the past, it has been a very uneven struggle. It is still uneven. But this has changed and is changing. Theoretical sophistication is one of the changes which has begun to even the struggle.

Local Research

There is quite an extensive Aotearoa/New Zealand literature on families and family life, but most of it is of limited value. There is much recycling of the overseas research literature, often without considering its applicability to our society (Swain, 1984). There is a great deal of opinion, with little reference to what data are available. There is little attention to theoretical perspectives and conceptual frameworks, although Cameron (1985) and Gilling (1988) discuss the definition (conceptualisation) of 'family'. Middleton (1984) criticises theorising about sex roles. Cameron (1984; 1986) does the same for research on childlessness and the value of children.

There is a similar lack of attention to methodology, although Lowe (1984) looks at discontinuities in the census. Fergusson, Horwood and Shannon (1984) present and use a valuable 'proportional hazards model' of family and childhood events. Duffin (1985) and Lamb (1987) illustrate more qualitative methodologies.

Much of the most valid and reliable information is demographic rather than sociological, and is not reviewed here. The Christchurch Child Development Study and the Society for Research on Women in New Zealand Inc (SROW) have produced valuable research within their chosen areas. We know from the former a great deal about children and their families, and the factors which affect their health and welfare. SROW has enlarged our knowledge of the family and household experience of women. There are useful research reports from government departments (especially the Departments of Social Welfare, Statistics, Justice and Education) which touch upon family life, although these tend to be based on implicit and unexamined theoretical perspectives.

Some of our history (and herstory) is being re-presented in recent publications. Eldred-Grigg (1984) has researched areas such as substance abuse and prostitution in the nineteenth century, while Phillips (1981) has changed our view of marital and family breakdown at that time. The nineteenth century was not a golden age of family life.

Nor is the twentieth century, although it is a great improvement! Kedgley (1985) describes our male-female relations as a sexual wilderness; Colgan and McGregor (1981) claim to disclose our tawdry sexual secrets. There is a growing literature outlining sexual harassment and child sexual abuse. Family violence is now more widely acknowledged.

The notion, from American functionalist sociologists, that the modern family is small and isolated has been challenged here as elsewhere. Meade (1984), Rosemergy and Meade (1986), Mill (1987), and O'Regan and O'Connor (1989) show networks of kinsfolk, neighbours, and friends sharing mutual support, although James (1982) suggests that for Pakeha such aid takes a limited range of forms. Traditional sex roles are alive and well, even among young people professing changed attitudes (Koopman-Boyden and Abbott, 1985). The male sex role is receiving attention (Phillips, 1987) with the promise of a better quality of life for men and women if it changes.

We are learning that the transition to parenthood (especially motherhood) in Aotearoa/New Zealand may be different from other Western societies, in that a number of independent research studies (Swain, 1978; 1985) have generally shown lower levels of crisis than in the USA and UK, although the evidence of stress and indeed real distress where support is lacking is clear (Phillips, 1983; 1988). This is one area where the theoretical perspective clearly shapes data interpretation.

The mutual influence of childcare and families has been explored with the finding (Swain and Swain, 1982; Smith and Swain, 1988) that childcare enhances the quality of family life for all, including the children. Patterns of childrearing have also been well-documented. This may not be a great place to bring up children, but the way we do it – while sharing features with other Western and Polynesian societies – has its particular character.

For families with children presently of school age, we now have useful information about the chances and patterns of change and reorganisation (Fergusson, Horwood and Shannon, 1984a), and their implications for the children (Fergusson, Horwood and Shannon, 1984b). These researchers can show one pattern of family variables which predict a 1 per cent chance of family breakdown in the first five years after the first child is born; another pattern of variables increases the chances of breakdown to 99 per cent. Some of these variables we can change, some we cannot. They also show whether, and if so how, these family events affect children and their mothers. More recently, the same researchers (Fergusson, Horwood, Kershaw and Shannon, 1986) have been able to identify two groups of factors associated, respectively, with no chance and with a one-in-three chance of violence by men towards their partner.

Conclusion

We all have available plenty of material on families and family life, from the intensely personal through a bewildering variety of media artefacts to the austerely academic. We do, of course, need more data, both to test ideas about families and family life, and to inform public policy and private practice. However, in this chapter, I have argued that the family scholar above all else needs a broadly eclectic acquaintance with the theoretical perspectives and conceptual frameworks available in the family field. This knowledge plays a crucial role in shaping our understanding of families and family life. Other attributes are of course important – technical competence both in the general and in the particular methodological requirements of family research (Rodgers, 1973), acceptance of the daunting complexity of the family field of study, even an ability to recognise the dangers inherent in taking one's work home – but this theoretical sensibility is essential.

Further Reading

Department of Statistics, 1992, *New Zealanders At Home*, Wellington, Department of Statistics.
James, B., 1982, 'Family', in P. Spoonley, D. Pearson and I. Shirley (eds), *New Zealand: Sociological Perspectives*, Palmerston North, Dunmore Press.
New Zealand Planning Council, 1989, *From Birth to Death II*, Wellington, New Zealand Planning Council.
Swain, D.A., 1987, 'Children, Families, Law and Social Policy in Aotearoa/New Zealand', *Journal of Comparative Family Studies*, 18(2):175-206.

2 Community

David Pearson

'Community' is one of those words we all know the meaning of until confronted with the question – how do you define it? At this point, we are inclined to move on to the next question on the examination paper. All definitions, as Anthony Cohen reminds us, 'contain or imply theories, and the theory of community has been very contentious' (Cohen, 1985:11). Nevertheless, there is general agreement that community, as its Latin origin *communis* suggests, is about similarity and sharing. We readily refer to 'our community' to evoke a sense of place shared by others; politicians are fond of the phrase 'in the community interest', whilst academics may speak of a 'community of scholars'. All of these examples express a sentiment of sharing and something held in common, but they also illustrate a diversity of contexts and usage which has prompted the criticism that the community concept, whilst readily used, is decidedly ambiguous – some might say to the point of redundancy (Stacey, 1969).

Despite the array of possible definitions, it is still feasible to identify certain general areas of common usage. Most students of community have been concerned with three parameters. First, a definition of community as a locality or place; second, the form and content of social organisation within 'real' or symbolic boundaries; and finally, community as a form of human relationship.

The first strand of community suggests that people use topographical and other physical features of the landscape to place themselves in the social and natural world. Traditionally, this conception of community is drawn from illustrations of rural or small-town life. For example, tribal and peasant 'folk' societies are viewed as communities because of their size, stability and isolation. This geographical sense of a finite and bounded physical location is often reinforced by the sociological perception of community as a local social system (Bell and Newby, 1971; Stacey, 1969). The 'locality' is not only a spatial referent for those who reside within it; it is a geographical setting for shared social lives. Within this perspective, the confines of place are reinforced by locally autonomous, cultural and social institutions.

Bonds of interdependence are forged by close family and kinship ties, systems of land tenure, or local stratification patterns, within which there may be an indivisibility between home, work, worship and recreation. This social matrix provides a common framework of authority patterns, social values and forms of association.

A sense of a small and unchanging social microcosm is firmly captured by the often over-romantic flavour of the third major usage of community, namely, community as a form of social relationship. Bell and Newby (1971: 22) suggest that 'community' occupied a position in the minds of many nineteenth century intellectuals similar to the idea of 'contract' in the Age of Reason. Most notable in this regard was Ferdinand Toennies, whose classic work *Gemeinschaft und Gesellschaft* (loosely translated as Community and Society), set the tone for much subsequent urban and rural sociology. For Toennies, *Gemeinschaftlich* relationships were intimate and enduring; epitomising an interdependence of blood, mind and place (Mellor, 1977: 179). The closeness of extended family ties, the intimacy of neighbouring relations and the values of religion and friendship shaped the human will in settings of mutual co-operation. In contrast, *Gesellschaftlich* relationships heralded the collapse of traditional communality as people became entrapped within the competitiveness and individualism of capitalist market relations and the impersonality of the urban landscape. Toennies was careful to draw a distinction between models and reality, and between places and relationships. *Gemeinschaft* and *Gesellschaft* were 'pure' types that analytically separated what Toennies conceded was a set of interrelated processes of communality and association that could never be neatly parcelled into 'rural' and 'urban' compartments.

Echoes of Toennies' work are to be found in Robert Redfield's (1947) conception of a rural 'folk' society, Louis Wirth's (1938) contrasting urban archetype, and the Chicago School tradition that influenced so much subsequent urban sociology (see David Thorns' chapter). However insightful and ethnographically rich these studies were, their perspective was fundamentally flawed. As Cohen (1985: 28-37) has argued, they perpetuated the myths of rural communal simplicity, egalitarianism and conformity in contrast to the complexity, inequality and heterodoxy of urban life. Such studies, often forgetting Toennies' sensitivity to the dynamics of social life, tended to promote a somewhat static method of comparing past and present that inevitably provokes an image of the destruction of small-scale, simple societies. Whether we are talking about a type of place, a form of social microcosm or a quality of human relationships, 'community' is all too often conceived of as a frozen entity that melts away as local becomes cosmopolitan, communal becomes individual, at a particular moment in history.

In contrast, I believe the community concept is best conceived of as incorporating three central processes – boundary, interdependence and ideology – that provide useful measures of social transformation in all settings. These:

Facets of community.....need not be described as static elements which disappear at a particular historical juncture. They are themselves constantly changing as societies do so – and, as such retain great utility for framing important aspects of social change. The study of community thereby becomes a general method of analysis rather than an examination of a specific thing in itself (Pearson, 1980: 148).

Boundary, Interdependence and Ideology

Before examining some New Zealand examples of the community study genre, let us have a closer look at the three processes mentioned above. The boundary process seeks to describe the way men and women construct geographical and social reference points wherever they live. Social life is always spatially patterned (Giddens, 1984). Consider the design of your house and the way you use the living spaces within it. Think about land and property and how different systems of usage and ownership promote various forms of boundary – geographic, symbolic, and possibly, legalistic. How do we conceive of divisions between neighbourhoods, towns, regions and nations?

These are difficult questions but we can at least point out some pitfalls in the provision of answers. First, 'locality' is not the same as 'community'; second, spatial characteristics should not be separated from the social actors that give them meaning; and third, one should not assume that spatial patterns necessarily determine social patterns (Urry, 1987). Let us look more closely at these three statements in turn.

We might use the word community to describe the township we were born in, or the suburb we live in now, but these localities are places which may not have communal characteristics. 'Community' is something more than the place in which it might be found. We also talk about the relationships between Wellington and Auckland, possibly in uncomplimentary terms! But, at the risk of seeming pedantic, cities do not have social relationships, citizens do. Finally, and this was a stumbling block of many classical approaches to community, it is an open question whether where you live has any direct influence on how you live. For example, if some outer surburbs of New Zealand cities are described as 'nappy valleys', is this because suburban living promotes child raising; or is it, simply, that many households which contain young children move to the suburbs because that is where they prefer or can afford to live?

What we have to consider is the way in which the social and the spatial are interconnected. The boundaries that people use to place themselves in the world are often a guide here. Some boundaries are physical or geographic – if we cross that bridge, ford that creek, pass over that mountain, we have moved beyond our territory in local terms. More often boundaries are symbolic, and 'communities' are imagined

(Anderson, 1983). We cannot know all those who live in our town, who embrace our ethnic group, or who form our nation, but we have a sense of 'them' and 'us'. This sense may be a permanent feature of one's existence. The black novelist, George Lamming (1979), can write of living within 'the castle of my skin', and the metaphor powerfully evokes the permanence of a lived experience within ethnic boundaries. Men and women's perceptions of locality and community may differ according to their experience of domestic and paid work, kin and friendship networks, participation in voluntary associations, and the power relationships within local systems of social stratification and differentiation (see Hall *et al.*, 1984; Levine, 1987; Mahar, 1985).

Other senses of boundary, and their connection to community, may be more transitory. Our sense of 'the nation' may only arise, ephemerally, during some political event or sporting contest. The sinking of the *Rainbow Warrior*, or another victory for the national netball team, brings our New Zealand identification to the fore. The boundaries are closed between 'us' and our political or sporting opponents, but perhaps for only the duration of the game.

If boundary creation and reproduction is a wide-ranging process, what other facets of social life do we need to consider to bring us closer to 'community'? This leads us to the question of interdependence – a central feature of community analysis which focuses on the links between local and extra-local interconnections. Norbert Elias (1974), for example, has described a community as a locality with its own tangible or symbolic boundaries within which groups of people are socially interdependent through shared obligations. The test of community is whether these interdependencies are closer within the locality than the 'interdependencies of the same kind with other groups of people within the wider social field to which a community belongs' (Elias, 1974: xix). One should note that Elias does not restrict his definition to particular places or historical periods, nor does he stress stability and consensus. Elias freely acknowledges that individual and group reciprocities involve conflict and co-operation. Essentially, we are asked to study the tensions between those forces that integrate social groups and those which divide them. When these tensions are locally based and produce territorially bounded interdependencies, then we can speak of community formation (Pearson, 1980: 151).

Hall, Thorns and Willmott (1984) suggest that propinquity, property and kinship are key sets of defining relationships within localities that may, combined or in isolation, provide the basis for community in an objective and subjective sense. They also acknowledge that gender and ethnic relationships could serve the same purpose. In effect, these are the potential or actual bases for interdependence. Whether interdependence is actualised in communal form depends on the presence of solidarity and group consciousness. And so we come to our third strand of 'community' – its ideological significance.

Images of community are evoked by individuals or groups to describe how things are or should be in their locality. Community ideologies may also be foisted on people by outsiders. The interaction of processes of categorisation and identification are vitally important in this respect. Categories are essentially abstractions, and they are often imposed on people – not least by sociologists! We often speak of women or men, Maori or Pakeha, young or old. Statisticians might draw out comparisons between such categories on the basis of some measure of aggregation – for example, the educational attainment of young, female Pakeha. But there is no sense here of these 'youngsters' constituting a group, let alone a community. For group qualities to exist, there must be a semblance of indirect or direct social interaction. If groups become communities, social bonds are drawn even tighter to the point of solidarism.

If we accept W.I. Thomas's dictum that if people believe situations are real, then they are real in their consequences, 'community' as an ideology has a resilience that extends its use far beyond the confines of its classical traditions. A sense of 'belonging' (Cohen, 1982), or what Schmalenbach (1961) describes as 'communion', can arise out of long-established and deep-seated social attachments. Thus, the boundaries between 'locals' and 'outsiders' in some communities are almost caste-like (Hall, 1987: 8). Conversely, this sense of 'us' might only be a fleeting reaction to changing social circumstances. For example, at times of crisis when a locality is threatened by invasion or some natural disaster, an external threat or internal upheaval produces a common awareness or consciousness that brings together our three strands of community (see Luketina, 1986: 79). 'With the development of communion, 'latent' community becomes 'manifest' in the consciousness and collective behaviour of the local inhabitants' (Hall et al., 1984: 208). Communal boundaries, shared interdependencies and a common consciousness are intertwined, perhaps only momentarily, in a meaningful illustration of 'community' in the contemporary world.

Communities and Change

Thus far I have described three important dimensions of 'community'; namely, boundary, interdependence and ideology. At this point it will be useful to illustrate their usage by examining a selection of local community studies that portray important social changes in New Zealand.

If one takes a backward glance at the early nineteenth century, we find Maori communities, that in many respects contained *Gemeinschaft*-like qualities, providing a striking contrast to the greater individualism of Pakeha lifestyles. One needs to be cautious about over-generalisation and romanticism with respect to patterns of Maori settlement as with their Pakeha counterparts. Davidson (1981) notes that Maori settlements in the late eighteenth century varied greatly in size and shape. Such variation depended on 'the subsistence pattern, the climate, and the social and political situation of the time' (Davidson, 1981: 15). As Ritchie (1992: 114) recounts: 'Maori lived in bands who roved a territory, moving from one resource or habitat to another in a more or less regular way. Some sites were permanent but even these would have no more than a few hundred regular dwellers'. Broadly speaking, however, at the extended family (whanau), sub-tribal (hapu) and iwi (tribal) levels, the boundaries of communal land ownership were firmly linked with kinship ties and common ancestry (Metge, 1976: 1-16). Such boundaries had cosmological significance and were defended militarily (Kawharu, 1977). Hence, Maori groupings were both internally and externally competitive but displayed many of the classical features of community alluded to above. The coming of the European severely disrupted traditional mores. Dramatic changes in land use, possession and ownership, the escalation of warfare with the introduction of the musket, and the influences of Christianity all threatened, and indeed, often destroyed traditional ways of life. But blood, mind and place were co-existent in long-established Maori communities, in contrast to the social patterns in the emergent settler society.

Hamer (1979: 6) suggests that New Zealand was 'fragmented into many small pockets of nineteenth century space, the bounds of which were determined by the distance that could be covered in the course of a day, and each such pocket needed a village with certain basic services and amenities for the traveller'. The subsequent expansion or demise of a locality depended on a variety of local, regional and national contingencies. Franklin (1969), for example, provides a useful study of the evolution of village communities in Wellington province. He distinguishes between three phases of village growth and decline. The first phase (1870-95) is described as the period of establishment when settlements were carved out of the bush, transport links were established and the rudiments of local institutions were created.

During the second phase (1895-1925), the village becomes stabilised, most notably because improvements in the dairying and sheep farming industries promoted a close interdependence between township and countryside. Economic viability provoked occupational diversity and a growth in the associational life of the community. Gradually, however, Franklin (1969: 139) notes how: 'The industrialisation of the economy, the increasing technological nature of society (and) the mechanisation of farming, have all entailed a swing in emphasis towards the larger urban community'.

Franklin's perspective is exemplified by Pearson's (1980) study of Johnsonville, and is given added weight by Miles Fairburn's (1989) recent work on nineteenth century New Zealand Pakeha society. Fairburn argues that rapid, sizeable and socially attenuated patterns of immigration between the 1850s and 1880s produced an atomised society. The swift expansion of the frontier, the lack of kinship ties, the dearth of social association amongst scattered, remote and privatised households, and, above all, the high degree of social and geographical mobility and an attendant ideology of individual achievement, delayed the eventual emergence of 'community'. In an atomised society, close-knit communities are aberrations, not the norm. Ritual events, such as annual race meetings or township festivals, are deemed (by Fairburn) to be 'too diffuse, fleeting and infrequent' to provide social bonding. The lack of extended kinship ties within a predominantly young, single, male, itinerant immigrant population is hardly conducive to communality. And evidence of low levels of participation in a variety of local voluntary associations supports his argument that neighbourliness is at a premium among social and geographical isolates too concerned with their individualised lives to worry about establishing cohesive and lasting formal associations.

Fairburn's view of an atomised society is still the subject of great debate. Other historians have stressed the presence of more cohesive social arrangements in mid-nineteenth century New Zealand (see Arnold, 1990), especially in particular localities, although regional variation makes generalisations difficult. It may be appropriate to see the period between the 1850s and 1880s as a stage of establishment within which atomisation and settlement are processes that coexist in the same society. In some rural townships or city suburbs, a core of settlers and institutions provide the communal frameworks which exist despite the high levels of transience within these localities. Such frameworks will differ according to the local history of settlement, the patterning of male (Phillips, 1987) and female (Daley, 1991) lives, and the size and isolation of specific places. But the possibility of Toennies' classic sense of *Gemeinschaftlich* communities existing beyond the confines of the Maori population is highly questionable.

By the turn of the century, as cautious use of Pearson's (1980) Johnsonville study reveals, some semblance of a local social system was emerging in the suburban township period. The main street with its local stores, and nearby public buildings, provided a focus which enabled distinctions to be drawn between 'us' and neighbouring localities. During the period between the First and Second World Wars, local neighbouring, kin and friendship networks overlapped in various forms of interdependence. Much of the local population pursued family and leisure activities, if not necessarily their employment, within the locality. The local school and village hall had multi-functional purposes and symbolised community participation (Shaffer, 1973), whilst the sports clubs were a focus for parochial sentiment. Above all, the social bonds of marriage, friendship and common association, consistently shaped by the warp and weft of gossip networks, promoted a sense of communion.

But wider social changes, together with local expansion, shaped and reshaped socio-spatial limits. Suburban expansion and transportation improvements weakened local attachments, although an enlarged population maintained the viability of many local businesses and the ease of commuting enabled a core of residents to remain in the suburb whilst working elsewhere. Nevertheless, economic and political autonomy, always scarce commodities in Johnsonville, have been further eroded in recent years. National and regional centralisation of retail distribution and other economies of scale led to the partial demise of the small shopkeeper and the parallel ascendency of chain-store big business. An image of local economic dependence is mirrored by the loss of what was always a limited degree of local political control.

Despite the recent growth of progressive associations and service clubs, regionally and nationally based political parties, trade unions and city bureaucracies largely control the destinies of local inhabitants.

State welfare policies and more secular lifestyles brought the demise of the lodges and a decline in church participation. The advent of mass car ownership widened leisure pursuits beyond the locality, whilst television and video keep many households within but not of the community. A plethora of voluntary associations still exist, but they serve a growing specialisation of leisure interests which need not overlap with those of one's neighbours. The ubiquity of the telephone still maintains meaningful social ties (Bell, 1968: 85), but at a distance. In short, present Johnsonville, in contrast to its working-class past, now exhibits more middle-class lifestyles reminiscent of 'suburbia' elsewhere in New Zealand as well as overseas (Thorns, 1972). The class composition of Johnsonville has changed, and with it associational life and the nature of communion.

Class and community consciousness may be congruent or contradictory. In some localities, particularly fishing or mining communities where deep traditions of shared labour, leisure and residence coexist, class and community consciousness may be thoroughly intertwined in a working-class subculture (Pearson, 1963; Williamson, 1982). In other localities, where 'the community' lacks these subcultural traditions, is internally class differentiated, and/or reflects the greater individualism of middle-class life, the relationship between class and community is far more complex (see Hall et al., 1984: 211). This, indeed, proved to be the case in Johnsonville (Pearson, 1980: 173), for whilst the locality now possessed few features of communal boundaries and interdependence, the 'idea' of 'community' was freely drawn upon.

Social divisions were therefore often set aside by communal sentiments. A glance at other New Zealand community studies confirms that the Johnsonville experience is by no means atypical, although we need to be ever-watchful for regional and cultural variations. Local studies of rural communities are a case in point. For example, the 'eclipse of community' refrain (Stein, 1960) is echoed in Somerset's (1938) study of 'Littledene', a small farming centre on the Canterbury Plains.

Littledene's origins, at least in physical terms, were somewhat different to Johnsonville's. As Somerset relates: 'In Canterbury the relation between city and country was more intimate than in any other part of New Zealand. On the smooth Canterbury Plains there was no natural feature to tell where the provincial capital ended and the hinterland began' (Somerset, 1974: xi). It was physical isolation rather than the natural landscape that fixed the limits of social habitation. In the nineteenth century, Littledene was 'a long day's journey by bullock wagon' from Christchurch (Somerset, 1974: 63), so the tyranny of distance forced residents to create and maintain social institutions in their immediate locality.

The yearly farming cycle set the scene for local work patterns and much else besides. The farmers maintained the cultural continuity of the small country town, provided much of its political leadership and most of its economic viability. In common with Johnsonville, the framework of interdependence between work, family and leisure in the 1930s readily evoked the communality of a local social system, but much had changed when Somerset returned to Littledene in the early 1950s.

Christchurch could now be reached in two hours and was becoming increasingly important as a commercial and recreational centre for Littledene residents. The radio 'brought the once isolated settlement into continuous touch with the world' (Somerset, 1974: 63), and television cemented this process. Nevertheless, a strong sense of loyalty to local businesses and voluntary associations remained.

Paradoxically, the mechanisation of farming not only partly destroyed the pattern of Littledene life but also maintained it. Mechanisation reduced local employment, promoted larger acreages and changed the pace of the farming seasons. It also kept the farmers tied to their properties and the locality (Somerset, 1974: 153).

A core of farming families, local representatives of a land-owning class, underpinned the salience of community. This aspect of many New Zealand rural localities is echoed in the work of Hall (1987) on Kurow, Hatch's (1992) study of 'South Downs' (also in Caterbury) and, to a rather lesser extent, in Willmott's (1985) study of Tinui. These localities are different in many respects, although each have clear boundaries and a rich associational life within their environs. But what is striking in Kurow, for example, even to the present day, is 'the fact that landownership both defines a class of farmers that predominates in the rural district and dominates its structure of voluntary associations (this) provides a more salient basis for the emergence from relations of propinquity of community identity and loyalty' (Hall *et al.*, 1984: 211).

If the presence of 'old-timers' in Littledene cemented continuity, many other residents, especially the young, became caught up in the urban drift from country to town, from South to North island. These demographic and social trends swiftly closed the gap between 'rus' and 'urbs'.

By the early 1970s Littledene, like most New Zealand rural townships, had become subject to a range of international, national and regional constraints that rendered the idea of local autonomy increasingly anachronistic. As Catton notes in his Epilogue: 'The changes in Littledene between the 1930s and the 1950s were part of a worldwide evolution. Towns in which people's lives had been shaped largely by local influences were becoming strands of a far-flung but ever more tightly-knit web in which people's lives would be increasingly shaped by trans-local forces' (Somerset, 1974: 213).

Littledene, Johnsonville, South Downs and Kurow represent longstanding New Zealand settlements, but what of more recently established 'communities'? One such place is Tokoroa. This timber town, that grew into prominence in the early 1950s when the giant mill at Kinleith was constructed, is the subject of Chapple's (1976) study. He portrays the single-industry settlement in the 1960s, akin to other hydro (Burch, 1969; Campbell, 1957) and neighbouring forestry towns (James, 1979), as a largely artificial creation. As Chapple (1976: 137) says: 'Industrial communities in the new world are synthetic communities'.

Job opportunities at Kinleith attracted a wide range of migrants from within and beyond New Zealand. Many of the newcomers were single males or young families and hence highly sensitive to the ebb and flow of industrial needs and human aspirations. Inevitably, both the work setting and the residential environment seemed to militate against putting down permament roots in the area. Not surprisingly therefore, unlike Littledene, Tokoroa lacked a core of prominent local identities to provide cultural continuity and a sense of common ancestry. This ethnic and generational mix, together with the occupational hierarchies found in a large industrial plant, promoted socio-cultural and residential segregation and the separation of workers and management.

Communality, therefore, is a quality of ethnic, class and gender relations in these industrial towns – and these relationships are sufficiently cross-cutting to undermine any wider sense of a 'community'. Tokoroa residents, Chapple argued, may verbalise, indeed seek, the 'community' idea, but their privatised lifestyle is more reminiscent of suburbia than closer-knit village life. His study confirms, therefore, the oft-noted axiom that geographical proximity is not automatically conducive to social propinquity (Pahl, 1968).

Similar gender, class and ethnic backgrounds or positions in the life cycle are frequently more salient bases for communality than mere co-residence. If single-industry towns represent new forms of social and spatial arrangements where 'community' is hard to find, perhaps Maori settlement in New Zealand still represents the closest approximations to traditional conceptions of communality. As we noted earlier, the coming of the European severely disrupted tribal lifestyles. However, a number of contemporary studies of Maori settlements vouch for the resilience of community within a framework of considerable social change.

For example, Ritchie (1963) in his study of Rakau, traces the impact of the European, the loss of autonomy caused by the sale of tribal land, and the more recent influences of education, occupational changes and migratory patterns. Despite these incursions, he argues, the small settlement of Maori families has retained a sense of place and communion through its symbolic remembrances of Rakau ancestors.

· This is no romantic conception of things past but a Maori sense of continuity best illustrated by the saying, 'Men [sic] pass away, the land remains' (Hohepa, 1964: 22). Territorial symbols reinforced by tradition and semi-isolation provide the framework, whilst social interdependence fulfils the main requirement for community. As Ritchie notes: 'Rakau folk are not a community because of some sentimental desire to counteract the mass society of which they are a part; they do not seek to reconstruct some village ideal of togetherness; rather they are a community because to fight you must have someone to fight with; to gossip you must have someone to gossip with and about; to feel isolated you must have someone to be isolated from' (Ritchie, 1963: 190).

This sense of continuity and change runs through most studies of Maori communities (see Mahuta, 1978). For example, Hohepa (1964) in his description of Waima in Northland, reiterates the importance of topographical boundaries acting as a physical framing of communal relationships. The village has been affected by rural-urban migration and internal factionalism; but the interdependence of ancestral ties, the 'whaamere' or extended kin group, and the recurrence of seasonal events, fosters community. The meeting house fronted by the marae, the funeral gatherings (hui tangi) and the ritualised annual clearing of the local cemetery, all act as important foci for community sentiment. Metge (1964), in her study of Kotare, another Northland community, evokes similar images. She stresses that Kotare is not a self-sufficient, self-contained settlement. The push/pull factors of rural/urban migration patterns have forced or persuaded many Maori to move to Auckland. Kinship ties are spread far beyond the immediate locality and political and economic extra-local control is the norm.

But once again, the inter-meshing of boundary, interdependence and consciousness is present. Kotare is seen as a territorial entity 'defined on a traditional Maori basis'. Local associations, particularly the football club, evoke a sense of place. Moreover, an ethnic identity embodied in the concept of 'Maori heart' provide a communal focus − 'a boundary drawn around themselves as a common front vis-à-vis others − notably Pakeha' (Metge, 1964: 95). This sense of identity, evocatively recalled in Mihi Edward's (1990; 1992) account of her rural childhood in Maketu and later years in Wellington, may provide some continuity in the transition to the city.

A sense of ethnic exclusivity, reinforced by feelings of external threat, aids the adaptive process in the new urban environment. Metge reminds us that Maori residing in Auckland do not constitute a single or even a series of communities as such. Traditional Maori communities have been transformed by urban dispersal, residential and occupational mobility, new stratification patterns, and the divisions of tribe, gender and age. However, amidst these signs of organisational disunity, some platforms for emotional solidarity can be discerned (see Kernot, 1972). The construction of urban marae, Maori community centres and the development of ethnic-based voluntary associations provide tangible symbols of common purpose.

As Kawharu points out, when commenting on Walker's (1975) study of Maori associations in Auckland, 'there is some groping towards the idea of community − through committees of one sort or another, honorary welfare officers and wardens, cultural and religious groups and not least, struggles for leadership' (Kawharu,

1975: 14). Hence, ethnic inclusivity reinforced by tangible or intangible perceptions of external threat from racism or racial discrimination, act as the mainstay for new forms of 'community' for Maori and other urban migrant groups in the major cities of New Zealand, a fact well illustrated in the 'ethnic revivals' of the last two decades (see Paul Spoonley's chapter).

Categories like 'Maori' and 'Pacific Islander' disguise the presence of ethnic groups and communities within. They are labels originally imposed by outsiders; but through the processes of racial categorisation and ethnic identification, such terms take on new meaning for those so labelled. New forms of communion arise out of the sharing of the experience of social exclusion. The origins of 'community' in ideological parlance are therefore often found in the search for a sense of place in a world where boundaries and interdependencies change in swift and bewildering fashion. Thus, as Cohen suggests, 'people assert community, whether in the form of ethnicity or of locality, when they recognise in it the most adequate medium for the expression of their whole selves' (Cohen, 1985: 107).

Conclusion

The above discussion of a variety of settlement types – suburban, rural, single industry and ethnic-based – confirms that localism and traditional forms of interdependence have been transformed, if not completely destroyed in New Zealand. The increasing influence of urbanisation, bureaucracy, mass communications and geographical mobility has eroded the economic, political and social autonomy of all but the most isolated of settlements (see Levine and Levine, 1987). However, community as an ideology is very much alive in the contemporary setting.

'Community' still has a high currency among those social planners who seek to invest some importance in 'locality' and its implied connection to communal social relations. Local ordinances are designed to protect 'the character of the community', and community centres are viewed as panaceas for every urban ailment from adolescent boredom to suburban neurosis. The idea of community policing evokes similar imagery. Recent devolutionary moves in education policy (see Roy Nash's chapter) are aimed at giving 'the community' more say. Local radio stations and newspapers commonly operate under the community rubric.

All these recent examples of the search for the Holy Grail of communality seek to maintain or recreate community within the city.

But others in the quest often look for the community idea beyond urban limits. For example, the communitarian movement, both religious and secular, dates back to pre-Christian times and many examples of modern communes are to be found in New Zealand (Jones, 1975). Whatever their aims, and most communes cover a range of intentions, all these groups constitute communal ventures to provide alternatives to the so-called urban or suburban way of life.

The social planning and communitarian strands of the 'community' process return us to the 'classical' assumptions that we described and basically rejected at the beginning of this essay. Social consensus and propinquity are not essential pillars of 'community'. Social interdependence and boundary formation are as much, if not more, the result of conflict as co-operation. In fact, they are often cooperative ideals or actions in the face of opposition (Cohen, 1985: 115). Most 'communities' in the urban-industrial milieu are imagined – and New Zealand is no exception. And imagination implies creativity as well as invention (Anderson, 1983: 15). Ideologies are belief systems that not only constitute and pattern social lives, they also reflect power relations in society (Thompson, 1986: 66). Conflicts over planning decisions, women's rights, conservation policies, factory closures or Maori land claims are frequently fought under the banner of 'community'. In these contexts, community becomes a clarion call for what some sociologists have described as 'urban social movements' (Castells, 1983). For example, in other words, New Zealand suburbanites can follow O'Reagan and O'Connor's (1989) recent advice to give it a go! In this guise, communion is a potent force for liberation.

But 'community' can also be used as a legitimatory tool to deflect attention away from sectional interests or personal gain by evoking images of 'the common good'. Property developers, for example, may advertise a new subdivision in sylvan tones that betray the muddy wasteland that their new suburban 'community' actually represents. A politician's bland allusion to the 'community interest' may be nothing more than an empty phrase, or worse, a direct attempt at concealment of distinct inequalities. In short, the extolling of 'community' virtues can just as readily be seen as a vehicle of external social control as a liberative device for the local urbanite.

Whether one delights in the elasticity of the community concept or despairs at its elusiveness, the current ubiquity of the term hints at its symbolic resilience. The staying power of 'community' should not surprise us, since the very forces which continually threaten to destroy it are the very source of its regeneration.

Further Reading

Cohen, A.P., 1985, *The Symbolic Construction of Community*, London, Ellis Horwood/Tavistock.
Hall, R.R., Thorns, D. and Willmott, W.H., 1984, 'Community, Class and Kinship – Bases for Collective Action Within Localities', *Environment and Planning: Society and Space*, 2:201-15.
Hatch, E., 1992, *Respectable Lives. Social Standing in Rural New Zealand*, Berkeley, University of California Press.
Hohepa, P.W., 1964, *A Maori Community in Northland*, Wellington, Reed.
Metge, J., 1964, *A New Maori Migration*, London, Athlone Press.
Pearson, D.G., 1980, *Johnsonville. Continuity and Change in a New Zealand Township*, Auckland, Allen and Unwin.

3 Urban

David Thorns

Early Sociological Study of the City

The study of the city has been an integral part of the study of the development of Western industrial capitalism. Cities, of course, existed well before the nineteenth century urban explosion, but they were of a different kind and were not where the majority of the population lived. Urban sociology has thus, for the most part, concentrated upon the structure and processes within the industrial cities which were a major feature of the nineteenth century. This century, the population of Britain changed from being one that was predominantly rural, with 64 per cent of the population living in the countryside, to one where 68 per cent lived in cities (Weber, 1963: 41).

The cities created during this period of rapid urbanisation contained sharp contrasts. There were the slums where the new industrial proletariat lived in conditions of terrible poverty and squalor, and there were the gracious, leafy suburbs of the newly emergent middle class of industrial entrepreneurs and financiers (Lambert and Weir, 1975, Part 3). Engels (1971), in his analysis of the condition of the working classes in England, provides one of the first and still one of the best pieces of urban sociology. In this study, he both describes the conditions in Manchester in the 1840s and attempts to show how these conditions were not the result of arbitrary forces, but the direct consequences of the emerging capitalist system built around the exploitation of the labour power of the working people. For Engels, the industrial city was the reflection in bricks and mortar of the capitalist relations of production. The apparent chaos which was the product of urbanisation was in reality not chaos at all, but part of the inevitable consequence of capitalist industrialisation.

The structure of the industrial city as it emerged in the nineteenth century and the relationships between the upper middle class, the lower middle class (petty proprietors and traders) and the workers, were all, for Engels, a direct consequence of the capitalist system of organisation and exploitation. The commitment to empirical study that Engels showed in his work was taken up by other early urbanists. However, the theoretical connections Engels made were less often followed by the later writers, and by the turn of the century, urban research had become more descriptive than analytical (Mellor, 1977; Smith, 1980; Saunders, 1986).

New Zealand cities, in contrast to the industrialising cities of Europe in the nineteenth century, mostly began as entrepôts, ports from which the products of the new colony were exported back to Britain and through which came the supplies required for the developing life of the new colony. The cities were therefore initially commercial rather than industrial cities (Johnston, 1973).

Nevertheless, living conditions in these early cities were also marked by contrast; from the early mansions of the wealthier upper-class settlers to the more humble housing of the working class, much of which was of a poor standard of construction. Consequently, although not primarily industrial, New Zealand cities were still segregated places. For example, Dr. Burns, the Assistant Surgeon at Dunedin Hospital commented in the 1860s that:

> ... the houses of labouring classes in Dunedin ... are ... of the slimmest possible construction compatible with some degree of shelter (quoted in Davis, 1981: 64).

Other commentators on Dunedin have drawn attention to the extent of residential segregation within the city in the nineteenth century. Olssen, for example, notes that:

> ... residential differentiation, rooted in different life chances and opportunities intensified class distinctions. Institutions such as lodges, churches, and sports clubs, which mediated between social strata in small communities, compounded class differences in the cities and provided a necessary though not sufficient condition for the growth of class conciousness (Olssen, 1977: 35).

In other New Zealand cities during the 1870s and 1880s, it was noted that many people lived in filth and that the problems of sewerage and drainage were chronic in some of the inner suburbs. Sydenham in Christchurch, for example, was one suburb where people continued to drain their slops into the side gutters of the street, a practice which led to problems of disease (New Zealand Federation of University Women, 1977). In fact, Christchurch was probably only saved from a major epidemic in these years because of its artesian water supply which, because of the depth of the wells, remained unpolluted. As the city grew during the latter years of the nineteenth century, new industries were located near to the city. Housing for the workers quickly moved out and surrounded the factories, creating industrial and residentially mixed working-class suburbs to the south and east of the city in contrast to the more affluent middle-class residential suburbs to the north and west (Hall *et al.,* 1983).

By the end of the nineteenth century, New Zealand cities contained for the most part single-storied, detached dwellings, many owned by their occupants who often had built their homes with their own labour (Sutch, 1973). The general climate was one of laissez-faire so there were limited restrictions or controls over land development and building activity. The cities were mostly ill-planned and the standard of much of the housing was poor. As a result, there was pressure for more stringent and extensive planning controls in the early decades of the twentieth century culminating in the passing of the first formal town planning legislation in 1926. The associated concern to improve the quality of housing available to the workers led to the passing of the first piece of explicit housing legislation with the 1905 Workers' Dwellings Act. This Act provided for the setting apart of land and the building of dwellings for workers. The 1905 Act, however, was not particularly successful at increasing public provision of workers' housing, and by 1919, only 648 houses had been built under its provisions (Wilkes and Shirley, 1984; Trlin, 1977; Commission of Inquiry into Housing, 1971).

Early Social Theory and the City: From Founding Theorists to Chicago

The founding theorists of the discipline of sociology, Marx, Durkheim and Weber, all agreed that cities were important in the transition from feudalism to industrial capitalism and were created by the necessity to house workers near to the emerging factories. Further, they also saw the city as a contingent factor in influencing social change, with urban living as a necessary condition for the development of class consciousness. The study of the city was thus one of the earliest foci of the developing discipline of sociology. However, despite this initial recognition, little explicitly urban analysis was undertaken by early European sociologists and the base for twentieth century urban sociology was really laid through the work first of Engels and then of the 'social reformers' such as Booth with his study of London's poor in the 1880s. Urban research reflected the empirical rather than the theoretical traditions of the early sociologists (Dunleavy *et al.*, 1981; Kilmartin *et al.*, 1985).

Robert Park (1921), the leading theorist and founder of the Chicago School which developed in America in the 1920s, was concerned to explore the internal characteristics of the city and how the processes of residential segregation operated to distribute the population around the urban area. Park's explanation was built around two basic processes: those of competition and communication. Competition for Park was the harsh struggle which selected the fittest to survive. In developing his ideas, Park was clearly influenced by the Social Darwinism which was making its impact upon social analysts in the early part of the twentieth century. In addition to this notion of competition, Park utilised classical economics. This economics emphasised the importance of market competition and therefore the relationships of supply and demand as a major mechanism guiding both land use and the distribution of population across the various suburbs and inner city areas of Chicago. Park's view of competition left little room for a consideration of culture or social values in the shaping of behaviour. Competition was complemented by communication in human society and it was this social process which tied people into society. As social beings, people organised themselves co-operatively through communication. There was thus a socio-cultural level of experience which permitted the development of distinctive 'sub-cultures' within the city where distinctive modes of living could emerge. Consequently, Chicago was seen as made up of separate social areas characterised by particular land uses, population mix and exhibiting particular ways of life.

Students of Park took up these ideas and developed them to form two sub-schools of urban analysis which dominated the field until the 1960s, not only in the U.S.A. but also more generally. The first group can be referred to as structural ecologists, as they focused their attention on the spatial structure of the city and the identification of its various zones and natural areas. The second can be called behavioural ecologists as their focus was upon the ways of life which emerged in the city and the extent to which particular sub-cultures formed (Smith, 1980; Mellor, 1977; Pahl et al., 1983; Saunders, 1986).

The most prominent member of the first sub-school was Ernest Burgess who engaged in the social mapping of Chicago (Burgess and Bogue, 1964). Burgess took a whole series of indices of physical and mental disorders – housing conditions, crime rates, psychiatric illnesses – and by mapping their incidence demonstrated that there was a concentration of disorganisation, and therefore social pathology, in certain areas of the city. Burgess concluded it was the disorganised nature of social life in these areas arising from the physical conditions which led to the social problems. Such conclusions stimulated the growth of urban reform movements committed to the improvement of the physical structure.

The history of urban intervention within the twentieth century saw initially a commitment to physical improvement and then, when this failed to produce a reduction in 'social problems', a move was made towards community development which aimed at social intervention. In both cases, the direction of the intervention was aimed at those who were experiencing the problems and thus deflected attention from the question of how their condition was in fact produced.

The question which was central to Engels' analysis of nineteenth century Manchester, that of the connection between industrial capitalist development and urban structure and ways of life, was one that was largely missing from the Chicago school. As this school developed, it became increasingly dominated by empirical analysis leading to description rather than explanation (Faris, 1967; Smith, 1988).

The zonal model of Chicago produced by Burgess, a dominant image in urban studies from the 1920s to the 1960s, was seen to represent the 'normal' pattern of the industrial cities fed as they were by growth from the expansion of their industrial/ commercial base and through successive waves of migrants (see Figure 3.1).

Figure 3.1
Urban Areas

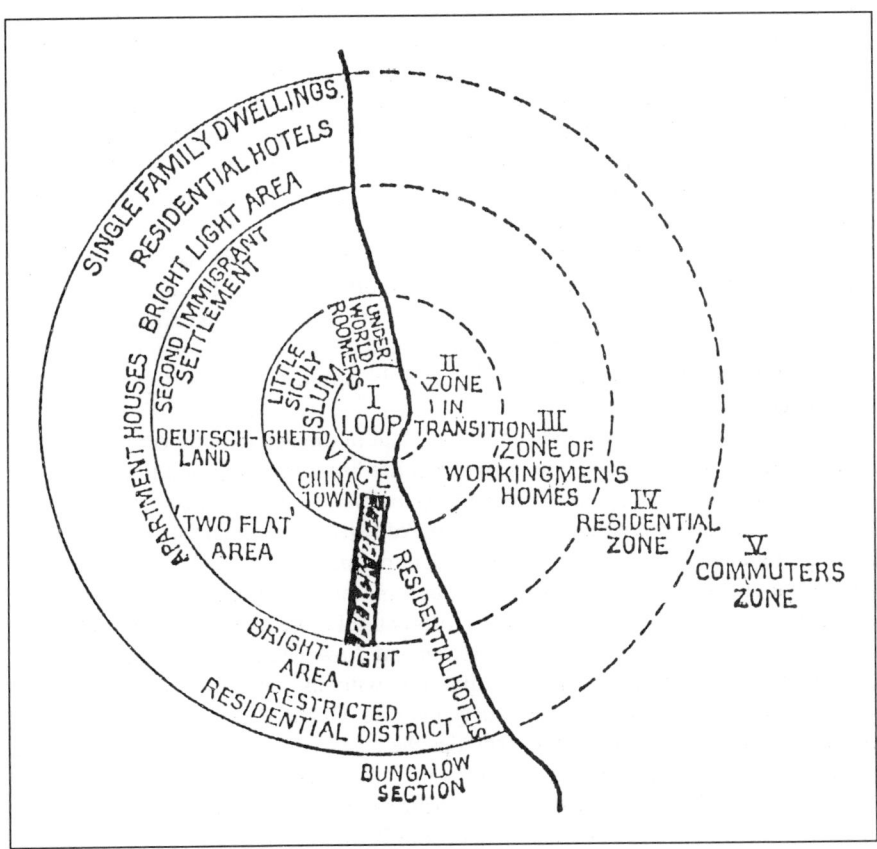

The model sets out five major zones. The first was the core of the city based around a central business area in which there was a concentration of offices, shops, banks, amusement and recreation areas. The zone had a high daytime population with flows of daily commuters, but a low residential population. It was the point of origin of the transport system and thus the focus of the road network which radiated out from the centre.

The second zone was one of transition in which there was a resident population, but it was being affected by the outward shift of the industrial and commercial activities leading to out migration of the population. Where such migration led to larger properties being vacated, a lodging house district formed which became the first point of entry for new migrants to the city. The area thus had many ethnic ghettos as the new migrants settled amongst those of their own ethnic group. It had an unstable social structure due to the mobility of the new migrants and had more singles and less families than the areas further from the centre.

Beyond the zone in transition there was a zone of working-class housing, an area of homes largely adjacent to areas of employment. The area was stable, made up of families with strong kinship ties and attachments to the locality.

The fourth zone was that of middle-class housing; as the distance from the centre increased and the industrial areas became more distant, so the size and amenities of the housing improved, and the workers were more likely to be white-collar managerial and professional than blue-collar workers. Finally, beyond the city would extend a commuter zone, the extent of which was linked to the mode of transport and depended more on time than actual distance. Consequently, over this century with the improvements in roads and the speed of transport generally, the size of such zones has increased.

The key writer in the second sub-school, that of the behavioural ecologists, was Louis Wirth. Wirth (1938) argued that urban life brought changes in the size of the city, its residential density and in its heterogeneity. This interrelated set of changes led to more secondary relationships and a breakdown in communal forms of solidarity leading to greater anonymity. It was no longer possible to know all the other people within the city and, therefore, social life became more formalised and contractual rather than spontaneous. The work of Wirth focused more on the behavioural rather than structural consequences of urbanisation and drew a contrast between urban life and rural life, often implying that rural life with its smaller scale and greater intimacy was intrinsically more satisfying (see David Pearson's chapter). The depersonalising influence of scale provides the basis for the development of public policy initiatives designed to personalise the city. These were attempted through both residential design and social engineering ventures based upon the advantages of social balance and population mix, and, latterly, through community development strategies.

Because of the emphasis upon technology, urban analysts within the ecological tradition focused attention on the way transport systems and communications improvements were crucial for urban expansion, taking cities from the walking cities of the early nineteenth century to those of the privatised car-using commuter cities of the late twentieth century. Such an approach now looks to the arrival of the micro-chip and the computer to bring about the decentralisation of the city as no longer will there be a need for the concentration of offices within the city centre. Such changes could render the role of the Central Business District obsolete and so radically transform the structure of land use and values (Castells, 1985).

The 1960s saw a number of analyses of the New Zealand city from within the ecological tradition (see Timms, 1972; Johnston, 1971; 1973a; 1973b). Working from census data, Timms sought to examine the degree to which cities are residentially segregated and therefore the extent to which distinctive social areas existed. Three main indexes were used in the study, those of socio-economic status, familism and ethnicity.

The first of these indices, socio-economic status, is a composite measure of occupation and income. Applying this index to the Auckland metropolitan area in 1961 and 1966, Timms found there existed a sectoral pattern across Auckland with areas of high and middle social rank in the south-eastern section of the North Shore (Takapuna and Devonport), the eastern section of the isthmus (Parnell, Kohimarama, St Heliers and Glendowie) and the east coast of the southern area south of the Tamaki River (Pakuranga and Howick). In contrast, the south-western and north-western areas provided sectors of working-class housing.

The second variable, that of family status, showed a zonal rather than a sectoral pattern, with low values characterising the inner city suburbs indicating a greater number of single-person households and two-person households without children. The inner suburbs of the city provided the initial housing for the new migrants to Auckland and were also undergoing transition as residential properties gave way to the outward expansion of the urban core and the development of improved roading to facilitate privatised commuting to the city centre.

The final index used by Timms was that of ethnicity. The pattern found here for Auckland was a bi-polar one, with the major concentration of non-Europeans in the inner city and on the southern edges of the Auckland metropolitan area, at that time Mangere and Otara. The inner city suburbs were the receiving areas for new migrants to the city whereas the southern suburbs were the areas that they moved to for more permanent residence. Many of these more permanent places were in areas of predominantly state housing. Timms, for example, notes that in 1969, 75 per cent of new state tenancies taken up in the Auckland area were by Maori and Pacific Island families.

The most striking correlation between the three indices was that between ethnicity and social rank which showed that as the social rank of the suburb increased, the proportion of non-Europeans decreased.

Similar analyses were also carried out for Wellington, Christchurch and Dunedin, which showed that the patterns of these three variables changed somewhat depending on the local topography (Timms, 1972; Johnston, 1971). However, the data indicated quite clearly that New Zealand cities were segregated residentially by social rank, family type and ethnicity. Research along these lines helped to establish a profile of the cities and raised important questions about urban differentiation and the distribution of facilities and services such as health services, access to general practitioners, libraries, community centres and local offices of government departments and agencies (e.g. Barnett and Newton, 1977; Bush and Scott, 1978; Davis, 1982). What they failed to do, however, was to provide a very satisfactory explanation for the origin and development of the patterns of inequality that were demonstrated.

In New Zealand as in other countries, there was a shift in public policy debate from a concentration upon physical amenities to social provisions and community development. The 1970s saw community advisers appointed within the larger local authorities with a wide-ranging brief from recreation through to advice on urban planning and locally based group activity (Shirley, 1979; Haigh and Gavin, 1977). In the mid-1970s, there was also the rise and fall of the public participation debate within the formal planning process of local and regional authorities. However, by the end of the 1970s, a move away from broad-based participation had occurred. Key factors in this shift were the passing of the National Development Act, providing fast-track planning procedures for major projects and the overall deterioration in New Zealand's economic conditions.

The work of those drawing upon the ecological tradition became subject to extensive critique in the mid-1960s and into the 1970s for failing to recognise either the role played by powerful social actors or the role played by conflict between the social classes that make up the city. All shades of ecological theory produce essentially apolitical theories of urban growth and development within which conflict and power imbalances as factors shaping the structure of the city are largely ignored. The critique of the 1960s and 1970s saw the emergence of new urban analyses which paid much greater attention to politics, power and class processes in shaping the city.

New Urban Sociology

The critique in the 1960s and 1970s of the urban research and analysis arising from the work of the Chicago School led to the reintroduction of European rather than American theory, beginning with a rediscovery of the contribution made by Weber and then Marx to an understanding of the city.

Weberian Urban Sociology

In *The City,* Weber (1921) drew attention to the city as a political entity in which the form that the city took reflected the values and goals of the dominant social group. This work clearly pointed to the importance of history, the social context of the time and the role played by key social actors in shaping the city.

In the 1960s, Weberian-informed analysis developed along two lines. The first was the study by Rex and Moore (1967) of race relations in Sparkbrook, an inner suburb of Birmingham in the British Midlands. In this study, Rex and Moore examined the place that the new immigrants occupied within Birmingham's housing market and argued that to understand this position, it was necessary to add to an analysis of economically determined classes the idea of housing classes, representing the degree of conflict and competition over access to housing resources. Life chances of individuals, with respect to their occupational and housing class, may well be different and thus require separate analysis. The work of Rex and Moore clearly showed that the urban system was one guided by competition between social groups for access to scarce and desired commodities, such as housing, which were allocated in part by the private market and in part by the bureaucratic processes of local government. Housing, given the substantial public housing stock in the 1960s, was a key area of local government activity. The rules and procedures adopted for allocating housing were a crucial determinant of the life chances of both the new migrants and the existing working class within the city. In New Zealand, this approach has been taken up and developed in the work of such writers as Myers (1975), Piesse (1978), Thorns (1981; 1989) and Dupuis (1989).

The second line of Weberian-informed analysis drew upon Weber's work on rationality and bureaucracy. The central concern of this work, the process of the allocation of resources, developed into a focus upon urban managers in the work of Pahl (1969;1977). The urban system was increasingly directed by urban managers within both the public and private sectors. Pahl's work placed emphasis upon three aspects of the city. The first was the way that resources were spatially distributed across the city. The work recognised that the resulting distribution was usually unequal and reflected the actions and positions within the power structure of the allocators. The second was the identification of the key actors within the city and the rules and procedures that they used in the urban allocation process. This group Pahl termed the urban managers. The final emphasis was upon the conflicts which occurred and the forms of urban action and protest. Such conflict was seen as inevitable given the differing values represented amongst the citizens. Consequently, urban analysis needed to examine the nature of urban conflict with a view to establishing who wins and who loses in urban decision-making.

The reformulation of urban research around the study of urban managers led to studies of local authority housing officials, planners, councils and councillors, town planning processes and procedures, banking and other mortgage institutions, builders and property speculators, and real estate agents. All of these groups were seen to have a role in shaping the access of individuals and social groups to desired urban resources and so affected life chances and opportunities.

The focus of the early work was mostly upon managers in middle-level positions, those who stand between the citizens and the dominant class. Such an emphasis led to a concern with the question of who controls the managers and how far they exert an independent influence upon the urban allocation process. Are the managers simply gatekeepers or do they materially affect policy outcomes? The concern with the amount of power managers possessed took the analysis and debate still further, into the controversy over the national and local role of the state in late capitalist society and its relative or absolute autonomy under capitalism (Saunders, 1979; 1986).

In the late 1970s and 1980s in Britain, under conditions of economic and social restructuring directed by the central government, resistance emerged at the level of local authorities. The resistance to and ongoing conflict between local and central government over the past decade has seen the demise of the Greater London Council and the implementation of a centrally directed programme to sell off local authority housing against the wishes of many local authorities (Murie and Forrest, 1988; Duncan and Goodwin, 1988).

The Weberian influence upon urban social analysis brought the study of the city within the wider debates of sociology which in the late 1960s and 1970s were about the nature of the state, power, class and social action. It thus made central what the previous ecological tradition had largely ignored. The city was viewed as an arena in which individuals and resources were distributed by social processes in which a key element was the action of urban managers operating within a system of domination and subordination. The extent, therefore, of managers' power became an important empirical question.

Utilising this approach for New Zealand cities, we would need to explore what resources are to be distributed within the cities, who distributes these resources and what is the result of the distribution in shaping the life chances of individuals and groups within the urban population?

Research operating within the neo-Weberian perspective has explored the structure and allocation of local resources and shown how access is restricted and choice is largely circumscribed. As a consequence, the nature of spatial inequality is interpreted as the result of socio-political procesess (Kilmartin and Thorns, 1978).

Marxist Urban Sociology

Marxist urban theory re-emerged within France in the late 1960s, particularly through the writings of Castells (1977). Castells began by attacking existing urban sociology as ideological because it did not possess any clearly identifiable object of study (Castells, 1976). Cities in advanced capitalism could only be understood within a more general analysis of the development of capitalist accumulation. The city was seen as shaped by the wider needs of the society and as derivative of broader economic processes. It could not be explained by the particularities of its territory and population mix as had been attempted by the ecologists, nor simply as a result of the actions of key social actors as had been attempted by the managerialists. Castells argued that advanced capitalism rested increasingly upon the processes of consumption. The post-war expansion of the welfare base of Western capitalist societies had created a large and growing arena of collective consumption covering health, education, housing and general community welfare. The important characteristics of these provisions for Castells is that they were not consumed by their users in the same way that food or clothing is consumed.

The fiscal crises which occurred within the states of Western Europe and the U.S.A. during the late 1960s gave rise to the need for fiscal austerity programmes which began to erode the levels at which the provisions of collective consumption could be maintained. This began the process whereby resources were returned to individual provision. The most widely studied of these resources has been housing with the growth of owner occupation through the sale of public housing (Harloe, 1981; Harloe and Paris, 1984). Castells considered this would lead to a politicisation of provision and an emergence of social movements opposing the cuts to welfare. Such social movements would be urban-based and would provide a major force for change (Dunleavy, 1980). For Castells, urban sociology's new agenda was to be constructed around the development of capitalism, the creation and restructuring of forms of collective consumption and the emergence of social movements.

Castells was not, however, the only Marxist writer to develop an urban critique. Another very influential writer was Harvey (1973; 1985; 1986; 1987). Harvey also brought the focus of analysis back to the logics of capitalist accumulation and the way in which these shaped the structure of the city. Harvey particularly drew attention to the role of finance capital and the part this played in the property booms and busts of the early 1970s, taking capital away from productive activities and into property speculation. A similar trend also re-emerged in the 1980s when there was a sharemarket and property speculation boom from the mid-1980s until the sharemarket crash in late 1987.

The examination of the logic of capital accumulation took urban analysis away from a focus simply on cities to that of regions, nations and international movements. Cities became the beneficiaries and victims of global movements. The decision to close a plant in one city was linked to the decision of multinational companies to relocate their operations from high-cost centres to lower-cost centres because of such things as tax rates or labour costs. New Zealand clothing manufacturers relocating to Fiji are an example of this kind of shift. Clearly such movements have a profound impact upon the urban infrastructure. Urban research has therefore moved progressively from a concern with the internal structures of individual cities to an appreciation and analysis of the role that cities play within a developing international system reflecting the new international division of labour that has been developing between the nation states and regions of the world during the 1980s (Smith and Feagin, 1987; Henderson and Castells, 1987; Thorns, 1989b; Smith, 1989).

Post-Fordist or Post-Modernist Cities?

The result of the restructuring of the cities that occurred during the 1970s and the 1980s has been the emergence of cities more dominanted by financial services and information than manufacturing production (Castells, 1989; Thorns, 1992a). These shifts have given rise to a debate as to whether a new 'post-Fordist' or 'post-modern' city form has resulted. Proponents of the 'post-Fordist' position see the changes within the city as primarily the result of economic and employment shifts leading to the restructuring of the gender, ethnic and class relations within the city. This creates a new high-consuming 'service' class of those employed in the new information and financial business service and a marginal 'servant' class of those involved in such areas as restaurants and fast-food outlets, entertainment and cleaning thus producing the 'dual city' (Harvey, 1989; Mollenkopf and Castells, 1990). Those who see the change more in terms of the rise of the 'post-modern' city place greater emphasis upon the shifts in architecture and style of building and the restructuring of the central city around consumption and recreational activity, with the emergence of 'yuppies' and a new round of gentrification (Watson and Gibson, 1993; Zukin, 1991).

This debate regarding the future shape of the city as a result of continuing restructuring is thus likely to dominate the urban agenda in the 1990s.

New Zealand Cities in the 1980s

To understand the present structure and form of New Zealand cities, it is necessary to examine them within a framework which allows us to see the cities as a product of the development and progressive reorganisation of capitalism. However, this is only a first step as these general processes have been influenced by New Zealand structures and institutions which have developed since 1840. An understanding of the shape and form of the cities needs both the analysis of capitalist accumulation and an exploration of local social and political structures, of class relations and economic conditions. The remainder of this discussion will sketch out how such an approach can illuminate the development of New Zealand cities over the 1980s and 1990s.

The 1980s has been a decade in which major restructuring has taken place within the economy as New Zealand has moved to adopt policies of economic liberalisation which have particularly affected the shape and size of manufacturing (Rosenberg, 1993; Britton et al., 1992). Such changes have impacted upon cities, both large and small alike. In this brief introductory discussion, it is only possible to point to some of the changes that have taken place.

The 1991 employment structure of the four main cities of Auckland, Wellington, Christchurch and Dunedin show the impacts of a decade of restructuring (see Table

3.1). The manufacturing sector has shrunk to a range of 24 per cent of total male employment in Auckland,' to 14 per cent in Wellington and, for females, from 16 per cent in Auckland, to 8 per cent in Wellington. The growth areas have been in business and financial services, especially in Auckland and Wellington which by 1991 comprised 14 per cent and 19 per cent of male employment and 19 per cent and 23 per cent of female employment. In all four cities, the service sector is now the dominant area of employment. However, Wellington emerges as the most dependent, with 74 per cent of male work in this sector and 73 per cent of female. The cities have taken on an increasingly 'post-industrial' character, where consumption and service-related activities form the core activities. In this respect, they have experienced similiar changes to those which have taken place within the industrial capitalist world (see Castells, 1989; Mollenkopf and Castells, 1991; Zukin, 1991).

Table 3.1
Percentage of Male and Female Employed by Sector:
Auckland, Wellington, Christchurch and Dunedin, 1991

	Males				Females			
	Auckland %	Wellington %	Christchurch %	Dunedin %	Auckland %	Wellington %	Christchurch %	Dunedin %
Agriculture	1.7	0.5	2.3	1.7	0.9	0.3	1.3	0.8
Manufacturing	23.7	8.7	24.3	20.4	16.5	4.7	15.7	12.3
Elect.Gas Water	0.9	0.9	0.5	1.4	0.3	0.4	0.1	0.4
Construction	10.4	8.2	9.6	10.2	1.2	0.9	0.9	0.9
Wholesale/Retail	20.8	17.2	20.9	18.7	21.7	16.4	22.3	19.9
Transport Communication	9.0	10.1	9.7	9.6	7.3	6.1	6.6	3.3
Business/Finance	13.8	24.6	10.8	11.3	19.1	26.3	15.4	13.9
Community/Social	17.5	28.2	20.3	25.3	31.2	43.4	36.5	47.4
Not Specified	2.2	1.6	1.6	1.4	1.8	1.5	1.2	1.1

Source: Census of Population, 1991.

The other side of these structural changes in the urban economies has been the uneven growth in unemployment rates across the various centres. Data from the three largest urban centres show that Wellington has been consistently below the national average, whereas Christchurch has followed the national trend. Auckland also followed the national trend in the early part of the 1980s, then in the mid-1980s benefited from the restructuring that occurred and its rate fell below that of the country as a whole, with the North Shore of Auckland being the area of the country with the lowest rate of unemployment. However, with the ending of the speculative property and financial boom towards the end of 1987, the unemployment rate increased in the metropolitan centres. Auckland in the 1990s has an unemployment rate which is now the third highest in the country after Northland and the Bay of Plenty (Britton *et al.*, 1992).

The growth of services and the deregulation of the financial sector in 1984 led to a speculative boom in both commercial and residential urban properties. Wellington was particularly affected by this boom of 1984-88 with 75 per cent of developements being carried out by four companies: Chase, Renouf, Cromwell and Realty Development Corporation. The activities of these companies and the concentration upon the central area fuelled the escalation of prices. The land values in the central office district in 1983 averaged $1,600-$2000 per square metre, whereas in late 1985 they had risen to $6000-$7000. The crash of October 1987 led to just as rapid a collapse, with the value of property company shares falling by 70 per cent in five months (Willis, 1992). A similar pattern also occurred in Christchurch, with commercial floorspace expanding by 2.43 per cent in 1986, 4.88 per cent in 1987, and 7.36 per cent in 1988. After the crash, the vacancy rate increased by 1347 per cent (Thorns, 1992b).

The result has been increased office space – much of it now empty – and a quite marked alteration in the visual image of the central areas of the three largest cities (Auckland, Wellington and Christchurch) as a result of this burst of construction.

Variations in employment structure and unemployment rates affect the overall income distribution within and between urban centres. In both Auckland and Christchurch, the overall distribution has become extended as a result of the structural changes. In turn, this has created a group of more affluent income earners and a growing welfare-dependent group made up of the unemployed and other beneficiaries. However, it is in Auckland where the greatest increase has occurred at the upper end, particularly during the mid-1980s boom years. A consequence of this was the development of a more conspicuous-consumption lifestyle among the city's newly rich, increasing the demand for such consumer services as restaurants, boutique shops and designer clothing.

Differentials in employment and income are also reflected in property prices. Auckland is the most expensive housing market in the country. The gap between Auckland and the other centres began to open up in the 1970s and has increased during the 1980s. The extent of this differential can be shown by examining the proportion of an average Auckland house that could be bought from the proceeds of the sale of an average property in other centres. In 1971, an average Christchurch house would have purchased 76.5 per cent of the Auckland equivalent. By 1986, this had fallen to 49 per cent. Again, the collapse of the property market as a result of the crash in October 1987 can be seen to have had the greatest impact on the Auckland area (see Table 3.2). By 1992, the differential between Auckland and the rest of the country had narrowed with, for example, the average Christchurch house purchasing 65 per cent of one in Auckland.

Table 3.2
House Price Changes in Main Urban Centres
1971-1986.

	Average House Prices ($)					
	1971	1976	1981	1986	1988	1992
Auckland	13,939	33,585	60,450	149,980	199,342	192,562
Wellington	13,865	30,844	43,286	107,125	155,039	166,328
Christchurch	10,660	25,818	35,777	74,258	91,585	125,994
Dunedin	9403	24,528	34,163	59,998	61,843	89,688

These changes indicate that the gap between Auckland and the other cities has widened and then narrowed again over the 1980s and into the 1990s. Such variations point to the difficulties likely to be faced by those moving from one region to another in search of employment. It is, in part, a reflection of these escalating housing costs that Auckland had not only the highest prices, but also the largest proportion of its households with severe housing needs during the mid- and late-1980s, with studies showing that Auckland's homeless grew from 1.3 per cent of all households in 1982 to 6 per cent by 1987 (National Housing Commission, 1988; Percy, 1982).

Significant changes have taken place within the structure and composition of New Zealand cities. There is a northward drift of population, employment and the more dynamic services sector. This movement has led to the occupational and income structure of Auckland undergoing modification leading to the emergence of an affluent service class which exhibits a quite different lifestyle and which in turn has stimulated the growth of new forms of consumption which have modified the streets and centres of the cities. The stockmarket crash of October 1987 has slowed the growth of this group rather than led to its disappearance.

The restructuring which has taken place has thus begun to produce a new urban landscape more characterised by consumption, festivals and displays and these have reshaped the ideas we hold about urban images and identities. Thus Christchurch has now become the 'city that shines' and its central planning is focused around the linking of Victoria Square, dominated by the Park Royal Hotel, through Cathedral Square, the traditional centrepiece, to the Botanical Gardens and Museum along the reconstructed 'Worcester Boulevard' complete with vintage trams.

The agenda, therefore, for the 1990s will be one of exploring the extent to which New Zealand's cities are now entering a 'post-industrial' or 'post-modern' phase of their development, and the implications this has for urban social relations.

Conclusion

In this chapter, we trace the growth of urban analysis from its nineteenth century roots in the examination of the impact of early industrialistion upon the lives and experiences of members of the working class. In the late nineteenth century, urban analysis was picked up by reform movements which led to the systematic studies of urban areas and cultures conducted under the guidance of the Chicago School. In the 1960s, a critique of these approaches developed, leading to the emergence in the 1970s of a new urban sociology with an agenda for research and analysis which focused much more upon the city as a set of resources to be distributed through political processes and involving key social actors who attempted to manage the urban system. Limitations within urban managerialism in the last decade have resulted in urban analysis moving still wider to try and understand how the cities of nation states are incorporated into the international processes of restructuring within capitalism. These international processes are, however, mediated through the particularities of place, both physical and social, demonstrating the continuing need for empirical analysis of the cities.

The new agenda for urban studies in the 1990s has been set by the restructuring of the employment and economic conditions within cities created by both global and local changes and leading to the debate as to whether cities are now entering a new 'post-industrial' or 'post-modern' phase more dominated than in the past by consumption.

Further Reading

Britton, S., Le Heron, R. and Pawson, E., 1992, *Changing Places in New Zealand*, Christchurch, New Zealand, Geographical Society.
Castells, M., 1989, *The Information City*, London, Basil Blackwell.
Harvey, D., 1989, *The Condition of Post Modernity*, London, Basil Blackwell.
Kilmartin, L. and Thorns, D.C., 1978, *Social Theory and the Australian City*, Sydney, George, Allen and Unwin.
Smith, M.P. and Feagin, J.R. (eds), 1987, *The Capitalist City: Global Restructuring and Community Politics*, Oxford, Basil Blackwell.
Thorns, D.C., 1992, *Fragmenting Societies?*, London, Routledge.
Watson, S. and Gibson, K. (eds), 1993, *Post Modern Cities,* Sydney, University of Sydney.
Zukin, S., 1991, *Landscapes of Power. From Detroit to Disneyworld,* Berkeley, University of California Press.

4 Rural

Ian Carter

On my first visit to this country in 1980, people kept asking me what kind of sociologist I was. After more than a decade writing about social relations in the Scottish countryside, the answer seemed pretty clear. Even though I knew that this description disguised some of the complexities that will emerge in this chapter, I answered with some confidence: 'I'm a rural sociologist'. 'How interesting', came the invariable reply, 'We've never heard of one of those'.

This was not what I had expected in a country that proverbially lives off the sheep's back. Since European colonisation made Aotearoa into New Zealand, export income has flowed principally from land-based activities. Whales and seals; gold; kauri timber and gum; wool; sheepmeat; butter, cheese and casein; beef; exotic timber; crayfish, snapper and orange roughy; apples and pears; kiwifruit: the product mix has varied over a hundred and fifty years of tenuous nationhood, but what has not changed is a national dependence on the land and sea. We would expect to be able to find inside sociology the empirical trace of this reliance. There should be a string of benchmark monographs; studies of the social organisation of fishing to set alongside Canadian work (Sinclair, 1988); studies of rural mining settlements to compare with Australian work (Metcalfe, 1988); or studies of the social relations of production in agriculture to set alongside work from many other nations (see, for example, Carter, 1979). Every collection of readings would have its statutory rural sociology chapter, boiling down these monographs for an undergraduate readership. None of this exists. We do have a couple of significant monographs, but they are not recently coined. Crawford Somerset's *Littledene* is the founding rural community study. It was published in 1938. W.T. Doig gave us a solid study of dairy farmers' life conditions, published in 1940. That is the lot as far as monographs are concerned. Summary collections for undergraduate sociology students routinely ignore rural New Zealand. So do the academic journals. After a long and diligent search, I found one academic paper with the magic title 'Rural Sociology in New Zealand'. It was published in that central sociological journal,

The Transactions of the Royal Society of New Zealand, in 1947. It runs to five pages (Jacoby, 1947). Thirty years later and we find another piece in *New Zealand Agricultural Science* (Gill and Gill, 1975). The rest, so to speak, is silence.

Why is this? Why have New Zealanders paid so little attention to their country's rural sociology (Franklin, 1978:146)? This chapter will argue two main theses. First, that rural sociology is not quite so absent as one might think, but that much of what exists was written by people other than sociologists. Second, that the notion of a New Zealand rural sociology is not as simple as one might imagine, for 'rural' is a deeply problematic concept within sociology.

The 'Rural'

Let us start with this second point. How do we routinely construct a notion of the 'rural' in New Zealand? One obvious way is to use economists' sectoral distinctions. Table 4.1 lists New Zealand's leading export commodities in 1986.

Table 4.1
New Zealand's Main Export Commodities, 1986

	$ million
Meat and meat preparations	1731.7
Milk and cream	564.8
Butter	538.8
Cheese	267.2
Casein	197.0
Hides, skins and pelts	319.5
Wool	1281.4
Fish	405.3
Sausage casings	66.5
Tallow	62.5
Fruit and vegetables	651.5
Pulp, paper and paperboard	431.7
Total (including other exports)	10139.0
Re-exports	432.7
Total Exports	10571.7

Source: New Zealand Official Yearbook 1987-8: 619.

Taken together, commodities in these twelve leading categories made up almost 65 per cent of all exports by value in 1986. Every one is sourced to the economy's rurally-located primary sector – agriculture, forestry, fishing and quarrying. But note that not all this value is crystallised in the primary sector. Country-grazed animals become meat, meat preparations, hides, sausage skins and tallow in freezing works and downstream factories. Country-grown trees become paperboard in mills. In judging the economic impact of agriculture, economists have to examine backward and forward linkages: agriculture's significance for input suppliers and for firms and industries that take and transform farm production (Easton, 1987: 2-2). Easton shows that while direct employment in agriculture made up some 9 per cent of the New Zealand labour force in 1986-7, a true measure of agriculture's economic importance, one that takes linkages with the secondary and tertiary sectors into account, increases the proportion of the labour force dependent on agriculture to 46 per cent. But dependence can cut two ways. Freezing works, the key element in the process of transforming animals into consumable commodities and a major bottleneck for farmers, are firmly classified as manufacturing plants. Thus linkages inextricably connect primary production with the secondary (manufacturing) and the tertiary (service) sectors of the economy. The primary sector may be located solely in 'rural' areas, but the secondary and tertiary sectors bridge urban and rural locations in an unpredictable fashion.

Economic space does not map cleanly on physical space. It maps no more cleanly on social space. Consider groups involved in primary sector industries. What social characteristics link farmers, hired or family farm workers, trawler companies, skippers and deckhands, miners and gold dredgers, foresters and forestry companies? Clearly, not very much. We might prefer to distinguish owners and controllers from direct producers in each of these cases, using class analysis to cut across tidy economic categories. We see that 'primary sector' is not a sociologically useful definition of 'rural'.

The second obvious definition of 'rural' has to do with the distribution of population in physical space. 'The rural population, of course, is that not defined as urban', the 1976 census report tells us (New Zealand Census, 1977: 3). Of course; how stupid of us not to realise. But note a couple of things. First, 'rural' is defined negatively here. We know what 'urban' means; in recent New Zealand censuses, settlements with more than one thousand inhabitants. 'Rural' means the bits left over when 'urban' areas have been abstracted. It is a residual category. Second, note that the census report writer's confidence in the self-evident status of this definition is misplaced. 'Rural' means different things in different countries. Other nation states use a different population cutoff for distinguishing rural from urban; 200 people in Iceland, 2,500 people in the U.S.A., 10,000 people in Portugal (United Nations, 1988: 186-189). More intriguing than this, however, is the evidence in Figure 4.1.

58   New Zealand Society

**Figure 4.1
Percentage Rural Urban Distribution of New Zealand Population, 1881-1986**

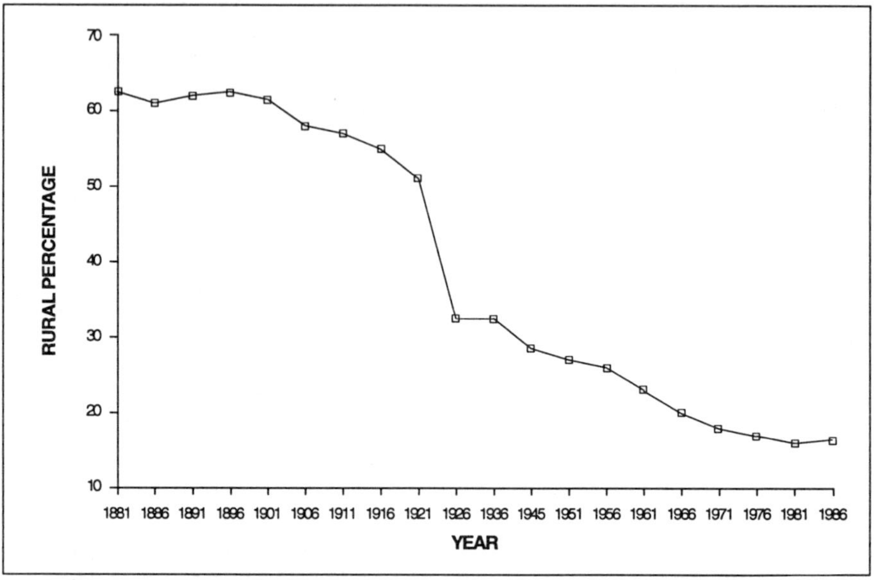

This displays New Zealand's rural population at each census since 1881. Until 1926, the implicit census definition of rural was 'county' rather than 'borough' population. The 1921 report was uneasy about this, noting that some unmunicipalised towns had considerable populations, while some of the smaller boroughs 'should strictly be classed as rural' (New Zealand Census, 1927: 16). The 1926 report replaced this constitutional distinction with a population threshold, and recalculated figures for the censuses between 1881 and 1921. It is these data, and another set from the 1976 census report that covers the years between 1926 and 1976, that form the basis for Figure 4.1. This figure shows a steady decline in New Zealand's rural population over the years; after 1971, more than 80 per cent of this country's people lived in towns and cities on census definitions. But what are we to make of the sharp change between 1921 and 1926, when the rural population apparently fell in five years from 51.2 per cent of the national total to 32.8 per cent? Was there rapid industrialisation in New Zealand during these years? No, that came with the import substitution policies introduced by the First Labour Government in the following decade. Is this the result of Maori people moving to cities and towns? No, that happened after 1945. In fact, very little happened between 1921 and 1926, except a change in the way in which census staff defined 'urban' and 'rural.' For 1926 and subsequent years, the cutoff point was set at one thousand people. So it was for 1881 also, but the 1926 census compilers used different thresholds for recalculating figures to 1921. The lower population level for an 'urban' settlement rose steadily: to 1200 for 1886, 1300 for 1891, and so on up to 2250 for 1916 and 2500 in 1921. This disrupts the census figures. It is clear that the compilers of the 1926 report were uneasy with a simple numerical criterion for 'urban'. Their progressively inflating criterion hints at an implicit 'way of life' distinction between rural and urban; certainly it destroys any notion that census figures provide a simple, sociologically valid conception of 'rural'.

This does not mean that a census definition of rurality is valueless for all purposes. Geographer-demographers may study changing population levels outside towns and cities (Bedford, 1980; Cloke, 1983). Geographers may seek to understand the pattern of services provided by state and private agencies (Gray, 1987). They can also study how planning legislation affects districts with different population levels, and examine the rural planning functions of central government departments (Moran, 1988). But what relevance does this hold for sociologists? What does it matter to us that some people live in settlements that contain fewer than one thousand people?

Twenty-five years ago there seemed to be an uncomplicated answer to this question. Sociologists assumed that social relations could be mapped on spatial relations. A 'rural-urban continuum' (Wirth, 1964) provided a measure of the extent to which any settlement was rural or urban. From this, one could predict what social life would be like in a particular settlement: tending to be kin-based, with overlapping sets of relationships in the country; sharply divided by class, with separate relationships for different life activities in towns and cities. New Zealand rural sociology could be built around community studies using varieties of ethnographic method to study country districts (Fox, 1980; Bell, 1983) and small country towns (Somerset, 1938, 1974; Oppenheim, 1976). Then Ray Pahl wrote his classic paper on the rural-urban continuum for the journal *Sociologia Ruralis*. Published in 1966, this paper destroyed the intellectual basis for an institutionalised rural sociology and a corresponding urban sociology. Pahl showed that the rural-urban continuum came from a misreading of Toennies' argument in *Gemeinschaft und Gesellschaft*. Toennies had distinguished two ideal typical forms of human mentality – usually translated into English as 'natural will' and 'rational will' – which were manifested as different forms of human sociability: 'community' and 'association'. He noted a *tendency* for the first to be found more often in villages, the second more often in cities. But things were much more complex than this (Newby, 1987; Saunders, 1981:81-3). For instance, there was a tendency for women to exhibit *Gemeinschaftlich* features and men *Gesellschaftlich*. To turn this distinction into a simple break between 'rural' and 'urban' was to disfigure Toennies' highly subtle attempt to understand the distinction between tradition and modernity. Further, Pahl argued, it made little sense in the light of empirical findings. If we can read of a densely kin-linked working-class community in east London (Willmott and Young, 1957) and a scattered farming parish without a nucleated village where class is the organising principle of social life (Littlejohn, 1963), then what price the mapping of social relations on spatial relations?

Rather clearly, not much. For a generation, urban and rural sociologists have been trying to find ways to put this particular Humpty Dumpty back together. Urbanists' attempts are treated in David Thorns' chapter in this book. What of rural sociology? Could a well-developed American literature provide the solution?

American Rural Sociology

If Crawford Somerset's *Littledene* (1938), a community study of Oxford in North Canterbury, which was written by a man trained in education rather than sociology, is most often seen to be New Zealand rural sociology's founding study, then close behind comes W.T.Doig's 1940 study. Given that a community study could not bear the weight for reasons stated above, then could Doig's be the real foundation for a national rural sociology? Some factors are not propitious. Doig was an economist, not a sociologist. He was recruited from Otago University to Wellington, his task to found a Social Science Section in the Department of Scientific and Industrial Research. With partial American funding, this section set out to study the living standards of New Zealand dairy farmers. But the central focus was on living standards, not dairy farmers; the section's second study, still unpublished because the dairy study proved politically chancy and led to the section's abolition (Robb, 1987), concerned the living standards of tramway workers. Once again, we find that there was no specifically rural focus in this work that could have provided the basis for an indigenous rural sociology.

This is a conclusion that would have surprised contemporary observers, for Doig's study was part of a push to establish American-style rural sociology in New Zealand (Carter, 1986; 1988). A leading American scholar, J.H. Kolb, was funded to assist Doig for a few months. Carnegie Foundation money brought Crawford Somerset's hero, the important American rural sociologist Edmund Brunner, to New Zealand to deliver a series of pep talks. In 1944 the Department of Agriculture established a Rural Sociology Section. One of the department's officers was tooled-up with the best available rural sociology training, a master's degree from the University of Wisconsin, Madison. The clear intention was to import an apparently well-established discipline and root it in New Zealand's fertile soil. It was a complete failure, for reasons which need not detain us here (Carter, 1988). What we do need to recognise, with the benefit of hindsight, is that American rural sociology never could have borne the expected intellectual burden.

American rural sociology emerged as part of a state-sponsored effort to mitigate the difficulties of family farmers in the early twentieth century (Nelson, 1969). Institutionalised in the severely practical atmosphere of the land-grant colleges and closely focused on client groups' needs, American rural sociology developed its characteristic emphases: heavily empirical, uninterested in theory, fetishising research methods, isolated from general sociology (Newby, 1980).

Change in the land-grant university system induced change in rural sociology. University research was funded by agro-corporations, which were concerned with maximising production through capital-intensive technological innovation. To rural sociology went the task of smoothing the brow of that dying class, family farmers. Interest in the labour process in agriculture, never strong after the briefly-flowering radical work of rural sociologists in New Deal agencies, was extinguished.

The leading features of American rural sociology are to be found in much New Zealand work. There is a complete absence of published work on the labour process in agriculture. We do have a string of studies on farm labour (Belshaw, 1933; Crothers and Loveridge, 1986; Guille, 1981; Harris, 1980; Martin, 1983a; 1984; 1987; Tipples, 1987), but none examines the social relations of hired or family workers with their employers or dominant relatives in the process of production. It is striking that the only published ethnography of farm work that we possess is a politics student's account of working as a cook for a shearing gang (Kraus, 1975).

The literature on farm labour has two interesting features. First, some topics have been done to death, notably the manner in which farm workers were excluded from the industrial conciliation and arbitration system (Belshaw, 1933; Martin, 1983a, 1987; Tipples, 1987), while other topics await any serious investigation. Second, we have directly comparable studies in some over-studied areas. Working on contract to the D.S.I.R., John Martin (1983b) investigated labour supply as a likely bottleneck for horticultural expansion in the Bay of Plenty. Working on contract to the Ministry of Works and Development, Evelyn Stokes (1983) considered the same topic in the same district. It is no surprise that they came to much the same conclusions. But Stokes wrote as a human geographer, Martin as a sociologist, although there is little to set his work apart as rural sociology.

This point can be generalised. While John Fairweather's (1982) interesting conceptual discussion of the transformation of nineteenth century land-holding patterns is both unprecedented and promising, there is no disciplinary *caesura* between historical geographers' detailed accounts of land settlement and tenurial reorganisation (see, for example, Franklin, 1969) and those provided by sociologists (Haythornthwaite, 1983). Sociologists' descriptions of the conditions controlling retirement from family farming (Kaplan, n.d.; Radford, 1983) are closely paralleled by geographers' studies (Moran and Anderson, 1988). The most determined recent attempt to find a specific object for a New Zealand version of American rural sociology – a technicist focus on social impact analysis (SIA) (Taylor and Sharp,

1983) – has collapsed for several reasons. One of these has to do with SIA's total dependence on state funding: not good news in these Douglas-inspired Friedmanite days. But SIA never could have supported a rural sociology. There is nothing specifically rural or sociological about the SIA enterprise: sociologists, geographers, economists, anthropologists and others have all been involved.

Thus, we see that empiricist American rural sociology shares with British community studies an inability to support a specific rural sociology in New Zealand. The former is in as deep a crisis as the latter. The empirical trace of crisis is the flood of agonised navel-gazing articles in the key American journal, *Rural Sociology*. In Britain, as in New Zealand universities, what passed for rural sociology was not institutionally separate from general sociology; there were no people who earned a specialised crust as rural sociologists. In America, things were very different. Staff in many universities' specialised rural sociology departments had found the ground cut from under their feet by Pahl's (and similar) arguments.

What, Then, is to be Done?

North American literature suggests that two current topics offer the possibility of a legitimate rural sociology. Astonishingly for that place and this time, both are rooted firmly in Marxist problematics. One concerns the internal dynamics of farm families, the other what has come to be called agribusiness. Both approaches merit much more serious consideration in New Zealand than they have received. Both presuppose that we should narrow the focus of 'rural sociology' to make it mean 'the sociology of agriculture'. Note that this shifts rural sociology to a mission built around economists' sectoral distinctions. A sociology of agriculture implies a corresponding sociology of forestry and a sociology of fishing. The focus moves to industries.

A Marxified populist programme for rural Russia; a book by Lenin, the arch-Bolshevik; a book by Kautsky, leader of the German SPD, the world's first mass Marxist political party: these are the unlikely building blocks for a new, adequate north American rural sociology. In a seminal article written from Toronto University, Mann and Dickinson (1978) glossed Kautsky's argument. The labour theory of value tells us that value is added to commodities in capitalist production only while labour is being applied. Hence, they argue, there is a critical difference between agriculture and other industries: a marked lack of it between agricultural production time and labour time. Only in those limited sectors where labour can be applied to a high proportion of production time – broiler chicken and egg production, intensive pig fattening are examples – will social relations of agricultural production take a fully capitalist form. In other branches, farming will be transformed internally to permit the realisation of surplus (if not surplus value) from a family farm sector trapped in a cost-price squeeze between fully capitalist input and output sectors (stock and station agents, feed suppliers, machinery suppliers, output merchants, and so on). In this view, North American family farmers are reduced to 'propertied labourers' (Davis 1980), precisely how Marx analysed the mid-nineteenth century French peasantry.

The parallels must not be pushed too far: in many ways and for many purposes modern American family farmers must be distinguished sharply from nineteenth century French peasants. Class analysis only makes sense in historically-specific social formations. A theoretically-sophisticated Marxist rural sociology is on the stocks (Newby, 1987). Kautsky's arguments have been developed in a case study of lettuce production (Friedland, Barton and Thomas, 1981) and in a recent important theoretical book on the developing nexus between farming and biotechnology (Goodman, Sorj and Wilkinson, 1987). None of this has sparked any work in New Zealand, although this country's economy is heavily, and increasingly, dependent on family farm-sourced agricultural exports which lie open to substitution as parts of agricultural production are industrialised. The continuous-process production of meat substitutes from single-cell vegetable proteins growing on a wide range of starch bases is a particularly threatening example.

Agribusiness merits close attention by New Zealand policy-makers and social scientists. There is little evidence that the first group has noticed what is happening. Social scientists have produced some useful marginal work. Historians and political scientists (Simpson, 1984: 147-174; Mulgan, 1984: 90-118; Vowles, 1985) have begun to put together evidence and argument on agricultural pressure group influence on the New Zealand state. This is an urgent matter in a political economy where most export crops are marketed not by private corporations – as the American agribusiness literature assumes – but by para-state producer boards. Bruce Jesson's (1987) account of intricate cross-Tasman corporate linkages – among stock and station agents and in the canned fruit and vegetable sectors for instance – needs constant updating as New Zealand capital is sucked more and more into an Australian union. The absence of this kind of work is astonishing and disgraceful. Richard Le Heron is working (in a geography department) on a study of the reorganisation of New Zealand food and fibre production, but even so we lack any serious work to set alongside major American studies or alongside a developing Australian literature. Given this academic weakness, currently burgeoning corporate integration, and New Zealand and Australia's common experience of dominion capitalism (Denoon, 1983), then the most promising short-term prospect for a critical sociology of agribusiness in this country is to piggyback on Australian work, developing consistent trans-Tasman comparative studies (Lloyd, 1987).

Things are scarcely less bleak in another sector. Mann and Dickinson's classic paper prompted another Toronto scholar, Harriet Friedmann (1980), to a critical response. Friedmann takes her bearings from the Russian populist/socialist debate. Her work, and the subsequent debate, centres on the dynamics and internal stratification of farm households. This work has barely penetrated New Zealand. There are two essays, one by a Canadian sociologist comparing Northland family farming with that in Ontario (Hedley, 1985; 1988), and the other an important doctoral thesis written for a British university by a New Zealand-born geographer turned rural sociologist (Pomeroy, 1985). In New Zealand the Friedmann debate is beginning to inform empirical work by local social geographers. Sociologists remain largely aloof from the entire rural sociology field. There is a growing stream of work on rural New Zealand women (Gill, Koopman-Boyden, Parr and Willmott, 1975; Grigg, 1987; Mahar, 1985; Maunier, 1985; Pomeroy, 1988). Some of this literature moves beyond documenting women's existence and experience to a feminist stance which challenges the frameworks through which existence and experience are captured, but none matches Sachs' (1983) feminist sociology of American agriculture.

There is much to do. Whether any volunteers will come forward to do it is a different matter. New Zealand sociology is ill-developed in so many of its branches. Again and again we find that we lack the benchmark studies on which a lively sociology focused on locally important issues could be founded. Particular difficulties inhibit the development of a good New Zealand rural sociology. The entry cost is high: one needs to understand both sociology and agriculture (or fishing, or forestry, or whatever). We have seen that much of the intellectual space that has fallen to rural sociology in other countries has been occupied in New Zealand by folk other than sociologists, notably human geographers.

Conclusion

What can we conclude from all this? Several things. First, that we should beware of nominalism. We can coin the term 'rural sociology' but this action does not mean the automatic creation of a new subject. We have seen that what should count as rural sociology is a surprisingly tricky problem. Second, we can choose to follow the most promising current route forward and redefine rural sociology as the sociology of agriculture. This has several implications. It implies the construction of parallel sociologies that are even less well developed in New Zealand: a sociology of forestry (Smith, 1981a, 1981b; Crothers and Macpherson, 1984; McClintock and Taylor, 1983) that could be seen as a sub-discipline of the new sociology of agriculture; a sociology of fishing that is completely undeveloped here and which would have to start from the industry's exploitation of a wild resource. All of this means, in the real conditions of 1990s New Zealand, overcoming engrained disciplinary prejudices to put together a critical mass of people interested in common problems. Geographers, political scientists, economists, sociologists: all have something to contribute and none has a monopoly of wisdom. The last point is important. One of the things that doomed earlier American rural sociology, and the attempt to transfer it to New Zealand, was a definition of the rural sociologist as the neo-classical agricultural economist's under-labourer. That we can do without. Finally, New Zealand sociologists interested in rural matters can and should stretch out in another direction to a different group of colleagues, to folk in disciplines like history, English literature and art history. 'Rural', like 'community', is a compendious term in everyday life (see David Pearson's chapter). People say 'rural' when they want to say something else but cannot find the right words. Like 'community', 'rural' is a metaphor that does sterling service in a huge range of contexts. To investigate these contexts is an entirely legitimate task for sociologists interested in New Zealand culture. Raymond Williams' *The Country and the City* (1973) provides a marvellous template for this task. What are the social meanings attached to 'urban' and 'rural' in New Zealand? How did and do these meanings change over time? How many of them came to these shores on emigrants' ships; how many arrived rather earlier, by canoe? What happened and happens when different meanings collide? Exploring these complexities is a major task for New Zealand sociologists with a humanistic bent. A little has been done (Carter and Perry, 1987): much more waits to be done. Who will do it?

Further Reading

Hussain, A. and Tribe, K., 1981, *Marxism and the Agrarian Question,* London, Macmillan.
Lawrence, G., 1987, *Capitalism and the Countryside,* Sydney, Pluto.
Wallace, L.T. and Lattimore, R. (eds), 1987, *Rural New Zealand – What Next?,* Christchurch, Lincoln College Agribusiness and Economics Research Unit.

5 Class

Chris Wilkes

Introduction

In everyday life the judgement of social difference is a commonplace. When we meet new people all of us have some preconceived criteria by which to evaluate the newcomers. If we are politically liberal, we may be interested to know if the new people we have just met have liberal political views themselves. If we have just been on a diet and lost a lot of weight, we may be judgemental about someone who is still overweight. If we spend a lot of time shopping for, buying and wearing clothes, we may judge the less well-dressed as not being up with the play. These judgements of social difference are so common that they are rarely mentioned, but they happen all the time. They are one of the mechanisms by which we place people and, having placed them, are able to manage them more easily. Of course, these patterns of judgement and evaluation are very varied and complex. What one group of people holds to be valuable and important may be of no importance to another grouping in society. In a university, for example, those who do the most research and write the largest number of articles and books are sometimes evaluated as outstanding researchers. In another setting, these same activities might be construed as a waste of time, and the people who do research labelled as worthless drones. Judgements of social difference are therefore very much dependent on the context in which the judgement takes place and on the individuals who are making the judgements.

These everyday events are of real interest to sociology because they provide examples of the stratification system at work ; the process by which human societies rank and evaluate themselves into an hierarchical order. Any socially accepted system of ranking and evaluation can lead to stratification and, as we have seen already, these systems of judgement and ranking may take on many forms. However, these processes of ranking, judgement and evaluation are more than just interesting anecdotes; they are also the basis for some enduring inequalities which appear to exist over time, and sometimes across cultures. Stratification means inequality. When we judge someone we establish a ranking in which their place is lower or higher than others. And this process of judgement is not merely an individual activity. The criteria we use to judge and rank others are embedded in wider social processes whereby New Zealanders as a whole judge other nations as well as each other.

Stratification as a process of ranking people in a socially accepted way is therefore a very widespread phenomenon. Whether we are male or female, black or white, young or old, rich or poor, each attribute can be used by other individuals, or by larger social groups, as a way of categorising us, a way of evaluating us and putting us at a certain level in the social hierarchy. The peculiar thing about certain attributes such as gender (the male/female difference), ethnicity (the black/white difference), age and class (the rich/poor difference) is that these particular characteristics appear to crop up in different societies and in many different historical periods. However, it is important to stress that even these apparently clear differences between people are not used in the same way wherever they occur. Age is a good example. It used to be the case that older members of a society were highly regarded as essential sources of knowledge and sustenance for the community; they were therefore highly ranked. We could not say that about contemporary New Zealand society. At the moment, one of the most contentious debates is whether we can afford as a nation to support the older generation through state pension policies. Clearly the process of ranking has changed, and age does not automatically attract esteem. The differences between men and women are also a product of social construction; that is, the meaning of being male and female varies in different societies at different times. Rosemary Du Plessis reviews these issues in her chapter. Similarly, the evaluation of ethnic difference is also highly variable. Paul Spoonley develops this theme more fully in his chapter.

In this chapter I am concerned predominantly with one form of stratification – social class. When sociologists talk of social class they generally refer to a system of economic difference in which property, wealth, money, exploitation and labour are the principal features up for discussion. In what follows, I am going to examine one of New Zealand's central myths about itself – the myth of classlessness. To examine this myth I will need to answer a series of smaller questions in the search for an answer. First, what were the origins of European settlement here, and did these original plans intend New Zealand to be classless? Second, what were the economic developments in the twentieth century which gave rise to the present class structure? Third, I will need to review New Zealand's present class structure and show how class acts as a form of stratification by creating and establishing social differences. These three questions will provide the necessary clues to the reasons behind New Zealand's evaluation of itself as a society without class. In the process, I will define class (in a somewhat different way from some other writers) as a system of structured social practices, shaping the form of our daily lives and maintaining a social hierarchy, against the vision of equality that we have of ourselves. I will conclude by suggesting that only by knowing its limits will class analysis demonstrate its considerable force as a social explanation.

The Origins of Class in New Zealand

The settlement of Aotearoa by European settlers, which gained momentum after 1840, was not an accidental affair; it was planned. The Britain of the early 1800s was a very disordered place; riots were not unknown in the streets of London, and the countryside was also in a state of unrest. Evans comments:

> The contrast between the pleasures of the rich and the privations of the poor could hardly have been drawn more starkly. For a Suffolk clergyman in 1849, poaching symbolised 'the antagonism of class against class in our rural districts' .... In East Anglia hardly a year passed without reports of rick-burning, cattle-maiming and destruction of farm out-buildings. The years 1816-1817 and 1822 were particularly disturbed. Targets, as with food riots, were carefully selected: farmers who paid below the going rate, harsh overseers of the poor, clergymen – magistrates who relished their judicial but neglected their spiritual duties (Evans, 1983: 146).

An English writer of this time, Wakefield, argued for the importance of colonisation as a way of solving the problems at home. Wakefield's argument was simple in outline; the problem with English society was that it was over-stuffed with people and needed room to expand. This expansion would allow those who owned property and money (capitalists) and those who wanted to work, but had no money or property (the working class and the unemployed) to find the right conditions for a new society. Wakefield thus championed a planned settlement of Aotearoa under the leadership of a private company, The New Zealand Company, and sought the British Government's help. He envisaged establishing a society in Aotearoa which would provide a happy balance between capital and labour, in which there would be enough money to invest and sufficient people to work the land for those with investments. All this, he argued, could be achieved by the use of a mechanism he called the 'sufficient price'. If the price of land was set at the correct level, it would mean that new settlers could look forward to saving for and eventually owning land, but they would need to work as labourers for several years before this happy outcome was achieved. In the meantime, they would provide the necessary workforce for the new settlement to succeed and, when the land was sold, the money would provide funding for the transportation of further new settlers. If the 'price was right', a happy balance of self-sufficient colonising, based on the principle of the 'sufficient price', would be established.

While there was much opposition to Wakefield's proposals, support eventually was gained for the general idea of a British colony, and members of the New Zealand Company set sail. The first 'Wakefield' settlements were in Wellington and in Nelson. Neither was a success, and both planned settlements had to be drastically changed so that the newly-arrived inhabitants could survive. However, the general principle of seeking to establish a new society, based on agriculture and closely connected to Britain, was followed during the course of the nineteenth century.

The acquisition of massive tracts of land by the settlers was essential to this plan. The history of the nineteenth century is predominantly the story of the struggle over land between Maori and Pakeha. Maori tribes throughout the country fought long and bitter battles, both directly – in a physical attempt to prevent the takeover of their ancestral property, and indirectly – through the courts, to try and find a legal basis for maintaining their control. These battles continue to this day (see Spoonley's chapter). For now, it is sufficient to underline the fact that European settlement in the nineteenth century was premissed on a large-scale alienation of Maori land. Without it, the emergence of farms, and the industries which developed from farming, would have been impossible to establish. This early source of inequality between the two ethnic groups lies at the heart of some our most pressing difficulties today.

In the earliest years of settlement, Maori traded with Pakeha. Maori provided the foodstuffs which kept the new settlers alive, while Pakehas brought the goods of the old world. As traditional workers of the land, the Maori were more expert than newcomers in gaining sustenance from the soil. By 1860, however, the balance of power was shifting from Maori to Pakeha. As European settlement developed, the new settlers brought in their own houses, some wealthy families going as far as bringing plate-glass windows. They brought their own farming animals, they brought their own seeds and grasses, they changed the soils with fertilisers until they became more like the soils they were used to at home. As well as changing the physical landscape, they brought a new language, a new culture, books, ideas, attitudes and ways of seeing the world which were from another place. In time, they brought their government, their legal system, their teachers to educate their children in Latin, music and ballet; their whole way of life. Conditions were very different in the new country, of course, but by attempting to transform the social and physical landscape in such a complete fashion, the newcomers hoped to make their new home as familiar as possible.

For early settlers, dumped on the beach in Wellington with little but their belongings and with few facilities awaiting them, the early society of New Zealand must have been completely unlike the life they were used to in Europe. Early Pakeha New Zealand was inevitably an unstructured and informal place. The rigid social structure that they had left in Europe had been dramatically changed during the space of the voyage. During the voyage itself, a hierarchy existed between those in steerage and those who could afford better. When they arrived, there were still those who were rich and those who were poor, of course, but the apparently closed society of England was replaced with a new society which was far more open (Fairburn, 1989). Occupations were much less specialised in the new country than in the old. Old patterns of deference between those in the lower and upper orders of society seemed to disappear. 'Jack is as good as his Master' (and 'Jill as good as her Mistress') were the slogans of the day. Opportunity beckoned for the landless. Those who arrived with money expected to increase their wealth rapidly.

The most familiar avenue which the new arrivals followed to improve their lot was to aim to buy a small, self-sufficient farm. In the earliest years this path was not easy to follow. Many people found the struggle an unequal one and walked off the land. There was widespread destitution and hardship, both in the rural areas and in the cities. An early urban settler commented:

> Work is not too plentiful, about two days' employment during the week for each ... Our credit being good we buy from natives and colonists, some of whom sell the clothes from their backs from destitution. Some in good circles in England have parted with everything, lead miserable and degrading lives, skulking in the bush and drowning their sorrows in drink – when able (Ward, 1928: 105).

In spite of the difficulties, by the last decades of the nineteenth century many small farms had been established and new rural settlements had been placed on a surer footing. Toynbee (1979) estimates that in 1882, almost half the adult male population were landholders. While many of these landholdings were not large enough to be self-sufficient farms, the figure nonetheless indicates the degree to which early settlers managed to establish small holdings. The small family farm thus became an important source of sustenance for the newcomers. Alongside such farms there developed large-scale sheep stations, and these larger holdings became sites of major wealth creation in some parts of the country, especially in the Canterbury region and in the Hawke's Bay (Eldred-Grigg, 1980). In addition, by the end of the nineteenth century, small towns were growing rapidly as sites where the developing volume of production could be serviced, exported and sold.

When we think of the class structure of the early years we must therefore think of several key groups. Maoridom was being rapidly disenfranchised of its land and many Maori forced into rural labour. Small farmers were developing their properties. Large-scale farming was emerging in which a complex hierachy of cooks, servants, shepherds, farm managers and a multitude of labourers were employed – some itinerant labour, others more permanently employed. The work of women was at the centre of these new developments, as it had been part of the old society. In New Zealand, women were expected to work on farms with the men, as well as keep the work of the household under control. On large stations, owners' wives took on the task of managers of large numbers of servants; women were employed as domestics (though they were hard to get and train, according to the farm owners of the day). In all walks of life, women were engaged in paid and unpaid labour in a more direct sense than in Britain. An example of an early class structure is provided by Auckland in 1843 (Table 5.1).

Table 5.1
Nominal Class Structure: Auckland, 1843

	%	Number
Owners (includes senior civil servants normally allocated to the middle class)	11.4	103
Self-Employed (shop-keepers, but excludes small farmers who are not separately categorised)	10.9	98
Workers (includes skilled workers, gardeners, farm employees, domestic servants and includes an unknown number of small farmers)	77.7	702
Totals	100.0	903

Source: Table 16 from Statistics of New Zealand, 1840-1852 (modified).

The vast majority of people were working class (approximately 60-80 per cent); perhaps 10-20 per cent were self-employed, the remainder were large land owners and owners of companies employing other people. These proportions were to change in the coming years, altering the balance between classes and bringing into being a new class, the middle class, for which there was little need in the nineteenth century. But the overwhelming story of the nineteenth century is the change in the mode of production. In 1800 the dominant pattern of economic production was the hunting and gathering economy of the Maori. Hierarchical, based on collective ownership and non-competitive, this pattern of production was demolished by the new mode of production the settlers brought with them. Based on private ownership, on a hierarchy of class rather than kinship and directed towards competitive profit-making, this new system of economic organisation established the pattern for the years to come. This tells us something about the first part of the question we have posed, namely to discover what the class structure of the nineteenth century was like. As we have seen, it was fluid, characterised by a loose hierarchy, predominantly working class, and dominated by agricultural production, both on a large scale and as a system of family farms. In addition, the towns were springing up and bringing with them all the new occupations which were needed to manage the vast agricultural wealth of the emerging society. Maori disenfranchisement set the scene for a pattern of disadvantage which was to endure into the twentieth century. By the end of the century, women's work was having a profound effect, not only in the household and on the farms where it had always been crucial, but also in the paid labour force as well.

But to typify the new colony as some glorious land of opportunity would be quite mistaken. As we have seen, the planners hoped New Zealand would be a successful capitalist society. It had never been planned as an equal society, but rather as a society which produced the inequalities of private property more successfully than had Britain. And while the early plans were shelved, there is little doubt that New Zealand in the nineteenth century exhibited a class structure that was unequal in terms of wealth and income, which grossly disadvantaged the indigenous people and discounted the contribution of women. Thus, while we are right in pointing out the fluid nature of early class society, vast divisions had developed between owners and workers, even if those who had suffered the most in Britain sometimes did a little better here. Another part of the answer about the myth of classlessness is therefore now clear. New Zealand was *planned* to be unequal, but at the same time, because of the fluid nature of nineteenth century society, it offered newcomers, used to being at the bottom of the ladder, a chance to escape. Even if the new society was unequal, the new settlers expected to be on top, not on the bottom. New Zealand was partly open, at least in comparison to Britain. And it was not until the twentieth century that class structures became more rigid.

Class in the Twentieth Century

The second part of our argument concerns the development of the twentieth century. Here, three trends are important as a background to an understanding of present class society – the rise of urbanism as a predominant way of life; the emergence of the working class and the development of the New Zealand Labour Party; the development of the middle class. First, the rise of urbanism. New Zealanders still think of themselves as a rural country, dependent on rural life as the backbone of the nation, a litany so often repeated that most of us believe it without thinking about it. Nonetheless, since the latter part of the nineteenth century, a majority of the nation's inhabitants have lived not in the rural areas, but in the towns and cities. Of course, many of the economic activities of these settlements are dependent upon rural production and are therefore closely tied to the country. But we have been a predominantly urban nation for almost a century, while simultaneously believing ourselves to be rural. Seeing ourselves as a rural society has meant we could identify with an image of ourselves far removed from the over-industrialised world which some of our ancestors left many years ago. This sense of difference was aided by the small scale of industrial production in the new country. Contrasting our own society with that of the old world means too that the problems of such societies – overcrowding, poor health, conflicts between boss and worker, centuries-long battles between the haves and have-nots – can all be left behind as part of another world. Ironically, New Zealand was thought to be a leader in industrial relations through the legislation of the Liberal Government of the 1890s (Hamer, 1988), which sought to put an end to strikes and to get beyond the problems of the old society. However, this programme was only possible because of the under-developed condition of the urban economy and the elemental form of organised class relations.

By 1910 the rise of the Labour Party and the increasing organisational power of the working class (the second theme we need to consider) was changing the shape of New Zealand society. As Olssen (1988) has shown us convincingly, by the end of the first decade of this century, social unrest in the workplace had reached a peak. The Liberal Government's attempt to legislate against strikes was faltering, and New Zealand witnessed widespread disruption in the workplace. Through an elaborate process which need not concern us here, this social discontent found a permanent voice in the shape of the New Zealand Labour Party. Labour began as the political voice of a single class, the working class. It did not gain power until 1935, and when it did it was not as a representative of just one class. Nonetheless, the development of the party signals a new stage in the history of class society.

Finally, we must point to the emergence, most importantly since the Second World War, of a new class, the middle class. Early New Zealand was based on small-scale productive units, whether as small farms or businesses servicing the agricultural sector, which either used only family labour in self-employed businesses or small numbers of workers usually supervised by the owner of the farm or company. The twentieth century changed all that. The average size of businesses began to increase, and together with the increasing size of government, a need developed for a managerial stratum in the workplace and bureaucracy. It was no longer possible for individuals to run companies on their own. The government had need of large state organisations – these also were too large to be organised by a single person. As the scale of organisations increased, and companies and the state became larger, it became more common to employ a group of workers whose primary task was to organise the work of others. Owners of companies delegated the running of businesses to managers and supervisors. Government departments became multi-layered bureaucratic institutions. Owners, workers and the self-employed were joined by a middle class, paid to manage the work of others. The rise of the middle class was accompanied by changes in the way in which we viewed ourselves as a nation. By the post-war period, talk of economic recession, the important defining feature of the 1930s, was receding. New Zealand enjoyed unprecedented wealth, relative political stability and unemployment rates which were infinitesimal compared to present-day levels. At the same time, intellectuals of the post-war period began to feel classes, class conflict, social disorder and differences between rich and poor had little to do with the New Zealand of the time. Consider this quote, for example:

> New Zealand has no class struggle, no poor, no intellectual tradition, no overt group conflict, little self-awareness as a social entity and has sought for similarity rather than diversity ... it is for these reasons that New Zealand has no sociology (Jackson and Harre, 1967: 125).

This description of New Zealand seems a little dated if not absurd to us in the 1990s, with high rates of unemployment, clear and widespread poverty and, one hastens to add, a lively New Zealand sociology! However, it is clear that political scientists, no less than other members of society, are as capable of coming to the wrong conclusions as the rest of us. And the myth of classlessness is very much part of the understanding we developed of ourselves as a nation in the relative cosiness of post-war affluence. Thus, a further part of the answer concerning the myth of classlessness must therefore lie in our failure to understand post-war trends as simply moments in history, rather than unchanging certainties. As we shall see, changed economic times made such attitudes harder to justify.

Contemporary Class Structure

Until now in our argument I have used a theory of class, based on ownership and control of the economy, without spelling out the details of my argument. As you will immediatetely realise when you read through this book, all sociological theories are subject to debate and class analysis is a highly contested area. In this section, my purpose is to set out the model of class analysis I have used, comment on why I use it, and compare it to competing models. The simplest way to set out the class model used here is by way of a table (see Table 5.2).

As we can see from the table, classes are created by asking four basic questions of people and by placing individuals accordingly. This is simple enough, but there are two things which need explanation. First, this hierarchy has two dimensions embedded in it – exploitation and domination. These terms are in common use but have a technical meaning in sociology. Exploitation refers to the expropriation of products from workers. Put simply, if I work all day writing something and at the end of the day someone comes along and sells it, paying me only part of what they get for it, I could be said to have been exploited because the value of the thing I made was not returned to me in full – some of its value went elsewhere. Of course, this process occurs all the time when people work producing things which are then

Table 5.2
The Criteria Used for a Class-Relational Model

	Class Criteria			
	Own Business	Purchase Labour	Managerial Supervisory	Wages or Salary
Class category:				
Owners	Yes	Yes	No	No
Self-Employed	Yes	No	No	No
Middle Class	No	No	Yes	Yes
Workers	No	No	No	Yes

sold by the company at a value higher than wages. Owners are those people who live off this surplus, generally termed profit. The self-employed work for themselves and thus avoid exploitation because they own the things they produce and thereby receive full payment for them in the market place. However, exploitation is only part of the story. Domination (control of the workplace) is also important in establishing a class hierarchy. Control in the workplace distinguishes the middle class from the working class because the job of the middle class is to direct, manage and control the work situation. Thus, the middle class both have authority over workers but are themselves exploited because, like workers, they do not own the things they produce and do not receive full value from them at the end of the day. Workers comprise the remainder of the workforce – they do not own companies, and they do not control the workplace. The members of the class hierarchy are thus connected by a system of exploitation and domination – twin mechanisms which work hand in hand. Unpaid domestic work in the home – maintaining a house and caring for children and spouse – can also be considered a criterion for membership of the working class. Here workers do not own a company and work with little control in the workplace. The placing of domestic work in a class hierarchy is a further subject for debate.

What alternatives exist to this form of class analysis? The above model derives in the first instance from Marx who saw the world divided into owners and workers, as well as from work by Erik Wright (Wright, 1978) who established the middle class as a distinct category. However, scholars influenced by Weber argue that status (the social prestige accorded to people) and 'party' (their political power) may be equally important in creating a class hierarchy. The particular mechanism which is applied here is the concept of the market and 'market situation'. It is argued that market allocation is responsible for creating class difference through the process of ownership, education and other market factors. Scholars in New

Zealand influenced by Weber include Pearson (1980) and Pearson and Thorns (1983). Earlier work on class in New Zealand followed what is termed a functionalist analysis. Here the central argument is on the function of occupational or socio-economic difference and the needs society has for inequality (see Congalton, 1966). A more orthodox Marxist account than the one I have proposed is offered by Bedggood (1980). The difference between Bedggood and the model used here is that Bedggood has no middle class but, like the present model, he includes domestic labour within the working class. I have argued elsewhere that it is misguided to limit analysis of the exploitation of domestic labour to class analysis (Wilkes, forthcoming).

I prefer a class-relational model for several reasons. I want to suggest, like Marx, Wright and Bedggood, that the four classes are connected to one another by processes of exploitation and domination. It is thus absurd in my view to talk of a single class, since classes only develop *in relation to one another.* It is meaningless to talk of a working class without an owning class, since one group is produced by its relation to the other in our kind of society. Second, I want to suggest, in contrast to functional accounts, that class inequality is not inevitable in all societies but, instead, is a product of the way we have chosen to live in New Zealand, an outcome of our particular history. Third, as distinct from Bedggood, I want to suggest that what is distinctive about the twentieth century is the rise of the middle class, along with an increasingly powerful and organised working class. Only an analysis which accepts the rise of the middle class can account for the politics of the twentieth century. Fourth, while I argue with Bedggood that certain aspects of the domestic labour situation may be similar to conditions within the working class, I reject a *reduction* of the condition of exploitation to class conditions, preferring to see it as a product of both gender and class relations (see Wilkes, forthcoming, Chapter 10).

Using such an analysis, how does the New Zealand population divide itself? Table 5.3 illustrates how including domestic work in the class structure influences the shape of our class map.

Table 5.3
Class Structure of the New Zealand Workforce

Class	Percentage in Each Class (Without Domestic Workers)	Percentage in Each Class (With Domestic Workers)
Owners	10.8	7.6
Self-Employed	8.9	6.3
Middle Class	39.3	27.7
Workers	41.0	58.4
Totals	100.0	100.0

As we can see, including domestic labour in the equation dramatically alters the balance of the class structure, giving the working class an absolute majority overall. In contrast to the paid workforce, where the middle class are almost the same proportion as the working class, the second model reduces the middle class to half the size of workers. But the important question is to ask what difference this class analysis makes. The answer to this question lies in the matter of social difference.

First, it is clear that classes are not homogeneous; each class category has subdivisions within it, generally termed class fractions. For example, women engaged in domestic labour are generally conservative voters, whereas semi-autonomous workers (workers with a great deal of control over their own work) are generally radical or liberal in their outlook. This means that any simple explanation which suggests that the working class will 'vote with one voice' is likely to fail. However, in spite of these complications, owners do tend to vote more conservatively than workers (Chrisp, 1986; Wilkes, forthcoming). The middle class do tend to act more moderately than owners and they become more liberal the further down the hierarchy you go. Workers overall do tend to vote more commonly for Labour (see Vowles' chapter).

When we turn to social life, people in the working class prefer their own company to that of other classes, while owners of companies say they prefer to spend their social hours with others who own companies and make few friends at work. There is evidence of spatial segregation between classes with members of classes more likely to live with people of their own group than among others. Attitudes towards society, relations between men and women, and between ethnic groups, as well as class identification, religious beliefs and other social factors distinguish one group from another (Wilkes, forthcoming; Vellekoop, 1969). Moreover, the class structure serves as a powerful mechanism in the exclusion of women and ethnic minorities, both groups being poorly represented in the owning class and under-represented in the upper reaches of the middle class. As we move down the hierarchy, more women and ethnic minorities are included. In the working class we find a majority of paid working women (if we include domestic work, women are a majority in the working class) and a majority of Maori and Pacific Islanders in paid work.

Of course, none of these divisions is clearcut and many ambiguities exist. But overall, there is clear evidence that many significant features of daily life are influenced and shaped by class difference (Wilkes *et al.*, 1984). This is hardly surprising in a society which was planned as a class society and which, since there has been no discernable revolution since 1840, is still structured in the same way.

But is it accurate to say there has been no revolution? Even if we use a strict definition of revolution as the violent overthrowing of a government, it is plausible to suggest that Maori government of the nineteenth century suffered just such a fate.

Closer to our own time, some writers have also spoken of the 'Quiet Revolution' (James, 1985). The argument is that recent changes resulting from the Labour Government's rise to power in 1984 may also be revolutionary. In the last section, I want to see if these recent changes in New Zealand matter for class analysis and answer the last part of our question about the myth of classlessness.

Conclusion

The Labour Government of the 1980s consistently followed a pro-market policy, freeing up the economy and letting capital and labour negotiate directly with one another without government intervention. This is an important change for class analysis because it alters the relationship between owners and workers, a relationship which has been closely monitored by the state since 1894. (See Nicola Armstrong's chapter on the state for further discussion of the relationship between state and class). In the present climate, the existence of inequality, rather than being hidden behind an apologetic denial of class, has been brought out into the open and celebrated, according to David Lange, as the driving motor of society. If class society has now become respectable, and a pillar of government policy, it is not surprising that the glorification of wealth has recently become a much more acceptable pastime in New Zealand, as the BMWs, mirror-glass buildings and the deliciously-satirical *Gloss* tell us. There have been several attempts to explain this change (Wilkes, 1988; Jesson, 1989; Wilson, 1989; Maharey, 1989). One suggestion is that the shape of the economy has altered from Fordism to post-Fordism (a phrase which requires explanation).

Traditional industrial (Fordist) societies, with large-scale production, mass employment, increasing wealth and little choice for consumers are sometimes said to be typical of the post-World War Two period. We might hypothesise that in New Zealand the post-war period between 1950 and 1970 was just such a period, with high productivity, increasing wages and low unemployment. Recent complex economic changes are said to have brought this era to an end. Now, in the present era (Post-Fordist), we see high rates of unemloyment, little economic growth, the development of a highly specialised economy making many different types of goods available in small runs, and increasing class divisions. Britain is said to be going through such a change (Jessop, 1986). Could the same be said of New Zealand? Certainly we have high unemployment, little growth and a collapse of the old economy, as the demise of the freezing works seems to indicate. What does this mean for class analysis? It means several things. First, there is a realignment among the fractions of the owning class, away from the dominance of the farming and manufacturing of the past, towards finance and services of the future – bankers have become overwhelmingly important. Second, the rise of the managerial middle class to a place of prominence is significant. It is sometimes forgotten that state expenditure has reduced very little in the last decade and that resources have often been lost by the working class at the expense of managers. In Auckland, for example, nurses have argued that consultants and managers of hospitals have got new offices and cars, while nursing numbers have been reduced and resources have dwindled at the ground level. Finally, the working class has been severely disadvantaged by these changes. The rates of unemployment affect this group most severely, thus also affecting women and ethnic minorities disproportionately.

The myth of classlessness is a changing phenomenon. In trying to explain it, I have suggested that the myth was a necessary part of the nineteenth century vision of New Zealand, as an invaluable part of the motivational landscape which led people here and, once here, drove them to seek material improvement. In the twentieth century the emerging organisational power of the working class dispelled the illusion that class could be ignored, and class remained part of the national debate until the Second World War. During the post-war era, class analysis was almost entirely absent from the intellectual agenda in a crucial period of our history when many contemporary social scientists were trained. And, in a unique turn of events, the 1984-1990 Labour Government saw something to celebrate in our economic differences.

Class analysis has the potential to be a disquieting political doctrine, capable, in the appropriate circumstances, of providing the basis for revolutionary action. It certainly had this potential for New Zealand in the early years of this century. But this revolutionary doctrine can also be turned on its head by those in power and used to explain how the rich are rich because they have more talent and work harder. The myth of classlessness has therefore acted as a spur to activity on some occasions, and a denial of unpleasant and enduring truths on others; it has been embedded in the way we have, as a nation, explained ourselves to ourselves. But classes have consequences, and it is these consequences which we have to consider when we study class structures. The consequence of class society is inequality; in wealth, longevity, health, quality of housing – in fact, with regard to all the social goods we need to survive. Class is a system of structured social difference. It is a system because it involves whole clusters of people. All society's members are part of a structure of relations. It is structured by the places people occupy in the economic system, based on exploitation and domination. It establishes social difference in all the arenas of social life which matter to us. Alongside gender and ethnic difference, as well as age and disability, class difference is one of the underlying reasons that our social world remains, and will continue to remain, unequal.

The paradox for class analysis therefore lies in its limited but powerful explanatory capacity. Indeed the strength of its explanation depends in part on writers knowing the limits of its field of analysis. When we try to use class analysis to explain every form of inequality which exists in the world, the shortcomings of a class-analytical approach are clear enough. Nonetheless, all societies are massively shaped by economic difference. All class analysis can do is to explain how those differences arose, who is advantaged by them and who suffers, and how shifts in resources take place. It can draw the lines of cleavage created by the emergence of class systems, it can suggest how the politics of societies might be shaped by class forces, and it can offer an account of the cultural, educational and ideological corollaries of class structure – which really should be enough for one theory.

Further Reading

Bedggood, D., 1980, *Rich and Poor in New Zealand,* Auckland, Allen and Unwin.
Jones, F.L. and Davis, P., 1988, *Models of Society: Class, Stratification and Gender in Australia and New Zealand,* Sydney, Croom Helm.
Pearson, D. and Thorns, D., 1983, *Eclipse of Equality: Social Stratification in New Zealand,* Sydney, Allen and Unwin.
Wilkes, C., (forthcoming), *Social Classes in New Zealand,* Auckland, Oxford University Press.

6 Racism and Ethnicity

Paul Spoonley

Few New Zealanders remain untouched by the issues of racism and ethnicity and most, given the opportunity, will express strongly held views about what is commonly referred to as 'race relations'. It is an exciting if somewhat fraught area for the sociologist to study, partly because of the emotive nature of public debate, partly because a sociological interpretation may offend, and partly due to the rapidly changing nature of the issues. As with notions like 'the community' or 'the family', many feel that they know what constitutes 'race relations'. They confidently identify the problems and what ought to be done. The sociologist should begin by asking questions about such commonsense perceptions and then proceed to develop critical and analytical arguments about the social processes involved.

This chapter begins by asking such questions and then by offering a terminology which encapsulates sociological arguments about the social processes in question. Those who would criticise sociological terminology as unnecessary jargon ought to ponder the difficulties associated with using terms which are not only highly emotive, but which tend to vary in meaning according to who is talking or writing. Sociology as a science requires a reasonably precise technical language which does not reflect the variability of commonsense terms.

Racism and Ethnicity[1]

One of the first matters a sociologist must address is the labels by which people make sense of their social and physical world. In the present context, the core concept is that of 'race', and those words such as 'race relations' which employ the meaning of the first term. Many sociologists are highly critical of the concept because of its commonsense meaning and the history of political and scientific racism which is associated with it.

The word 'race' was first used in the sixteenth century to classify humans into sub-species in the belief that physical differences (phenotypes) reflected basic (innate) cultural and intellectual differences. There evolved a number of forms of scientific racism, notably those offered by the racial typologists and Social Darwinists (see Banton, 1977; Miles, 1989) who dominated both scientific and popular thinking on 'race relations' in the latter half of the nineteenth century and well into this century. These scientific arguments played a major role in the process of European colonisation, and then in justifying slavery (particularly in the U.S.A) and other forms of racial oppression. Developments reached a climax in the Holocaust of the 1940s whereby Nazi Germany used scientific racism to legitimate the genocide of Jews and gypsies.

Since 1945, and at the bidding of UNESCO, biological and social scientists have taken a much more critical look at the popular and scientific use of the concept 'race'. Biologists now use terms such as *breed* or *sub-species* to avoid the assumptions implicit in the concept. It is considered to be inaccurate to talk of human 'races' because of the difficulty of establishing who constitutes a member of a particular 'race'. The interchange of genes makes racial boundaries a nonsense. Further, the assumption that physical differences provide an accurate marker of other differences, notably intellect, is scientifically invalid (Miles, 1989).

Despite the acceptance in scientific circles that 'race' is of little use, the term is still widely used as a commonsense way of labelling people according to physical appearance. It is this social or *ideological* use which interests social scientists. How such labels are employed, and why they continue to be used, are important sociological questions. However, there is some dispute as to how social scientists themselves ought to use the word 'race'. Some sociologists, including radical, black and Marxist sociologists, have continued to use the word while being highly critical of any form of racial oppression. Others have argued that such usage simply continues to reinforce the commonsense view that 'race' is a valid means of categorising people (Miles, 1989). Following Miles (1989) and Gilroy (1987), the word is put in quotation marks in the present chapter to indicate its ideological nature and the highly suspect assumptions which underly it.

If sociologists are to be critical of this term, then they need to provide alternatives. The first and now widely used term is *racism*. But its political use during the civil rights campaigns of the 1960s and the debates of New Zealand since the 1970s means that it, too, has a commonsense meaning and it is often deployed as a form of abuse. Anti-racist groups have used it to good effect in criticising Pakeha dominance and Maori disadvantage. More recently, its meaning has been inverted by New Right activists to refer to 'Maori privilege' and 'Pakeha disadvantage' (see the debate in 1993 about cultural safety). A particular sociological definition will be supplied here, but the political use of the same term can cause confusion.

As a result of the heightened awareness during the 1960s of the oppressive nature of concepts such as 'race', racism was increasingly used by sociologists to identify particular ideas. In the first instance, it was used to refer to the presence of racial arguments, or the idea that people could be categorised according to phenotype. Inevitably, prejudice, or the expression of negative or positive attitudes towards particular 'races', was either implicit or explicit. The meaning was altered by the term *institutional racism* which was coined in 1967 by black civil rights activists in the United States. It was used to focus on structural effects, or the way in which non-whites were systematically disadvantaged by major social institutions in areas such as justice, education or health. The assumption here is that organisations develop ways of operating, independent of the people involved, which function to deny access or resources to minority groups. Institutional racism was defined by the presence of discriminatory outcomes, of racial inequality. As a result, racism is often now defined as *power plus prejudice* (see Spoonley, 1993), to encompass both the existence of negative and/or positive ideas about 'race' and the structural dimension of racial disadvantage. The concept has been widely used by anti-racist groups such as the Auckland Committee on Racism and Discrimination (ACORD) and major reports on the state such as *Puao-Te-Atatu* (1986) as part of their critique of Pakeha and the state.

This broader political use of racism has tended to obscure its sociological meaning, and sociologists (Williams, 1985; Miles, 1989; Pearson, 1990) have been critical of the way in which the meaning of terms like institutional racism have become over-extended, being used to explain all racial disadvantage without precisely identifying the social processes involved. Miles (1989) argues for a more focused definition of racism and, in particular, that racism be defined by the ideological content of ideas. There are two important identifying features. First, there is the use of biological characteristics to define a group, underscored by the belief that such distinctions are natural and unchanging. Second, the group is regarded as having negatively valued characteristics, or that the group is seen as responsible for negative social consequences (Miles, 1989: 79). The above features must be present before the concept racism can be applied to ideas or activities. In some cases the ideas will be presented as part of a coherent theory (as in the case of the political views of right-wing racists), or they may be a less coherent assembly of stereotypes, images and explanations (Miles, 1989: 79). The point is, as Miles (1989: 80) notes, that racism 'makes sense' of the world in a way that is important for the holder of such views. But it should be also acknowledged that because of varying circumstances, different groups (class, ethnic, gender) will understand and use racism in different ways. Racism is not a single phenomenon but takes on a variety of forms in any given society.

· Miles (1989: 84-85) continues to use the term institutional racism but he limits its application to two sets of circumstances. In the first case there are exclusionary practices which arise from racist beliefs but which are no longer justified by such beliefs. In the second, an explicit racism is modified in such a way that the racist content is eliminated but other words carry the original meaning. So institutional racism refers to exclusionary practices which at some point were justified by racist beliefs although such beliefs may no longer be present.

Finally, the term *ethnicity* requires a definition. The term 'ethnic' became widely used from the late 1960s onwards as an alternative to the concept of 'race'. The idea of ethnicity, or a consciousness of cultural identity, provided a positive and less politically suspect way of classifying people into groups. In the case of ethnicity, group affiliation was self-claimed and not imposed according to phenotype as occurred with 'race'. This development was reinforced by the ethnic revival that has taken place in Western societies in recent decades. Contrary to the assumptions held by social scientists that capitalism would ensure that class and work-related identities would prevail, ethnicity gained a new importance, even displacing class politics in many situations. Black Americans led the revival but were soon followed by 'white ethnics', such as the Irish, Poles or Italians.

In essence, an ethnic group is one which shares cultural traditions, beliefs and behaviours, and whose members express a sense (consciousness) of belonging. The latter is termed ethnicity. Hence an identity is created and reproduced using certain cultural symbols and based on a shared history. Ethnicity is a malleable and often contested subjectivity (as the label 'Pakeha' illustrates; see Spoonley,1991), and there is often more than one way of expressing or practising a particular ethnicity. Pearson (1989) also suggests a range of concepts for describing different forms of ethnicity. Having provided some basic sociological concepts, we now turn to explanations of racism and ethnicity in the New Zealand context.

Colonialism and the Arrival of Capitalism

Sociologists have long seen the colonial and capitalist nature of New Zealand society in the nineteenth and twentieth centuries as critical to an understanding of contemporary patterns of racism and ethnicity. Foremost among earlier generations of such theorists was Bedggood (1980), who employed a classical Marxist approach. Bedggood identifies three stages in the penetration of the capitalist mode of production and the displacement of the Maori lineage mode of production. The period up to 1840 he labels *initial contact* to indicate the development of links with a capitalism based predominantly in Britain. The *colonial period* extends from 1840 until after the Anglo-Maori Wars and represents the period in which Maori society was destroyed in various ways and replaced by private ownership and other relations of production characteristic of capitalism. In 1840 only 1 per cent of New Zealand's population was Pakeha. By 1860, Pakeha equalled Maori in numbers and had begun to use the law and coercive force to separate Maori from their resources, particularly land. The *neo-colonial* period encompasses the development of a much more complete capitalist infrastructure and the ongoing marginalisation or destruction of Maori society.

Pearson (1990), in line with a Weberian approach, also examines economic relations but is concerned to give much more emphasis to the socio-political relations between coloniser and colonised. New Zealand is described as a settler society (as opposed to a sojourner society) because public and private interests encouraged the migration of entire families from Britain, primarily by offering land. This led to major conflict over land between settler and tangata whenua in the second half of last century. Pastoralism was the dominant form of production because it was suited to local conditions: ample land but no abundance of labour. Relations with the colonial centre, Britain, remained important and the government of New Zealand and the protection of settler interests were ultimately a responsibility of that country. These links, argues Pearson (1990), shaped local political and ideological relations, and produced quite specific class and ethnic relations. Included in the imported ideological and political baggage were certain beliefs about the superiority of British institutions and the desirability of destroying or curtailing Maori interests. Hence, in the latter part of the nineteenth century, a series of policies, acts and institutions were developed which either marginalised Maori interests (e.g. the creation of the four Maori seats in 1867, when in fact, equity required the establishment of at least sixteen seats), or demanded the adoption of British conventions (e.g. the 1867 Education Act which specified that English be the language of education).

Local settler interests eventually dominated the colony and supplanted the control previously exercised by Britain. Pearson (1990) argues that beliefs about their own cultural and/or 'racial' superiority led the settlers to develop institutions, including a centralised state, which allocated resources and privileges differently. In particular, Maori were encouraged or forced by such practices to discard their culture, and policies were designed to assimilate them into the majority-controlled society. He describes these ongoing policies as exclusionist not only of Maori but also of other non-white groups (e.g. Chinese and Indians in the latter decades of the nineteenth and first half of the twentieth century; see Leckie, 1985).

Both Bedggood and Pearson, from differing viewpoints, emphasise the introduction of capitalism to a non-capitalist society as a major force in disrupting the coherence and importance of Maori society. Bedggood tends to focus on economic relations, while Pearson is concerned to explore, in much more detail, the way in which the settlers sought to incorporate Maori into a Pakeha-dominated and newly established nation-state. Both authors point to the destructive nature of colonial capitalism and the way in which this history is essential to an understanding of contemporary intergroup relations. This approach has gained considerable support from the recent revision of our understanding of New Zealand history. Authors such as Orange (1987) on the Treaty of Waitangi, Belich (1986) on Victorian attitudes to New Zealand's race relations and Phillips (1987) on male culture all provide material on the racism of Pakeha officials and settlers. This revisionist history provides a necessary backdrop to an understanding of more recent relations.

Labour Migration

From the time of the Anglo-Maori Wars through to the Second World War, contact between Maori and Pakeha was limited. The groups were largely located in different parts of the country and in different communities. The main points of contact were the institutions of the state, such as education (although even here there were separate forms of schooling, including different curricula, for many), and when Maori labour was required for seasonal work such as shearing, fruit picking or meat processing. This situation changed dramatically in the 1950s and 1960s because of the capitalist need for labour. An important sociological approach to these issues is that offered by the political economy of labour migration.

The seminal work was by Castles and Kozack (1973) and it was expanded in the 1980s by Miles (1982), Phizacklea (1983), Castles *et al.* (1984) and Cohen (1987). This approach seeks to understand contemporary intergroup relations by relating them to the requirements of capitalism, notably the demand in the post-war period for unskilled and semi-skilled labour.

The political economy of labour migration begins its analysis by examining the process of capital accumulation within capitalism and the need to provide more profitable means of producing and exchanging goods. A key requirement in the process is labour. As Miles (1989:117) comments:

> Where the process of capital accumulation is obstructed by a shortage of labour power within the nation state, the state is faced with the possibility of permitting or organising the recruitment of labour from outside the nation state in order to effect its central role as the guarantor of the conditions for the reproduction of the capitalist mode of production.

In the post-war period, traditional sources of unskilled labour – the rural hinterland or neighbouring countries – could not supply the labour needed, and so capitalist economies, aided by state policies, attracted labour in large numbers throughout the 1950s and 1960s from former colonies or countries on the periphery of Europe or North America.

This migrant labour was characterised by several factors. It was largely unskilled, coming as it did from under-developed regions, and so migrants entered capitalist relations as part of the proletariat or waged labour. To begin with, the migrants were mainly males, but later stages saw family reunification and the establishment of demographically complete communities (involving male and female, and several generations; see Castles *et al.*, 1984). By the 1970s, when capitalism was experiencing a crisis, most capitalist countries quickly moved to limit the number of migrants and to reduce their rights as citizens. This gives rise to the interest in 'unfree labour', migrants who lack the normal political and civil rights of residents of one country or another. Such steps by the state were legitimated by the popular antagonism towards certain migrants. Whether it was New Zealand and 'Pacific Islanders', or Britain and Afro-Caribbeans and Asians, some migrants and their descendants were held responsible for such things as the decline of law and order, unemployment, deteriorating inner cities and the competition for resources such as health. As Miles (1989) says, some groups were racialised: they were defined as being 'races', which in turn were seen as a 'problem'.

In New Zealand the first group of labour migrants came from the rural hinterland. Encouraged by state policies (embodied in legislation such as the Maori Social and Economic Advancement Act, 1945), Maori migrated to the expanding urban sites of capitalist production. Prior to the war, in 1936, only 10.02 per cent of Maori lived in a city or borough. By the 1970s, three-quarters lived in cities or boroughs. In 1945 only one out of every 20 Maori lived in the Auckland urban area. By 1976 that figure was one in four and the numbers have continued to increase since.

The next source of unskilled and semi-skilled labour was provided by the Pacific Islands, and throughout the 1950s and 1960s the numbers coming to New Zealand steadily increased. By the 1991 Census there were 167,000 Pacific Islanders (or Tagata Pasifika; see Pulotu-Endemann and Spoonley,1992) in New Zealand, with less than half of these born in the Pacific. They, too, were concentrated in Auckland, with 67 per cent resident in the Auckland urban area (see Ongley,1991; Larner,1991; Bedford, 1988 for further information).

Both Maori and Pacific Islanders were disproportionately concentrated in unskilled and semi-skilled jobs in a narrow range of industries. In 1976, 58.7 per cent of Maori and 69.3 per cent of Pacific Islanders in the labour force were 'Production, Transport, Equipment Operators and Labourers' compared with only 34.4 per cent non-Polynesians. At the other end of the scale, only 4.6 per cent of Maori, and 3.7 per cent of Pacific Islanders were 'Professional, Technical and Related Workers' compared with 15 per cent non-Polynesians. Maori and Pacific Island labour force participation indicated their position as part of the working class, a position which was reinforced by where they resided and the resources they received from institutions in areas such as health and education.

The crisis of capitalism, which effectively began in New Zealand in 1973, encouraged the development of a much more public and significant racist discourse. In Miles' (1989) terms, both Maori and Pacific Islander were racialised, although in different ways. Both were seen as 'causing' a number of social and economic problems. Pacific Islanders were 'blamed' for taking New Zealanders' jobs (despite the fact that Cook Islanders, Niueans and Tokelauans are New Zealand citizens). Both Maori and Pacific Islanders were seen as 'creating' a law and order problem, especially in terms of gangs and rapes, which in turn produced a special police 'Task Force' in Auckland which targeted them as a problem (see Spoonley, 1982).

And both groups were also seen as responsible for 'problem areas' in the major cities: Otara and Ponsonby in Auckland, Porirua and Newtown in Wellington. Political and popular racism was transformed into highly discriminatory state policies and the legacy is still apparent. The 'overstayers' campaign of 1974 to 1976 saw police and immigration officials conduct dawn raids and random street checks to try and identify Pacific Islanders who were in New Zealand illegally. A decade later, the Race Relations Conciliator (1986) found that while Pacific Islanders only constituted one-third of all overstayers in the years 1985 and 1986, 86 per cent (270) of all prosecutions for overstaying involved Pacific Islanders.

In the period from 1945 to 1984 there are two distinct stages in the development of new forms of institutional and popular racism. From 1945 to the mid-1970s, the need for unskilled labour in an expanding urban industrial capitalist sector saw the migration of large numbers of Maori and Pacific Islanders to centres such as Auckland and Wellington. The migration was encouraged by employers and aided by the state. From 1973 there was quite a different reaction. The state, backed by popular racism, regarded these recent migrants as a 'problem' in various ways. Their 'race' and presence in the urban centres became a way of explaining social and economic problems. As a result, the state initiated policies which denied certain political and civil rights to these migrants, especially to Pacific Islanders. In the case of the Maori, these new circumstances were moderated by political developments from within their own community: the growth of Maori nationalism.

The Politics of Ethnicity

It was indicated earlier that ethnicity became more attractive to sociologists in the 1960s and 1970s. This gave rise to new sociological approaches, primarily Weberian in origin, which have been called ethnic mobilisation theories. They were characterised by two key arguments. First, they emphasised the importance of ethnicity as a key dimension of Western capitalist societies to the point where some, such as Parkin (1979), argue that ethnicity can displace class as the major cleavage in such societies. He is critical of Marxists who hold rigidly to the view that class is always the most important form of political difference and struggle. Second, these theorists regard ethnicity as an essentially political phenomenon which is used to compete with other groups for resources. So Parkin (1974:119) defines ethnicity as:

(i) the articulation of cultural distinctiveness,
(ii) in situations of political conflict or competition.

A recent and obvious example of the mobilisation of an ethnic group is the politicisation of Maori ethnicity. The current period of activism began in the late

1960s and early 1970s as those young Maori who had experienced life in Auckland and Wellington, and a number of whom had reached university, began to employ an analysis which used concepts such as institutional racism. Initially influenced by feminism and the black civil rights movement, groups such as Nga Tamatoa (1970) adopted protest tactics to publicise the concerns of Maori: land, language and culture. The momentum developed during the 1970s with annual protest action on Waitangi Day, the Land March in 1975 and the occupation of Bastion Point in 1977 and 1978. The 1981 'Maori Sovereignty' statement which appeared as articles in *Broadsheet,* and then as a book (Awatere, 1984), provided something of a manifesto for Maori nationalism and marked the break between Maori and Pakeha activism. After that, the concerns of Maori ethnicity became a matter for Maori, and was no longer confined to Maori radical politics but was very much part of mainstream and tribal/iwi politics. The adoption of concepts such as institutional racism in major reviews of the state (see Ministerial Advisory Committee on a Maori Perspective on the Department of Social Welfare, 1986, *Puao-Te-Atatu*), or the increasingly critical and activist stance of the Maori Council, indicate the acceptance of new arguments and strategies.

Greenland (1991) provides one of the best analyses of Maori sovereignty, or mana Maori motuhake. He argues that land alienation came to be seen as the key to explaining the current disadvantage of Maori, both for material and emotional (spiritual) reasons. The theme of Maori as tangata whenua stressed the common experience of Maori, whatever their tribal origins, and provided a basis for collective political action. The new politics of Maori ethnicity encouraged the positive aspects of being Maori, the need to preserve language and culture by separatist and exclusionist tactics where appropriate, and an emphasis on decolonising the mind by rejecting Pakeha/European values and beliefs. These politics have been reflected in state policies (see later) and have given new strength and direction to iwi and the need to retain Maori language and culture.

The politicisation of Maori ethnicity provides an excellent example of the arguments of the ethnic mobilisation theorists. But such ethnic assertiveness in other parts of the world has also produced new forms of white ethnicity (e.g. Polish or Irish in the U.S.A.), and there has certainly been a Pakeha reaction in the wake of Maori nationalism (Spoonley,1993). The response, however, is confused. Some accept that there is Pakeha ethnicity. It is defined by membership of the dominant group and by a particular relationship to the Maori and to the social and physical environment of New Zealand (King, 1985; *Sites*, No.13). Others deny that Pakeha are culturally different and indeed, reject the label 'Pakeha' completely. So the politics of Pakeha ethnicity are contradictory and it may be some time before sociologists are able to competently analyse its form and meaning (see Pearson, 1989; Spoonley, 1993).

State Policies

The growth of Maori nationalism encouraged the state to contemplate new forms of service delivery and policy directed at Maori. The changes began in 1977 when the Department of Maori Affairs adopted its Tu Tangata philosophy, but the much more extensive and radical changes took place in the 1984 to 1988 period. During these years and since, the state has sought to respond to Maori expectations and to meet its own agenda of reducing the size of its operations and, therefore, its financial commitments. In terms of the issues of racism and ethnicity, it has been a period of experimentation and radical reform.

Fleras (1989) describes the period from 1840 to 1977 as being concerned with the bureaucratisation of Maori policy administration based on certain principles: the protection, civilising, and assimilation of Maori. But the Tu Tangata programme reversed this emphasis and sought to 'debureaucratise' the Department by encouraging community development and control. The Department was now to be culturally sensitive and to be guided by the needs of the community it served. The restructuring 'indigenised the bureaucracy' (Fleras, 1989:218) and produced some innovative and progressive programmes including kohanga reo, kokiri (self-help schemes to develop community and work skills) and matua whangai (an alternative to institutional care for young Maori). The kohanga reo have been a success story, with almost 100 being established per year so that by 1989 about 12,000 children attended nearly 700 kohanga reo (*Dominion Sunday Times,* 29 October 1989). But they were run with minimal financial help from the government and, with devolution, iwi had to provide even more support (Fleras, 1991). In fact, Tu Tangata in general saved the government considerable expenditure and cleared the way for the complete disappearance of the Department of Maori Affairs in the late 1980s under a policy of devolution.

After 1984 the Labour Government continued the process of reform. The Department of Maori Affairs was replaced by a Ministry with a considerably reduced staff, no money for social and economic programmes, and a mandate simply to provide advice to government and its departments. Responsibility for a range of social services and economic development was transferred to iwi, with the help of the Iwi Transition Authority, so that the state had significantly reduced its role in terms of providing direct aid to the Maori community by the late 1980s. This process was continued by the 1990 National Government although there was an appeal for interventionist policies. In 1991 Winston Peters, as the Minister of Maori Affairs, released a report on Maori development, *Ka Awatea*, which argued that if Maori economic development was to proceed, then state intervention was required. This position was in stark contrast to the policies of the National Government and its advisors, notably Treasury. Peters lost his portfolio and the recommendations of *Ka Awatea* were largely ignored.

A Ministry of Maori Development (Te Puni Kokiri) was established in 1991 but with substantially reduced staff levels and limited responsibilities (largely policy advice). The justification has continued to be one of meeting Maori demands for autonomy, but there is little doubt that the state is reducing its costs and expenditure in line with neo-liberal policies.

Alongside this, however, the government also expanded the role of the Waitangi Tribunal in 1985 and again in 1988 by providing it with additional resources and giving it the power to investigate complaints back to 1840. This gave the Treaty of Waitangi new importance and a legitimacy to Maori complaints about the alienation of land and other resources.To reinforce the point, the courts did rule in favour of Maori complainants and defendants in landmark decisions in the mid-1980s. Cases have been brought in order to obtain legal rulings that resources such as fisheries or coal should be guaranteed to Maori under the Treaty. As a parallel to legislative and policy changes made during 1984 to 1986, Maori have initiated legal action to confirm their ownership of a range of resources and the courts or the Waitangi Tribunal have been used to settle questions concerning the rights specified in the Treaty of Waitangi.

Many Pakeha felt threatened by such developments and the government sought to restrict the dispersement of resources to Maori from 1988. In results that are typical of many polls, an NBR (11 October 1989) survey showed that while 37 per cent agree that the government should honour the Treaty of Waitangi (29 per cent disagreed), 77 per cent *disagreed* that Maori should receive a half share in fishing resources and 61 disagreed that Maori land claims are fully justified and must be taken seriously. The Treaty received some support as long as it did not mean a reallocation of resources. The government quickly moved to pacify these concerns. The Prime Minister's statement (July 1989) on the Crown and the Treaty of Waitangi emphasised the commitment to one legal system and the supreme right of government to rule (see Palmer, 1989). By the early 1990s this retreat was also apparent in the position adopted by the High Court and the Court of Appeal. For example, in 1991 both courts were reluctant to rule that the sale of the state's broadcasting assets were in breach of the Treaty of Waitangi. By 1993 the Waitangi Tribunal was also compromised. It had been undermined by a lack of resources and a political concern that it should exercise more restraint in its activities and recommendations (Kelsey, 1993: 279-291).

The most significant exception to these developments has been the government-funded deal to allow Maori to purchase half-shares in the fishing company Sealord. The mid-1980s saw the establishment of individual property rights for fishing resources established. This excluded many Maori from fishing and was a breach of Treaty rights. Various options were canvassed and implemented in the late 1980s to compensate Maori, including allocating quotas to the Maori Fisheries Commission in 1989, but none was very successful. At this point, 'iwi had identified two primary objectives: to restore their mana and tino rangatiratanga over fisheries, and to help re-establish an economic base' (Kelsey, 1993: 265). The 1992 deal meant that the government funded a half-share purchase of Sealord which had a 22 per cent share of the national fisheries quota (see Kelsey, 1993: 260-269). The Treaty of Waitangi Fisheries Commission was to receive $150 million on behalf of iwi; Brierley Investments Ltd is the other partner in the purchase. In return, the government anticipated that further Treaty claims would evaporate or be moderated and iwi would have an economic base from which to fund both further excursions into the market and social and cultural programmes. It has done little to resolve the issue of tino rangatiratanga.

> In the case of fisheries, they [National and Labour governments] had repackaged Treaty rights into a size and form that involved minimal long-term financial outlay, and which locked Maori economic development into contemporary market capitalism. In other cases they had eased the path to privatisation with payments worth a miniscule proportion of the total asset value, or offered symbolic gestures returning land for which they no longer had a use (Kelsey, 1993: 270).

The position adopted by both governments has exposed a number of contradictions. First, as Kelsey (1988; 1993) argues, the free market policies of the 1984 Labour Government, and the subsequent National Government, clash with policies on the Treaty of Waitangi. The provision of economic and welfare resources for groups runs counter to the individualistic and competitive emphasis encouraged by a 'free market'. Increasingly, government initiatives seek to encourage Maori to become petty capitalists (e.g. Tu Tangata small business and entrepreneurial schemes) or to establish links with major capitalist corporations such as Fletcher Challenge or Brierleys (e.g. Maori Development Corporation). Second, the process of devolution has meant that Maori iwi and communities have had to take considerably more responsibility for funding, not only for immediate community projects, but for welfare programmes in general. Scarce community resources are having to go further. Third, the Waitangi Tribunal has challenged the 'one law for all', and the 'legitimacy of the existing state and its legal apparatus' (Kelsey, 1988: 5). The possibility of legal pluralism has brought a critical and negative response from the government (Palmer, 1989), despite the fact that special legal provisions have long existed for Maori (Walker, 1989).

> [The]...failure to address the promotion of Maori collective rights, much less those of sovereignty and power, have left many unimpressed with the rhetoric of reform (Fleras, 1989:220).

After Monetarism

In the 1970s and 1980s, sociologists, in explaining racism and ethnicity, tended to focus on the way in which labour migration had structured intergroup relations in all Western capitalist societies. Labour migration theorists analysed the connection between the requirements of capitalism, notably for labour, and the way in which certain migrant groups were then racialised or seen as a social and political problem. Alternatively, those interested in ethnicity focused on the way in which cultural identity was politicised for both migrant and non-migrant as part of a general ethnic revival. But there is a need to move beyond both these approaches and to develop theories which help explain racism and ethnicity in the 1990s. Circumstances have changed, and they include: changes to the nature of capitalism, often described as a move from Fordism to post-Fordism; the presence of ethnic communities who are no longer migrants and who have established complex communal and political structures in capitalist societies (sometimes displacing the previously dominant structures and politics of class); and the creation of a 'new racism' by various New Right groups, thus altering the way in which many understand racism and ethnicity.

Theorists of capitalism and the state such as Lash and Urry (1987) and Jessop (1989) have noted a fundamental change in the nature of Western and global capitalism. The change is one from Fordism to post-Fordism (see chapters by Terry Austrin and Chris Wilkes for details). The first refers to a capitalism which is based on mass production, while post-Fordism is characterised by a high degree of flexibility in terms of both production and the supply of labour. Technology means less reliance on semi and unskilled labour, and if low-cost labour is required, then production is located in those countries where labour is cheap and non-unionised.

The social and political effects of these new forms of production are substantial. To begin with, there is a 'two-nations cleavage' (Jessop, 1989) between a core-workforce, skilled and well-paid, and marginalised groups of workers whose locality or industry can no longer provide jobs. If they do have jobs, they tend to be temporary and poorly paid. The effect is readily seen in New Zealand as a result of restructuring (see Britton and Le Heron, 1987). Manufacturing and primary sectors have lost jobs (9 per cent and 11.5 per cent respectively between 1977/78 and 1987/88; New Zealand Planning Council, 1989: 96), with more than 60,000 jobs lost to manufacturing in the years 1987 to 1989. The numbers of unemployed and those in part-time work have grown significantly, and will continue to grow.

A significant aspect of this 'two-nations' situation is that in New Zealand it is sharply differentiated along Polynesian/non-Polynesian lines. Many of those Maori and Pacific Islanders who came to the urban industrial centres during the 1950s, 1960s and 1970s in response to the requirement for unskilled labour in Fordist production, have become redundant. Young Maori and Pacific Islanders leaving school are simply unable to gain jobs. They do not even enter the workforce as full-time paid labour, as Maori and Pacific Island unemployment figures in Table 6.1 show.

Table 6.1
Unemployed as a Percentage of the
Full-time Labour Force

		1986 %	1991 %	Increase in Unemployed
Maori	15-64 years	12.2	23.3	+11.1
	15-24 years	19.9	35.5	+15.6
Non-Maori	15-64 years	3.8	8.4	+ 4.6
	15-24 years	8.1	16.9	+ 8.8

Source: Spoonley, Teariki, Newell and Taiwhenua o Heretaunga, 1993.

In effect, about one-fifth of the Maori working-age population lost their jobs in the two years from March 1987 to March 1989, and the loss is about four times higher than for non-Polynesian (see New Zealand Planning Council, 1989). This has major implications for this group's access to a whole range of goods and services, especially as privatising social services means that the quality of the service depends on the ability to pay. In important respects, the 'two-nations' of post-Fordism will be structured along Polynesian-non-Polynesian lines in New Zealand.

The response from iwi has been to develop new strategies that rely less on government-funded schemes and more on their own human and economic resources. Given the loss of paid employment as the result of a collapsing labour market, iwi have sought to identify new economic bases and to utilise these in the context of a communal system, mauritangata (see Spoonley, Teariki, Newell and Taiwhenua o Heretaunga, 1993), which operates in sharp contrast to the individualism which is assumed to be the base for a neo-liberal market economy. Whanau, hapu and iwi constitute the social and economic focus of development. Human and capital investment are meant to provide returns for all, and a basis on which to preserve cultural traditions. By the late 1980s this vision was to be seen in the expanding iwi participation in training, labour market supply, small business development, tourism, resource management and development and company ownership (e.g. Deka). Tino rangatiratanga is being given expression in Maori-directed programmes and in spite of neo-liberal government policies.

The second factor to briefly note is the change in the nature of the Polynesian populations. In relation to the Maori population, a significant proportion are located in the greater Auckland area, having been born and educated there. Their links and experiences with their tribal origins are limited, and new urban subcultures, based partly on international cultures (reggae, rap), are proliferating. Equally significant is the demographic profile of Polynesians. Pool and Pole (1987) show that in the late 1980s, Maori and Pacific Islander are predominantly young. Maori made up 19.7 per cent of all children under the age of 15 and they estimate that Maori will grow to become 19 per cent of New Zealand's total population by 2011. This means that those in the 'at risk' youth groups will be significantly Maori, and institutions such as education (at least those particular schools that deal with the Maori section of the population) will see more and more Maori. The politics of Maori will need to incorporate the concerns of young, urban-based Maori.

Similarly, for Pacific Islanders, the population is increasingly New Zealand-born, with less interest and fewer connections to the island cultures of origin. The 1986 Census indicates that 49.3 per cent of all Pacific Islanders were born in New Zealand (48.9 per cent were born in the Pacific Islands), and, like the Maori, the populations of the various groups are young and likely to face substantial social pressures in the 1990s. The politics of the older Pacific Islanders, based around age, maleness, the church, family and island links, will become less relevant and unable to mediate between Polynesian youth and New Zealand authorities and institutions.

Finally, the altered identity politics are represented in the new political groups and ideologies which have appeared during the 1980s. Between 1981 and 1987 the impetus lay with Maori in that their ethnic nationalism and the strength of tribal groupings continued to grow supported by critiques of the state such as *Puao-Te-Atatu*. The 1984 Labour Government underlined these developments by making such far-reaching changes as significantly extending the ambit and resources of the Waitangi Tribunal. But the New Right groups of the mid- and late 1980s were opposed to such 'concessions'.

Conservative and politically active Christians opposed taha Maori in the education system because it was considered anti-Christian. Middle-class conservatives (liberal during the 1981 Springbok Tour, conservative by the time of the Muriwhenua fisheries claim in 1987) were critical of 'social engineering in education' and the 'privileged' status of Maori generally. Libertarians regarded any policy or provision directed at a group as cutting across the individualism of the market place. While the New Right contained disparate groups, all were agreed that Maori should not expect or receive 'special privileges' and they became increasingly hostile during the late 1980s to anything Maori. A new set of arguments appeared. Racism was something that Maori practised against Pakeha, the 'new disadvantaged', while 'institutional racism' was used by the New Right to refer to Maori 'privilege' and Pakeha 'disadvantage'. The language of the 1970s was inverted. By 1989 even the Labour

Government was reworking its stance to accord with Pakeha/New Right politics on these issues. Since then, there has been a significant retreat by political parties and sectors of the state from the goal of biculturalism or tino rangatiratanga. A collapsing labour market, the move towards a minimalist state and the commitment to an enterprise culture in which the market distributed various 'goods' which were purchased by individuals, cancelled out many of the moves made to recognise the particular interests of iwi. The economic divisions between Maori and Pakeha under post-Fordism were being underscored by the politics of the New Right. The response of iwi was to establish new pan-tribal organisations (National Maori Congress) to restore or expand the economic base of iwi and to develop new managerial strategies which ensured that resources were used for iwi development.

Conclusion

In 1940, Sutherland (1940: 21) wrote:

> ... if we now correlate this rapid growth in the Maori population with the diminished material resources and the progressive landlessness of the Maori people, the inability of some districts to support their Maori population on Maori lands, the limited opportunities for engaging in other and varied forms of employment and the general lack of vocational training for young people, we realise that the Maori situation is in many ways critical and urgent.

While many of the characteristics of New Zealand society have changed, including the geographical location of Maori (urban versus rural in 1940), the outlook has not. A market-oriented capitalism which venerates an enterprise culture and which requires high levels of skills continues to marginalise Maori. A soft form of biculturalism, represented by the Waitangi Tribunal and certain policy changes, has moderated some of the impact of monetarism but has been unable to transfer significant resources or power to Maori communities. As Sissons (1989) points out, the state has manipulated the issues of Maori nationalism via the institutionalisation of procedures, neutralising land claims, co-opting people as advisors rather than decision-makers, and retaining control over budgetary items. Kelsey (1988) talks of the challenge to the state posed by Maori nationalism and organisations such as the Waitangi Tribunal, but this challenge had been diverted and substantially weakened by the late 1980s. The hegemony of certain Pakeha is easily seen in the dominance of a particular form of production (free market capitalism), a political consensus between the major political parties (broadly libertarian in its sentiments), a move away from a Keynsian welfare state and the conservative, nationalist politics of a dominant Pakeha. This has delayed but not diverted iwi ambitions for tino rangatiratanga, and new strategies have emerged in the 1990s which seek to establish economic independence for iwi as a way of maintaining and extending cultural traditions and identity.

Note

1. Parts of the discussion in this section have been adapted from an article (Spoonley, 1989) published in *Sites* No. 18. The material is reproduced here with the permission of *Sites*.

Further Reading

Ihimaera,W. (ed.), 1993, *Te Ao Marama. Vol. 2. He Whakaatanga o te Ao. The Reality*, Auckland, Reed Books.
Miles, R., 1989, *Racism*, London, Tavistock.
Spoonley, P., 1993, *Racism and Ethnicity*, (2nd edition), Auckland, Oxford University Press.
Spoonley, P., Pearson, D. and Macpherson, C. (eds), 1991, *Nga Take. Ethnic Relations and Racism in Aotearoa/New Zealand,* Palmerston North, Dunmore Press.
Pearson, D., 1990, *A Dream Deferred. The Origins of Ethnic Conflict in New Zealand,* Wellington, Allen and Unwin.
Walker, R., 1990, *Ka Whawhai Tonu Matou. Struggle Without End,* Auckland, Penguin.

7 Gender

Rosemary Du Plessis

Introduction

Gender is a social phenomenon which shapes our sense of personal identity, the nature of our everyday interactions with others and the sets of social relations embedded in institutions such as the family, the workplace, the school, the hospital, the criminal justice system and the state. The social significance attached to being female or male and the use of gender as a component of social structures varies between societies and over time.

The sociological study of gender entails a search for patterns and trends that cut across cultures, classes, ethnic groups, historical periods, socialist and capitalist economies. At the same time, it demands an openness to discovering differences between what it means to be a woman or a man in different societies, in different ethnic groups within the same society and in different classes. In the New Zealand context, it demands that we look at the way being female or male in this society varies between Maori and non-Maori, skilled and unskilled workers, heterosexuals, lesbians and gay men as well as the differences between the 1890s, the 1950s and the 1990s. It involves trying to discern what is unique about the New Zealand context and the ways in which the relations between women and men in the family, the workplace, the school, political parties, sports organisations, and the entertainment industry are similar to those in Australia, Japan, the United States, Germany, Brazil or the Soviet Union. This chapter begins with a discussion of gender, sociology and feminism. It then focuses on attempts by some New Zealand sociologists to analyse the dynamics of gender in ways which connect the personal and the political, the particular and the general.

Gender and Sociology

C. Wright Mills argued that sociology should enable us to grasp the connections between the day-to-day experiences of our own lives as individuals and the wider structures which shape those experiences, sustain and reproduce them. It involves exercising what Mills referred to as the 'sociological imagination' – the capacity to sense the connections between biography, social structure and history (Mills, 1959, reprinted 1976).

This is also the conception of sociology embraced by the Canadian feminist sociologist, Dorothy Smith, who has argued that the task of the sociologist is:

> ... to develop a sociology capable of explicating for members of the society the social organisation of their experienced world .... we begin from where people are in the world, explaining the social relations of the society of which we are a part, explaining an organisation which is not always fully present in any one individual's everyday experience... (Smith, 1987: 89).

Dorothy Smith's particular interest is the development of a sociology *for* women. This is a sociology rooted in women's everyday lives, the details of their day-to-day existence and the understandings they bring to it. At the same time, this sociology should reveal the connections between a woman's 'everyday' world and 'the larger socio-economic organisation to which it is articulated' (Smith, 1987: 88-97). This sociology is 'necessarily local', arising out of particular contexts, and 'necessarily historical' (Smith, 1987: 89).

According to Dorothy Smith, sociologists should not see women as the 'objects' of inquiry but 'subjects', and sociologists should locate themselves as subjects in the social contexts in which they live their lives. This involves a self-consciousness about their own 'bodily and material existence' and their everyday lives. It challenges the view that sociologists are ideally neutral observers of the social lives of others who impose order on the confusion of lived reality by applying to it sociological theories written for an audience of those initiated into academic discourse. It means revising the idea that sociology is an academic discipline detached from the personal issues we confront as social actors or 'subjects'.

The personal, structural and historical aspects of gender in New Zealand society have been explored by Bev James and Kay Saville-Smith in a slim volume which sketches the development of gender relations between women and men at the time of colonisation and their persistence into the 1980s. They argue that New Zealand is a 'gendered culture', a culture in which the structures of masculinity and femininity are central to the formation of society as a whole (James and Saville-Smith, 1989: 6).

Understandings of what it meant to be men and women are seen as integral to the processes whereby settlers assumed control of Maori land and developed political, economic and cultural dominance. These definitions of masculinity and femininity were also inseparable from the development of class relations in this context and the way wage-workers began to organise themselves into trade unions and political parties (James and Saville-Smith, 1989:16-46).

The argument advanced by Bev James and Kay Saville-Smith focuses on the consequences for women of a 'gendered culture' – lower wages, dependency on social welfare benefits, domestic violence and sexual abuse. They also, however, address the costs for men of their higher levels of motor car accidents, alcohol abuse and imprisonment. Men, privileged in some respects on the basis of their gender, are also seen as bearing the costs of the social significance given to physiological differences between women and men in this society.

Changing our 'gendered culture' demands not just the abandonment of the constraints of femininity by women but a redefinition of what it means to be a man (James and Saville-Smith, 1989: 89). Feminist sociologists have tended to focus their critical attention on women's experiences and the implications for women of the pervasiveness of gender as a way of structuring social relationships and access to resources like money, housing, health care, jobs and power inside and outside the home. However, more attention is now being directed by sociologists of both sexes to the dynamics of masculinity and power. Alternative and subordinated masculinities which do not entail male dominance over women or assumptions about heterosexuality are being explored (Connell, 1987; Brod, 1987; Brittan, 1989; Morgan, 1991). Others have tried to identify the links between racism, sexism and class divisions (Hoch, 1979; Brittan and Maynard, 1984). Recent work by Bob Connell, an Australian sociologist, has explored the development of a 'protest' masculinity embraced by young unemployed men in contexts such as bikie gangs (Connell, 1991).

Gender is not just a set of structural relations imposed on us by impersonal outside forces but a key component of our personal identities. In a variety of social contexts we 'do' gender as expressions of self, and maintain gender differences within institutions. Change in New Zealand as a 'gendered' society therefore involves people assuming individual responsibility for change as well as working with others to change insititutions like workplaces, schools, sports organisations and political parties (James and Saville-Smith, 1989: 89-94). An understanding of the ways in which gender operates personally, structurally and historically can help us assess what sort of changes we might want to make and how change can be achieved.

Analysis of Gender in the New Zealand Context: Some Examples

The investigation of gender as a social phenomenon involves understanding the personal, micro-level experience of being male or female, the structures or sets of relations between people within which that experience occurs, and the way particular historical contexts influence those experiences and the sets of relations. What follows is a discussion of some of the work done in New Zealand which makes these connections between personal experience, social structures and historical context.

Gender and Jobs

Women and men in New Zealand tend to do very different sorts of jobs. Not only do women do most of the unpaid housework and childcare (McKinlay, 1992: 77-79), but when they are in paid work they are concentrated in a narrower range of occupations than men (Department of Statistics, 1990: 62-64). These occupations are predominantly female. A third of women in employment are in clerical work while most of the rest are found in saleswork, teaching, nursing, and clothing and textile manufacture. Maori and Pacific Island women are less likely to be in clerical work and more likely to be production workers in factories, agricultural labourers or service workers in kitchens, motels and restuarants (Novitz, 1987; Horsfield, 1988; Horsfield and Evans, 1988; NACEW, 1990: 61-83). Men, on the other hand, are involved in a wider range of occupations. They are more likely to be in admininistrative and managerial jobs than women. A higher proportion of those in the skilled trades, factory and agricultural work are men (NZCEW, 1990: 63).

The association of women and men with certain types of work is both a personal and a structural phenomenon. Certain occupations are seen as appropriate for women on the basis of assumptions about their personalities and skills. Others are seen as ideally done by men. At the same time, the definition of certain occupations as 'male' or 'female' is not just a matter of personal choice; insititutional mechanisms perpetuate these definitions and the distribution of people into jobs. Until the mid-1970s, women could not serve apprenticeships in other than ladies hairdressing. Certain branches of medicine are less likely to be pursued by female medical graduates because training in those specialties is difficult to combine with the responsibilities women often have as parents. Since women have been defined as men's economic dependants, the pay for those in jobs traditionally done by women has been low (Du Plessis, 1992: 212-213). This has been to the advantage of those employing women workers. It also discourages men from embarking on work in occupations in which women are the majority of those employed.

There has been little work done in New Zealand and elsewhere which shows how gender operates in the workplace at the micro-level of personal identity and the macro-level of social structure. An exception is Roberta Hill's research into the transition from the use of 'hot metal' to 'cold type' technology in the New Zealand newspaper industry. Her study of the way the *Christchurch Star* introduced computer technology into the printing of its newspapers between 1979 and 1983 highlights the significance for change in the workplace of ideas about gender and the dynamics of relations between women and men (Hill, 1983; 1984a; 1984b; Hill and Novitz, 1985; Hill, 1989).

Many of the men who had worked the big linotype machines under the old 'hot metal' system of newpaper production saw that work as uniquely masculine. As one of the printers put it, work on the old linotype machines was 'somehow more manly'. The transition to 'cold type' production which involved using qwerty (typewriter) keyboards to work the new visual display terminals entailed doing work which the male printers had traditionally associated with women. As one of the printers put it: 'the job's more for girls' (Hill and Novitz, 1985: 15).

The men were aware that if they did not acquire typing skills and retrain on the computer terminals, their jobs would be taken by women typists. A number of the printers felt undermined by doing work which they saw as 'jobs for girls', but they also saw themselves as having more right to those jobs than women typists, not just because they were trained printers, but because they were *men*. This claim to jobs on the new machines was based on their structural position as 'breadwinners' in their families.

By negotiating a retraining programme for the exclusively male printers, the predominantly male Printing Union was able to ensure that the most skilled and highly paid jobs using the new computer technology were the preserve of men. No printing tradesman was replaced by a typist. At the same time, the new computer technology stripped the male printers of the traditional symbols of their status as skilled craftsmen which for some of them had also been the symbols of their masculinity. They did, however, manage to retain a privileged position for their occupational group which was consistent with traditional gender definitions of men's responsibilities as 'providers' within the institution of the family.

The New Zealand Printing Union was able to achieve this because they were operating within a particular historical context. While their employers could significantly reduce their labour costs by employing female typists to do the typesetting work on the visual display terminals, they were negotiating with the printers against the background of the extensive costs of strike action by printers resisting 'cold type' technology in Britain. Knowledge of the likely costs of action by the printers shaped the decision to retrain the more expensive male printers who had worked the linotype machines or worked as compositors boxing the metal type into the pages of the newpaper (Hill, 1989: 274-5). Since there was little competition from other evening newspapers directed at the same group of readers in a particular city, employers were also reasonably confident that they could also pass on to advertisers and readers any extra costs associated with this decision to retrain male printers and retain their rates of pay.

The structural position of trade unions in the New Zealand context in the early 1980s also contributed to this outcome. A state-regulated national award system, compulsory unionism and a lack of contestability with respect to the coverage of workers in a particular occupation all enhanced the chance of the printers negotiating continued access to highly paid printers' jobs, even when the technology made possible the employment of another lower paid occupational group. It was not insignificant that the group which was excluded was female.

The printers were not, however, able to resist the retraining of a different set of women workers – the telephonist-typists. They were taught to use a series of formats to typeset most of the advertisements that they received from clients over their headphones. Having advertisements typeset by the telephonist-typists (renamed telead operators) involved significant cost savings for employers and reduced the work available for printers. Printers were, however, able to ensure that the telephonist typists were restricted to the use of a limited set of pre-coded formats. They also had to send the more complicated advertisements to the printers for setting. The telead operators were trained by the retrained printers at the very end of the period of transition to computerised printing (Hill, 1989: 277).

Control over what work was to be done by the telead operators was achieved by incorporating them into the Printing Union. This involved the union arguing that they were doing the work of printers – an argument many in the union found hard to accept. However, they also argued that this work was less skilled than that of printers who had served their apprenticeships. The telead operators therefore became 'non-journeymen' members of the union with lower rates of pay. Faced with a tension between acknowledging that typists were doing the work of printers, and control over the extent to which the telead operators did typesetting, the printers decided that control was more important than preserving the exclusivity of the definition of 'printer'.

This case study of technological change in a particular workplace illustrates the way gender operates at the level of the self-definition of individuals and at the level of organised attempts to secure the interests of those in a particular occupational category against the interests of those of the other gender in a different occupation. While the men, at least temporarily, managed to secure their jobs and their higher rates of pay as skilled tradesmen, a number of them had to undertake work which they saw as work for 'girls', work which did not have the 'manly' qualities which had attracted some of them into printing as a skilled trade. The particular historical context of compulsory unionism and national awards in the early 1980s also shaped the way cold type production was introduced into this gendered workplace. These outcomes would have been very different under the industrial relations environment created by the Employment Contracts Act.

Gender and the Household

Gender is not just a key factor in the distribution of women and men into different occupations in this society, it is also the basis for the allocation of unpaid work in the home (Craig, 1992: 106-107). Most unpaid domestic work in New Zealand is done by women. The New Zealand pilot time-use survey revealed that on average unpaid work accounted for 20 per cent of a 24-hour day for women and 12 per cent of the day for men (McKinlay, 1992: 78). A much larger time-use study in Australia suggested that marriage increases women's unpaid work by 60 per cent (Bittman, 1991: 4). A variety of different studies have revealed that, while some men may 'help' with cooking, cleaning and childcare, most of this work is done by women (Novitz, 1987: 44-49). This is consistent with a National Council of Women study done in the mid-1980s which revealed that only 14 per cent of the women surveyed reported that housework was divided equally between them and other members of their family (Bell and Adair, 1985: 49).

In the late 1970s, Bev James researched the experiences, thoughts and feelings of women doing this unpaid domestic work. The study was based on individual and group discussions with women living in the milltown of Kawerau – a town dominated by the timber industry and the pulp and paper mill (James, 1985; 1986; 1987; 1989). Like Roberta Hill's study of the transition to the use of computer technology at the *Christchurch Star,* it enables us to set the personal experiences of individuals in the context of social structure and history. The women interviewed revealed that they saw the town as 'a man's working town' in which men did work that was 'tough, demanding and dangerous' (James, 1987: 109). They often had little understanding of the exact nature of the work done by their husbands because many of the men wanted to 'switch off' when they came home from work (James, 1987: 109). The consequence of this was a sharp division between men's public world of work and their private world of home and family. Women's paid and unpaid work was done both inside and outside this 'private' sphere.

Many men handed over their pay packets to their wives but women's access to this income depended entirely on the decision of their husbands to give them this control over the household finances. Men were recognised as the most significant contributors to the family income even when their wives had paid work. One of the women in part-time employment put it like this:

> Doesn't mean just because I've got a job I can shirk what's at home. Mum should be in charge of all what's at home, and he goes out and makes money and takes care of us all in that way ... he wants to know that he's providing for us (James, 1987: 112).

The shift work of many of the men who worked at the mill had a major effect on how women organised their days. The women said that 'the wife does that shiftwork as well' (James, 1987: 113). Housework was done at times when it did not disturb sleeping husbands and meals were often timed to fit in with when men were available to eat with the family. One woman descibed how she would prepare a cooked tea just after 3 in the afternoon in order to have the main meal of the day before her husband left for the 4 o'clock shift (James, 1987: 114).

Women organised their involvement in paid work around their housework, childcare responsibilities and their husband's shift work. This was partly a consequence of the male breadwinner ideology articulated above, and partly a response to the higher earnings associated with the jobs in which the men were involved and women's limited opportunities for paid work in what was essentially a 'company town' where over 60 per cent of the local workforce was employed at the mill.

The separation of men's work from the world of home and family had a major impact on the way women responded to the industrial disputes that occurred in Kawerau in the late 1970s. They had no say in whether their husbands would strike or how long they would stay out but the strike directly affected their work in the home, particularly their responsibilities to provide food for their families. The strike highlighted their vulnerable position as people dependent on the earnings of others and undermined their ability to perform their domestic roles. As a result, some of the women resented the way the strike disrupted their lives. They wanted to be more involved in public debate on the issues, to attend union meetings and to be better informed about union strategies. Women's involvement was not welcomed by union officials. While women might be affected by the outcome of union action, officials argued that it was workers who should make the decisions, not their economic dependants (James, 1987: 120).

Bev James' study of women in Kawerau also raises issues about the relationship between ethnic divisions and gender divisions in New Zealand society. This research was done in a town in which a third of the population was either Maori or Pacific Islanders. Many of the women interviewed were Maori. Bev James has reflected critically on the likely distortions of Maori women's experience which are a consequence of white feminist women researching the experience of women of other ethnic groups. The lives of the Maori and Pacific Island women who participated in this study were shaped not just by gender but also by their ethnicity. This had a major impact on their experiences with respect to education, employment and housing. The mill site had been bought from its Maori owners who continued to have misgivings about this. Maori and Pacific Islanders were over-represented among the unemployed and among those in the least skilled and lowest paid jobs. Since housing and housing loans were allocated on the basis of occupational status, the concentration of Maori and Pacific Island men in the lowest status jobs affected the housing available to their wives and children. Occupational status, ethnicity and gender interacted in Kawerau, as it does elsewhere in New Zealand, to produce different outcomes for women and men, Maori and non-Maori, skilled and unskilled (James, 1986: 26-29).

Gender and Ethnicity

Attention to the interaction between ethnicity, gender and class in the context of Kawerau highlights the need to explore differences between women of different cultures in Aotearoa/New Zealand. Most of the work on gender divisions has involved an analysis of Pakeha society by Pakeha social researchers. Much work remains to be done by Maori researchers on the dynamics of gender within Maori in households and more public contexts such as the marae.

Some authors have suggested that women and men in traditional Maori communities did very similar tasks. Rangimarie Mihomiho Rose Pere (1987: 57) has written about her childhood in Waikaremoana where she saw women and men doing the same tasks, caring for children, ploughing and digging roads. Whatever the original gender divisions in pre-European iwi, the establishment of a Pakeha dominated economy and state bureaucracy ensured that few Maori women could remain unaffected by the way gender has been used to structure paid work, politics, education, entertainment, sport and social services in Aotearoa/New Zealand.

In the 1990s, Maori women are providing new analyses of the roles of Maori women in pre-European society as well as analysing issues of ethnicity and gender in the current context. Kathie Irwin has analysed gender differences with respect to speaking rights on the marae – an issue which she argues is 'one of the most misunderstood and abused cultural issues of our culture and time' (Irwin, 1992: 8). Her analysis of the convention in many iwi that only men whaikorero on the marae atea involves a rejection of claims that this is a sexist practice. At the same time, she looks critically at the way Maori men have bent tradition to provide Pakeha men of status with such speaking rights, and the way these traditional practices have been used by Pakeha bureaucrats to exclude able Maori women from positions in the public service on the grounds that 'they can't speak on the marae'. She suggests that 'many of the "newly traditional" Maori cultural practices that are emerging serve the interests of Pakeha men whilst disempowering Maori women, in the name of "Maori cultural practices" ' (Irwin, 1992: 16). Her analysis attends to the way in which traditional gendered customs can take on new meanings in different contexts.

Gender and Education

The interaction between personal biography, social structure and historical context is illustrated in a study of feminist educators completed by Sue Middleton in the mid-1980s (Middleton, 1985; 1987). Her life history interviews with feminist educators provide us with a range of insights into the interaction between their personal biographies and the constraints and possibilities they encountered as they moved from girlhood to womanhood in the 1950s and 1960s.

Sue Middleton's use of the life-history method in her research was based on her desire to do the sort of sociology that represented people as 'creative strategists who devise means of resisting and resolving the contradictions they experience' (Middleton, 1988: 128). She argues that recent research into the process whereby gender expectations are communicated has revealed that we are not exposed to a simple and consistent set of understandings about what it means to be male or female but contradictory sets of expectations. Women are expected to be nurturers and skilled in domestic tasks as well as successful at school and prepared for paid work. In their teens, they are expected to be physically attractive, but not sexually active. These contradictory ideas generated in some women 'visions of both the desirability and the possibility of change in their own lives and the lives of other women' (Middleton, 1987).

The existence of these contradictory expectations (which occur for men as well as women) in a society which attaches considerable importance to whether we have penises or vaginas enables us as individuals to be differently affected by the social expectations associated with our biological sex. While we may all be 'gendered' individuals, we do have some flexibility in the way we respond to gendered expectations. This flexibility can also explain why change is possible in the way people define the implications of being female or male.

Sue Middleton chose to look at a group of women who, as feminist educators, were critical of the constraints women and men, boys and girls experience as a consequence of the significance attached to gender in this society. The focus of the study was the lives of a group of women who were born in New Zealand in the late 1940s and who started their formal education in the 1950s. The purpose was to explore the relationship between these individual biographies and their social context – the institutional structures and the specific historical periods in which these lives were lived.

The research on feminist educators revealed that in the 1950s and early 1960s 'attitudes towards girls in secondary schools, particularly those in the "academic" (or "professional") streams were contradictory' (Middleton, 1988: 72). Girls who did well at school were encouraged both to be academically ambitious, preparing themselves for professional careers (albeit within a narrow range of jobs), and expected to prepare for lives as efficient, unpaid homemakers.

The 1942 Thomas Report provided the blueprint for post-war secondary education in New Zealand. It argued that a 'core' curriculum consisting of social studies, mathematics, English, general science, music, art and craft was to be undertaken by all pupils. Agriculture, engineering shopwork and woodwork were refered to as 'boy's subjects'. Girls were to receive a different form of manual training:

> We think that the course of every girl attending a post-primary school should contain studies and activities directly related to the home (Thomas et al., 1942: 46).

The post-war plan to make secondary education accessible to a wider range of girls and boys than ever before in New Zealand was therefore also a means of reinforcing the significance of gender. Compulsory lessons in clothing and cooking were to remind young women that their true vocation was in unpaid domestic work at home. On the other hand, there were also pressures on academically able girls to train as teachers. In the 1960s the Currie Commission concluded that the teacher shortage demanded that one in every two girls in the Sixth Form should be recruited into teacher training (Currie *et al.,* 1962: 585).

The shortage of teachers prompted the development of studentships for trainee teachers to enable them to support themselves while in training. For many women whose parents could not afford to support them in any post-school training, this was the only means to further education (Middleton, 1988: 83). This form of support during training was, however, contingent upon women not marrying while they were in training. If this occurred, they immediately lost their studentships, a provision that did not apply to men. The implication was that marriage signalled responsibilities incompatible with further education for women (Middleton, 1988: 85).

The contradictory expectations academic girls were encountering in New Zealand secondary schools occurred in a context in which married women were increasingly involved in paid work outside the home, while other aspects of New Zealand culture elevated full-time domesticity as the ideal for all married women, but particularly mothers. Helen (Cook) May's research into the experiences of the women who were mothers during the post-war years and her investigation of the way expectations of women were presented in the *New Zealand Listener* and the *New Zealand Women's Weekly* provide us with an understanding of some of the deep ambivalences which existed at that time about married women in paid work in the 1950s (Cook, 1985a; 1985b; 1986; May, 1988; 1992).

Women in the post-war period 'yearned for peaceful domesticity' (May, 1988: 58). However, access to the new consumer items like vacuum cleaners, washing machines and fridges often necessitated women's involvement in paid work, at least in a part-time capacity (May, 1988: 59). Many women and men in the post-war period were therefore confronted with contradictions between the ideal of women's full-time domesticity and the reality of the need for them to undertake paid work if they were to enjoy the material symbols of post-war prosperity.

The life history approach adopted by Sue Middleton deliberately challenged conceptions of the social researcher as the objective observer of the behaviour or responses of others:

> As a woman, a 'post-war baby', and educationalist and a feminist, I shared many political and theoretical assumptions, as well as common experiences, with the women studied.... It was important to develop a

methodology which would enable the women being interviewed to assist in the analysis of their own tape-recorded life histories and to avoid imposed alien constructions on their experiences (Middleton, 1986: 132).

She discussed her analysis of the interviews with the women who participated in the study. In this way, she was able to involve them in the process of connecting their life experiences and the ways families, schools, sexuality and work are organised in this society.

Sue Middleton's work, like that of Bev James and Roberta Hill, is grounded in the experiences and understandings of the people she interviewed. The women have unique biographies but they also share some common experiences which are the outcome of their participation in the New Zealand education system in the 1950s and early 1960s. Biography, the structure of institutions and a particular historical context intertwine to produce the lives that Middleton documents. In a more recent book, she explores the connections between her personal biography as a feminist educator, the institutions within which she lives and works and the specific context of the rapidly changing New Zealand society of the late 1980s and early 1990s (Middleton, 1993).

Gender and Sport – the Case of Rugby

Much of the work on gender in the New Zealand context has been done by feminist researchers interested in discovering the mechanisms which have produced and sustained gender divisions in this society. Their focus has been predominantly on women's experience. Increasingly, however, both male and female sociologists have analysed the construction of male gender identity, particularly the place of rugby football in the articulation of understandings about being male in the context of this society.

The most detailed analysis of the development of rugby as an institution in this society and its part in encoding certain ideals of masculinity has been offered by the historian, Jock Phillips. He argues that the Pakeha male stereotype was the outcome of the need to integrate the 'muscular virtues of the pioneer heritage' and to contain that masculine spirit within respectable boundaries in order to provide the emerging colony with a conscientious, well disciplined workforce (Phillips, 1987: 86). Rugby football became the context within which that stereotype was best expressed. It occupied a special place in New Zealand society because it encouraged toughness, endurance and physical daring, while demanding that these expressions of masculinity were played out in an organised and regular way. It provided the combination of raw physicality and discipline which was seen as the key ingredient of male settler character in the late nineteenth and early twentieth centuries.

While in Britain rugby was the sport of the élite, in New Zealand it was played by all social classes. As Geoff Fougere has pointed out, its success depended on its cutting across divisions of class and ethnicity and providing a symbolic expression of 'mateship' and unity consistent with New Zealand's egalitarian ideology (Fougere, 1989: 115). Piet de Jong's study of rugby as an institution in a small New Zealand town suggests that through rugby 'men with differing access to social and economic resources are reconstructed into something approaching a rugby family' (de Jong, 1987).

Rugby was, of course, always problematic as an expression of national unity in New Zealand. The rugby 'family', the mateship, unity and camaraderie of the rugby field excluded women, whose job it was to wash the dirty jerseys, shorts and socks and provide 'the plate' at club socials. Geoff Fougere and Christine Dann have suggested that this was one of the reasons why rugby came under attack in the early 1980s. The anti-tour protests of 1981 were not just about the politics of sporting contacts with South Africa but about the rejection of the traditional place of rugby in New Zealand society and the way it has shaped the personal and national identity of many New Zealand men (Fougere, 1989: 112; Dann, 1982). This was why emotions ran so high during the 1981 Springbok Tour. What was at stake was the institution of rugby as a key facet of New Zealand society, an institution which has had a major impact on the character of most New Zealand males who have participated in it at primary and secondary school, even if they were not adult players of the game. As Geoff Fougere suggests:

> The cultural freight carried by rugby – its powerful embodiment of particular relationships between men, the forms of identity they carried and the national ethos they suggested – helps explain why the challenge to rugby generated by the Springbok tour drew on such deep emotions ... what was at stake ... (was) nothing less than the defence of individual and collective identity, a symbolisation of a way of life, suddenly threatened (Fougere, 1989: 117).

Geoff Fougere argues that this attack on rugby can be explained by shifts and changes which had been occurring in New Zealand since the 1970s, changes which meant that rugby could no longer act as the symbol of New Zealand masculinity and egalitarianism. Women's increasing involvement in paid work, feminism, and Maori activism around issues of land and language, had disrupted old assumptions about what it meant to be a New Zealander and the appropriateness of the All Blacks as national icons. According to Fougere:

> ... changes in social context meant that, for increasing numbers of New Zealanders, the values and practices embodied in rugby were felt

to be at odds with patterns newly emerging in New Zealand culture (Fougere, 1989: 120).

Another New Zealand sociologist, Lynne Star, has argued that the Rugby World Cup of 1987 which attracted major coverage on TVNZ was an attempt to resurrect rugby after the battering it had taken during 1981. She suggests that the New Zealand Rugby Union and the International Rugby Board went to enormous lengths to present their act as 'well and truly cleaned up'. TVNZ's handling of the World Cup ensured that the focus was once more on rugby as a spectator sport, cleaned of the political stigma attached to it through its association with South Africa (Star, 1989b). What emerged on our television screens was 'sportsopera', a male equivalent of soap opera, a serial in which we wait from game to game to find out about the fortunes of our favourite characters. Will they exhibit heroism and be crowned with success, or will they experience illness and disability? (Star, 1989a).

While Geoff Fougere has argued that rugby slipped from its place of significance as the symbolic representation on New Zealand manhood and the ideal relations between men in this society in the early 1980s, Lynne Star asserts that in the late 1980s it re-emerged in a dynamic televised form as the 'civil religion' of New Zealand complete with iconography (mascots, special clothes, flags) and ritual performances. As an institution, it is fueled by the quest for 'manhood, individuality and national competition' and packaged as 'entertainment' (Star, 1989c).

While the euphoria of the 1987 World Cup has been superseded by less spectacular All Black performances in recent years, rugby football continues to absorb television time. Simultaneously, new versions of the game, like touch rugby, have attracted increasing numbers of women and men to a sport which has some of the pleasures of rugby but does not entail the old gender divisions. Does this reflect some of the challenges to traditional gender divisions which are a feature of the late twentieth century?

Conclusion

We have looked at the way a number of New Zealand sociologists have explored the personal and structural dynamics of gender. All of these reflections on gender have attached importance to the particular historical context in which gendered expectations and the social practices associated with them have occurred. All have explored the way gender differences shift over time and the way they are affected by changes in work, economic relations, politics and culture.

Our experience as gendered people varies across generations, between ethnic groups and classes, between heterosexuals, lesbians, gay men and bisexuals. The messages we get about how we should behave as women or men, boys or girls are not always consistent and uniform. This enables us to make certain choices or struggle to fulfil contradictory expectations. It also makes possible the development of new understandings of what it means to be male or female, and the actualisation of social practices which will change the structures of the family, the workplace and the state.

Further Reading

Briar, C., Munford, R. and Nash, M. (eds), 1992, *Superwoman, Where are You? Social Policy and Women's Experience*, Palmerston North, Dunmore Press. (See chapters by Celia Briar, Robin McKinlay and Robyn Munford.)

Cox, S. (ed.), 1987, *Public and Private Worlds : Women in Contemporary New Zealand,* Wellington, Allen and Unwin. (See chapters by Novitz, James, Robinson and Saville-Smith.)

Du Plessis, R., Bunkle, P., Irwin, K., Laurie, A. and Middleton, S. (eds), 1992, *Feminist Voices: Women's Studies Texts for Aotearoa/New Zealand*, Auckland, Oxford University Press. (See chapters by Kathie Irwin, Anne Opie, Lynne Star, Ruth Habgood, Anne Else, Ngahuia Te Awekotuku.)

Horsfield, A. and Evans, M., 1988, *Maori Women in the Economy: A Preliminary Review of the Economic Position of Maori Women in New Zealand,* Wellington, Ministry of Women's Affairs.

James, B. and Saville-Smith, K., 1989, *Gender, Culture, Power,* Auckland, Oxford University Press.

Middleton, S., and Jones, A. (eds), 1992, *Women and Education in Aotearoa 2,* Wellington, Bridget Williams Books. (See chapters by Karen Newton, Lise Bird and Bill Rout.)

Olsson, S. (ed.), 1992, *The Gender Factor: Women in New Zealand Organisations*, Palmerston North, Dunmore Press. (See chapters by Bev James and Kay Saville-Smith, Janet Holmes and Maria Stubbe, Judith Pringle and Nicola Armstrong.)

8 State

Nicola Armstrong

There are two quotes that epitomise the debate which is currently taking place regarding the role of the state in New Zealand society. The first is from the Royal Commission on Social Policy:

> As the ultimate expression of our collective responsibility, the State is the major force in achieving a more just society (Royal Commission on Social Policy, 1988: 25).

The second is from the National MP, Ruth Richardson:

> You have believed the state is your friend; look how it has betrayed you, now try the market (cited in James, 1987: 5).

This chapter analyses the relevance of both of these statements to an understanding of the changing role of the state in New Zealand society. At one end of the political spectrum is the Royal Commission's portrayal of the state as the guardian of 'collective responsibility', positively intervening in the economy and providing the public services we associate with the 'welfare' or 'social democratic' state. From the opposite end of the political spectrum comes a 'negative' model of the state where it is portrayed as betraying New Zealanders by 'artificially' protecting the country from the international marketplace and encouraging welfare dependency.

Between these two models of the 'interventionist' and 'minimalist state' lies a middle ground which acknowledges both the important role the state plays as the guardian of collective responsibility, *and* agrees that there is a need to encourage a 'democratisation' of the state to ensure greater accessibility, diversity and accountability. This analysis suggests that the changing role of the state in New Zealand society is highly contestable and that *all* groups within New Zealand society, including women and Maori, have an important role to play in defining what the state is and can be.

What is the State?

The state is defined in basic terms by its key institutions and the functions they perform. Ham and Hill (1984) summarise these institutions as follows:

> ... *legislative bodies*, including parliamentary assemblies and subordinate law-making institutions; *executive bodies*, including government bureaux and departments of state; and *judicial bodies* – principally courts of law – with responsibility for enforcing and, through their decisions, developing the law (cited in O'Brien, 1988: 34, my emphasis).

In addition, political institutions employ the police and armed forces to support and maintain legislative, executive and judicial institutions and to guarantee internal and external security (Ham and Hill, 1984).

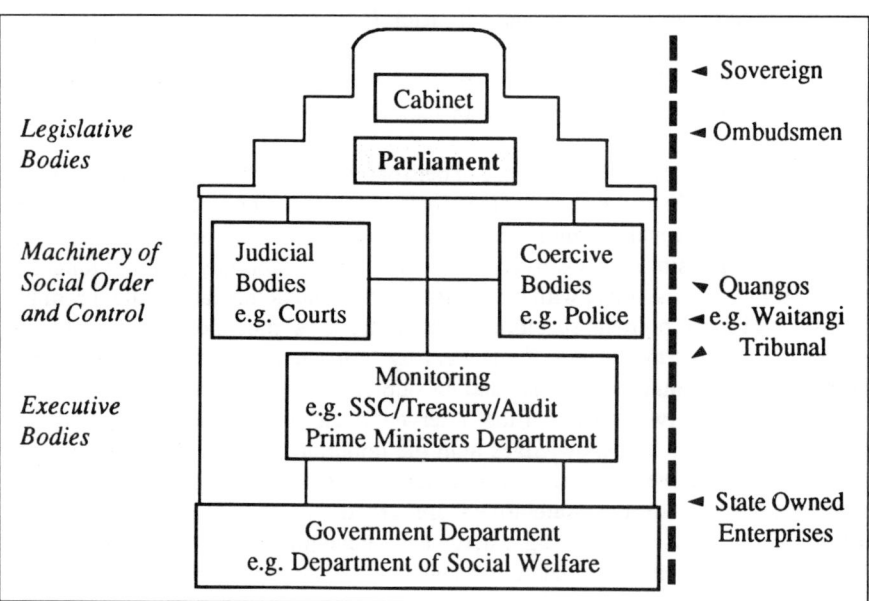

**Figure 8.1
Central State Apparatus**

Legislative bodies are comprised of Cabinet (the main body which adopts policy and initiates action on it) and its committees; the Government Caucus which is in turn supported by committees; and the Government Research Unit. In addition, Select Committees, made up of Members of Parliament and appointed by the House, exist for the life of a parliament or a specified time (for example, the Select Committee on Contraception Sterilisation and Abortion). These legislative bodies are the central and most important arena for law and policy formulation and act as the key decision-making apparatus of the New Zealand state.

At a second level is the *machinery of social order and control*. Judicial bodies in New Zealand consist of a hierarchy of courts from the Privy Council, Court of Appeal and High Court to District Courts, Small Claims and Rent Tribunals, etc. (see Palmer, 1987: 181). *Coercive bodies,* such as the police and military, exist primarily to ensure internal and external security, one of the oldest functions of the state. A third category of agencies of social control (in addition to judicial and coercive bodies) exist in the form of the regulatory agencies of the state which operate at a national and local level. These agencies, while not possessing the same degree of legal or coercive power as the courts or the police, do maintain social order and enforce the law. Examples include health inspectors or television licencing authorities.

These regulatory agencies often work from within, or in conjunction with, *executive bodies*, such as government departments which in turn perform the dual role of devising policies and administering programmes to implement them. Government departments both directly provide some services, or fund other agencies to provide them on their behalf.

There are four central departments within the executive level of the state apparatus which act as key *monitoring* agencies, namely the Treasury, the State Services Commission, the Audit Office and the Prime Minister's Department. These four organisations have specific functions – the Treasury in terms of the supervision of expenditure; the State Services Commission in relation to the management of state personnel; the Audit Office in the task of auditing the accounts to ensure public monies have been spent in the manner authorised by Parliament; and the advisory and liaison group which is part of the Prime Minister's Department.

In addition, there are a number of other important elements of the state apparatus that operate outside the framework of the central state (to a certain degree), but which have important monitoring or accountability functions to, or for, the central state apparatus. For example, according to the Constitutional Act 1986, the British Queen is Queen of New Zealand, and the Governor-General the Sovereign's representative in New Zealand. The Governor-General's legal powers are by 'constitutional convention and democratic principle exercised on the advice of Ministers' (Palmer, 1987: 25). The *Ombudsmen* are similarly connected to Parliament as a check on the power of government and are able to investigate (on their own or the public's initiative) any administrative decision, recommendation, act or commission of government departments, related organisations and local authorities.

Quangos, or quasi-autonomous non-governmental organisations, are public bodies which are not government departments, and which experience a degree of autonomy from government jurisdiction, although they are still part of the state. They may be more or less free from direct ministerial supervision or Treasury control of their expenditure, although Ministers usually appoint their members. Quangos may take the form of corporations, (for example, the Accident Compensation Corporation); commissions set up by statute (for example, the Human Rights Commission); tribunals also set up by statute and empowered to decide questions in the same fashion as a court (for example, the Waitangi Tribunal); or committees, such as the Advisory Committee on Education (Palmer, 1987:90).

State Owned Enterprises similarily experience a greater or lesser degree of autonomy from government. The 1986 State Owned Enterprises Act commercialised state trading activities, giving the managers of these organisations more publicly answerable responsibilities and greater control over the use of the resources allocated to them. SOEs are, however, directly accountable to Parliament for their administrative performance, although their principal objective is to operate as a successful business. The Electricity Corporation is a well known example of an SOE.

Given the diversity of institutions which form the state apparatus, it makes sense to conceptualise the state not as a single or monolithic entity, but as a:

> ... complex of relationships, embodying a certain form of power operating through various institutional arrangements (Burton, 1985: 104).

The state, according to Burton, is essentially a *socio-political process*, the result at any given historical moment of various and competing struggles and demands.

How this socio-political process is understood theoretically has been the focus of much debate in the sociological literature, and the following discussion will briefly outline four key theoretical approaches: pluralist, libertarian right, Marxist and feminist analysis.

Sociological Approaches to the State

Pluralist theories of the state emphasise the democratic nature of the state in mediating between competing groups. Dahl's (1961) book, *Who Governs?*, portrays the state as being like a honeycomb, open to pressure upon its structure from various interest groups and responding to these pressures through appropriate structural change. Dahl argues that a *plurality* of interest groups such as unions, women's groups and employer associations, can influence government through lobbying and political organisations at a local, regional and national level. In New Zealand, pluralist theory informs work such as the New Zealand Planning Council's (1982) document *Who Makes Social Policy?* Here, the Planning Council emphasises the plurality of interests represented in the political process, the open and accessible nature of government structures, and sees the state as benevolently acting in the public interest in order to reflect public needs.

Clearly, this version of pluralist theory has little to say about conflict or disagreement about policy, or the differential power between competing interest groups (for example, the Business Roundtable compared with the Clerical Workers Union), because of an over-riding emphasis on the consensus of interests in society.

The *libertarian right* offer an alternative account of the state which is, in essence, *anti-pluralist*. They contest that aspects of a liberal democracy lead to the 'distorted' growth of the state '...beyond the level necessary to satisfy citizens' demands for publicly supplied "goods" ', (Dunleavy, 1981: 134). The libertarian right argue, for example, that party political competition and interest group activity, rather than enhancing democracy, lead to unrealistic promises to voters and the wholesale acceptance of 'packages' of policy which do not have a positive overall effect on social welfare.

The state is portrayed by the libertarian right as 'captured' by bureaucrats committed to maximising their bureau's budget and staff allocation, rather than pursuing policy goals voted by citizens. The libertarian right attacks Keynesian understandings of the state as an economic regulator and instead portrays it as an imposition on the free individual and a constraint on free enterprise. The pluralists' key decision-making processes of party competition, interest group influence and an independent bureaucracy are understood by the libertarian right, not as the cornerstone of a democratic society, but as pathological tendencies within liberal democracies which lead to the creation of a monolithic state apparatus.

At the opposite end of the political spectrum, *Marxist* theories offer critical approaches to the state and also oppose the consensual nature of pluralist theory. For *orthodox Marxists*, the state is understood as an *instrument* through which the bourgeoisie control other classes in society. Miliband (1977), for example, argues that the state and class are closely connected, as demonstrated by the ways in which the ruling class 'get their way'. According to Miliband, the bourgeoisie fill up senior government positions with their cronies, ensure that the right people (from the right schools and the right clubs) are appointed to positions of power outside the government, and use state power to extend class power by using state policies to further their own pecuniary gain.

In contrast, *Neo-Marxist* accounts of the state argue that the process by which the modern state has developed has demonstrated the way in which class conflict is managed by co-operative rather than coercive methods through the process of *hegemony*. According to Gramsci (see Simon, 1982: 21-3), hegemony is the process stabilise, thus distributing the goods and services of society to the maximum benefit of the maximum number.

The inadequacies of neo-classical economics led to strong political support for state intervention to protect citizens from the anarchy of capitalism's 'boom and bust' cycles. New Zealanders, who had suffered through the Depression, did not wish to return to the 'unemployment and destitution that came from having few or no social benefit supports' (Maharey, 1987: 74), or to the idea of the state as a 'night-watchman with very limited functions' (Gamble, 1988: 180).

The New Zealand state was increasingly looked to as the means to deliver a more secure future, a future free from the instability of the market, where the state played a *positive* and *necessary* role in the regulation of the economic system and the provision of social welfare. In other words, state intervention was seen as necessary to further capitalist accumulation without the 'anarchy' of the market.

The theories of John Maynard Keynes were to justify the development of a programme of greater state intervention in the economy as a means to promote full employment, minimise inflation and '... curb the volatility of private investment using an active fiscal policy (government spending and taxation policies) and monetary management policy' (Sharp and Broomhill, 1988: 34). Keynesian economics were not, however, a radical departure from earlier neo-classical economic theory. Keynes continued to accept the dominant role of the market in allocating resources; in the principle of competition; in the importance of consumers furthering their own self interest and maximising their economic choices; and in the principle of firms pursuing private profit. The social democratic consensus was therefore always based on a settlement between 'equality and efficiency'.

Marrying the collectivist principles of democracy and the individualistic principles of the market economy was a settlement attractive to many New Zealanders. This was clearly indicated in the 1935 General Election when Labour captured 69 per cent of the vote on a platform of greater state intervention.

However, the settlement between the market and democracy that the social democratic consensus represented was always just that, a *settlement*; a trade-off only possible when the underlying rate of economic growth was strong and able to pay for social reforms. In New Zealand, this consensus never challenged capitalism *per se*, although the state did assume control of some industries and the welfare state was greatly expanded. Such intervention heralded the coming of the social democratic state, but there were real limits to what the consensus could achieve while still maintaining the legitimacy of the state. The attempt to socialise medical care, for example, did establish that such care was a social right but could not and did not break the hegemony of doctors over the health system (Maharey, 1987: 75).

Walter Nash's 1936 Budget was a manifesto for the role of the social democratic state in New Zealand society. According to Nash, the aim of the state was to:

> ... organise an internal economy that will distribute the production and services of the Dominion in a way that will guarantee to every person able and willing to work an income sufficient to provide him and his dependants with everything necessary to make a 'home' and 'home life' in the best sense of the meaning of those terms (Nash, 1936, cited in McKinlay, 1988: 15).

This quote is very interesting in terms of clearly stating the dual aspects of the social democratic consensus. The state's role was to further both capitalist accumulation and sustain the legitimacy of the state's own power by maintaining public order, in part through the patriarchal family. Public order was particularly problematic when trying to deal with the increasing financial and social burden of the 'victims of social disruption' particularly 'the elderly, the destitute and the deserted' (James and Saville-Smith, 1989: 31). By fostering a greater and more rigidly defined domestic role for women, the state could impose domestic order on men and children. This domestic role was promulgated in what feminists have now come to recognise as the 'Cult of Domesticity'.

James and Saville-Smith (1989) describe the 'Cult of Domesticity' as a:

> ... particular construction of femininity which emphasises almost exclusively women's alleged nurturant and maternal capacities, ... (where) 'women come to be seen as more morally responsible and, of course, more chaste than men' ... (and through which), women's lives are structured as dependent and privatised... (as) opposed to masculinity which situates men as actors in the public sphere where they are providers for and protectors of women (James and Saville-Smith, 1989: 32).

James and Saville-Smith suggest that the Cult of Domesticity provided the state with a means to control and educate children, to '... reassert the obligations of individuals to care for kin' (James and Saville-Smith, 1989: 32) and to reinforce the nuclear family. As Walter Nash suggested, men worked (for money), women and children were dependent upon them and the female role was to create a secure and stable 'home life' to assist the breadwinner in his task.

For women then, the social democratic consensus was characterised by a belief that their role was firmly within the home. For example, women drawn into paid labour during the Second World War were encouraged from as early as 1941 to return to their proper place of 'hearth and home' so that '... men returning from the war could have 'their' jobs back' (Jesson *et al.*, 1988: 27). If women chose instead to move into other available paid employment (usually that more traditionally associated with 'women's work'), they found that women's wages and the cost of childcare made their paid work simply unprofitable.

The social democratic 'consensus' then, even in its more progressive form, contained political features which were conservative and even reactionary. Jesson *et al.* note that:

> ... New Zealand went where Britain went. A woman's place was in the home. Children were supposed to know their place. Anyone of non-British origin was a 'hori', 'wop', 'nigger', 'wog', [and] catholics were 'tikes'... (Jesson *et al.*, 1988: 32).

Crisis of Consensus (1966-1984)

By the late 1960s the economic basis of the 'consensus' had begun to seriously erode. Britain's entry into the Common Market ended the long-standing and profitable exchange that had existed between the two nations and this, combined with the oil shocks, 'stagflation' (declining employment and increasing inflation) and the development of a global market place, subjected New Zealand to a 'double instability', both internal and external (Jesson, *et al.*, 1988: 33).

The years 1966-1984 broadly represent a period of transition and the attempt to maintain the increasingly fragile 'consensus', at the same time as the state responded to the inevitable repercussions of national and international change. The political arena was similarly characterised by a high degree of volatility.

The 1970s, for example, saw the re-emergence of an overt feminist movement with 'women's liberation' conferences and conventions held throughout the country between 1972 and 1979. The development of the first women's centres (1974), refuge and rape crisis centres (1975), the establishment of the Women's Studies Association (1977), the Working Women's Charter campaign (1978), the first Trades Council Women's Sub-Committee (1979) and the National Black Women's Hui (1980) are just a few examples of the many and varied political organisations and campaigns that characterised the seventies (see Dann, 1985: 1-27). The 1970s also saw the re-forming of Maori activism within groups such as Nga Tamatoa (formed in 1970), and a high degree of political activity, particularly the 1975 land marches, the occupation of Bastion Point (1977-8), and the refocusing of attention on the Treaty of Waitangi (Spoonley, 1988: 5-6).

The Rise of the Libertarian Right

At the same time, Muldoon's government was restructuring the economy in fundamental ways. Reforms in tax, Closer Economic Relations with Australia and product diversification, signalled a '...general shift towards 'more market' policies' (Edlin, cited in Maharey, 1987: 74). This restructuring in turn stimulated the rapid expansion of entrepreneurship, particularly for those involved in property development, finance and industry directed at national and international markets. This group, which lacked political representation, was joined by a small but significant section of the electorate, including business people and bureaucrats influenced by laissez-faire ideas (Maharey, 1987: 78).

The interests of this disparate but powerful group coalesced around the articulation of what Jesson *et al.* (1988: 10) have defined as *'libertarian right'* ideology. This ideology brings together *classical liberalism* which values, above all else, individual freedom from government interference; *neo-classical economics* (and the belief in the 'natural' tendency of capitalist economies to reach equilibrium); and *monetarist* economic theory associated with 'supply side' economics.

Classical liberalism understood 'liberty' as freedom from interference, especially state interference. The demand for liberty did not require the abolition of state authority, but demanded that such authority be 'grounded on the consent of the governed' (Jaggar and Rothenberg, 1984: 83). The sphere of legitimate state authority was clearly delineated as the 'public' sphere of life, the state was seen to have no authority to intervene in the private sphere of home and family. Classical liberalism contained a '...social vision which saw the private world of the individual as more satisfying and valid than the public world of community affairs' (Jesson *et al.*, 1988: 10).

Middleton (1989: 18) argues that Treasury analysis originates from this libertarian perspective, although, through political necessity, this doctrine is modified because 'unfettered free competition' and the associated inequality it produces is not, in its extreme form, acceptable to New Zealand voters. Moreover, the increasingly vocal call for the ratification of the principles of the Treaty of Waitangi in legislation has also acted as a brake on libertarianism. Despite these modifications, Treasury continues to argue, in classic liberal style, that the 'collective good' can only be realised through private individuals acting in competitive isolation, pursuing their self interests with minimal state interference (Hall and Held, 1989: 19).

Neo-classical economics, developed in the late nineteenth century which similarly emphasised the importance of the individual, particularly 'individual consumers in an atomised market place' (Jesson *et al.*, 1988: 11). Jesson *et al.* argue that classical liberalism and neo-classical economics are mutually reinforcing ideologies because liberalism advocates the supremacy of the individual which is central to neo-classical economics whilst the latter's emphasis on the free market 'justifies the anti-state beliefs of classical liberalism'.

As discussed earlier, neo-classical economic theory was largely eclipsed in New Zealand by Keynesianism and a desire for the state to intervene to establish and guarantee individual rights. However, throughout the period of the 'consensus', certain theorists maintained an interest in, and advocacy of, libertarian right ideology.

Two key figures in this debate were the Austrian economist, Friedrich von Hayek, and his American counterpart, Milton Friedman, who promoted *monetarist* economic policy. Monetarist theory at 'the most conservative end of the spectrum' (Wilkes and Shirley, 1984: 13) argues that state activity should be opposed outright. It is, essentially, 'theory *against* the state' (Wilkes and Shirley, 1984: 13, my emphasis) because it claims that the state is unnatural, inefficient and costly.

These three strands inform 'libertarian right' or 'market-liberal' thinking on the state, and in the 1970s, gained increasing currency within the political arena.

Rolling Back the Welfare State? 1984 Onwards

The state's response in the 1970s and early 1980s to the social, political and economic upheaval that New Zealand was experiencing was the imposition of the social democratic consensus through 'authoritarian statism', that is, the imposition of increasingly unpopular measures to secure the objectives of the consensus through the state apparatus (Gamble, 1988). The wage, rent and price freeze is one example of the attempt to enforce the consensus, and its failure opened up a political space for the articulation of a new libertarian right project in New Zealand.

The libertarian right draws upon an increasing discontent with aspects of the welfare state and government intervention in the economy. Fougere notes that in this critique of the state:

> Analysts competed to show how those who were white, male and middle class were likely to benefit from the system while others were subjected to extensive social controls and disadvantages by the same mechanisms (Fougere, 1987: 2).

The libertarian right propose an alternative explanation of economic and social change which is, by its very nature, anti-statist, anti-collectivist and anti-socialist (Gamble, 1988: 193). Maharey argues that the libertarian right approach makes the following arguments to justify an 'anti-state' approach:

> It suggests that the people of New Zealand do not really want the welfare state because they are individuals who prefer to look after themselves. They like to take chances and achieve their personally defined goals. Standing in the way of the true people of New Zealand is a past built up of over forty years of interventionist governments ... New Zealanders have allowed themselves to become over regulated and over protected ... (the New Right) demand that the income earners be given back their taxes so individuals can choose how they want to spend their money. If people want health care, education, accident

insurance and unemployment benefits should they not, the argument goes, provide for themselves through insurance? (Maharey, 1987: 79).

The libertarian right's vision of society capitalises on the existing critique of the state by creating a powerful dichotomy between the state and collective provision, (associated with uniformity, inefficiency, indignity and a lack of choice), and the market and private provision, associated with self sufficiency, choice, efficiency and rising living standards (Leadbeater, 1988: 18).

According to this New Right vision, the state should be actively opposed and the market economy, with its institutions of private property and free voluntary contract, protected from state intervention as the 'most important sphere of individual freedom' (Gamble, 1988: 154). The 'free' and 'natural' operation of the market economy in satisfying human needs is understood as essential to prevent domination by the state, where the state is understood as '...'unnatural' and artificial and therefore costly and unnecessary' (Wilkes and Shirley, 1984: 13). There is no justification, according to the libertarian right, for intervening in the 'free' market because 'those who end up with little or nothing have not been coerced', they will receive 'whatever rewards [are] determined appropriate by the market' (Jesson *et al.,* 1988: 15).

Libertarian right theory asserts the supremacy of the market to provide goods and services as opposed to the public sector, a preference for individual rather than collective action (for example, individual health insurance as opposed to a publicly funded health system) and, particularly, an emphasis on the free individual acting in competition with other self interested individuals. Given this vision of society, social justice is clearly not a priority. As Wilkes and Shirley (1984:15) argue, economic inequality *presupposes* a lack of freedom, because people can hardly be free when they are poor and starving.

A powerful source of this new ideology comes from *within* the state apparatus, in the form of Treasury advice to government. Treasury warns that the government must avoid interrupting the 'natural' cohesion that exists between people in the provision of welfare services. The state is reduced to a safety net, so that:

> ... government involvement is required only when there is a breakdown in the two natural channels through which (all human) needs are met – the family and the market... (Koopman and Scott, 1984: 88).

However, as Novitz (1987: 3) has pointed out, social relations are frequently 'coercive rather than voluntary'. Women who care for children, the disabled and the elderly are less likely to do so because of 'voluntary and spontaneously developed networks' than because of the structure of unpaid labour and the economic and ideological factors which define this work as largely the responsibility of women.

Furthermore, libertarian right theory understands the individual as essentially *rational* and *acquisitive*. Middleton (1989: 20-21) notes that in the Treasury document having children is seen as an 'irrational desire' because of the cost and 'dependency' of the caregiver and child to the family. Furthermore, the interests of mothers and children are seen as conflictual and competing because the child's needs for care are clearly in conflict with the mother's needs to compete in the market economy.

As Jesson *et al.* (1988: 16) point out, 'if human relationships are measured only in terms of their worth as determined by the market, then many relationships are excluded and marginalised'. The libertarian analysis of motherhood (or indeed any domestic or reproductive labour) reflects this marginalisation of women's work. The energy, creativity and skills such work requires are rendered either invisible or irrational, despite the enormous contribution they make to society's wellbeing.

Reproductive and domestic labour is however, an 'essential prop' for the 'free market', a prop which provides goods and services in the home as well as a pool of 'free' voluntary labour in the community to provide the services the state once provided. As Wilkes and Shirley (1984: 15) comment:

> Are all freedoms including the 'freedom' to remain unemployed, the 'freedom' not to get into a hospital, the 'freedom' to own a house, are all these worth having?

To this list I would add: is the freedom to become a provider of 'community care' in its many senses, without adequate resources, training, information, and support, is this a 'freedom' worth having?

Wither the Welfare State?

This chapter began by suggesting that the state is a site of struggle and clearly the state is, at this moment in New Zealand society, in the midst of such a struggle. The question remains, however, as to whether this struggle represents the growing pains of the welfare state or a profound structural crisis which will result in the state's radical transformation (Fougere, 1987: 3).

The continuing popularity and hegemonic nature of the libertarian right's remaking of the state is an ideological response to the changing social and economic context which New Zealand faces. The nation-state has become increasingly permeated by global financial markets, mass media and the internationalisation of production, distribution and consumption. Under these new conditions of capitalist accumulation, the old basis of the state's legitimacy is called into question. In the context of criticism of the public sector from many different groups, the libertarian right's critique has magnified the 'crisis' of state legitimation.

The libertarian right's 'solution' to this crisis is to 'roll back' the state. In the 1990s this 'rolling back' of the state has been heightened. Most directly, the cutting and capping of benefit provision in 1991 saw, for the first time in New Zealand's history, the decreasing of most welfare benefits and the cessation of forms of universal provision (such as the family benefit). In addition, the shape of the state itself was radically transformed in terms of the continuing sales of state-owned businesses and assets and the massive reduction in core government service employees from 88,507 in 1986 to 36,374 in 1993, a 59 per cent decrease (Edwards, 1993: 5). As O'Brien and Wilkes (1993: 170) note:

> ... the rationales for these cuts ... were the increasing government deficit, a thrust toward family and individual independence and self reliance, and a reconstruction of the welfare state as a safety net.

However, if there is criticism of the paternalistic interventionist state, *and* a concern for the inequities of the market-driven minimalist state, then what is the possibility of a third alternative? Maharey (1989: 6) suggests that a 'democratic alternative' is possible, an alternative which, Leadbeater (1988: 17) argues, acknowledges the inadequacies of the paternalistic state and speaks to the new social aspirations of 'choice, autonomy, decentralisation and greater responsibility'. At the same time, such an alternative acknowledges that the welfare state, has been and still is, 'a source of liberation for most New Zealanders in areas such as housing, education, employment and social support' (Maharey, 1989: 6). As O'Brien and Wilkes (1993:180) suggest:

> The first and most substantial principle which needs to be reintroduced is that there must be an *active role for the state* in planning the future direction of New Zealand society.

Maharey (1989) suggests that there are two ways to construct the democratic alternative state. The first is to restore the concept of *citizenship,* and the second is to democratise the state, that is, to change the role and function of the state in order to enhance the principles of *diversity, accessibility* and *accountability.*

Citizenship

The libertarian right approach to the issue of citizenship is couched in terms of the individualism discussed earlier, where citizenship is understood in terms of a narrow model of 'consumer sovereignty' which assumes people can have whatever they can afford (Maharey, 1989: 101-2). If the passport to participation in society is increasingly focused around the possession of a credit card then, inevitably, large sections of our society will become further disenfranchised, particularly many people who are working class, unemployed, young, women, Maori...; the list goes on.

The libertarian right's vision of the individual is not compelling, not only because some cannot afford to participate, but also because of the collective consciousness fostered by 50 years of the welfare state. To adapt Leadbeater's argument, people do not work and live in families, whanau, communities, factories, trade unions, health collectives, iwi authorities *as individuals, they work together*. Because of the collective nature of our lives, the libertarian right has failed to extinguish the collective culture which surrounds our health and education systems.

Given the collective nature of our lives, it makes sense, as Maharey (1989: 6) has suggested, to '...foster collective forms of organisation that will allow people to co-operate with one another to solve problems of common interest'. It is simply not possible for many of the problems of individual security and advancement to be overcome by individuals acting on their own. Inadequate investment in housing, training, education and health 'can only be overcome by sustained collective action' (Leadbeater, 1988: 15).

Collective action, however, should not simply collapse into the problematic notion of 'community care' which masks the 'collective sacrifices of women as carers' (James and Saville-Smith, 1988: 101). Community care feeds off the appropriated labour of women as carers for the young, the old, ill or differently abled and thus perpetuates the marginalisation of women from the paid workforce and their confinement to unpaid domestic labour. Instead, the concept of the individual's citizenship rights and responsibilities must be redefined in terms of the need to ensure the *public* provision of social services and the protection of civil and political rights to all citizens free from the abuse or potential abuse of state power.

To see these collective needs as the rights and entitlements of *all* individuals, not just those possessing the prestige, power and wealth to 'buy' them in the market, creates both a basis to critique the libertarian right's narrow focus on the 'consumer' and an opportunity to promote an 'expanded notion of what it means to be a citizen in New Zealand society' (Maharey, 1989: 6).

Diversity

Diversity acknowledges the need for the state to service the 'widest possible range of interests and needs' (Maharey, 1989: 7) by taking into account the interests of all groups, including (for example) women and Maori. It would require the reprioritising of issues of importance with, for example, sexuality being an emblem of the diverse society New Zealanders wish to nurture, not a 'side' issue.

Such diversity would also include strategies such as devolution, where the central state is no longer seen as the most appropriate body to deliver services to communities. Although the current debate concerning devolution has indicated some of the problems of devolving responsibility (for example, the need for adequate information, resources, support, accountability and/or autonomy from central state 'rule-making'), such strategies do create the possibility for greater local decision-making, resource allocation and the recognition of diverse needs within communities.

Accessibility

Accessibility requires that the state ensures that no one is 'barred from participating in society because of income, gender, ethnicity or location' (Maharey, 1989: 7). This may mean removing areas of public interest from the market to guarantee access, for example, through a state-operated and funded cervical screening programme.

It may also mean that the state, rather than directly providing all services, creates a 'publicly provided regulated space' (Leadbeater, 1988: 19) in which both private and public activities are possible. The state, Leadbeater (1988) argues, would be vitally concerned to ensure that this space exists (through legislative regulation and accountability), but its direct role in the provision of services would 'depend on whether it is the most efficient provider of the services'. The state would need to become more responsive to individual and group needs rather than providing standardised goods and services from a centralised bureaucracy (Maharey, 1989: 7). In the above example, the provision for marae-based cervical screening programmes would be an example of this kind of flexibility.

Accountability

Making the state more accountable would mean both the day-to-day opportunity for consumers of public services to make their opinions and needs felt to the providers of those services, as well as the opportunity for the input of diverse groups into the overall policy formulation of the state (Maharey, 1989: 8). Fougere argues that mechanisms for making the state more responsive and accountable include:

> ... *exit*, essentially the exercise ... of voting with one's feet and *voice*, the attempt to bring pressure to bear on the institution to improve the quality of its output (Fougere, 1987: 12).

Without the ability to affect political and policy decisions, individuals and local communities have limited opportunities to create a more democratically accountable system. The move away from elected Area Health Board representitives to Crown Health Enterprises, whose board members are appointed by the Minister, is a worrying example of a trend towards a less democratic system for the articulation of local needs and aspirations. Furthermore, if more articulate, discerning and/or wealthy users exercise the option of 'exit' from public welfare provision, then the continuation of good quality public services freely available to all is increasingly endangered. As Fougere (1987: 10) notes: 'it's better to keep the "sharp elbows of the middle class" inside the system pushing it outwards than to have them knocking it down'.

Conclusion

Many of those currently discussing the 'third alternative' argue that there needs to be a reassertion of the state's ability to represent, in the words of the Royal Commission on Social Policy, 'collective responsibility'. There is a need to restore the link between individual entitlement and collective action. In the creation of an alternative vision of the state, there must be an acknowledgement of the attractiveness of choice, diversity and responsibility, where *people* make decisions, not the state, the council or the expert. The task for the future is to renew confidence in the belief that collective social action *can* fulfil individual needs and deliver value, efficiency, flexibility and choice and to create the 'third alternative' between the activist and minimalist state.

Let us end the chapter as we began, with a quote from the Royal Commission on Social Policy (1988: 26):

> We believe that the state's role is to give a chance to everyone... to lead a fulfilling life. At some time in their lives many New Zealanders need the state's support to help them become self-determining, to look after themselves and others.... Changes... [to the state]... far from increasing dependence, would increase partnership, let more people share power and decision-making and enhance their chances to show initiative and exercise choice in their own destinies.

Further Reading

Else, A., 1992, 'To Market and Home Again: Gender and the New Right', in R. Du Plessis *et al.* (eds), *Feminist Voices: Women's Studies Texts for Aotearoa/New Zealand,* Auckland, Oxford University Press.

Jesson, B., Ryan, A. and Spoonley, P., 1988, *Revival of the Right. New Zealand Politics in the 1980s,* Auckland, Heinemann Reed.

O'Brien, M. and Wilkes, C., 1993, *The Tragedy of the Market,* Palmerston North, Dunmore Press.

Saville-Smith, K., 1987, 'Women and the State', in S. Cox (ed.), *Public and Private Worlds: Women in Contemporary New Zealand,* Wellington, Allen and Unwin/ Port Nicholson Press.

9 Social Policy

Ian Shirley

Social policy concerns the way in which society meets its collective responsibilities by enhancing human development and advancing social wellbeing. All societies have social policies which vary over time and space reflecting the political and cultural forces from which they evolved. The earliest forms of social policy can be traced back to the way in which human beings devised systems for the satisfaction of basic needs such as water, food, shelter and sanitation. These early production and distribution systems were based on primary institutions such as the family and the tribe, both of which played a crucial role in the maintenance of social order and control. The spiritual values and norms of traditional societies were embodied in tribal rituals and taboos and the social needs of the poor were addressed in accordance with cultural tradition and precedent.

What we in the twentieth century refer to as social security was evident in India more than 2,000 years ago when provision was made for the maintenance of children, widows and the elderly (Siddiqui, 1987). Similarly, in the Islamic world income maintenance was defined by the principle of Zakat which regulated individual charity and governed the collection of public funds for distribution to the poor. During the feudal period, the Aztec and Inca civilisations used legislation to compel their local communities to farm communal plots in order to provide for the needy, whereas in Africa, culturally-based reciprocal agreements rather than legislation have been used for many centuries as a means of enhancing the welfare of the family and the community. The British tradition of social policy goes back to 1547, when the City of London imposed a compulsory tax on the rich in order to alleviate poverty, and over the next 400 years a range of policy initiatives saw the establishment of workhouses and voluntary hospitals, private charities and public services (Fraser, 1973). Many of these welfare systems continue, albeit in modified form, to the present day.

It was the Industrial Revolution and the doctrine of Mercantilism which substantially influenced the development of social policy throughout Europe from the sixteenth to the eighteenth centuries (Litchtheim, 1971). Early Mercantilist writers promoted the economic and political independence of the nation state and they argued in favour of repressive poor laws and low wages as a deterrent to idleness and as an incentive to industry. In the seventeenth century, a more socially attuned version of the doctrine was developed in response to the growing problems of poverty and social unrest. The declining demand for labour encouraged the Mercantilists to find new ways of diversifying the national economy, including schemes for the employment of paupers and training for the children of the poor.

The main challenge to Mercantilism came from classical economics and the doctrine of laissez-faire. Although Adam Smith is often viewed as the founding father of the laissez-faire tradition, the term was first used by a group of French political economists known as the Physiocrats, who were opposed to government interventionism and control. Adam Smith was clearly influenced by this philosophy, and in his classic text, *The Wealth of Nations* (1776), he argued that human welfare would be advanced so long as goods and services were allowed to move without hindrance between nations, and labour could find its own price in the market. If these factors, along with the creation of money, were allowed to operate in a self-regulatory way, then there would be a natural coincidence between self-interest and the welfare of all. To the classical economists, the free market was in effect the welfare society (Pinker, 1979).

Conflict between these two doctrines was partially resolved in the first half of the nineteenth century as there was a gradual loss of confidence in the capacity of the free market to enhance individual welfare. As confidence in the efficacy of the market declined, the citizenry demanded that the state should play a more active role in the collective provision of welfare. With the onset of the Great Depression in the 1870s, the doctrine of free trade receded and welfare collectivism became associated with protectionist economic policies which owed much to the Mercantile tradition.

The Evolution of The Welfare State

The evolution of the welfare state can be understood as a response to two fundamental developments: the formation of national states and their transformation into mass democracies after the French Revolution, and the growth of capitalism which became the dominant mode of production after the Industrial Revolution (Flora and Heidenheimer, 1987). Whereas the production and distribution of social wealth within traditional societies was based on kinship, the industrial revolution tore at the bonds of collective responsibility and undermined those social and economic relationships which tied class to class, occupation to occupation, and individual to family and community. The kinship system gradually surrendered its central functions of power and control and as family gave way to church and voluntary agencies in the provision of social services, so these services in turn were secularised and incorporated within the framework of the national state.

The historical transition from *residual* to *institutional* forms of social policy (Wilensky and Lebeaux, 1965) began as the emergency service of primitive industrialism and culminated in the welfare state of the twentieth century. It was a transition which was marked by conflicts of interest between different collectivities and classes and by varying perceptions about economic and social systems and how they enhanced human welfare and social wellbeing. Early forms of state intervention were limited in scope, merely providing the conditions under which the market economy might expand and flourish, but the persistence of grinding poverty in the midst of industrial wealth enhanced the role of the state in providing for the destitute and in maintaining social order and control. Whereas some national states subsidised private charities and voluntary social services, others chose direct intervention through labour legislation, the inspection of factories, compulsory insurance and the provision of public services in the form of health, housing and education (Briggs, 1961).

Two dominant interpretations pervade the history of the welfare state, each seeking to explain the way in which modern social policy became institutionalised in the latter part of the nineteenth century. The first can be described as a form of social management from above with emphasis on the preservation of social order and the retention of power by the controlling elite. Germany is often used to illustrate this approach. In the late nineteenth century, the German state was built around military strength reinforced by a desire on the part of its hereditary rulers to preserve political and economic stability. One of these rulers, Otto von Bismarck, introduced the first social insurance programme in the modern world, but this scheme was primarily designed to stem the rise of socialism and forestall the organised demands of the working class. Bismarck was neither a democrat nor a reformer; his social policies were concerned with what was commonly termed the 'worker problem' (Higgins, 1981:100-129). A variant on this social management approach was provided by liberal capitalism which sought to minimise state interference in private property and simultaneously limit the use of distributional mechanisms outside the market. In the nineteenth century, Britain exemplified this approach insofar as those who applied for state support were generally regarded as deviants who were as much in need of training or punishment as of assistance. Moral distinctions were commonly drawn between the 'deserving' and 'undeserving' poor with the undeserving being both feared and despised (Ditch, 1987). The state provision of residual services for the destitute was treated in the same way as the provision of sewers and drains, which as Jordan suggests probably explains 'why the architect of the New Poor Law of 1834 was also an expert on sewerage, and an advocate of drains' (Jordan, 1987: 41).

An alternative interpretation of social history places emphasis on the urban proletariat of the nineteenth century which fought against the exploitation of factory labour, the unsanitary housing and working conditions of the industrial centres, enforced unemployment, and the insecurity and impoverishment of the elderly. These working-class movements viewed the welfare state as a natural extension of the co-operative societies, self-help organisations, friendly societies and trade unions which emerged in the wake of industrialisation. Among the most successful examples of working-class power were the catholic worker movements of Belgium, The Netherlands, Germany, Italy and France. These movements had a significant impact on the political economy of the wealthy continental democracies in that they placed emphasis on labour legislation and social security and on an economic order based on worker participation in industrial ownership and management (Wilensky, 1987). Although the existing citadels of power generally adopted defensive and even repressive strategies in order to stem the development of these 'socialist' movements, they were eventually forced to accommodate the demands of the working class in order to avoid industrial and social distress. When the working class combined its industrial and political wings in the twentieth century, it became a major force in the development of social democratic states.

Modern Social Policy

The origins of modern social policy are therefore associated with an amalgam of contradictory ideals and interests: of crusading liberalism with its confidence in individual human progress and self-determination; of traditional conservatism with its emphasis on paternalistic charity and social order; and of democratic socialism with its faith in the benign power of the state to exercise collective responsibility on behalf of the citizenry. These contrasting philosophical objectives characterised policy debates during the final decades of the nineteenth century, and although the state eventually accepted increasing responsibility for economic and social wellbeing, conflict continued over basic values such as liberty, equality, justice and security.

The circumstances which changed the nature of this debate in the twentieth century centred around the 1930s Depression, the Second World War, and the social and economic imperatives of post-war reconstruction. These events helped shape political assumptions about the nature and form of state involvement in social and economic planning. It was the Depression which undermined confidence in the private sector to deal with social problems such as poverty and unemployment and, as a consequence, state activism became not only politically viable, but widely expected. In Britain, Lord Beveridge (1942) insisted that there should be minimal protection for all citizens against the evils of idleness, want, disease, ignorance, and squalor, and he advocated cooperation between the individual and the state. Beveridge's notion of a welfare society was one in which the major agencies of the state, funded through social insurance and taxation, were complemented by a wide variety of voluntary services catering for the special needs of distressed minorities. The factory and the family were seen as the main systems of co-operation meeting the common requirements of the citizenry, with other basic needs such as education and health care being met by social services funded through taxation. Health, education, housing and social security became major programmes of the state as democratic governments gradually extended universal guarantees on basic needs to all citizens. This was not a new way of thinking about citizenship or the role of the state – rather it was an extension of those tendencies which had existed before the war. However, the war provided the impetus for increasing state powers in the mobilisation of resources, industrial self-sufficiency and in the drive for technological innovation in production. The aftermath of war generated demand for consumer durables and for the physical reconstruction of industry, housing, and public services. International agencies, such as the World Bank and the International Monetary Fund, were established ostensibly to restore a war-torn Europe and prevent further economic or military conflicts, and national governments in the Western world initiated radical social reforms in response to the needs and demands of the labour movement.

The theoretical tradition which provided the rationale for reconstruction was Keynesian economics, which offered an approach to national economic management that was consistent with the liberal democratic tradition. In formulating his general theory, Keynes (1936) looked back to the once discredited mercantile doctrine and took from that tradition certain insights which had relevance in the development of social policy. Keynes believed that the enhancement of welfare was contingent on a reconciliation between the public interests of the state and the private interests of entrepreneurs. He argued that the state could exercise a guiding influence on consumption by adjustments to taxation and the rate of interest and by the provision of social services sponsored jointly by state and private agencies. He prescribed direct taxation which would lead to increased consumption and ultimately to the creation of employment opportunities and he advocated a greater degree of income equality which would lead to increasing wealth and prosperity. Keynes placed considerable emphasis on the role of entrepreneurship in the creation of wealth, but he was equally convinced that private initiative had to be complemented by the active involvement of the state in economic policy. Spending for social purposes was designed to increase productive growth and investment, and secure stable fiscal policies in the provision of social services. These expansionist policies became equated with the welfare state.

The comparative success of welfare states during the 1950s and 1960s was credited to Keynesian economic management and to what is commonly called the 'post-war consensus'. In the Western world, a series of post-war settlements saw the trade unions, employers and social democratic parties reach a compromise with respect to national development. Labour movements gave their support to new social institutions in anticipation of full employment and a share in growing national prosperity, and employers accepted industrial arbitration and conciliation in return for a profitable and stable political environment. A broad consensus appeared to be established right across the political spectrum and although this compromise varied from country to country, the major political parties accepted the notion of a mixed economy – that is, a market system of production and distribution with the state accepting responsibility for economic management and the enhancement of social wellbeing.

Although the notion of consensus tends to ignore the serious conflicts which characterised post-war reconstruction, the achievements of the industrialised world were considerable. In a period of 23 years (1950 to 1973), output in the advanced industrialised societies increased by 180 per cent, with more being produced in that period than in the previous 75 years (Maddison, 1964; 1982). Real wages rose in line with productivity and reserves of unemployed labour were progressively exhausted. Civil spending on goods and services such as health and education increased by 50 per cent more than total output and transfer payments in the form of social security also accelerated. The welfare state established (in principle at least) minimum standards of income, nutrition, health, housing and education for every citizen, and social policy was credited with having contributed to the higher levels of consumption and wellbeing experienced by affluent nations throughout the post-war period. So successful was this new pattern of social and economic policy that in the 1960s sociologists, such as Daniel Bell (1973), predicted an end to ideological and political differences and the advent of the post-industrial society.

In the 1990s we can be more circumspect about these achievements. While few doubt the accomplishments of the affluent Western nations in achieving unprecedented standards of social protection for their citizens, poverty was not eliminated from these societies and inequalities continued despite increasing expenditure on health, education and social services. By the end of the 1970s, public expenditure on social welfare in the OECD countries averaged 25 per cent of gross domestic product (GDP) and 60 per cent of total public expenditure (OECD, 1978; 1985). Tax revolts and anti-bureaucratic movements emerged and frequent reference was made to the fiscal crisis of the state (O'Connor, 1973; Mishra, 1984; OECD, 1981).

The Fiscal Crisis of the State

The crisis was subject to alternative interpretations. Socialist writers, such as Armstrong *et al.* (1984), associated the deteriorating financial accounts of the welfare state with a decline in the profitability of capital. The 'over-accumulation crisis' as it was called was attributed to low productivity and growth, to the increasing costs of materials and labour, and to the consequential squeezing of profits. Although these conditions were temporarily masked by the economic boom of the 1960s, business confidence was undermined, investment collapsed, and this led to what is commonly termed a classical capitalist crisis. Habermas (1975), a member of the Frankfurt School, expanded on this interpretation. He questioned the ability of the welfare state to act as a steering mechanism for the capitalist economy when it was required to meet the mutually incompatible needs of labour and capital. Although Habermas believed the welfare state had been relatively successful in dealing with the worst excesses of market forces, he pointed out that these interventionist policies had embroiled the state in conflict, thus politicising its role in meeting the collective needs of its citizens. Rather than acting in the *public interest,* the modern welfare state had served the *private interests* of capital and, as a consequence, the economic crisis had become a crisis of legitimation. If the state acted on behalf of one class rather than another, then, said Habermas, how could it continue to maintain that it was advancing policy which would enhance the wellbeing of all?

Whereas socialist interpretations of the crisis focused on production, the modern heirs of laissez-faire concentrated on the distribution mechanisms of the state, and especially its welfare provisions. New Right theorists such as Hayek (1960) argued that slower rates of economic growth, aging populations and an escalation in welfare benefits had not only imposed financial burdens on Western economies which could not be sustained, but the state itself had become an impediment to individual liberty and freedom. Charles Murray (1987) went even further, arguing that state welfare had created an under-class of permanently dependent citizens who had neither the ability nor the incentive to take responsibility for their own affairs.

By the 1980s the combined effect of these alternative interpretations was evident in widespread criticism and unease within the affluent nations over the purpose and efficacy of the welfare state. While few doubted the accomplishments of the advanced and democratic societies in achieving unprecedented standards of social security, there were widely divergent views about the future of social policy in general and welfare services in particular. Some argued that despite progress in the post-war period, problems of poverty and disadvantage remained and thus, they argued, that traditional forms of state intervention should be extended and sustained. Others saw social policy as having become a burden, both on the state in the form of public expenditure and on the market economy in that welfare had a depressing effect on incentives, thus reducing economic efficiency.

It was the latter perspective which seemed to gain the ascendancy in the 1980s as New Right policies were implemented in Britain, North America, Australia and New Zealand. Based on the works of Friedrich Hayek and Milton Freidman, New Right economists argued for market solutions to economic and social problems and a scaling down of the activities and services of the welfare state. 'Thatcherism' (Britain), 'Reganomics' (U.S.A.) and 'Rogernomics' (New Zealand) became misleading abbreviations for a return to the doctrine of laissez-faire and the consequential reduction of social policy to a residual role within the market economy, reminiscent of the reluctant state of the nineteenth century (King, 1987).

Comparative Social Policy

There are many parallels between these international trends in social policy and historical accounts of New Zealand's social history which graphically describe the unique circumstances out of which social and economic policy emerged (Oliver, 1988; Tennant, 1989). The British domination of an indigenous people and the imposition of European customs and beliefs; the fracturing of family and communal systems and the establishment of church and voluntary services in administering charitable aid; the increasingly important role of the central state in the provision of public works, labour legislation, and the delivery of social services; and the moral judgements and controls which accompanied the selective distribution of benefits and services to the deserving and undeserving poor; these trends and the attitudes which accompanied them were consistent with the international experience.

In other respects, New Zealand deviated from these international tendencies and thereby justified its reputation as a social laboratory (Shirley, 1993). Legislation such as the Industrial Conciliation and Arbitration Act of 1894 attracted overseas scholars to these shores to study the concept of a basic minimum wage and the arbitration provisions for employers and employees which were markedly different from the West European experience. So too, the Old Age Pensions Act of 1898 and the enfranchisement of women in 1893 – these initiatives identified the new colony as an innovator and leader in social policy legislation and reform. It was a reputation which was substantially endorsed by the first Labour Government in the wake of the 1930s Depression. Labour's social philosophy embraced free education, a community-based preventive health scheme, a salaried medical service, a free public hospital system, adequate standards of housing, a basic minimum wage and full employment. The cornerstone of these reforms was the 1938 Social Security Act, which was hailed as 'a bold and daring experiment that deeply influenced the course of legislation in other countries' (Briggs, 1965: 67). Despite the fact that Labour's philosophy in practice was severely compromised by powerful sector groups such as the Medical Association (see Geoff Fougere's chapter on Health), the expansionist programme based on Keynesian economics did produce full employment as well as a degree of economic and social security, and New Zealand's reputation as one of the leading welfare states in the immediate post-war period seemed justified.

From the late 1960s on, New Zealand's reputation declined. The country's vulnerability as a trading nation became much more apparent as Britain (New Zealand's major export market) forged closer economic relations with Europe. The New Zealand economy was slowly opened up to overseas competition and industry was reorganised through mergers, takeovers and amalgamations (Pearson and Thorns,

1983). Whereas other advanced nations appreciably expanded their welfare provisions, New Zealand's overall commitment to public services declined (Castles, 1985). Even isolated reforms (such as the 1972 Accident Compensation Act) could not disguise the fact that whereas New Zealand was among the eight largest welfare spenders in the early 1960s, by the 1970s it was rated among the welfare state laggards.

These crude comparisons between welfare states based on levels of public expenditure were later extended by more sophisticated studies. Two broad approaches were adopted. The first was articulated by writers such as Lipset (1963) who suggested a *convergence* in both the form and purpose of the 'welfare state'. Countries as diverse as Sweden, Germany and New Zealand were used to illustrate a global trend toward universal coverage in the immediate post-war period, with an increasing proportion of national income being devoted to the social services. Convergence is a rather simplistic notion however, given the wide variations evident both within and between nation states. Not only are there enormous differences between welfare states in terms of the proportion of GNP[1] spent on social services (OECD, 1981), but there are wide discrepancies between countries when it comes to comparing public and private services and the consequential impact of these services on the living standards of the citizenry.

A second group of writers (Mishra, 1977; Jones, 1985) turned therefore to *comparative* studies in order to emphasise differential patterns of social and economic policy. The most comprehensive measures for comparing the living standards of national populations emerged in the 1960s and 1970s when several international agencies established social indicator systems, and a wide cross-section of nation states produced social trend documents and social reports (Zapf, 1972; Shirley, 1981). These systems were designed to provide a comparative picture of social wellbeing by measuring national standards of health, education, work and housing, and by including qualitative factors such as participation rates, safety records and individual security (Davis, 1988). Esping-Andersen (1990) used this approach in his comparative study of eighteen welfare states. Based on 1980 figures, he constructed an index in order to measure the way in which modern welfare states guarantee standards of living for their citizens regardless of individual differences such as employment record or financial contribution. The composite indicators drawn from this study were then ranked, leading Esping-Andersen to conclude that three distinctive patterns of social policy have emerged in the post-war period (see Table 9.1).

In the top group are the *Social Democratic Welfare States* dominated by Scandinavia and exemplified by Sweden. These countries provide a comprehensive network of social services as an unrestricted and unconditional right of citizenship. A defining characteristic of the Swedish welfare state is the absence of clear boundaries between social and economic policy, with national development strategies

Table 9.1
Three Social Policy Patterns that have Emerged in the Post-war Period

Welfare States	Composite Score[1]	Patterns of Social Policy
Sweden	39.1	
Norway	38.3	
Denmark	38.1	Social Democratic
Netherlands	32.4	Welfare States
Belgium	32.4	
Austria	31.1	
Switzerland	29.8	
Finland	29.2	
Germany	27.7	Conservative
France	27.5	Welfare States
Japan	27.1	
Italy	24.1	
United Kingdom	23.4	
Ireland	23.3	
Canada	22.0	'Reluctant'
New Zealand	17.1	Welfare States
United States	13.8	
Australia	13.0	

[1] Rank order of welfare states based on composite indicators. Composite scores were derived from a standard of living index emphasising citizenship and security.

Source: Adapted from a De-Commodification study by Esping-Andersen, 1990.

based on a social partnership between employers, the labour movement and the state. The pursuit of full employment and high productivity are seen as socio-economic priorities with the attainment of these goals dependent upon the provision of unconditional social rights and universal social services. In the delivery of these services, Sweden has set the quality of public provision at levels sufficiently high to discourage private alternatives.

The second group comprise the Continental European countries, Finland and Japan. These countries are described as *Conservative Welfare States* in that they are generally prepared to extend a modicum of rights outside the market, but within a framework of strong social controls. In these countries, economic and social policies are viewed as complementary rather than interdependent, and this relationship is demonstrated by West Germany's *Sozialplan* which attempts to harmonise resources and needs in meeting national economic priorities. The labour movements in these conservative states have had mixed success in influencing social policy. This ambivalence is most evident in Japan where factories of more than five thousand employees provide health insurance for 99 per cent of their workers and company housing for 93 per cent of their workforce – by contrast workers in small firms, women, casual workers and the unemployed are dependent upon the vagaries of occupational welfare which means calculating benefit levels on the basis of an individual's 'work record'.

A third group of countries comprise the new nations of the Anglo-Saxon world, including the U.S.A., Britain and New Zealand. These nations are described as the *Reluctant Welfare States* in that they have largely avoided unconditional social rights by separating economic and social policy and by treating welfare as an adjunct to the market economy. America provides a good illustration of this model in that it represents a dual society, with one labour market providing high salaries for professionals and for those supported by stronger sections of organised labour, and a second labour market paying low wages to a casualised and fragmented workforce consisting mainly of unskilled, short-term or part-term employees, many of whom are women, blacks or migrants from Latin America. Social services are adapted to this two-sector economy, subsidising low wages or paying 'workfare', which is public assistance made conditional on some form of compulsory employment. Not only are benefit levels in the public sector low and designed to provide minimal coverage, but many services are means-tested, punitive, and aimed at deterring 'undeserving' applicants.

These different patterns of social policy as described by Esping-Andersen (1990) confirm earlier comparative studies by Mishra (1977) and Furniss and Tilton (1977). While there may be some disagreement over the precise ranking of welfare states and the terms used to describe the social and economic policies which have emerged, there is little evidence of convergence. Not only are wide variations evident between countries when the *outcome* or impact of social policy is examined (George and Wilding, 1984), but the *process* by which policies are implemented differs from country to country according to the relative distribution of power both within and between national states. From a sociological perspective, it is *the distribution of power* between different individuals, collectivities and classes which establishes the conditions for bargaining as well as the context in which strategic and tactical choices are made.

The Distribution of Power

Over the past two decades a vast array of studies have attempted to explain how the distribution of power in society conditions both the aims and consequences of social policy. Feminist writings have concentrated on patriarchy and the domestication of women (Wilson, 1983); ethnic studies have emphasised cultural invasion and the impact of economic and political domination (Walker, 1982); and critical theorists have focused on class relations and the way in which welfare states attempt both to ameliorate and legitimate the structural inequalities of the market economy (Offe,

1984). Whereas some studies have focused on particular domains of social policy such as inequality (Townsend, 1979), unemployment (Therborn, 1986) and housing (Donnison and Ungerson, 1982), others have set out to explain the broad patterns of development (Fordism/post-Fordism) in order to understand the changing relations of production (Jessop, 1984; Lipietz, 1987; O'Brien and Wilkes, 1993). In contrast to these studies which emphasise the distribution of power, the social administration tradition in Britain and public policy writings in America tend to accept power relations as given and they concentrate therefore on changes in legislation and descriptive studies of management. The social administration approach is the one which dominates policy reports published by agencies in New Zealand such as the Institute for Policy Studies and the now defunct New Zealand Planning Council. A critical appraisal of these various approaches and the theoretical traditions on which they are based is contained in an 'Introduction to Social Policy' by Wilkes and Shirley (1984).

From those studies, which emphasise the dynamic relationship between individuals, collectivities and classes in the development of social policy, the two major sources of power which are most frequently cited are *capital* and *labour*. As Esping-Anderson and Korpi (1984) suggest, these sources of power inevitably produce two alternative interpretations of social policy. Whereas labour movements attempt to create institutional welfare states in which politics assumes a natural role in the production and distribution of goods and services, the owners of capital strive for marginal types of social policy which only come into play when the market or the family fail to fulfil their 'natural' responsibilities. The conflict between these two sources of power produces interesting results when we compare the development of social policy in a social democratic state such as Sweden (Esping-Anderson and Korpi, 1984; Gould, 1988) with a reluctant welfare state such as New Zealand (Castles, 1985; Davidson, 1989).

Although social policy in Sweden continues to be characterised by ongoing conflict between the two centralised federations (employers and workers), these two sectors have consistently endorsed the twin goals of prosperity and security by effecting a compromise in which employers accept the goal of full employment, while workers accept the need for wage moderation and high productivity. The mechanisms for achieving these goals have centred around an active labour market policy, centralised wage bargaining practices, and a state economic policy designed to support industrial investment and expansion. The social philosophy which has accompanied this programme has emphasised *universalism* by eliminating status differentials with respect to conditions and benefits, and by divorcing the allocation of social services from moral judgements or individual performance. The outcome is a society with one of the highest standards of living in the world, relatively low unemployment, and a high degree of economic and social security (Gould, 1988).

In recent years it has become fashionable for New Right politicians in New Zealand to claim that this country has adopted Swedish policies and practices but in reality there are few similarities. The New Zealand labour movement has always been relatively weak when compared with its counterparts in Scandinavia and Europe, a weakness which stems from the size of productive units in this country and the dispersed nature of both capital and labour within the rural and industrial sectors (Martin, 1981). The working class has therefore sought tangible benefits from the state in the form of wage and employment security rather than the more comprehensive systems of welfare which emerged in Scandinavia. These factors have been important in establishing what Castles (1985) has called *a wage earners welfare state* where the emphasis has been on an economic defence of the working 'man' supplemented by a modicum of relief for the less fortunate. Whereas the relationship between employment and income security seemed adequate for the majority of citizens during periods of full employment, once this relationship was fractured, the deficiencies of a selective welfare system became transparent. Thus since 1967, New Zealand has become an increasingly fragmented society with wide spatial and social divisions (Thorns, 1988). These trends are reflected in escalating unemployment, in the unequal distribution of income and in the declining value of the social wage.[2] Rather than emulating social democratic states such as Sweden, New Zealand has developed an approach which conforms much more readily with the American pattern - a dual society in which social welfare is used to subsidise low wages or provide temporary relief on the basis of selective, and at times punitive, criteria.

Social Policy: Prospects

These different patterns of social policy have continued through into the 1990s. Despite recent changes within the structure of the Swedish welfare system, the historic compromise in that country between labour, capital and the state has now been institutionalised and thus Sweden is unlikely to revoke the concept of citizenship on which its social and economic policies are based. New Zealand, by contrast, has consistently linked economic and social security to an individual's status as a wage-earner and with the balance of power in this country moving noticeably in the direction of capital, the reluctant welfare state is clearly becoming both more reluctant and punitive.

The core of this reluctance stems from the way in which social policy in New Zealand has been progressively reduced to an ancillary role within the market economy, so placing increasing emphasis on economic policy as the major determinant of national development. 'The economy' has been equated with production, whereas social policy is seen to be concerned with the ends and means of distribution. This artificial distinction between economic and social policy ignores the fact that 'the economy' is the manifestation of human relations and activity. What we regard as the economic system is a particular historically limited answer to the fundamental question about how human beings should interact with regard to what is produced for survival and development. We cannot refer to the economic system as though it is somehow distinct from our daily lives, for at root, 'the economy' is a patterned set of individual and social relationships. It follows that the welfare of a nation cannot be reduced to a narrow economic construct as conveyed by the level or rate of economic growth. Welfare is determined by the character and quality of living conditions, by the way in which human beings are able to participate in the decisions which affect them, and by cultural and political determinants of wellbeing such as work, fellowship and social solidarity. These fundamental concepts of social living are the areas which have been most severely undermined by the economic policies of the New Right.

Although the trend toward economic liberalisation in New Zealand began in the 1960s, the free market revolution sponsored by the fourth Labour Government (later endorsed by National following the 1990 election) carried the doctrine of laissez-faire to its logical conclusion. The extreme version of economic individualism which was ideologically driven by Treasury (1984; 1987), the Business Roundtable (1987) and by leading politicians in the Labour (Douglas, Prebble, Bassett) and National (Richardson, Upton, Luxton) cabinets, undermined the 'historic compromise' which was forged between capital and labour in the immediate postwar period. The disinflationary programme of the late 1980s and early 1990s saw income and employment security traded for an inflation rate of 0-2% per annum, a low wage regime and a highly speculative development path. Short-term profitability and financial speculation gained at the expense of productive economic growth, while competition between individuals for resources in health, education, housing and employment progressively reduced the value of the social wage (Shirley, 1990; O'Brien and Wilkes, 1993).

The reshaping of the welfare state in New Zealand was supposedly designed to shift responsibility for social welfare from government to 'the family' (Boston and Dalziel, 1992), in line with the concept of a minimalist state. The aim was to provide a 'modest safety net' for those in 'need', and while this general proposition does not differ radically from the selectivist approach to welfare traditionally pursued in New Zealand, it has been implemented at a time when the corner-stone of the welfare state (namely, employment and income security) is no longer a reality for an increasing proportion of the population. As a consequence, the social costs of economic liberalisation (Shirley, 1993) have been extremely high, as evidenced by growing inequalities of income and lifestyle, and a range of negative social indicators such as a 100 per cent increase in the child abuse and neglect rate in less than three years, a 40 per cent rise in the number of households living below the poverty line (Easton, 1993) and the highest youth suicide rate of all OECD nations.

The minimal benefits which have occurred from economic restructuring have been inequitably distributed. Women have born the brunt of 'community care', while the negative consequences of unemployment and financial deprivation have impacted most severely on Maori, Pacific Island Polynesians and working-class families on low incomes and social security. These social conditions have prompted widespread disenchantment with politics in general and the policies of the New Right in particular. Whether or not the implementation of a Mixed Member Proportional (MMP) system of government will lead to improvements in the political system remains to be seen. In policy terms however, we can be sure, that concepts such as freedom, equality, justice and security will continue to dominate public debate over the direction of economic and social policy toward the twenty-first century.

Notes

1. Gross National Product (GNP) is an economic construct representing production, income derived from production, and the expenditure of income. As a composite statistic, GNP omits certain transactions such as production from unpaid work (housework) and production costs incurred by workers (investment in education and travel time). 'Costs' such as pollution and congestion and 'benefits' such as leisure and the standard of living are also not included.
2. The social wage includes income security and those goods and services which confer a personal benefit on individuals – that is, services such as education, health and social security which would otherwise have to be bought from private incomes.

Further Reading

Castles, F., 1985, *The Working Class and Welfare: Reflections on the Political Development of the Welfare State in Australia and New Zealand, 1890-1980*, Wellington, Allen and Unwin.

Davidson, A., 1989, *Two Models of Welfare: The Origins and Development of the Welfare State in Sweden and New Zealand 1988-1988*, Uppsala, Sweden, Political Science Association.

Oliver, W., 1988, 'Social Policy in New Zealand: A Historical Overview', in Royal Commission on Social Policy, *The April Report*, Vol. I, Wellington, Royal Commission on Social Policy.

Shirley, I., 1990, 'The Advance of the New Right', in I. Taylor (ed.) *The Social Effects of Free Market Policies*, London and New York, Harvester/Wheatsheaf.

Tennant, M., 1989, *Paupers and Providers: Charitable Aid in New Zealand*, Wellington, Allen and Unwin.

Wilkes, C. and Shirley, I., 1984, 'An Introduction to Social Policy', in C. Wilkes and I. Shirley (eds), *In the Public Interest: Health, Work and Housing in New Zealand,* Auckland, Benton Ross.

10 Health

Geoff Fougere

Health and health care are shaped by the larger social contexts in which they occur. Social contexts are characterised by enduring relations of economic, ethnic, gender and political power. This chapter explores some implications of combining these two, deceptively simple, statements. Three kinds of issues are explored. Who gets sick, who stays well and why? Who claims control over medical work and how are such claims achieved, sustained or undermined? How is access to health care negotiated within the context of the New Zealand welfare state?

The chapter aims to develop questions rather than resolve them. The coverage of issues and of relevant theoretical approaches is brief and incomplete. Still, I hope to make two important points. What sociologists have to say about health has important practical implications for health policy, for the work of health professionals and for citizens. Second, just as the chapter draws on general sociological concepts and theories to make sense of its empirical material, so analyses of health and health care speak to central issues in sociology. As Turner (1987) eloquently argues, health and health care are important sites for sociological analysis.

Who Gets Sick and Who Stays Well[1]

Who gets sick and who stays well, the distribution of health and illness within and between societies, is largely determined by social rather than biological facts. Life expectancy in New Zealand is much higher than life expectancy in third world countries such as Honduras. This is not because of genetic differences between New Zealanders and Hondurans. Nor is it because diseases in Honduras are more virulent than their counterparts in New Zealand. Instead, differences in mortality are due to differences in economic, social and political organisation between the two societies. Access to such things as good nutrition, clean water, adequate housing and safer, less back-breaking work mean that New Zealanders are much less likely to suffer illness or injury than Hondurans. And, if they do get sick or injured, New Zealanders have better access to medical care. Societal differences, rather than biological constants, explain differences in the kinds of illness, the amount of illness and in life expectancy among countries. (For a good overview of differences in first and third world health status, see Susser *et al.*, 1985).

The same is true historically. The genetic characteristics of New Zealanders are much the same as in the nineteenth century. The micro-organisms blamed then for causing disease, with the addition of H.I.V. and the possible exception of smallpox, are still present today. Yet New Zealanders die of different causes, for example, heart disease and cancer rather than pneumonia and tuberculosis, and at a much older age (Davis, 1981). Explaining these differences requires a focus on what has changed in New Zealand society rather than on the enduring features of human biology.

If social factors largely explain differences in the causes and rates of illness and death between societies, they also explain differences within societies. Illness and death are distributed within societies on the basis of general patterns of social inequality. Work by Neil Pearce and his collaborators on New Zealand men shows that social class, as measured by occupation, makes a big difference to life chances (Pearce *et al.*, 1985). Mortality rates increase with movement down the class scale; the mortality rate of those in the lowest social class category is approximately double that of those in the highest. This difference is greater than that found for England and Wales, societies that New Zealanders think of as much more class stratified than their own.

If class matters, so does ethnicity. Within each social class category there are, '53 per cent more Maori deaths than there would have been if Maoris had experienced the same mortality rates as non-Maoris in each class and each age group' (Pearce *et al.*, 1985: 11). In other words, if working in a lower-status job, being poorer and less educated already significantly increases the risk of death, the social consequences of being Maori adds further to that risk. (For an exhaustive survey of Maori health status, see Pomare and de Boer, 1988). How can these differences in who gets sick and who stays well be explained? The issue is of practical as well as theoretical importance. Different theories of causation imply different strategies for the prevention of illness. While good theories will focus attention on factors that make a difference to health, bad ones will result in failed programmes.

Germ Theory

Germ theory has become the most pervasive theory of health and illness. In this view, human beings are locked in battle with nature and sickness results from the invasion by hostile micro-organisms. Medical science aims to identify and deal with the organisms responsible. Eventually, illness will be prevented by vaccination or cured by drugs. In the meantime, it is important to support biomedical science and to provide ample resources for medical work, particularly in the hospital where medical science is applied to human beings (Stacey, 1988; Tesh, 1988). The theory is one with obvious appeal to doctors seeing that much of their practice (and the justification of their occupational privilege) is based on it. Less obviously, it appeals to many governments and to dominant groups in society as well. The idea that sickness reflects the impact of nature on society and that it will eventually be solved by biomedical science means that health can be seen as a personal and technical problem rather than a political one (Tesh, 1988).

Germ theory has given rise to important advances. In the twentieth century, medical care often makes significant differences to the health status of individuals. Consequently, few people choose not to see a doctor when they are sick. As an explanation of the levels and distribution of illness within societies, however, germ theory is entirely inadequate (and injury falls completely outside its range) (McKinley et al., 1989). First, McKeown's (1979) work shows that it has been rising standards of living with their impact on nutrition, housing and other variables, rather than interventions based on germ theory, which have been most important in lowering mortality rates in the nineteenth and twentieth centuries. Thus, mortality from infectious diseases began to decline long before effective medical therapies were developed. Second, cancer and heart disease have replaced infectious diseases as the leading cause of death in New Zealand. But despite much research, the role of micro-organisms as contributory causes to these conditions remains uncertain (Tesh, 1988). Third, germ theory does not explain why mortality should be patterned along lines of social inequality within societies. Being poorer, less educated, doing lower-status work is associated with a greater chance of dying from all causes: from injury as well as from illness and from chronic as well as infectious diseases (MacIntyre, 1986).

Lifestyle Theory

Dissatisfaction with germ theory has led to the rise of lifestyle theories. In this view, illnesses are the outcome of many causes, chief among which are bad habits: too much stress, too little exercise, bad nutrition, unsafe sex, smoking and even drinking. Here human beings are at war not with an external nature but with their own psyches. Adopting healthy lifestyles is the necessary preventive measure. What is required is not more doctors or hospitals but better information, more health educators and, above all, more will power. The theory offers people a sense of control over their lives in a world where much seems out of control – if only they seize the opportunity. It also gives an apparently scientific endorsement to elements of an upper middle-class lifestyle: exercise, concern with weight, healthy living and so on (Tesh, 1988). Less attractively, it suggests that if people get sick then it is their own fault, a phenomenon that William Ryan (1972) has accurately described as 'blaming the victim'. The theory has had increasing appeal to governments and to dominant groups. If building more hospitals is expensive and has not seemed to make much difference to health, the advocacy of changes in lifestyle costs governments little and deflects the issues of health policy into issues of personal choice (Ratcliffe *et al.*, 1984; Tesh, 1988). Lifestyle factors are clearly important in determining health status and the causes of illness are indeed more complex than the uni-causal focus of germ theory. In a nutshell, smoking matters! But the emphasis on personal choice is overdrawn, making the theory at best a partial and incomplete one. Human beings make choices, but always within particular social contexts.

The social structural contexts of choice enable some kinds of choices but constrain others. Systematic differences in nutrition or, for that matter, smoking among social classes reflect systematic differences in the resources, constraints and opportunities that go with social position rather than simply differences in individual will power. At its simplest, having more money in a market society means a greater choice of food and housing, insulation from the fluctuations of the economy and greater resources for dealing with adverse life events (Hart, 1986).

The problem of abstracting choice from social context arises in a second guise: lifestyle theories focus attention on those who make risky choices while obscuring the behaviour of risk imposers (Ratcliffe *et al.*, 1984). Lung cancer provides a good example. Is the problem smoking or the production and distribution of the hazardous substance, tobacco? A lifestyle formulation, with its focus on smoking, obscures the fact that the regulation of tobacco companies may be a more powerful means of reducing risk than hundreds of smoking cessation programmes.

Another problem in abstracting choice from social context is that many risks are simply imposed on people, quite apart from any personal decision. The depletion of the ozone layer, with its associated risks of skin cancer, is not materially affected by my personal decision to avoid fluorocarbon-based aerosols. In a country dependent on agriculture, everyone is affected by risks posed by pesticides (MacIntyre *et al.*, 1989). Being born into a Maori or working-class family in New Zealand increases the risk of death, quite apart from any 'choices' a baby may have. Individuals can sometimes shield themselves from the consequences of environmental hazards: in these examples, by covering up in the sun, by being careful to wash food, or by the use of vaccination against childhood diseases. But reduction in the hazards themselves is dependent on collective action rather than individual choice.

Social Structural Theories

The problems of lifestyle theories point toward the need for theories that focus on the interplay between biological phenomenon, social context and persons (in the current jargon, structure and agency). In health, such theories have been the province of the public health perspective. They have traditionally focused on exposure to physical hazards such as impure water or workplace chemicals. But the creation and regulation of such hazards and the processes which determine who will be exposed to them are always set within a larger nexus of social structural relations. The degree of danger in the work place, for example, generally reflects the conditions for profitability in an industry together with the patterns of state regulation of workplace hazards. Patterns of regulation depend in turn on features of the state's structure and on the balance of power in society between unions and business (Carson, 1989; Dwyer, 1991; Elling 1986). Similarly, who ends up exposed to such hazards is an outcome of the allocation of jobs by labour market processes which systematically reflect lines of gender, ethnic and class privilege (Granovetter and Tilly, 1988).

Social structural theories of health and illness exhibit both a long history and a serious lack of development (Engels, 1975; Waitzkin, 1981; MacIntyre, 1986). If historical evidence generally supports the idea that social structural changes have been the most important in changing patterns of mortality and that social position largely determines life chances, then why has theoretical and practical development of these ideas been so stunted? One reason may be the lack of creativity of the theorists. Another would point to the reception of such theories. In Tesh's (1988: 55) words, they, 'wear [their] politics on [their] sleeve'. Such theories tease out the connections between social inequalities and patterns of health and illness. They suggest an intimate connection between social justice and health and imply that the solution of health issues may have less to do with laboratory science than with successful collective action by disadvantaged groups. (For a brilliant, brief, social structural analysis showing how babies and very young children rather than those belonging to the usual risk groups have been the chief victims of AIDs in Romania, see Rothman and Rothman, 1990).

Control Over Medical Work

The focus of modern medicine has been on the treatment of illness rather than its prevention. The twentieth century has seen the elaboration of a vast 'medical-industrial complex', centred on the modern hospital and the university, backed by the pharmaceutical and other medical supply industries, and funded by elaborate systems of taxation and private insurance. In 1989 in New Zealand 7.4 per cent of GDP was spent on health care (Muthumala *et al.,* 1989). Hospitals are generally the largest single employers in the major cities and towns.

Presiding over the creation and expansion of this 'medical-industrial complex' has been the medical profession. In the twentieth century, doctors have won the almost exclusive right to define the meaning of symptoms, the treatments appropriate to them and, more generally, the meaning of health and illness (Belgrave, 1991; Starr, 1982). Complementing this cultural authority is the social authority wielded by doctors over nurses, physiotherapists, laboratory technicians and all of the other partly autonomous and partly subordinate members of the health care 'team'.

Typically, doctors dominate health care markets and public and private health care institutions (Starr, 1982; Willis, 1983). The creation of these relations of symbolic and structural power have in turn provided a vehicle for the profession's considerable social mobility. Unlike the bulk of their nineteenth century counterparts, doctors enjoy high incomes, high social prestige and often wield considerable political power. They do so not by virtue of their individual brilliance or capability (although sometimes these are real enough) but because of their common training and their status as accredited members of the medical profession (Starr, 1982; Larson, 1977).

How has the medical profession achieved such a central position not just in the health system but in society? And in what contexts is its centrality likely to be reproduced, eroded or even overturned? Processes of 'professionalisation' and 'deprofessionalisation', the development or dismantling of professional dominance, centre around the control of work (Abbott, 1988; Freidson, 1970). But work is not simply given. As Abbott (1986: 190) argues: 'Professions don't just find things laid out for them: they construct their problems as they work with them'. Moreover, work is always the subject of contestation: occupational groups compete to gain control over its definition and content. The outcomes of these conflicts are inter-related: shifts in the control of work by one professional group create corresponding shifts in the work of related groups (Abbott, 1988).

The Case of Midwifery

So far, there is no systematic, sociological account of the waxing and perhaps current waning of the medical profession's power in New Zealand. But useful insights on the achievement of professional dominance is provided by an analysis of Philippa Mein Smith's fascinating historical case study, *The Struggle Over Maternity*. Smith shows how the medical profession developed and defended its dominance over pregnancy and birth in the 1920s and 1930s, with fateful implications not only for the medical profession and for women, but also for midwives, nurses and the state.

By 1920 a double transformation of the birth process was under way. Women were no longer attended at birth simply by a midwife, but increasingly by a doctor. At the same time, more and more births (35 per cent by 1920) were occurring in hospital, rather than at home. Birth was becoming increasingly medicalised. Medicalisation did not, however, bring a reduction in maternal mortality. Instead maternal mortality peaked at 6.48 per 1000 live births in 1920, a rate higher than in any other developed country except the United States. The most important single cause of death was puerperal sepsis (known also as septicaemia or blood poisoning), a condition which, since the work of Semmelweis in the nineteenth century, was known to be largely preventable. These statistics were soon dramatised by a small epidemic of deaths from puerperal sepsis in Auckland. Maternal mortality became the subject of public outcry.

The task of doing something about maternal mortality fell to the state and specifically the newly reorganised Department of Health. From the beginning of the twentieth century, the New Zealand state, like its counterparts in Britain, Australia and elsewhere, had manifested a growing concern about the health and size of its population. This concern was rooted in geopolitical concerns. Threats to British hegemony fuelled fears of military defeat and of challenges from non-whites. These fears were given concrete expression in the discovery of the falling birth rate and of the poor standard of health of many New Zealanders. If the risk of maternal death was great, women could hardly be encouraged to bear more children. The Health Department launched its campaign against maternal mortality under the slogan, 'Perfect motherhood is perfect patriotism' (Smith, 1986: 23).

The Department argued that the chief causes of maternal mortality were the unsafe practices of doctors and midwives and the low standard of hospital care. The Department set out to organise antenatal care for all mothers, to disseminate a standardised aseptic technique for the management of birth, to regulate and inspect private hospitals and to improve the training of doctors and midwives.

In different ways, each of these measures posed a threat to the medical profession's control of birth. The provision of antenatal care together with better training for midwives challenged medicine's claim to be the appropriate provider of maternity care. Worse, it laid the basis for the expansion of an alternative midwife-based service, an option known to be favoured by some leading officials. (There were already St Helen's Hospitals offering a midwife-based service to the wives of working men in each of the main centres). The requirement of aseptic technique and the inspection and regulation of hospitals threatened the livelihoods of doctors who owned and operated private hospitals. More important still, such measures potentially subjected the clinical practices of doctors to scrutiny and control. In its efforts to deal with maternal mortality, the Department of Health was attacking the profession's control of its work head on. The doctors' fightback came quickly. It was led by Dr Doris Gordon, general practitioner and founder of the Obstetrical Society, an organisation set up in 1927 explicitly to deal with the threats posed by the Health Department's campaign.

The Society's first task was to restore public confidence in the profession. Against the Health Departments' claim that puerperal sepsis was the result of infection transmitted from patient to patient by doctors, the Society argued a theory of autogenous causation. In this view, the problem of puerperal sepsis lay not with doctors but with the women themselves: the infection was something that arose spontaneously within a woman's body quite independently of the doctor's actions. (If this theory was not convincing then there was always the backup theory that the problem lay with the maternity nurses, often untrained, who assisted general practitioners at births). Meanwhile, quite independently of the outcome of this theoretical debate, the spread of aseptic technique and the improved standards of hospitals (both promoted by the Health Department) brought about a rapid reduction in maternal mortality after 1927.

The doctors' second task was to stop the development of an alternative service funded by the state and staffed by trained midwives. Pregnancy and birth, doctors argued, were pathological conditions fraught with danger. Their safe negotiation was well beyond the capability and training of midwives and required medical supervision. The most obvious problem with this argument was that the doctors' training in midwifery was actually inferior to that of trained midwives. To bolster the doctors' skills, a Chair in Obstetrics and Gynaecology was created at Otago Medical School in 1931 and the training of medical students improved.

The doctors' third task was to push back scrutiny of their practice by the state. The battle was fought on a number of fronts all aimed at winning for themselves the powers of regulation the state had assumed. By undercutting the powers of the Department's nurse inspectors, by gaining the right to direct consultation with the Department and by stopping maternity nurses providing information directly to the Department about their work, the threat of the effective regulation of doctors was beaten back.

Doctors had one further important card to play, one which according to Smith (1986), secured their dominance of birth. Unlike midwives who could offer only small doses of chloroform, doctors were licensed to administer effective anaesthetics in childbirth. Consequently, while both doctors and trained midwives could offer safe births by the 1930s, only doctors could offer the freedom from pain that women also wanted. This ushered in the New Zealand version of 'twilight birth', a technique which was to become the subject of considerable controversy by the 1960s.

By the time Labour became the government in 1935, the medical dominance of pregnancy and birth had been secured. Labour responded to the demand that all women should have access to safe and pain-free childbirth by negotiating a system of maternity benefits with the medical profession. These benefits continue to underpin free access to medically supervised births in New Zealand.

An Analysis

What points can be drawn from this highly abbreviated case study? A good theoretical understanding of what occurred would have to deal with at least the following issues. The case makes clear that medical control over birth was not driven by the advances of medical science but occurred quite independently (Willis, 1983; Starr, 1982). Medicalisation did not lead to a fall in maternal mortality. That fall only occurred once the medicalisation process was well underway. It was a result not of scientific developments, but of the complex pattern of medical response to state intervention. Moreover, while medical dominance was briefly threatened by unsafe practices, what actually cemented medical control was an artefact not of medical science, but of occupational licensing: doctors but not midwives could administer effective anaesthetics. The uses of science in public debate had more to do with the interests of participants than with its supposed 'objectivity'. The Department of Health, seeking to regulate doctors, argued a theory of causation that implicated doctors' practices in maternal mortality. Doctors seeking to defend themselves turned to the alternate scientific theory of autogenous causation, effectively absolving themselves from blame.

The real process by which birth was secured as medical work in the 1920s and 1930s was complex, minimally involving interactions between doctors, other professional groups, the state, educational institutions and the wider public. Most obviously, doctors mobilised under the banner of the Obstetrics Society to defend and extend their control of the birth process. By improving their training and techniques, by successfully promoting the idea of birth as pathology and by fending off the efforts of state officials to promote a midwife-based alternative, the doctors' own efforts were important in securing their position.

The role of nurses and, more puzzling, the role of the trained midwives themselves, are barely explored in Smith's account. But if an independent profession of midwives posed a threat to doctors, it can also be seen to have posed a threat to the claims of nurses (Willis, 1983). Unlike doctors, nurses do not seem to have opposed the registration and improved training of midwives, but they did seek to incorporate midwifery into their own domain by requiring that midwives have prior nursing training. Such a solution may have implicitly aligned the interest of doctors and nurses: both found themselves with an interest in undercutting midwives as an independent profession and each could favour a solution which by incorporating midwifery into nursing, subordinated it to medical direction while enlarging the work domain that nurses could claim. These issues require further research.

The state's role was equally crucial in what happened. Occupational licensing allowed doctors but not midwives to offer pain-free childbirth. More significantly, the failure of state officials to expand the role of trained midwives meant that doctors faced no significant competition for their services. Although the reasons for this failure are not explored by Smith, it is likely that they had as much to do with broadly-based constraints on state expenditure as on the lobbying of the medical profession. The result was that when the problem of maternity was posed in a new way in the 1930s – not so much maternal mortality as the problem of equal access to health services – the state found itself involved in an elaborate and conflictual set of negotiations with doctors rather than midwives.

While the reasons for state policies cannot be traced here in any detail, it is important to note a number of points. First, at no time was there a simple convergence of the interests of state officials and doctors. In the 1920s the attempts of officials to solve the problem of maternal mortality meant that doctors were faced with the threat of a state-promoted alternative to their services. In the 1930s, doctors resisted the maternity benefit scheme because they thought that it would allow the state to regulate and control their work. Doctors only consented to the scheme after a major modification of it. Second, the pressures shaping public policy on maternity reflected the embedding of the state in structural contexts far more inclusive than the health care system. The concerns pushing the state in the 1920s had a Bismarckian flavour: defending the Empire from its enemies on the one hand and undermining the appeal of the Labour Party on the other. In the 1930s, external threat may have been less important than the internal politics of class and gender which shaped not just health legislation but, in good measure, all of the other policies of the first Labour Government. Third, the case study makes clear the important role of state officials and of the institutional structures in which they are embedded. The reorganisation of the Department of Health was crucial to its attempts to modernise the health care system. Finally, the public's role was important in what happened. To deal only with the 1930s: it was the support of women's organisations and trade unions for the access of all women to safe and pain free childbirth that underpinned the Labour Government's maternity policy and with it, the medical dominance of childbirth.

Through all of this, gender relations are implicated through important but apparently complex and contradictory processes (Tully, 1993; Witz, 1990). A largely male medical profession won control of birth from professional female midwives. But the doctors were led by a woman and may have found their strategies coincident with those of the female dominated profession of nursing. Popular demands from women's organisations seeking to guarantee all women safe and painfree childbirth led to changes in state policy. These gave all women free childbirth services but simultaneously cemented the dominance of doctors and confirmed the midwives' loss of professional autonomy and control.

The general practitioners' victory in gaining control over birth has hardly proved final. Almost immediately they faced competition from within their own profession as an emerging cadre of obstetrics and gynaecological specialists sought to carve out their own sphere of work (Donley, 1986). Then an unlikely conjuncture occurred and it involved the following: a determined and articulate group of midwives; the demands of women's organisations for more control and choice for women in the management of birth; a major medical scandal at New Zealand's premier obstetrics and gynaecological hospital, National Women's Hospital in Auckland, which undermined the legitimacy of the medical profession; the diffusion of neo-liberal economic ideology favouring market competition for professional services; a courageous and innovative Minister of Health; and the grasping by a desperate and unpopular government at means to shore up its support among women voters and activists in election year. The result was the beginning of the Nurses Amendment Act in August, 1990. This Act restored to midwives the right to independent practice (McLoughlin, 1993; Stirling, 1990; Tully, 1993). No event could more graphically demonstrate the contingency of medical dominance and the ways in which its scope is shaped as much by changes in the larger society as in the health system. (For quite different renderings of this simple but useful idea, which stands in contradiction to much earlier theorising about professions in sociology, see Abbott, 1988; Fougere, forthcoming (a); Sarfatti Larson, 1977; Starr, 1982; Willis, 1983; Witz, 1990).

How are Claims to Health Care Negotiated Within the Context of the New Zealand Welfare State?[2]

The year 1993 marked the introduction of major funding and highly controversial reforms in the public provision and funding of health care in New Zealand. Central to the new system, a form of 'managed competition', is the split between the purchase and provision of health services. Newly created Regional Health Authorities and eventually private Health Care Plans are charged with purchasing a specific range of primary and secondary health services (the 'core') for their members. These services are provided by a mix of public and private providers, the largest of which are publicly owned Crown Health Enterprises (CHEs). Providers compete with each other to win contracts from purchasers (Upton, 1991). Competition in purchasing is also envisaged as private Health Care Plans are set up and begin to compete with Regional Health Authorities for members. While everyone is initially a member of a Regional Health Authority, those dissatisfied with this coverage will be able to opt out, taking a risk-adjusted, tax-paid voucher to a rival Health Care Plan (Upton, 1991).

The system is expected to work in the following way. Competition for contracts among providers pressures them to develop innovative, efficient forms of health service delivery – on pain of going out of business. Similarly, competition among purchasers for members forces them to drive hard bargains with providers and to pay careful attention to the services their members want. The result is intended to be a system which is flexible and innovative in its development of health services and efficient in their production. In fact, there is no *a priori* reason to believe the system will operate this way. The only existing health system with a significant degree of competition is the United States (Culyer *et al.*, 1990). This health system is notoriously characterised by high costs and rapid cost escalation, large and growing inequality of access and poor performance in terms of health indices such as infant mortality.

Will the reform of the New Zealand system have the same consequences? The evidence from the United States suggests that the outcomes of reform cannot be assumed. Instead, careful examination of the particulars of the new system and of the different ways in which elements may combine is required. This task is inherently problematic and provisional. As Chris Ham, Professor of Health Policy and Management at the University of Birmingham argues in examining similar proposals across a number of European countries: 'The difficulty for independent analysts is how to make sense of these changes when evidence on their impact is incomplete and when a fierce debate still rages about their desirability' (Ham, 1992: 32).

The move to split purchasing and service provision, in the form of Regional Health Authorities contracting with competing public and private providers, offers a number of possible advantages. First, it may render the connection between what is paid for health services and what is delivered much more transparent, making purchasers and providers more accountable to each other and to the wider public. Second, the split may work to counterbalance aspects of provider control of the health system, shifting strategic control (the initiative for deciding what services it will provide) from provider groups to purchasers whose role it is to act as agents for their members. Finally, the ability of purchasers to induce competition among providers for contracts may spur a rapid productivity improvement in the delivery of services. But the split is not without its problematic side. The negotiation of contracts, with providers specifying price, quantity and quality, is difficult and costly, mirroring precisely the complexity of the services delivered. In many services and regions, there is little choice of providers, thus giving providers the balance of the bargaining power. Competition may encourage providers to skimp on those aspects of quality least visible to purchasers (Weisbrod, 1991).

The American experience is instructive. Grappling with a system in which complex contracts and extensive monitoring is used to link purchasers and providers, Americans currently spend an estimated 22 per cent of every health dollar on administration, an amount that increased as more competition was injected into the system through the 1980s (Evans, 1986). Ironically for New Zealanders, one key American response has been to seek to lessen these costs by fusing, rather than further separating, purchasing and providing. The result has been the rapid growth of Health Maintenance Organisations which directly supply health services for those they insure.

These considerations suggest that a rigid separation of purchasing and providing is unlikely to be efficient (Williamson, 1975; Granovetter, 1985; Ashton, 1992; Howden-Chapman, 1992). Instead, the system is likely to evolve toward close, long-term, highly interdependent relations between purchasers and providers. In such relationships, the fact that purchasers can ultimately but not easily go elsewhere provides incentives for purchaser and providers to work together so as to improve the productivity and quality of health services (Hirschman, 1970; Ham, 1992; Sabel, 1982).

The development of competing purchasers, a mix of Regional Health Authorities and Health Care Plans, is intended to provide members with 'the ultimate sanction against RHAs which fail to respond to their concerns: the ability to take their custom elsewhere' (Upton, 1991: 62). It is likely to have much wider ramifications.

Creating multiple purchasers may shift the balance of power toward providers, raising the overall cost of health care. In a series of provocative papers, the Canadian health economist Robert Evans argues that the much lower cost of health care in Canada than the United States is the direct result of the construction of a single, dominant public system for the purchase of health care in Canada, compared to the continuing reliance on a multiplicity of purchasers in the United States (Evans, 1986). If Evans' argument can be generalised, then a shift toward competing public and private purchasers of health care in New Zealand is likely to increase health costs without any compensating benefits.

Competition between Health Care Plans and Regional Health Authorities for members is likely to result in wide inequalities of health service entitlement. The process will work like this. Private Health Care Plans may attempt to compete with Regional Health Authorities by wringing more productivity from providers but they will find it much easier to compete by selecting low-risk, rather than high-risk, members. RHAs, responsible for insuring everyone except those who opt for Health Care Plan membership, are unable to compete in this way and will find their lists disproportionately filled with poorer, older and sicker people. As a result, Health Care Plans will be able to offer their clients more attractive bundles of services (and their providers more attractive returns) for the same cost of premium as the RHAs.

This problem of risk selection is explicitly recognised by those implementing the new system. They argue that the problem can be dealt with adequately by risk rating the vouchers available to those opting out of the RHA. Still, given the high incentives for effective risk selection by the Plans, the enormous and as yet unresolved theoretical and practical difficulties involved in effective risk rating and the insurer of last resort status of the RHAs, it seems likely that the Plans and the RHAs will come to serve quite different segments of the population and offer them quite different health care entitlements.

What outcome can be expected from the new system? Is the path, as some claim, one which leads to a reinvigorated, publicly funded health system where access to good health care is a basic entitlement of citizenship? Or does it, as others claim, lead to something more closely resembling the American system with its high costs and grossly unequal distribution of access to health care? The argument I have sketched suggests that different aspects of the reform, differently combined, may make either outcome possible.

Implemented one way, the new system may provide the basis of a more effective publicly funded system. The process of purchasing is developed at a speed which allows those involved to learn how the new system works and to modify their plans accordingly. At the operational level, limited forms of competition for contracts generates information about the range of costs of health services and facilitates purchasers and providers working together to enhance the efficiency and quality of the service delivered. At the strategic level, the purchaser-provider split provides the flexibility required to shift the mix of health services so as to best meet the health needs of the populations served. The core set of mandated, tax-funded services remain widely defined so that few feel the need to buy additional insurance and all share an interest in maintaining a publicly funded system. Overall, the system manages to be consistently innovative, combining the efficient production of high quality health services with equitable access. As among the first fully working systems of 'managed competition', it becomes a model for others to emulate and a point of pride for New Zealanders.

Implemented another way, the new system simply lays the basis for a modified but essential American-style system. The result could come about as an outcome of direct government intention. More likely it will result from a subtle process of interaction between the legislative and regulatory framework of the new system and the particular, situated responses of purchasers, providers and users to this framework. In this scenario, the creation of competition among different kinds of purchasers leads to a stratification of risk and entitlement with the poor, the elderly and other high-risk groups largely confined to RHA coverage and everyone else covered by private Health Care Plans. Competition among the purchasers weakens their bargaining position *vis-à-vis* providers, leading to a steady escalation in the overall costs of health care and great difficulty in enforcing quality standards. Caught between continuing fiscal pressure and a disproportionate rise in health care costs, the state defines downwards the core set of services it guarantees everyone. Those who can afford it consequently increase their privately purchased additional insurance to ensure adequate coverage for themselves. Meanwhile, the state's regulatory role is increasingly compromised. This is because its motivation to intervene is reduced as its fiscal stake in the system contracts and as its wealthier and most demanding citizens increasingly turn to private forms of insurance. It is also because the state is increasingly buffeted by the rapid growth of new pressure groups which seek to enhance their control of the profitable opportunities the new system offers.

Overall, the system evolves toward a high-cost, low-efficiency outcome with wide differences in access to health care. New Zealand again becomes an international showcase, but of a different kind. The lesson drawn by some from the dismal results is that the concept of managed competition is inherently flawed, while for others the problem is argued to lie with the particulars of implementation. Eventually, a new reform coalition is set in motion, seeking to restore strong public management of the health care system.

Notes

1. This section draws heavily on Tesh (1988).
2. This section is drawn from my discussion of the new health system in Fougere (forthcoming (b)). For excellent complementary and overlapping overviews, see Ashton (1992), Borren, P. and Maynard, A. (1993), Easton (1991).

Further Reading

Abbott, A., 1988, *The System of Modern Professions*, Chicago, University of Chicago Press.
Boston, J., and Dalziel, P. (eds), 1992, *The Decent Society*, Auckland, Oxford University Press.
Davis, P., 1981, *Health and Health Care in New Zealand*, Auckland, Oxford University Press.
Dwyer, T., 1991, *Life and Death at Work. Industrial Accidents as a Case of Socially Produced Error*, New York, Plenum Press.
McKinley, J. et al., 1989, 'Trends in Death and Disease and the Contribution of Medical Measures', in H. E. Freeman and S. Levine (eds), *Handbook of Medical Sociology* (4th ed.), Prentice Hall, Englewood Cliffs.
Oakley, A., 1986, *The Captured Womb: A History of the Medical Care of Pregnant Women*, London, Basil Blackwell.
Tesh, S., 1988, *Hidden Arguments,* New Brunswick, Rutgers University Press.
Upton, S., 1991, *Your Health and the Public Health*, Wellington, GP Print.
White, K., 1990, 'Health: Medicalizing Social Problems', in P. Green (ed.), *Studies in New Zealand Social Problems*, Palmerston North, Dunmore Press.
Willis, E., 1983, *Medical Dominance. The Division of Labour in Australian Health Care*, Sydney, George Allen and Unwin.
Witz, A., 1992, *Patriarchy and Professions,* London, Routledge.

11 Education

Roy Nash

Tomorrow's Schools (Lange, 1988) have now been a reality for several years. Following the recommendations of the Picot Report (Task Force to Review Education Administration in New Zealand, 1988), the government abolished the ten Education Boards which had administered primary education since 1877 and placed each school under the authority of a parent-elected Board of Trustees. At the same time, the Education Department was replaced by a smaller Ministry of Education with a remit to concentrate on policy-making functions, and a new institution, the Educational Review Office, was created to assume most of the functions of the inspectorate. The Boards of Trustees, working within the terms of a Charter – basically dictated by central guidelines but allowing some room for the particular educational goals of individual schools – are responsible for the appointment of teachers and almost all aspects of financial management. But although the Boards of Trustees have brought a greater degree of local and parental managerial control to education, public and professional concerns with the effects of market-driven competition between schools and the proposed introduction of bulk-funding are indications enough that debate over the Picot reforms is still unfinished. Broadly similar reforms have been introduced in many developed countries – Australia, Canada and the United Kingdom – and may be seen as being prompted by an underlying crisis affecting mature educational systems everywhere. It may be difficult for observers rooted in the day-to-day experience of school life to grasp the nature and magnitude of this over-shadowing crisis but it is tangible nevertheless. Let us step back and take stock of this system – a system which is projected to soak up $5.06 billion dollars in the financial year 1993-1994 – and attempt to grasp its essential social features.

Education, Equality and Efficiency

Educational provision in New Zealand has long been supported by a dual rhetoric of equality and efficiency. As Minister of Education in 1939, Peter Fraser declared the basis on which the expansion of secondary education would take place. His words are quoted again and again:

> Every person, whatever his level of academic ability, whether he be rich or poor, whether he live in town or country, has a right, as a citizen, to a free education of the kind for which he is best fitted and to the fullest extent of his powers (Currie Report, 1962: 11).

Ten years ago it was worth pointing out that this highly qualified statement of principle rather casually glosses over the issues of how, and by whom, those 'best fitted' might be selected. Today's students, however, who are charged a contribution towards tuition fees and are burdened with long-term loans rather than provided with adequate maintenance grants, might be willing to forgive even its conventionally sexist expression. The Currie Report (1962) endorsed this principle and went on to offer an additional reason for continuing to support the development of education:

> In a world that has suddenly become more competitive ... it will be necessary for any country which considers itself advanced, to make every effort – educational as well as economic – if it wishes to improve or even maintain its present position. Those who hold this view call for the maximum educational opportunity for all, since they regard the people as a whole as an important part of the natural wealth of the country; not to educate them to their maximum capacity is to leave at least part of the country's resources underdeveloped. (...) Equality and expediency appear, therefore, to point in the same direction (Currie Report, 1962: 12).

This sanguine doctrine has ceased to be credible (McCulloch, 1988). It collapsed under attack from all directions. In criticism of this liberal-democratic position, Marxist-inspired sociologists of education (Bourdieu, 1974; Bowles and Gintis, 1977) developed the thesis that schools in capitalist societies functioned essentially, and inevitably they seemed to suggest, to reproduce the existing social division of labour by rewarding the habits and dispositions learned in the middle-class family and termed by Bourdieu 'cultural capital'. A more romantic set of anarchist-minded critics (Illich, 1971) popularised the notion that schools perverted the true relationship between teacher and students and transmitted a narrowly institutionalised form of knowledge as credentials. These 'de-schoolers' had a brief, but influential presence. Then, and most powerfully by the mid-eighties, these themes were adopted by the conservative New Right which had always opposed the 'over-expansion' of education on frankly élitist grounds and now found itself with a ready-made body of critical studies questioning every assumption of the liberal belief in the ability of the school to promote either social equality (to which it had no great commitment anyway) or economic efficiency. The Treasury's (1987) remarkable *Education Briefing* provides a fascinating source of this New Right thinking on education which should not be neglected by New Zealand students (see also the commentaries by Lauder, 1987 and Lauder, Middleton, Boston and Wylie, 1988). These remarks will be elaborated in the next section, but it is important at this point to understand the sea change in the discourse of educational politics.

Traditional policies, such as those put into effect by Fraser, were directed towards the provision of equality of educational opportunity. This meant the provision of equivalent schooling in urban and rural areas, a more or less standardised curriculum, and a national examination system. Such policies were, of course, intended to create not only the necessary resource conditions for equality of educational opportunity but the real achievement of social equity in education. Equality of opportunity was always understood as a means to an end. That end, however, has quite plainly not been attained (Nash, 1993). As a result of this evident failure of the policy of educational opportunity, the ultimate aspiration has been pressed more directly by the Maori community and organisations representing women and the working class as a specific demand for social equality of educational outcome. It is not supposed that the achievements of each and every child can be made identical, but it is most definitely supposed that the average achievements of students from different ethnic groups should be more equal and can be made more equal. There should, again, be no difference between the educational performance of boys and girls. Average differences between students from different social classes are also regarded as evidence of the failure of equality of opportunity policies.

Differences in educational outcomes of an ethnic, class and gender character have been reported in New Zealand by every researcher to investigate these problems. The position of Maori pupils continues to disturb those within the Maori community and people of goodwill throughout New Zealand. Although there are real indications of a gradual but steady improvement in the general level of educational attainment reached by Maori pupils (Benton, 1987), the mean level of attainment remains considerably below that of their non-Maori counterparts. But improvement there is: the qualifications of Maori school leavers are now about the same as those of non-Maori only a dozen years ago – and the 'gap' is, in fact, closing. The attainments of Pacific Islands students are distinctly higher than those of Maori students, but not comparable to those of European students (see Table 11.1).

Social class differences are relatively well documented. The children of professional parents perform significantly better than others even at the age of five (and before they have attended school), and this initial advantage is never lost. At every stage of the educational system, middle-class students consolidate their relatively superior performance in an apparently inevitable manner. On standardised

Table 11.1
Qualifications of Maori and European Students on Leaving School

	Maori		European	
	Boys %	Girls %	Boys %	Girls %
University Bursary and Scholarship	4.7	5.5	25.5	28.8
High School Certificate	9.1	9.9	17.5	18.6
Sixth Form Certificate	21.0	24.6	27.6	29.3
School Certificate	25.3	26.0	17.5	13.5
No Award	39.9	34.0	11.9	9.8

Source: Ministry of Education, 1992

reading scores, for example, children from professional backgrounds reach an average of 109 compared with 93 for those from the unskilled working class. The difference is more than a standard deviation, and although well-established programmes like Reading Recovery are successful in their limited aims, they are unable to eradicate this substantial class-linked variation in educational performance. These basic differences are probably more deeply rooted in forms of cognitive socialisation than many sociologists like to acknowledge – and they do not by any means account for all of the social differences that can be observed in educational performance – yet they cannot be neglected. Data on the relationship between education and post-school destinations are more difficult to obtain and the last large-scale survey of school-leavers was conducted more than a decade ago. However, an indication of contemporary trends can be gleaned from the Access and Opportunity on Education Survey (Nash, Harker and Charters, 1991). It seems that by the age of 18 or 19, the great majority – 82 per cent – of students from broadly professional backgrounds had either entered higher education or gained employment in a non-manual occupation. This proportion fell to 50 per cent in the case of students from white-collar backgrounds and to 37 per cent for working-class students. It is true that students from the higher social classes had higher mean qualifications, but this does not entirely account for these characteristically different patterns of post-school destination. Middle-class and working-class students with similar levels of school performance typically report similar aspirations while they are at school – we can say that aspirations are a function of ability – but whereas almost all middle-class students actually realise their aspirations, this is true for only about half of the working-class students. Some possible explanations of these patterns will be offered in the next section. In any event, there is strong evidence to suggest that middle-class and working-class students with similar school qualifications, although they articulate common aspirations, do not realise them to the same degree.

The educational performance of Maori students is reported annually by the Ministry of Education, and statistics for school leavers have already been reported. When 27.1 per cent of European students and only 5.9 per cent of Maori students achieve the highest level of school qualification, we are a long way from equality of educational outcomes. Nevertheless, the educational position of Maori students is undoubtedly improving. In July 1991, 6.8 per cent of students enrolled for a bachelor's degree were Maori, and recent internal university surveys report figures between 8 and 10 per cent. Of course, true equity would demand a figure of about 20 per cent, but it seems that more than half of all Maori students reaching the seventh form do go on to enter university and that is a much higher ratio than observed for the non-Maori population. At the same time, it must be remembered that rather more than one third of Maori students, compared with barely more than 10 per cent of European students, leave school with no formal qualifications. Naturally, this affects the ability of these students to obtain employment and in the prevailing conditions of a collapsed youth labour market, such an aspiration can scarcely be a reality for a considerable number of unqualified school leavers. This feeds back into the processes of decision-making by structuring taken-for-granted, culturally located expectations (for teachers, parents and pupils alike) which then generate a certain additional self-fulfilling effect.

Differences between boys and girls are of a quite different character. To a small but significant degree, girls out-perform boys on all subjects right through to intermediate school and there are now no significant differences in the perfomance of boys and girls in mathematics and science at least until the end of the fourth form. To a very considerable extent, the patterns of differentiation which may be observed after that must be seen as caused by traditional class and sex-differentiated labour markets. It is only necessary to reflect on the historical development of clerical work for women and the specific educational provision which followed it, in direct response to market demand, to appreciate this. The rapid growth of women's employment in the commercial sector, for example, has brought about a dramatic increase (from 26.4 to 42.7 per cent between 1978 and 1991) in the proportion of girls gaining accountancy at Bursary level. At the lower level, these traditional divisions are proving only slowly amenable to change – trade apprenticeships are taken overwhelmingly by boys – and within the university, humanities and education attract more women while engineering and agriculture attract more men. But rapid progress is being made in certain professional occupations, including law and medicine, where students numbers are now at least equal – if they do not actually favour women. There is a belief that girls attending single-sex schools perform rather better than girls in co-educational schools, but research in this area generally fails to take into account the positive association between high social class and single-sex schooling, which undoubtedly complicates this issue.

This summary of ethnic, class and sex-linked educational differentiation has been able to report only the essential elements of a growing body of New Zealand empirical research. One crucial conceptual difference may be offered before taking up the discussion of causal mechanisms. The French sociologist, Raymond Boudon (1974), has drawn our attention to the nature of secondary effects. The easiest way to illustrate this concept is by reference to the phenomenon mentioned earlier – that equally qualified school leavers from different social backgrounds tend to have different destinations, even though their aspirations might have been similar. There are probably three reasons for this: the expense of full-time further education can more readily be managed by middle-class families; working-class students are perhaps more likely to modify aspirations for non-manual work as a result of specific class values; and middle-class and working-class students stand in an objectively different position in relation to non-élite institutions and courses which represent, for the former, a distinct lowering of social status, whereas for the latter, they may even represent a relative advancement. The final argument is Boudon's thesis and it is worth a little elaboration. High Socio-Economic Status (SES) students with University Entrance typically chose high SES destinations (including tertiary education) whereas low SES students typically choose middle level SES destinations (broadly clerical positions). These choices reflect secondary effects in that they cannot be explained by scholastic ability or by level of school qualification. Such effects pose a distinct explanatory problem for the sociology of education and focus attention on the processes of decision-making practised by young people. Such decision-making must be understood, it is suggested, as most typically embedded within the taken-for-granted framework of expectations generated by sub-cultures shaped by ethnic, class and sex-linked determinants. Cultural Studies has, for this reason, assumed an integral and important place in contemporary sociology of education.

A Brief Introduction to the Sociology of Education

It is worth knowing a little of the recent history which has brought the sociology of education to its present position. The fundamantal concern of this sub-discipline is with the extent and causation of socially differentiated access to education. I have stated that the expansion of educational provision, at least since the 1930s, had been predicated on the assumptions about the contribution liberal-democratic thinkers believed education could make to economic growth and social equality. The sociology of education was essentially developed by academics (Halsey, *et a.,* 1981; Gray, *et al.,* 1983) who set themselves the task of monitoring the progress of that great experiment. Their fundamental tools were the large-scale survey and, at first the card-sorting machine, and then the computer. What emerged from this methodology was a great deal of useful information but a theory which produced one-way 'hurdles of disadvantage' accounts (one-way in that educational failure among 'disadvantaged' pupils was left 'obvious' whereas success was explained away in terms of 'chance'), which invariably fell back on common-sense knowledge. All too often researchers advanced a frankly circular 'causal' interpretation in which the statistics of class access stood for the 'class chances' which in turn were supposed to explain them. The methodology itself was indispensible since only large-scale surveys could provide the necessary information to monitor the social performance of the educational system. But the less said about the ad hoc theoretical forms which accompanied this methodology the better. They certainly provoked considerable dissatisfaction in the young sociologists who entered this field towards the end of the 1960s.

At the beginning of the 1970s, twenty years ago but as yesterday in the minds of most sociologists who are all of a generation, there emerged a self-conscious 'break' with this 'social arithmetic' tradition. Young academics, the heady hopes of the student movement still a living force, rejected the implicit or explicit notion that British working-class and American black families were 'disadvantaged' in any sense which implied cultural deficiency (which almost always *was* implied) and turned their attention to the contribution of the school and the educational system. For a decade or more, until this enterprise was all but crushed by a particularly gritty social and political reality, the 'new sociology of education' (Young, 1971) criticised the socially constructed nature of knowledge, investigated the construction of pupil identities by teachers' practices, and generally defended the thesis that socially differentiated attainment was a product of the educational system at all levels. Some writers continue to maintain this thesis arguing, bravely but perhaps absurdly one may think, that the world may be different when New Zealanders realise that the calling of a refuse collector is as honest and as important as that of a lawyer. I have already suggested that many elements of this romantic critique, much to the dismay of those responsible for it, have been appropriated by the New Right and advanced as a reason for subjecting teachers to greater control and restraining state expenditure on education. Even Labour politicians have argued that if middle-class students benefit most from 'free' education, it is only fair that all students should contribute through fee charges and a loans system.

It has become clear at last that this radical 'new sociology' has profound theoretical weaknesses. In the first place, all our experience and all our research forces one conclusion and one only: most educational differentiation is rooted in the home. Bane's (1975: 287) stark observation that, '[ex]perience suggests that full compensation would require either massive interventions in the home or measures to retard the progress of the well off', has been reluctantly endorsed by an increasing number of scholars. This is not to say that there are no differences between schools in their effects on students' attainments, but it is to say that the difference in educational attainment we see between social classes is not created in the school to any great extent. And in the second place, all our sober moments incline us to the realist conclusion that true knowledge of the physical and social world is necessarily of a given character and can only be learned by a more (rather than less) restricted range of functional pedagogies. What space we make for cultural differences in education must be made within that real constraint. No one doubts that the ethos of, say, a French *école* and a New Zealand high school are characteristically different in ways that those familiar with both cultures will instantly recognise, but such differences are in a technical sense 'arbitrary', whereas the culture of literacy and science represents a scholastically 'necessary' culture which if the school lacked it would not be a modern school at all. The task for the sociology of education is now to move forward with a materialist theory of the family which transcends the old 'cultural deficit' thinking which rightly offended the radicals of 20 years ago, and with a theory of the scholastic necessary which respects the cultural arbitrary. Applying this to our own circumstances in New Zealand is, of course, a far from mechanical business and it is difficult to avoid positions tinged with the hues of propaganda on all sides.

An Acceptable Theory of Social Reproduction

The radical credentials of Pierre Bourdieu's theory of social reproduction have made the reconstruction of a family-centred theory of social reproduction easier than it might have been. While this leading French sociologist's theory has in fact been criticised as just another deficit theory (Bisseret, 1979; Baudelot and Establet, 1981), its links to Marxist thought, its powerful concept of 'cultural capital' and its recognition of knowledge as 'symbolic violence' has gained for Bourdieu's work a general acceptence amongst sociologists of education in New Zealand as elsewhere. It is a wide-ranging, historically sensitive, basically anthropological theory capable of generating profound insights. This section will examine some New Zealand material relevant to social reproduction and discuss this within the context provided by Bourdieu's theory.

The reproduction from one generation to the next of the social relations of production and the cultural symbols ordering those relations are as essential to the maintenance of society as biological reproduction itself. The institutions with the major responsibility for ensuring the successful reproduction of existing social patterns are the family and the school. In the conventional perspective of structural functionalism, the reproductive functions of social organisations were analysed by the concept of pattern maintenance (Parsons, 1954). Structural functionalism tended to understate the importance of conflict in social relations but its concerns with pattern maintenance were essentially the same as those of sociologists who prefer to speak of the processes of social reproduction. Families have always been seen as primarily concerned with socialisation, that is with the reproduction of social values and status, and the end results of these processes have been most extensively studied by sociologists interested in social mobility. Only enough is known of social mobility in New Zealand to enable tentative conclusions to be drawn.

The family is concerned to maintain and, if possible, to improve its social and economic position both in the present and the future. Families are in the business of social and cultural reproduction, and most are fairly good at it. Jones and Davies's (1986) retrospective cohort study of social mobility in New Zealand provides evidence in support of the belief that the patterns of inter-generational mobility in this country are quite similar to those in Australia and the U.S.A. Between 60 and 70 per cent of sons with fathers in either routine non-manual or small business occupations maintain their position above the manual/non-manual division but downward mobility for this group is not uncommon. Of class 1, however, the upper 10 per cent of the population, only 9 per cent are demoted to the manual working class. Conversely, less than 8 per cent of sons with working-class fathers, almost 35 percent of the population, reached class 1. At the same time, there is sufficient upward mobility to ensure that the professional élite is broadly based and, indeed, a more recent survey reported by Nash (1993) indicates that there may be at least as many men of working-class origin in the professional and upper managerial positions as there are from that class itself. These studies deal with the post-1945 period and are based on limited samples, but they strongly suggest that most social mobility in New Zealand is accounted for by movement between socio-economic categories within the broad divisions of the middle and working classes. Moreover, the degree of mobility that can be observed – which after all is not negligible – is generated by the educational system.

The means by which families attempt to maintain and improve their status are various. The classes engaged in private business enterprise are most obviously reliant on their ability to transmit property in the form of real or financial capital, and the skills and personal contacts to manage it profitably. Mobility within this group is achieved through the successful expansion of the enterprise, through marriage, or through various forms of family assistance. The professional sector of the middle class, who either lack substantial capital, or who are engaged in work for which the possession of knowledge is more important than the ownership of capital, are almost entirely dependent on the educational system for the reproduction of their class position. The skilled working class has traditionally been able to pass on superior positions in the labour hierarchy by a process of direct local negotiation. Promotion within the occupational structure from labourer through to supervisory status is also possible, but it may safely be assumed that most mobility from the working class is achieved through the educational system. It is clear that the educational system although by no means the only agency of social mobility, and for some sections of the community perhaps not even the most important, is crucial to the social reproduction of the majority sector of the middle class, and offers the most certain avenue of mobility for working-class individuals. This discussion has emphasised the reproductive character of the school and also its apparent inability to do other than certify family status. It is important, therefore, to consider the school as a specific agent of transformation.

Bernstein (1977), in particular, draws attention to the potential of the educational system to act as an interrupter and a reproducer of cultural systems. That is to say that the school can provide a curriculum which changes the cultural patterns of its students or one which reinforces the cultural patterns its students already possess. The achievements of the early New Zealand missionary schools, described by Barrington and Beaglehole (1974), afford a striking illustration of the power of schooling to change or disrupt culture. This dual potential should not be overlooked. Schools do, in fact, have some autonomy in the areas of organisation and curriculum, but the main concern of this discussion is with social and cultural reproduction and that, as the Treasury realises full well, is their dominant current function (Dore, 1977). This is to speak within the framework of sociological investigations of a particular kind – schools perform many other functions including the transmission of knowledge, but it seems a stubborn truth that they seem unable to act as other than agents of reproduction.

Bourdieu's theory is fundamantally materialist. In effect, Bourdieu stands the conventional explanations in the sociology of education on their heads. It is not that working-class (or ethnic minority) pupils fail because they are 'disadvantaged' or lack middle-class culture, the point is rather that middle-class pupils succeed simply by being better resourced. These resources (or 'capitals' as Bourdieu calls them) are of three kinds: financial, symbolic, and social. Families are to a very considerable extent differentially endowed with these material resources as a result of their location in the class structure. These resources, coupled with long-term strategic planning, prove to be extremely potent. We should not see this as classical deficit theory. The concepts of resource theory are not 'cultural deprivation' and 'linguistic restriction', but ones which recognise a class-structured continuum of resource levels. It is not especially difficult to understand how those best resourced are able to dominate the competition for the limited provision of educational credentials and the most influential and well-paid occupations. To deny such a self-evident observation for fear of being challenged as a deficit theorist is pusillanimous. Amid the competing theoretical claims of this and that 'perspective' within the over-specialised and fragmented discourse of educational theory, resource theory is often, however, 'forgotten': it is a peculiarly middle-class forgetfulness.

Bourdieu's thesis declines to accept the school's passive role in reflecting and rewarding the symbolic capital of the middle class (i.e. its characteristic class-related modes of thought), and has advanced an influential critique of the school in this respect. This highly influential element of Bourdieu's theory may be introduced by a local illustration. A former Director General of Education writes:

> A quarter of a century ago I sat in a remote corner of New Zealand, trying to persuade the chiefs and elders to accept for their district a secondary school providing technical courses the area so clearly needed rather than the academic course on which they had set their hearts ... I retired defeated, when an old chief, having shrewdly elicited that I had taken Latin, clinched the argument, with 'And look where you got to'. The proper reply still eludes me (Beeby, 1966: 30).

It is likely that everyone, rural and urban people, Maori and Pakeha alike, took this view in the 1940s. The core of Bourdieu's theory is an analogy between economic capital which is transmitted within the family by inheritance and invested in order to generate profit and a certain status in the world, and cultural capital, which is knowledge transmitted within the family through socialisation and invested in the school system to produce the qualifications (the academic capital) necessary for entry into the professions. In Bourdieu's theory, the true (as opposed to the apparent) nature of the educational system is to discriminate in favour of those who are the inheritors of cultural capital. It thus follows that the representation of the educational failure of certain social groups as due to lack of talent and intelligence must be seen as an ideology serving the maintenance of the system. Children in the middle-class home gain through socialisation a system of mental habits – 'habitus' to use the term Bourdieu has borrowed from the medieval scholastics – which organises thoughts and perceptions in such a way as to constitute an integrated set of mental categorisations which structure each social member's conception of reality within the great order of the cultural code. The forming of the habitus may be regarded as the programming of the individual and of the group to which he or she belongs. School does not and cannot compensate for an 'inferior' habitus; it merely continues to reward what the 'well-endowed' habitus produces. Making this crucial point, Bourdieu states:

> To penalise the underprivileged and favour the most privileged the school has only to neglect, in its teaching methods and its criteria when making judgements, to take into account the cultural inequalities between children of different social classes. In other words, by treating all pupils, however unequal they may be in reality, as equal in rights

and duties, the educational system is led to give its de facto sanction to initial cultural inequalities (Bourdieu, 1974: 113).

Thus the school system converts cultural capital into academic capital (for example Latin) which can 'objectively' qualify its possessor for entry into the élite. We can appreciate at once how the role of Latin was understood by the Maori elders in discussion with Beeby, but we are also aware that circumstances have changed. The question of whether other subjects, or groups of subjects, continue to perform this class gatekeeping function is one that should be considered on the evidence. What actually constitutes the habitus of the dominant social group at any particular historical moment is contingent on a unique set of determining factors and, in this sense, middle-class cultural capital may be regarded as arbitrary. However, overt arbitrariness at the level of *academic capital* exposes the legitimation process, by which cultural capital is transformed into 'objective' qualifications, to unanswerable criticism.

The sociology of education has now to work through just which elements of the school regime are, in fact, arbitrary in this Bourdieuian sense. It might be necessary to conclude that such elements are no longer (if they ever were) a mechanism of overwhelming importance in New Zealand. At any rate, Latin no longer serves this purpose. Those aspects of Bourdieu's theory which emphasise the material resources of those competing within the school for its quota controlled credentials may offer a more powerful explanatory system. Bourdieu has a useful theory – he is, one critic has put it, 'good to think with' – but it is asolutely necessary to treat this theory as such and interrogate it within the light of empirical evidence from our own contemporary educational system.

Implications for Practice Within the New Order

If it is the case that socially differentiated educational attainment largely reflects familial resources inalienably possessed by individual families as a result of their location in the division of labour, and if it is the case that the effective elements of the symbolic cultural capital are not arbitrary but necessary to the acquisition of real knowledge, then it may be to time to rethink some of the most popular academic theories in this field, particularly theories of self-concept and peer group pressure, together with the policies derived from them.

As far as first-level effects are concerned, that is differences in reading and other school attainments which reflect initial school entry differences and the support of a literacy-focused home socialisation, the school must respond (within the cultural arbitrary appropriate to its pupils) with an emphasis on reading and reading recovery programmes. Community Literacy Schemes, initiated in some urban areas, offer the potential to interrupt and reorganise lived familial cultures which, for one reason or another, give literate forms of knowledge a low priority. It should go without saying that the agencies of such cultural interruption must be organic to the community, reflecting and representing internal developments within it. But there should be no room for a compromised cultural relativism where literacy is concerned. Secondary effects, that is the emergence of average differences between social groups due to differential subject or destination patterns within ability categories, are likely to be particularly sensitive to the arbitrary culture of the school. School counsellors with responsiblity for careers advice might gain much from a greater understanding of the concept of secondary effects. Boudon suggests, and what local evidence we have seems to bear him out, that effects of this kind are more important to the maintenance of socially differentiated attainment than the more obvious differences of primary origin. Moreover, secondary effects must be conceptualised within the framework of knowledge provided by contemporary cultural studies which has demonstrated how destination trajectories are essentially collective in character as young people come to create their self-identities in the general production of distinctive sub-cultural forms.

Social theorists do not doubt that the differences in educational attainment and occupational destination between New Zealanders of European and Maori descent are exclusively social in origin. Few doubt that differences between social classes can be more than marginally, if at all, determined by genetic factors (Olssen, 1988), and the same applies to sex differences. It is not disputed by anyone that some families are better resourced than others, that they are richer or poorer, more or less well socially connected to the systems of cultural and political power, and more or less centred around a culture of literacy. What we still lack in this area is research directed towards a more precise understanding of how these different resources have specific effects at different stages of the educational system. There is also a considerable dispute about the ability of the school to nullify the effect of such home endowments. Radical optimists challenge the school to transform its cultural practices at the level of the specific local ethnic and social class arbitrary, the better to reflect bicultural realities, with the argument that such changes will generate a new confidence and a new power with resulting gains in the educational performance of currently underachieving groups. The more pessimistic, however, while supporting the need for schools to reflect the cultural arbitrary of their pupils, continue to doubt the power of the school to massively interrupt differences produced by initial literacy socialisation. The impetus of such socialisation does not cease on entry to school, but on the contrary, continues to gain force, providing a stimulus which should be understood as continual and cumulative. Were there convincing evidence from research conducted anywhere in the world to support the thesis that schools possess some hidden potential to negate the continual power of family resources, it would be easier to drink from the optimists' cup. Unfortunately, the entire history of theoretical and practical pedagogy lends itself to no such interpretation.

It is difficult to know what more can be done with the school system. That it not only fails to interupt family resource-driven attainment differentials but actually depresses the attainments of many pupils, particularly working-class Maori pupils, far below what they are capable of even within the terms of that extra-school resource difference, is widely acknowledged. To identify peer group culture as the source of this relative decline (Mitchell and Mitchell, 1989) is probably correct at one level but needs to be conceptualised within the wider contexts of social inequality and racist practices by the majority community which do nothing to discourage the production of such subcultures. A dual thrust is necessary: the development of a literacy-focused culture throughout the community, and the fullest degree of effective local control of the school necessary to establish the specific arbitrary culture required if the development of counter-productive sub-cultures of resistance is to be inhibited (Walker, 1988). For that is without doubt the most successful way to reshape the subcultural forms which seem so powerfully to determine destination trajectories. In this respect, the growing number of Kura Kaupapa Maori schools – about 45 by the early 1990s with a total roll of at least 500 students – stands as an example of one initiative that has been greatly facilitated by the educational reforms.

The correct conclusion to take from the thesis of educational differentiation based on class resources is not that nothing can be done, but that what can be done must be concentrated on the effective mechanisms of differentiation at the sites where they are active. Socially differentiated educational performance is not all of a type. This provokes the thought that the school may not be the most fruitful site to interrupt the processes which translate school credentials to occupations and further education places. It may be necessary to work here for a greater degree of popular acceptance for policies which assist all social categories of excluded students to gain access to education through 'second chance' systems, targeted courses, and perhaps by a deliberate attack on the arbitrary elements of the credentialling system at the level of occupational entry. It is worth making the point also that systems which privilege middle-class students from ethnic minority groups to the even greater disadvantage of working-class students throughout the New Zealand community are most unlikely to gain the degree of popular acceptance necessary to the success of positive discrimination policies. There are no instant solutions in this area, but certain policies are more likely to make a difference than others. Moreover, the differences that can be made are worth making. Research from Australia (Graetz, 1988), for example, indicates that the effects of social background on years of completed education are declining over time and that ability is becoming more important. This is probably because of the increased level of tertiary educational provision which delays and lessens the potency of those secondary effects which have been identified as so important an element in translating formal educational opportunity into real educational access. This move towards meritocracy must always be interpreted, of course, within the context of a theory which recognises the social determinants of scholastic ability, but it is definite progress.

This chapter began with a review of the administrative changes to the educational system introduced by the fourth Labour Government. Most academic commentary has been highly critical of these reforms (Bedggood and Bedggood, 1988; Codd, Gordon and Harker, 1988; Munro, 1989), and some have seen in them little more than a desire to reduce central government educational expenditure by shifting a further portion of the financial burden to local communities. While fiscal constraint should not be ignored, there is a more important set of reasons underlying this action (Nash, 1989). What the government will gain through these reforms is increased political control over the educational system. The areas which must be controlled will be more controllable and those which cannot be controlled will be removed from the state's area of responsibility. In effect, the government has withdrawn from 'no win' areas, and the problem of socially differentiated attainment is not the least of these, in order to regroup around a strengthened centre. The power of the civil service has been effectively restrained and a more manageable, biddable, state apparatus, responsive to government direction, brought into being. It is necessary to analyse the social and political origins of these reforms and account for the government's success in producing a package which, if it has not generated unrestrained enthusiasm, has to many seemed better than nothing. The New Zealand government appears to have reached the same conclusion as Gramsci (1985: 39):

> The problem of the school is at once both technical and political. In a parliamentary-democratic state there can be no technical and political solution to the problem of the school.

The state has attempted to abdicate its social responsibility and throw the problem of the school back to the 'community' – but since there is and can be no 'community' in a class-divided social formation, there will be intensified struggle. But Gramsci leaves a token of hope. If there is no technical and political solution to the problem of the school there might, in the long term, be a cultural solution. And the reforms have certainly thrown open the school as a site for renewed cultural struggle. We have experienced – and are likely to continue to experience – a period of vigorously contested struggle within the new framework of administration. Whether we see further movement in the direction of New Right market principles, or towards genuine collective practices, will be determined by the strength of the forces engaged in the struggle.

Further Reading

Bourdieu, P., 1986, *Distinction,* London, Routledge.
Codd, J., Harker, R. K. and Nash, R. (eds), 1990, *Political Issues in New Zealand Education* (2nd edition), Palmerston North, Dunmore Press.
Nash, R., 1993, *Succeeding Generations: Family Resources and Access to Education,* Auckland, Oxford University Press.

12 Politics

Jack Vowles

After a phase of descriptive and legalistic analysis of political institutions prior to World War II, for the next forty years or more, political science was dominated by sociological explanations. The sociological fashion had the effect of more usefully redefining politics so that it was seen as a process penetrating throughout society. But many political scientists of this era also tended to minimise the importance of the government institutions previously at centre stage, and sought political explanations in social and economic forces. For example, the development of the welfare state was viewed as the result of economic development and demographic change, rather than as the outcome of the efforts of reforming governments (Wilensky, 1974).

By the 1980s, however, intellectual fashions had changed once more with a reduction in the importance of sociology to political explanation (Evans *et al.*, 1985). There are now more sophisticated assumptions about the reciprocal interaction between the state and society, even among those who oppose the new focus on 'state autonomy' (Roper, 1991). Thus, the evolution of welfare states is now more frequently seen as underpinned by a mixture of economic, social and political events in combination (Hicks and Swank, 1992). There is a greater stress on agency and less on structural determination (which, in turn, is now conceived of in more subtle terms as relative constraint).

Of central importance is the acceptance that political agents may themselves make choices which lay the foundations for future structural constraint. For example, an industrial relations system legally established by a particular government may subsequently shape the form of class conflict, the nature of industrial organisations, and the effects of these on subsequent policy outcomes. In New Zealand, this was one effect of the Industrial Conciliation and Arbitration (ICA) Act of 1894 (Holt, 1986; Walsh and Fougere, 1987). Similarly, the consequences of particular electoral systems indicate equally powerful institutional effects on incentives for political action, the development of party systems, political participation, election outcomes and subsequent patterns of public policy.

Despite this new and more complex understanding of the relationships between society and politics, concepts employed in the analysis of social structure, social organisation and historical sociology still remain as part of the indispensable contribution of the sociological tradition to political science. Thus a contemporary account of the sociology of New Zealand politics must begin with historical sociology and move on to the key elements of social structure: class, ethnicity and gender. To investigate the social organisation of politics outside the state itself requires an examination of political parties and organised interests. For reasons of space, the latter cannot be dealt with here, but there is a recent accessible analysis for further reference (Vowles, 1992a), and other work (Deeks and Perry, 1992; Roper, 1992). The approach taken here will emphasise agency and strategic action operating within a context of structural constraint rather than structural determination. And it will also attempt to indicate the significance of reciprocal interaction between social forces, political agents, and politically-determined policy patterns and institutions.

Historical Background

As a society originating in nineteenth century British colonial rule, New Zealand can be placed into a model of 'settler capitalism' (Denoon, 1983). As imperial rule faded into settler autonomy, Maori, through war, demographic marginalisation, and constitutional neglect, were forced into the margins of politics. Settler society was initially highly disorganised (Fairburn, 1989). A rural working-class soon emerged but was highly itinerant, making class formation slow and halting (Martin, 1990). Politics was parochial and, until 1891, dominated by a small class of merchants and large landholders divided by personal, regional and business interests.

The processes of class formation were well under way by the 1880s as the tide of immigration receded, industry and infrastructure developed, urban communities expanded, and organised interests began to coalesce. Meanwhile, the lack of entrenched political and social privilege and thus little opposition to radical democratic ideas made it possible for New Zealand to become one of the world's first fully-fledged representative democracies.

Political and social cleavages at the time of democratisation set the stage for the institutionalisation of political competition for decades hence (Lipset and Rokkan, 1967). In the case of New Zealand, regional and parochial conflicts were declining and the state was already well on the way towards becoming one of the democratic world's most centralised and unified. Religion was to enter politics but more at the margins than as a central feature. With respect to Maori, tribal division, social disruption and demoralisation, spatial isolation in rural communities and political marginality all combined to minimise the ethnic dimension of politics. Thus, the emerging class structure provided the only significant foundation for the institutionalisation of electoral politics.

With the advantage of exceptional state autonomy, the Liberal Government's policies helped to create a framework for class politics, as well as institutions, economic interests and patterns of state intervention, which would shape future structural constraints on public policy development. Assisting the settlement of small and medium-sized farmers, and with a preference for leasehold rather than freehold tenure, the government provided an emerging farming and petty bourgeois class, both with an economic base and an ideological cause to support. By 1912, a new Reform Party based on an alliance between the petty bourgeoisie and what remained of the old bourgeois élite was able to defeat the Liberals. Having given trade unions a legally guaranteed platform and a wage-fixing process through the ICA Act, the Liberals promoted union organisation so that by the early decades of the new century, New Zealand had become the world's third most unionised country. Union organisation, social democratic ideology and a need to defend workers' interests politically, provided the conditions for the making of a New Zealand working class.

Because the political support of the working class alone is almost never sufficient for electoral victory, the entry of the working class into politics in democratic capitalist societies creates a situation where social democratic or working-class parties face a trade-off between seeking middle-class support and consolidating or holding their working-class support. It is a trade-off which becomes particularly acute when a party begins to attract the higher proportion of voters necessary to propel it into power. It follows that the trade-off decision can be made more acute if there is a working-class party to the left of a social democratic party; it may be less acute where a strong union movement operates within a centralised wage-bargaining system, thus keeping levels of working-class organisation and consciousness at a relatively high level (Przeworski, 1985).

In outline, the political trajectory of the New Zealand Labour Party is consistent with these arguments. Militant trade unionism in the years prior to World War One provided both class organisation and class consciousness, despite industrial defeat (Olssen, 1987; 1988). At its first election in 1919, and with a programme to the left of both the British Labour and the German SPD parties, the New Zealand Labour Party captured 25 per cent of the vote, concentrated highly in the urban working-class. Yet it could not advance significantly above that plateau until it had effectively abandoned its objectives of extensive socialisation under workers' control which occurred from the early 1930s onward. The socialist objective was formally dropped from the party constitution in 1951. Increasingly aware of its inability to recapture power save for brief interludes, the party leadership repudiated particularistic class politics in 1963. After another short-lived period of power, the Labour Party adopted a liberal constitution in 1976 with only a hint of its former socialist heritage (Vowles, 1987: 20-21). Until the formation of the New Labour Party in 1989 and its capture of a parliamentary seat in 1990, the New Zealand Labour Party has never been seriously challenged by a left-wing rival.

During the 1920s New Zealand trade unions were weak and were either unable or unwilling to provide the Labour Party with substantial assistance (Fairburn, 1985). The disorganising effects of conservative governments and unemployment weakened the strength and consciousness of the working class, and helped to make it more necessary for the Labour Party to seek middle class allies. Between the 1930s and the late 1960s, the institutionalisation of centralised wage-fixing and compulsory unionism built on the foundations of the ICA Act and, guaranteed union security. Yet because union organisation was underpinned by the state, it did not necessarily facilitate autonomous or genuine class organisation or consciousness. In the 1970s the centralised wage-fixing system began to collapse and, with the size of the traditional working class declining, and highly conscious of the trade-off problem between working-class and middle-class support, the Labour Party appeared to become, as Przeworski (1985: 122) puts it, 'indifferent to its class composition'.

The most successful period for the Labour Party was between 1935 and 1949, when it first held power and constructed the world's first comprehensive welfare state. The length of this period of political hegemony still stands unequalled by any other Labour Party in an English-speaking society. Yet, despite this, the New Zealand Labour Party has had limited success in gaining power since 1949, and more particularly, holding it. Winning in 1957, Labour lost the next election in 1960, and repeated the same pattern from 1972 to 1975. The fourth Labour Government's re-election for a second parliamentary term in 1987 was therefore a significant achievement.

Since 1949 New Zealand's most successful political party has been the National Party. Formed in 1936 from the ashes of the Reform and Liberal parties, as well as the short-lived right-wing Democratic Party, National began as a party to oppose Labour. Its principles emerged as a compromise between liberalism and conservatism. Its membership and support were derived from rural and urban business interests, although it was also successful in appealing to white-collar workers (Gustafson, 1986).

In government, National has acted as a party of the status quo, accepting the welfare state and the highly regulated economy constructed by the first Labour Government. After 1990 a new National Government similarly adapted to the new and very different policy pattern established by Labour between 1984 and 1990, although by seeking to further advance certain policies, National seriously threatened its survival at the following 1993 election. Normally National's 'free enterprise' principles have been less to the fore, although still important as a background influence. Thus National's period of longest dominance in the 1950s and 1960s was one in which real welfare state provision did not expand significantly despite modest economic growth, and New Zealand was transformed from welfare leader to 'welfare laggard' (Castles, 1985). This is consistent with international evidence that governments of the right act as a brake on welfare state development, particularly where economic conditions are favourable for expansion (Castles, 1987).

Since 1938 New Zealand politics has been dominated by National and Labour, but that dominance has been steadily eroded. Figure 12.1 shows minor party and independent voting at successive general elections, and indicates a steady, albeit fluctuating increase in that phenomenon since the early 1950s. In 1954 the Social Credit Political League took just over 11 per cent of the votes but no seats. In 1966 it secured a single MP who survived for one term only. In a 1977 by-election, another Social Credit MP was elected and survived the following general election, and in 1980, a second was elected. Both seats were retained in 1981 with an overall national vote of nearly 21 per cent.

Because of the small parliamentary margin between National and Labour, and in a situation where some National MPs no longer supported the government, Social Credit was able to exercise the balance of power on the issue of special legislation to provide for the construction of the Clyde dam. But Social Credit's backing of the government ran against the tide of public opinion, and the consequent collapse of its electoral support illustrates the vulnerability of a small party if it makes a strategic

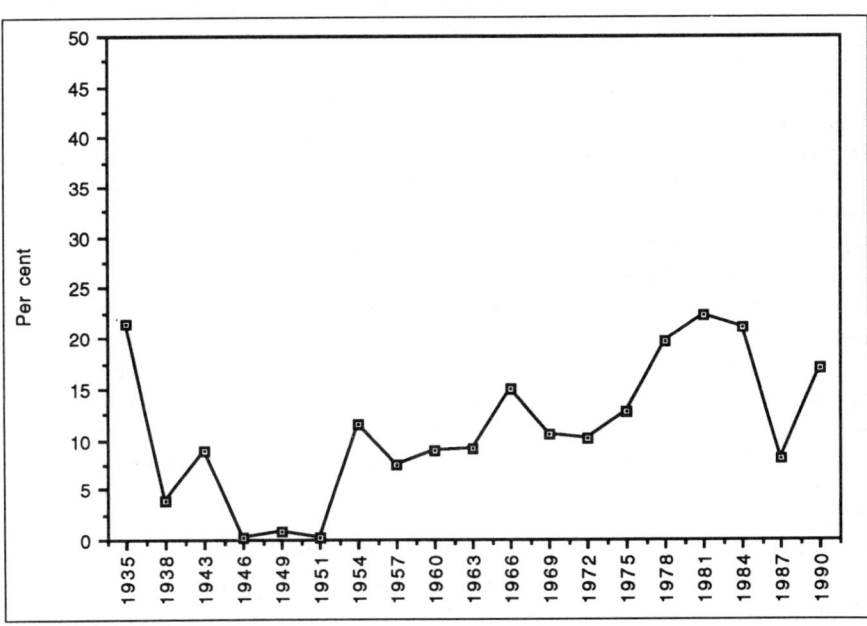

Figure 12.1
Minor Party and Independent Voting 1935-1990

error in such circumstances. Social Credit has tended to appeal to less successful members of the petty bourgeoise in rural and, more recently, suburban areas. Its popular support peaked at just over 30 per cent in opinion polls in 1980.

Other small parties have had shorter histories. The world's first national Green party, Values, achieved two per cent of the votes in 1975 and five per cent in 1975. By the end of the decade it was an empty shell, although it was to be another ten years before its organisation was formally dissolved (Rainbow, 1989; 1993). A right-wing party, the New Zealand Party, gained 12 per cent of the votes in 1984 but no seats, and quickly faded away. In 1990 New Labour secured five per cent of the vote and one parliamentary seat, but the new Green Party's seven per cent of votes delivered no representation at all.

Increasing support for minor parties has not yet been translated very effectively into political representation although minor parties did manage to obtain four seats in the 1993 election. Given New Zealand's first-past-the-post or plurality system, minority parties find it very difficult to secure representation unless their support is concentrated spatially. With a proportional electoral system, a party gaining, say, 10 per cent of the vote secures representation, an established foothold from which to move forward, and certain payoffs which may include status, influence, media attention and resources which assist organisational continuity.

By contrast, plurality provides minor parties with a very high threshold, a highly vulnerable position even where seats may be temporarily gained, and very limited payoffs. Meanwhile, voters are discouraged from voting for minor parties which they might otherwise prefer because they know the chances of small parties exercising political power are so small. Given this, voters have an incentive to choose to support the major parties they feel closest to, or, in the absence of a preference between them, they will perhaps not vote at all. Indeed, voting participation does tend to be higher where electoral systems are proportional (Blais and Carty, 1990). The very high threshold over which new parties must cross to effectively contest for representation provides both major parties with monopoly status in their respective sections of the democratic marketplace.

It was the plurality system which provided the key incentive for the formation of the National Party in 1938. Labour had advocated proportional representation from 1916 until the early 1930s. Its subsequent acceptance of plurality probably ensured that Labour's years of government have been fewer than might have been the case with a proportional electoral system. Where proportional electoral systems operate, there is a general tendency towards a divided right and an independent centre although, of course, specific conjunctures within individual countries can bring about other circumstances.

In New Zealand, Labour has been significantly disadvantaged by the plurality electoral system. While an otherwise sophisticated analysis of all elections since 1946 shows there has been no general or consistent bias in favour of either major party (Johnston, 1992), this fails to isolate the particular and very politically crucial effects detrimental to Labour which have been apparent where elections have been close contests. For example, in 1954, a tight margin in votes for the two main parties nevertheless delivered National a ten-seat majority. In 1957 a more healthy four percentage point popular vote margin to Labour gave the party only a very small three-seat majority. Worse, in 1978 and 1981 Labour polled slightly more votes than National but it was National which gained the most seats and formed the government. Only in 1987 did a four percentage point margin of Labour over National deliver Labour a healthy majority, and did so largely because of the increased organisational sophistication of the Labour Party and the targeting of its resources in those electorates it most needed to keep or win.

Thus it was a Labour Government which set up the Royal Commission on the Electoral System which recommended a Mixed Member Proportional (MMP) system for New Zealand, and Labour partisans, followed by third party supporters, provided the largest body of public opinion in favour of change in the critical period 1990 to 1993. Nevertheless, for the most part, Labour's parliamentary leadership opposed a change to MMP, apparently prefering the objective of gaining shorter periods of 'unbridled' majority government, rather than the likely alternative of more consistent and possibly greater long-term influence as a dominant partner within coalition governments.

Social Structure and Political Parties

As class has hitherto provided the most fundamental political cleavage in New Zealand, most of the work on social structure and voting has centred around that concept (for a more detailed theoretical and empirical review, see Vowles, 1992b). Even the most sceptical assessment estimates that Labour had 75 per cent of the working-class vote in its city seats in the 1920s (Chapman, 1962; 1969; Fairburn, 1985). Survey data collected since 1963 indicates a pattern of moderate class voting which weakens dramatically after 1975 (Bean, 1988).

The concept of class is, of course, both complex and contested. The traditional distinction has been between manual and non-manual households. Persons are classified according to the occupation of the male worker in the household into broad 'blue-collar' (working-class) or 'white-collar' (middle-class) categories. From these admittedly crude categories, the Alford index of class voting is constructed. This simply subtracts the proportion of middle-class voting for the left from the proportion of the working-class also voting for the left. Where all the working-class and none of the middle-class voted for the left, the index would score 100. Where voting for the left was the same in each class, the index would score zero. Internationally, the highest levels of over 50 were recorded in Scandinavia in the 1950s and 1960s. In New Zealand, the index has been calculated at 30 in 1963, falling to 16 in 1981 (Bean, 1988), nine in 1987 and five in 1990 (Vowles and Aimer, 1993:35).[1] Thus the New Zealand party system is undergoing 'class dealignment', a process common to most other capitalist democracies. Whatever class categories are employed, support for this assertion remains robust (Vowles, 1992b).

Class dealignment has been accompanied by the declining size of the traditional working-class and the increased size of the new 'service class' or 'salariat', thus making it increasingly desirable for Labour parties to seek support outside their traditional social bases. The 'service class' is essentially made up of professionals and managers whose social position is based more on education, knowledge and skills, than on the ownership of capital. But it is divided by various factors including the sector of the economy, and the extent of managerial or supervisory authority (Lash and Urry, 1987: 162).

Because the class structure is changing, and increasing levels of skills are demanded by the labour market, there is a tendency for some children of working-class parents to move into routine non-manual or service class positions. British evidence, which probably applies to New Zealand as well, indicates that increased social mobility is more a reflection of a changing class structure than of a more widespread increase in social fluidity (Marshall, Newby, Rose and Vogler, 1988). Indeed, the 1990 New Zealand Election Study (NZES) indicates that having a parent who was a wage worker was a significant predictor of Labour voting, whereas being a wage earner oneself was not! (Vowles and Aimer, 1993: 36). A form of class voting thus appears to survive, one generation removed. Meanwhile, of all occupational categories, farmers are those most prone to cast a vote for the party that represents their interests, indicating a remaining strength in one aspect of class voting for the National Party.

Indeed, the strength of National versus Labour party control, electorate by electorate, still reflects traditional urban-rural cleavages which remain remarkably potent. There is a very high correlation between the partisanship of electorates and a petty bourgeois variable, the percentage of employers in the adult population (which tends also to correlate with rurality). The more National, the more employers there are; the more Labour, the fewer (Vowles, 1989; Vowles and Aimer, 1993: 28). Detailed analysis indicates that this is not a true 'contextual' effect, which would imply that where people live is an important predictor of their voting choice. If it is, the effects are very small. More likely, it is due to a combination of the effects of aggregation which hides a significant variance among individuals, and the effects of other social characteristics of individuals who tend to live in particular electorates (Bae, 1991; Vowles and Aimer, 1993: 36-37).

Another important voting choice is the decision to vote or not to vote, and class tends to have a bearing on this. Persons in manual wage-earning households were less likely to vote in 1990, although these effects are accounted for more indirectly by other class-related variables such as income, ethnicity and housing status (Vowles and Aimer, 1993: 55-56). Over the longer term, and despite a recovery in the turnout rate between 1975 and 1984, Figure 12.2 shows that non-voting has tended to increase in New Zealand, a tendency which is more pronounced if measured on an adult population base, thus filtering out variations in the effectiveness of electoral enrolment (Nagel, 1988). The comparison of data from the 1963 and 1981 elections indicates that it is distributed across all social groups. Non-voting had become only a little more associated with class variables in 1990 than it had been in 1963 and 1981 (Vowles, 1994).

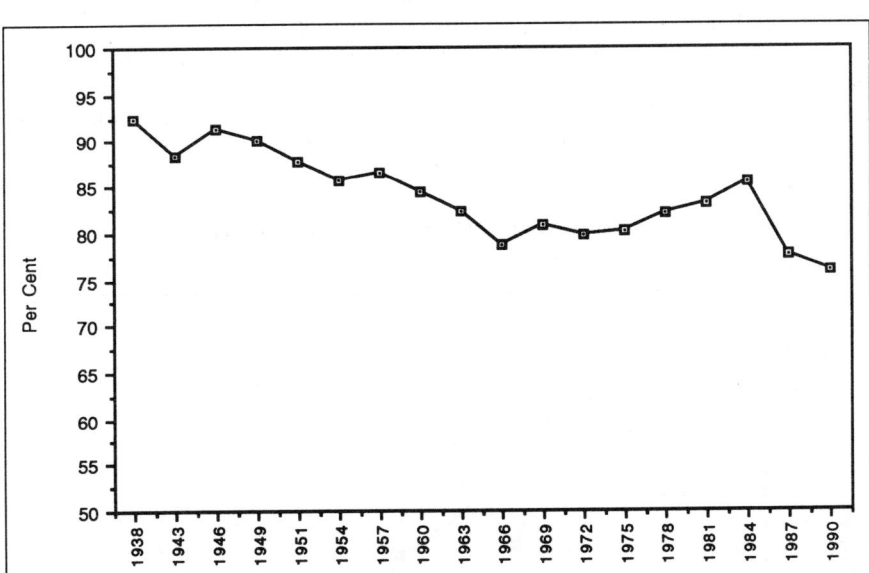

Figure 12.2
Election Participation in New Zealand 1938-1990

Location in the public sector has little or no association with voting choice for the major parties but was a modest predictor of a Green vote in 1990. In 1990, after controlling for class, ethnicity, education and income, union members were 12 per cent more likely than non-unionists to vote Labour (Vowles, 1992b: 110-111). Housing tenure was of little or no relevance in 1987 (Gold, 1989), but had modest influence in 1990. The receipt of multiple benefits was, as expected, mildly associated with a vote for Labour in 1990 (Vowles and Aimer, 1993: 36-37).

While the effects of social structure on voting choice have both diminished and become more complex, they have not disappeared. Neither has class dealignment had a great effect on the electoral success of the two major parties and the survival of a party system erected on the basis of the class conflicts of the period 1912 to the early 1920s. Much of this stasis is due to the electoral system with its excessive threshold against new political forces. Falling turnout fails to have a substantial influence except at the margins, although over the long term, it is a signal that the party system itself may be in a process of dealignment. Figure 12.3 supports this thesis, placing voting support for the two main parties on a base of the age-eligible voting population. This builds in the accumulating and combined effects of support for minor parties, non-voting, and a failure to enrol to vote, another indicator of declining political involvement. National and Labour may continue to dominate Parliament, but do so from an increasingly narrow popular base.

Where electoral systems are proportional, new political issues such as those brought into the political arena by new social movements based on environmental, peace, and other such issues can be effectively expressed through the formation of

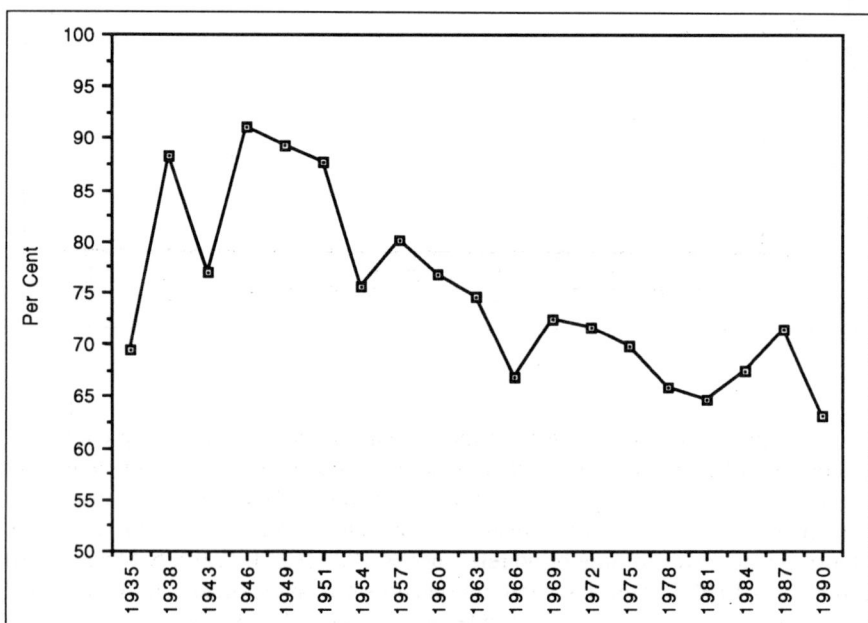

Figure 12.3
Votes for Labour and National as % Adult Population

new political parties, such as the Greens. With plurality or broadly similar electoral systems in both Australia and New Zealand, a combination of minor party discouragement and major party desire to expand voting coalitions has permitted relatively successful attempts to incorporate the 'New Politics' into the existing party system (McAllister and Vowles, 1994). Thus, after 1975 Labour sought to appeal to voters with anti-nuclear, environmental, and feminist sympathies and thus to expand into a voting coalition beyond a shrinking working-class, many of whose members were also attracted by the populism of the Muldoon-led National Party.

Until 1984 there were signs of a partial realignment of the party system, with class voting declining and voting participation increasing. But after 1984 the fourth Labour Government followed a strategy based on economic policies normally associated with the right, losing further working-class votes. In 1987 it was able to make up the deficit with a combination of New Politics voters concerned with peace, feminist and environmental issues, and economic liberals who applauded and supported the policies of Minister of Finance, Roger Douglas (Vowles, 1990), but voting turnout nevertheless fell dramatically. By 1990 Labour's coalition of the 1980s was in fragments.

Sociological explanations may provide a framework for class dealignment as an international phenomenon, although the different trade-off options and contexts in each country must be given attention in order to give agency and strategic action their due weight. In these terms, rather than changing class composition in itself, it is perhaps more convincing to identify party strategy in response to social change and the consequent effects on voter loyalties as the stronger explanation for the new sociology of electoral choice in New Zealand. Evidence consistent with the effects of party strategy on attitudes associated with voting support emerges when voters are separated out into those who subjectively identify as working-class or middle-class. Controlling for other aspects of social structure, in 1990, working-class identifiers were more likely to vote Labour the older they were, while the opposite held for middle-class identifiers. Labour's electoral strategy of moving beyond its working-class roots is likely to have had a long term impact on voting choice, working indirectly through the class identifications of those younger voters most affected (Vowles, 1992b: 114).

If the strategy of a party's political leaders can shift the foundations of its electoral support, one might also expect the composition of party membership to alter in the same direction, to become more middle class. However, party members have more opportunities than voters to act effectively in the process. Voters opposed to a party strategy can either vote for another party or not vote at all, although they also have the option of joining the party to seek to influence its strategy. Members opposed to a leadership strategy meanwhile can act in at least two different ways. A 'voice' option involves pressure within the party through policy promotion and candidate selection. An 'exit' option involves resignation, thus helping to reduce the party's financial and organisational resources. It may also involve the setting up of a new party to contest the old party's political monopoly of its traditional constituency. Some members may choose one option, and others the alternative. In 1983, the National Party found itself in this position of internal dissent and external challenge from the New Zealand Party, and again in 1993, with the formation of Winston Peters' New Zealand First Party; and in 1988 and 1989, the Labour Party faced a similar potential crisis.

Studies of party conference delegates in 1983 and 1988 were timed fortuitously to explore possible change over that period, and provide data profiling the social composition of active members of the National and Labour parties (Vowles, 1985; Miller and Vowles, 1989; Vowles, 1992c).[2] Consistent with earlier studies (Gustafson, 1976), the Labour Party in 1983 was already, to a large extent, a middle-class party. Nevertheless, union officials were 14 per cent of delegates and blue-collar workers 16 per cent. By contrast, blue-collar workers made up only three per cent of the National delegates. The National Conference contained no union officials at all. Members of unions and other organisations representing wage and salary earners provided 62 per cent of Labour's delegates compared to 27 per cent of National's. In 1988, the few notable changes included an increase in union officials at Labour's conference to 21 per cent, which was mainly due to the smaller size of the 1988 conference because of a steep decline in branch membership.

Membership of one or more business organisations rose marginally among Labour delegates to six per cent, but the comparable National figure was 29 per cent. Attitudes to unions were very different between the two sets of delegates. Three-quarters of National delegates expressed opinions which ascribed the worst motives to trade union leaders. The proportion of farmers among National conference delegates increased from 23 to 30 per cent from 1983 to 1988. Employers and the self-employed (at 46 per cent) were heavily over-represented among National delegates. National's role as a party representing bourgeois and petty bourgeois values and interests is confirmed by the data. Employers and the self-employed were under-represented in the Labour conference, but public sector employees substantially overrepresented.

These findings indicate that the composition of Labour's active membership did not become more middle-class over the period of the fourth Labour Government; indeed, there are hints of a movement in the other direction. As a social formation with an organisational life, an ethos, and an ideology, a political party can apparently resist tendencies towards a changing membership consistent with a new leadership strategy.

Data from the 1987 election and the 1988 conference surveys can be put together to summarise the relations between active party membership, voter profiles and the class structure. Table 12.1 employs Goldthorpe's neo-Weberian classification which puts the data in a form which is theoretically grounded and also comparable with the

British literature (Goldthorpe and Hope, 1974; Goldthorpe *et al.*, 1980; Heath, Jowell, and Curtice, 1983). All respondents are classified on the basis of male household heads.

Table 12.1
Active Party Members 1988, Voters 1987,
and the New Zealand Class Structure 1987

Class	Labour		All electors	National	
	Members	Voters		Voters	Members
Service Class	63	33	33	35	50
Routine Non-manual	10	17	19	21	6
Petty Bourgeois	7	11	12	16	40
Supervisors/Technicians	4	7	7	7	1
Workers	17	32	29	21	3
Total	349	383	945	342	334

Sources: Voters, the 1987 NZES; Conference Delegates, the 1988 Party Conference Survey.

The service class is relatively evenly split between the two sets of voters and is the largest section in each party conference. Its greater dominance in the Labour Party conference is, to a large extent, due to the classification of union officials as service-class members. But 80 per cent of Labour delegates were either workers or in the service class. Ninety per cent of National delegates are in the service or petty bourgeois classes. As expected, differences between the two sets of voters are minor except for the under-representation of workers among National voters.

The two parliamentary parties tend to reinforce the characteristics of party activists, albeit in a more extreme form. An MP is, of course, a member of the service-class by definition, but data on former occupations indicates that over 70 per cent of Labour's 1984 caucus had service-class occupations before entering Parliament, just over five per cent were working class, and just under four per cent were union officials (Gustafson, 1989: 211). Combined, workers and union officials rose from 9 to 14 per cent of the Labour caucus after the 1987 election, and 21 per cent of the much depleted 1990 caucus were former union employees. The National caucus, like the National conference, is a mixture of the service class and the petty bourgeoisie, the latter group mostly represented by farmers (Gustafson, 1986: 241). In government, National's farmer MPs have provided as much as a third of the caucus; with National in opposition after 1984, the figure increased to nearly 50 per cent but after the 1990 election it fell to 21 per cent reflecting National's capture of numerous urban electorates. But in National's post-1990 Cabinet, at least eight out of the 20 Ministers were farmers.

During the 1980s, as class has become at best a minor element in predicting voters' choices between the two major parties, ethnicity and gender have been more clearly identified as theoretically significant elements of the social structure. The alliance between Labour and the Ratana movement in the 1930s was cemented by the urbanisation of the Maori. Maori became concentrated heavily in the urban unionised working class, and Labour gained a political monopoly over the four seats set aside for Maori electors. Immigration into New Zealand of other Polynesian peoples was also disproportionately channelled into working-class occupations. Thus, on class grounds alone, it was highly likely that both indigenous and immigrant Polynesians would tend to support the Labour Party. As class has faded as a predictor of voting choice, Polynesians appear to have continued to support Labour, while the Pakeha working-class has become more evenly split politically. Meanwhile, the proportion of Maori in the voting age population has grown significantly, to about 10 per cent in 1990. In 1990, Maori and other Polynesians were less likely to vote National than for other parties, but no more likely to vote Labour once controls for other aspects of social structure were applied. Labour's dominance of the Maori vote has also been challenged by Mana Motuhake, a Maori party founded in 1980 to promote Maori culture and self-determination, which became part of the Alliance of minor parties with NewLabour, the Greens, the Democrats, and the Liberal Party in 1992. In 1993, three of the four minor party MPs elected were Maori, and Labour lost Northen Maori and Central Auckland to minor parties.

Gender equality has also become a major theme in New Zealand politics since the 1970s. While both parties have sought to meet demands for change, Labour was the most active in promoting pay equity and in the formation of a Ministry of Women's Affairs. In the Parliament elected in 1987, Labour had 11 women MPs to National's three, and in 1990, each major party had 8 women members. With 16 per cent of its MPs being women, New Zealand has the highest level of female participation in a legislature of any English-speaking country with a plurality electoral system. Within the Labour Party the female proportion of active members rose from a third to almost a half between 1983 and 1988.

Despite Labour's greater attention to women's issues, there is little evidence that women are significantly more likely to vote Labour. The earliest surviving data from 1963 indicates a small but statistically significant gender gap with women more likely to favour National than Labour (Vowles, 1993). From the 1980s some data indicates an equally minor tendency for women to favour Labour, but at levels too low for statistical significance and with no controls applied (Julian, 1992). At the 1981, 1987 and 1990 general elections, there were no statistically significant gender gaps in support for the major parties (Vowles, 1993). However, there is evidence that women's voting choices are more volatile than those of men, being more weakly rooted in social structure (Vowles, 1992b). Between elections, women tend to be more politically uncommitted than men, which may account for the more substantial gender gaps reported in polling between elections (Vowles and Aimer, 1993:177).

The relation between structural influences and political parties in New Zealand is complex, and weaker than many sociologists might expect. Regional differences in political support are relatively minor[3], and urban-rural differences overlap with class and have only limited independent effects. Ethnicity is a factor, but because Polynesians still form only a relatively small proportion of voters, the overall variance involved is also small. And a consideration of gender gives findings apparently opposite to those for class. Labour's strategy on gender is associated with changes in party membership and increasing caucus representation, but not with significant electoral effects.

The salience of class has decreased, although some voting behaviour, party membership and the electoral map still indicate remaining links between class and political choice. Party strategy has combined with broader social change to bring class voting to very low levels. Meanwhile, the dealignment of the party system further intensified during the 1980s, with increased volatility in voting choices, increasing levels of political non-commitment and new heights of support for minor parties in opinion polls (Vowles and Aimer, 1993: 217-218). Combined with the residual but eroding traditional political loyalties of voters, the institutional arrangements of the plurality electoral system had by the early 1990s been the most effective barrier against a political realignment which might otherwise recast the social foundations of party politics of New Zealand, reverse the trend toward political nonparticipation, and transform the nature of New Zealand politics.

Notes

1. Details of both the 1987 and the 1990 NZES can be found in Vowles and Aimer, 1993: 228-230.
2. The 1988 Party Conference survey was designed by Raymond Miller and Jack Vowles, and conducted by post after each conference. The co-operation and assistance of the parties involved is gratefully acknowledged. Funding was provided by the University of Auckland Research Committee, and further support by the Department of Political Studies, University of Auckland, and the Department of Politics, University of Waikato. Bridget McPhail's assistance with the questionnaire preparation is also gratefully acknowledged. For more details of the study, see Vowles, 1992c.
3. Regionalism is not discussed here, as New Zealand politics is national rather than parochial in focus, with swings between parties normally roughly parallel in all electorates and regions (Chapman, 1963), the 1981 election being the best documented exception for quite specific reasons (Bean, 1982). While party support varies by

region in New Zealand (Bean, 1991; Johnston, 1992), recent evidence suggests it does so largely on the basis of the socio-economic differences between regions. After allowing for those effects in 1987 and 1990, what regional effects that remained were inconsistent (Bae, 1991).

Further Reading

Bean, C., 1988, 'Class and Party in the Anglo-American Democracies: The Case of New Zealand in Perspective', *British Journal of Political Science*, 18: 303-321.

Holland, M. (ed.), 1992, *Electoral Behaviour in New Zealand*, Auckland, Oxford University Press.

Vowles, J., and Aimer, P., 1993, *Voters' Vengeance: the 1990 Election in New Zealand and the Fate of the Fourth Labour Government*, Auckland, Auckland University Press.

Vowles, J., 1991, 'Party Strategies and Class Composition: The New Zealand Labour and National Parties in 1988 and Beyond', *New Zealand Sociology*, 7(1).

Vowles, J., 1994, 'Dealignment and Demobilisation? Non-voting in New Zealand 1938-1990', *Australian Journal of Political Science*, 29(1).

13 Mass Media

Brennon Wood and Steve Maharey

Introduction

The mass media – print, radio, television, recorded music, film, advertising – have only recently begun to receive significant sociological attention in New Zealand. The many books dealing with New Zealand society reveal very little about them. Only slightly better results are gained from a survey of the *Australian and New Zealand Journal of Sociology* and *New Zealand Sociology*. This situation is not confined to sociology alone. As Farnsworth (1984) suggests, this neglect of the mass media is due to the educational system and to the beliefs of those who decide what should and should not be studied. The media sit uncomfortably within the traditional system because they raise questions best dealt with by an interdisciplinary approach. In addition, they are usually thought of as entertainment and therefore unworthy of serious study.

Over the last few years, the media have begun to attract more attention. Indeed, a sudden surge of interest is signalled by the rapidly expanding number of publications, courses and qualifications emerging at all levels of the education system, from primary schools through to universities and polytechnics. Study of the media, however, is a relatively new feature of our intellectual life. The field has grown so rapidly that it has proved haphazard and disorganised.

The emergence of media studies is a fascinating process for sociologists. The media offer new and important avenues of study. They offer an opportunity to participate in what Lumley and O'Shaughnessey (1985), following Bourdieu, call the formation of a distinct 'intellectual field'. Those interested in media studies have to mark out the field's central concerns, theories, concepts and methods. Such a process is not straightforward. It involves a 'struggle' over the definition of what media studies should be. The mass media are a diverse array of apparently quite different things. To begin with, we need some definition of the field. The main purpose of this chapter is to outline the definition offered by sociology. If media studies in general is rapidly growing but unsystematic, then sociology can make a valuable contribution by helping to organise the field of study.

Sociology approaches the media by placing them within a wider social context. The mass media are organised communications bringing together people from diverse walks of life, people who might otherwise remain largely unknown to each other. This is obviously a rough definition that leaves many questions unanswered. Indeed, it is less an answer than a way of asking sociological questions. The key issue is the focus on social organisation. This definition implies that how we understand the media depends on what we think social organisation is. A definition of the media, then, is also a definition of social life. Sociologists study 'media society'. They seek to understand mass communications by embedding them in the wider society to which they belong.

To understand New Zealand media, we need to understand New Zealand society at large. While that may seem a daunting task, the equation can also be reversed. Investigating the media is one way of finding out more about the society in which we live. Ultimately, this is why they are worth studying. The media are more than diversionary entertainment; they are not an 'escape' from important social issues. Rather, they are closely woven into the fabric of our collective life.

The Media Matter

The mass media's prominence in New Zealand culture cannot be denied (see *New Zealand Official Yearbook*, 1992). For those who can spare the time, 50-60 hours of television are provided every day by TVNZ and TV3. Another 60 hours of daily television are available to subscribers of Sky's three channels. There are also more than 130 radio stations to listen to. There are 29 daily newspapers and 104 (usually weekly) 'community newspapers' to read. Over 2,300 magazines are regularly available in New Zealand. Advertisements, moreover, are hard to avoid, not least because of the $1,500 million spent producing and circulating them. It is not just the sheer volume of media output that is striking. The mass media are very dynamic. Their output is rapidly growing, both in amount and type. Every few months brings new developments and promises of future possibilities. Among the recent arrivals in New Zealand broadcasting, for example, are some 30 iwi-based radio stations, 'pay television' by satellite, regional television, Education TV and TAB television.

As the mass media grow in volume and scope, they insinuate themselves ever more deeply into all aspects of our daily lives. From the radio alarm in the morning to the car radio, from advertising at the indoor cricket complex to magazines on the coffee table and the videos we watch – our lives have become infused with the media in ways we have yet to fully understand (Masterman, 1986). One thing, however, is clear. In modern societies, the mass media have become increasingly important.

In part, this is due to the fragmented way people live. People experience the world within narrow boundaries. They move from home to work, from the sports club to a friend's house, and directly encounter only a tiny amount of what goes on in the world around them. Modern life is fragmented by its emphasis on private experience and by a complex division of labour which separates and specialises the various things people do. This division of labour, however, does more than just pull people apart. Paradoxically, it also draws them together by creating far-flung interdependencies. This is why the mass media are important in modern life. They provide glimpses of the wider world. While everyday experience is narrow and fragmented, people nevertheless know of an enormous array of events because of the media. The media, then, are pivotal to any wider sense of collective life – a sense of our town, our nation, our hemisphere, our planet.

This does not mean that the media merely inform people. The media *select* what people learn. It could not be otherwise. It is impossible for all experience to be delivered unedited to the radio, newspaper or television screen. Reality is too big. What is worth covering in the news and what should constitute entertainment must be chosen. The media must establish an agenda of issues and concerns. They must decide what is important and entertaining. These decisions, imposed by the necessity of selection, mean that the media cannot simply inform us about events. Events must be interpreted. Such interpretations are inevitable even in so-called factual areas such as the news. Along with information comes guidance on how to understand the surrounding world.

The America's Cup Challenge of 1986-87 exemplifies the importance of the media as it moulds people's understanding of events. Prior to the Royal New Zealand Yacht Squadron challenge, New Zealanders knew little of the event. Yet the success of the challenge, the organisers knew, depended on the willingness of the public to open their hearts and wallets. The campaign now stands as evidence of the role of mass communications in constructing reality.

> First there was the parade. According to Radio 89FM's news report, thousands of Aucklanders had lined Queen Street to cheer a procession of marching girls, celebrities and a pristine white yacht on the way to the waterfront where the boat would be launched. The reality as witnessed by several people that wet Saturday morning was something different. It rained non-stop during the parade. Marching girls in sodden uniforms and bedraggled hats could barely drag their company flags out of the gutter by the time they reached the bottom of Queen Street.... Brave shoppers peered out glumly from under umbrellas as the drivers of the convoy looked vainly for the 'cheering thousands' (O'Meagher, 1986:24).

From this contradictory beginning, the yacht challenge went from strength to strength. The campaign used a wide range of media – a song, a roadshow, advertising, merchandising – in the cause of producing a continuous flow of publicity. Relations with the media were astutely managed to ensure journalists always had something to write about and that the story had a positive angle. As the promoters pointed out, it would not have been possible to push the Cup had it not been a 'good product'. Kiwis taking on the world in yachts provided something people could 'get in behind'. What is important here is that without the media, the challenge would have had limited appeal.

There were critics. John Kennedy, editor of the *Tablet*, took exception to the way the media were openly being used to build 'a vast tide of nationalistic fervour', all in the cause of the rich sailing boats. But in the debate, the role of the media became secondary to any criticism of 'rich people at play'. In sociological terms, however, the America's Cup campaign clearly highlights the need for people to understand how the media select and construct 'reality'.

An ability to interpret how the media work will become more important in the years ahead. More and more of our everyday existence is being mediated through their various forms. The main campaigning of the 1987 General Election, for the first time, took place in the media. This was not just a case of politicians doing something and the media relaying what happened. Rather, campaigning was conducted as a series of media events. As Misa (1987:57) reported:

> Millions have been spent in the cause of mass persuasion as voters are targeted and bombarded with researched policies and professional packaging. Campaigns full of showbiz and razzmattazz have been carefully structured around The Leader and the 6:30 news. This is undoubtedly the most high pressure, image-conscious, television oriented and professionally-driven election campaign New Zealanders have ever seen.

In the six months prior to the 1987 Election, the fourth Labour Government was responsible for some $3.7 million spending on advertising by state departments and corporations. The subsequent National Government spent $2 million producing and publicising its June 1991 Budget (Rudd, 1992: 122).

This shift in the conduct of politics is not confined to New Zealand. Television is already the key element in any political campaign. It is therefore essential for voters to become adept at interpreting political campaigning in mass communications. Indeed, it is hard to overstress the increasing importance of media literacy. As the above examples show, people must learn how the media are used to shape perceptions. They must learn, not just *through* the media, but also *about* the media. Critical analysis of the media is something all people should be able to do. Education should develop skills to understand how the media make sense of the social world.

Theory of Media and Theory of Society

The media mould perceptions and are highly integrated with such significant events as the election of governments. It is important, then, to understand how they work. But how is this understanding to be reached? Just what are the mass media? A number of different things – newspapers or radio and television sets – first spring to mind. Such a common-sense definition is fair enough, but limited. A more useful definition focuses on the mass media as a communal 'flow' between people. They are social interactions, processes rather things.

Communication often seems to involve no more than using your mouth or ears, opening a newspaper or switching on the television. The media are so pervasive they are often taken for granted. Mass communication seems so easily done that there appears to be no problem here worth investigating. But communication is problematic. Although often taken for granted, it is nevertheless an achievement. Communication brings together or co-ordinates. One way of understanding this process, then, is to break it down into smaller pieces. The achievement lies in making these various parts hang together.

We can think of any communication as having three distinct parts. Corresponding by letter, for example, involves a writer, the words written down and a reader. This idea can be extended as a general model. Such a model has been influential in what are called 'communication studies', and is associated in particular with the work of Lasswell. According to Lasswell, all communication involves the following components:

Lasswell's model suggests that a sender relays a message along a channel to a receiver. Something may interfere and thus distort the message along the way. The sender may get feedback from the receiver and thus learn whether or not the message got through. This model has proved very popular, especially within complex organisations (such as big businesses) where the accuracy of information flows is seen as important. From a sociological point of view, however, it has many faults.

The Lasswell model is very abstract. It claims to describe all types of communication at all times and all places. It provides a formal model which applies to everything from love-letters exchanged by hand between individuals to the broadcasting of an Olympic Games to billions of people. That is, it cuts the media off from the particular contexts in which they make sense. This has some unfortunate results. The people involved are defined solely in terms of their place in an abstract process, as 'sender' and 'receiver'. Moreover, this is a model of 'pure' communication. The actual content of the message is largely irrelevant. The media are seen as empty channels through which a message passes, to be assessed only in terms of whether or not they allow it to get through 'undistorted'. For sociologists, such a formal approach is inadequate. The media can be understood only by being placed in the social context to which they belong. Accordingly, understanding mass communication requires a fuller picture of the people involved. 'Sender' and 'receiver' are two specialised roles among the many other roles that people hold as members of society. Just what is communicated is important. It cannot be judged against some pure model of an undistorted flow. Rather, the message and the media play an important part in actually constructing the interaction between communicators.

Like the Lasswell model, sociology approaches the media analytically. It also distinguishes between various parts of the communication process, so that how it works as a whole can be investigated. But once this process is placed in a social context, Lasswell's three components appear in a different light. They become less abstract and more socially situated. The 'message' is conceived as a *representation*, as something which makes sense of the world in a particular way that needs to be figured out. 'Receivers' are conceived as *audiences*, as groups made up of people with distinctive social backgrounds. 'Senders' are conceived as particular *institutions* which organise the production of mass communication. The remainder of this chapter sets out these three dimensions of the mass media in more detail. First, however, a little more is needed on the character of the sociological approach in general.

We cannot understand the media by artificially separating them from the other things that people do. Social processes bind these activities together. Our understanding of the mass media, then, must be sociological. A theory of the media must inevitably be a theory of society. Sociology, however, offers a number of competing views of society. These viewpoints underpin different theories of the media. While the range of sociological theory is considerable, it can be focused on the issue of *power*. Power is the ability of a group to define and enact its interests, often in opposition to others attempting to do the same. Accordingly, different theories of the media can be interpreted as different ideas about the distribution of power in society.

Structural functionalists argue that 'the media have an integrative role, maintaining consensus through reinforcing central values in a way which is beneficial to society' (Dutton, 1986: 2). A similar perspective is offered by liberal pluralists, who think that the media assist democracy by meeting the competing needs and interests of their consumers. These two theories are alike in that each interprets the media as part of a society which distributes power equitably. Alternatively, there are those who see power as unequally distributed. Some people oppress and exploit others. According to such a view of society, the media are a means of social control. For these sociologists, often members of Marxist or feminist schools, the media further the interests of ruling groups. They benefit such people as the capitalist class, city-dwellers, men, those of 'mature' age or the members of a particular ethnic group.

Interpretations of the media as means of social control can be divided into two basic types. There is the theory of domination, which holds that power is massively concentrated and that the media are at one with this system of total command. Theorists of hegemony, however, focus more on struggles for leadership. While social powers are unequal, domination is never total. Oppression and exploitation are always contested. Just who rules society is a matter of ongoing conflict. Accordingly, the media are not so much a tool of command as a place where leadership battles between unequal powers take place.

The point of view offered in this chapter is more in sympathy with the theory of hegemony than any other approach. The mass media participate in the inequalities which characterise all social life. Domination theories, however, argue for an overly simplistic connection between power and the media. Social relations are not rigid; they constantly change as groups struggle with each other. The media, then, are more than the tool of some ruling faction. Rather, they are sites of conflict between unequal groups.

Representing Reality

Each of the theories considered above offers a different interpretation of the culture communicated by mass media. For structural functionalists and liberal pluralists, the media operate within a society that evenly distributes power. Media content, they argue, reflects this situation. The media are a 'window' or a 'mirror'. Whilst they must selectively reconstruct reality, they do so in ways which are authentic to what is actually going on. The social control school advances a different interpretation. Media representations are inhibited. They are culture in the service of power inequalities; they are ideologies. Some people are able to shape media content in order to promote their own interests. The media support the most powerful groups by making sense of the world in a distorted or biased way. They provide only a partial picture of reality and, in so doing, attempt to overcome opposition from the less powerful. This can be seen by asking questions about who gets represented and who gets left out, about how things, people, events and relationships are portrayed (Hall, 1986). Answering such questions shows that far from providing a neutral 'window', the media present a particular image of society (see Media Women, 1988).

The two types of social control theory have distinctive ideas about how the media serve power. According to the theory of domination, mass media are the tools of those in control. They justify the rule of the dominant. The media, then, are largely passive. Consequently, the media speak with one voice, the voice of these dominant groups. The theory of hegemony interprets media content in a different way. The media neither 'reflect' the world nor transmit a 'dominant ideology'. They are not so much tools of domination as places where things are done. The media are caught up in battles for social leadership. Unequal powers contend with each other to define social reality and to get these definitions accepted. The media, then, speak in more than one voice. They make sense, not as some monolithic 'dominant ideology', but rather as a conflict-torn and inherently unstable 'hegemonic ideology'.

What the media produce can be understood as texts. Texts are complex representations of the world around us. We are used to thinking of books as texts because we have been taught to acknowledge that a book has been produced by an author. We have been taught the skills to find out how books convey meaning. Books use language to draw on shared understandings of how the world works. Television, radio, newspapers and other mass media require the use of similar skills. These texts also draw on shared understandings. For sociologists, this sharing is organised by social conventions or rules, which in media studies are commonly called *codes*. How a mass communication is coded determines its meaning. It is these codes which produce a sense of the world in which we live. This is easily illustrated by thinking of the way television shows are introduced. The opening images combine music with rapid cutting from one shot to another to tell us whether we are about to see adventure, romance, comedy or current affairs. These various pictures and sounds are put together according to codes of what is meaningful in our society. The codes enable a programme to convey messages.

Those who work in the media, consciously or unconsciously, use codes to produce what we see and hear. The language they use, for example, actively constructs social reality. Any word has both literal and implied or connotative meanings. Take the words 'girl' and 'woman'. Commentators' preference for calling adult female athletes 'girls' has provoked a good deal of controversy in New Zealand sports broadcasting. Critics have complained that this is demeaning. Adult male athletes, they point out, are always referred to as men rather than boys. To many, this may seem a trivial issue. But in the context of wider efforts by women to gain recognition in a world constructed around the interests of men, it has considerable significance. In choosing the word 'girl' or 'woman', broadcasters draw upon shared understandings within our society which provide quite different ways of talking about the same people. The experiences of females can be situated within one of two different ways of representing reality. Which of these two alternatives is chosen is a matter of ongoing conflict.[1]

The concept of a code is valuable because it forces us to acknowledge that all media *re*-present the world. They are not transparent windows through which people simply see whatever is going on. This applies as much to the news as to television comedies and radio plays. From the opening to the closing sequence, the news is a particular construction of the day's events. New Zealand television news and current affairs journalists take the codes of balance, impartiality and objectivity seriously (Loader and Bosshard, 1987). They use many conventions to suggest that what they show is indeed the truth. The presenters talk straight to camera and wear middle-of-the-road clothes. They use phrases like 'Many New Zealanders think ...' to give the impression that what they say is of concern to everyone, despite the fact that they have no way of knowing what people generally think. An authoritative tone of voice is required of newsreaders, and those who do not measure up are removed. Perhaps most importantly, television takes us to the scene being discussed so we can 'see for ourselves' what is going on. While considerable effort goes into making news and current affairs look 'the way things are', these programmes are actually constructed views of some events of the day.

This may come as a surprise to those who regard the news as presenting the facts pure and simple. Indeed, it is the appearance of immediate 'truth' which makes the news such a powerful ideology. Codes like balance and objectivity are designed precisely to create the sense that we are seeing the world as it is, without the interference of some particular point of view. By concealing their own constructedness, such representations make some things appear natural and others alien or invisible. The media have choices to make and will usually decide upon what they consider to be the middle ground – the most acceptable view. After all, the media are guided by notions of neutrality and lack of bias; the majority view is the one to take. But in so doing, the media reinforce a particular world view by making it appear natural and unquestionable. Of late, the media have been made to realise just how tenuous this hold on reality is. Maori spokespeople, for example, have powerfully challenged the way they are depicted, or ignored. As a result, there have been small but significant changes in Maori media representation (see Fox, 1988; McRae, 1986-87; Spoonley and Hirsh, 1990).

The central issue here is not overt bias. While media bias is a problem, it is often easy to spot. It is important to move away from the simple idea that the media offer a 'false' picture, a picture of reality as it is not. A more useful approach holds that the sense of reality conveyed by the media is produced through the conflict of alternative definitions. Rather than bias, it is these battles for representation which should be the target of sociological study. As Bonney and Wilson (1983: 11) argue:

> A penetrating analysis of media outputs [concentrates] ... on the way they represent reality and the complex relations between those representations and the surrounding social, political, cultural and economic climate.

The media construct a particular viewpoint, but they do so through 'complex relations'. They operate within a 'surrounding climate' of ongoing conflicts over how to make sense of the world. The importance of this wider social context applies not only to the interpretation of media content. It also extends to how we conceive the role of audiences.

Audiences

When it comes to studying the audience of mass communications, the importance of the wider social context must not be forgotten. As discussed earlier, communication models such as that provided by Lasswell cut the media off from the society around them. This has some rather unfortunate results in terms of interpreting the role of audiences. The debate about the effects of violence in the media provides a useful illustration of this point.

It is often said violent acts directly result from individuals consuming violent material. The (usually implicit) theory is that the media have modified an individual's behaviour to the extent of causing a violent act to be committed.[2] The wider public has proved so concerned by the influence of media violence that of all the areas of social science research, this is the one with a good deal of financial support. The results, however, have not been very clear cut. Research by the Mental Health Foundation of New Zealand found that the correlation between television violence and a tendency to engage in violent behaviour does exist. Like most researchers, the Foundation found it necessary to qualify these conclusions. It acknowledged that boys who are inclined to violence for other reasons are most likely to be affected. It also identified a range of other causes, such as racial and social inequalities, economic injustice, interpersonal problems and parental behaviour (Mental Health Foundation, 1984; Barwick, 1990). Media violence is a matter of increasing public concern. The ambivalence of research results does not mean that television has no effect on behaviour. However, it does imply that we need to carefully think about the relationship between the media and their audiences.

How, then, should the relationship between media and audiences be understood? We must begin with the idea that people are active users of the media. The theory usually associated with this idea is the 'uses and gratifications' approach. This has produced some interesting research showing that mass communications can be used to satisfy a wide range of needs. Studies of radio, for example, report that listeners find it 'takes my mind off things, is like a friend calling in, helps keep me cheerful, keeps my mind active, helps keep me going, allows me to get involved' (Lewis and Pearlman, 1986). Audiences are not only active users; they also use the media in different ways. The people who make up audiences differ greatly in their reactions to the same mass communication. Some accept the programme, others reject it; some ignore it because they are too busy, while others switch it off or do other things while watching. On the basis of such findings, many researchers have concluded that it is not so much a matter of what the media do to people as what people do with the media. Contemporary thinking argues that the media help form people's views, while stressing that interpersonal experience provides a basis for action independent of the media. The media and their audiences interact with each other.

The codes which organise media representations reach out to audiences, inviting them to adopt a certain point of view. This process is called 'positioning the audience'. It is one of the most important ways in which the media shape perceptions. Televised sport clearly illustrates this construction of a viewpoint. As Bassett (1983: 9) notes:

> Many judgements go into shaping 'live' television coverage of sports events. Not only are the images that finally appear on our screens only a sample selected from those available, but other decisions are made by camera operators about what is of interest in the game as the action unfolds before them .... In rugby, one operates from the 'ideal spectator's' position at the halfway line. Other cameras are located on the side-line and at the ends of the field. Additional cameras may roam the crowd seeking interesting shots to fill moments of inaction in the game.

The types of camera shots which are selected put together a point of view from which the game can be followed, known about and enjoyed. This position, then, promises the viewer knowledge and pleasure. Bassett argues, for example, that the 'look' of televised rugby celebrates strength, dexterity and more-or-less controlled violence. Such programming positions audiences behind the values of an aggressive masculinity. It is through such positioning, then, that the media mould audience perceptions.

By positioning audiences, the mass media shape the way people get access to the world. Media representations are *encoded* with a certain point of view. However, this is not to say that audiences must passively adopt the encoded point of view. As Hall (1980) argues, audiences actively make sense of, or *decode*, media messages. The mass communications' audience is made up of many different types of social groups. These groups can interpret the message in their own ways.

Televised rugby, for example, may be encoded to sustain aggressively masculine points of view. But Star's (1992: 136) work suggests that New Zealand women make 'complex and often contradictory responses' to such sports coverage. While the 'fans' affirm 'their men', feminists can enjoy these pictures by identifying and resisting the views they convey. 'Rugby viewing', Star (1992: 135) points out, 'can be a lesbian occasion' which takes pleasures from the spectacle of male bodies in action. Viewers with different gender identities, then, can furnish their own decodings. In a similar vein, Zwaga (1992) found that responses to television depend on the flow of domestic activities in the household. Television is 'a background resource from which viewers tune in and tune out' (Zwaga, 1992: 124). In general, for example, audiences find advertisements neither pleasurable nor informative, and so routinely ignore them. Such revelations have understandably provoked concern from the advertising-dependent media. Sociologically, they are of interest because they demonstrate the extent of audience activity. Audiences do not sit open-mouthed, passively absorbing whatever the media show them. Rather, they participate in mass communication in terms of their own particular social contexts.

Hall's encoding/decoding model provides the basis for a fuller understanding of the relationship between the media and their audiences. The media mould perceptions by offering a constructed point of view. But how do audiences fit into this process? Do they actively use the media to organise their own sense of the world? Or do other people use the media to shape audience perceptions as they want? Theories of domination tend to think the latter. Theories of hegemony, however, point to a more complex interplay in which the audience plays an active part.

Private and Public Ownership

Most media research has focused on what the media produce and its effects on audiences. This undoubtedly reflects the concerns of the general public. However, more recently researchers have begun to look closely at the process through which mass communications are produced. Indeed, some have gone so far as to argue that until more is understood about this process, any further study of effects should cease (Barratt, 1986). As there is not the space in this chapter to explore all aspects of media production, the following discussion concentrates on one area of particular concern in New Zealand today – the issue of the relationship between private and public property (Wood, 1984).

The institutions which produce mass communications fit into a wider social context, the society they share with their audiences. There are two main power bases in this society. There is economic power, which in New Zealand is primarily a matter of private property. And there is political power, organised as a democratic state in possession of public property. The mass media are embedded in society through their relations with the institutions of private and public property. The mass media can be privately owned and run for monetary gain along capitalist lines, as is the case with newspapers. Or they can be organised as a 'public service' within the representative state, as has historically characterised broadcasting in this country. The merits of private and public ownership have become an issue of heated conflict in New Zealand. As a result of these conflicts, the mass media have become increasingly influenced by the profit motive. This is particularly so in broadcasting, though important trends have also taken place in the ownership of print media. These developments have given rise to a series of debates about the impact of commercialism upon mass communications.

Any understanding of the media must include the notion that they are commercial businesses. This is often difficult for people to understand, those who work in the media industry included. It is often thought that the media are something special, a 'fourth estate' which emphasises truth, neutrality and impartiality. This is taken not just as a worthy aspiration but as a matter of fact. Such a view ties in well with the liberal pluralist position. Liberal pluralists think of society as a complex of competing groups and interests, none of them predominant all of the time. Given that society is seen as a free-wheeling plurality of powers, there is no particular group to which the media can belong. There is no ruling group which the mass media serve. Media organisations are seen as bounded systems, enjoying an important degree of autonomy from the state, political parties and institutionalised pressure groups. Control of the media is said to be in the hands of a self-reliant managerial élite who give considerable independence to media professionals.

If the media are autonomous from other social powers, then other parts of society are also autonomous from the media. This is the case, for example, with the audience. For liberal pluralists, a basic symmetry exists between media institutions and their audiences. As McQuail (1977: 91) puts it, the 'relationship is generally entered into voluntarily and on apparently equal terms'. Liberal pluralists, then, tend to espouse ideas of 'consumer sovereignty'. Audiences are seen as capable of manipulating the media in an infinite variety of ways according to their prior needs and dispositions. They have access to what Halloran calls 'the plural values of society', enabling them to 'conform, accommodate, challenge or reject' whatever they are told (Gurevitch *et al.*, 1982: 1).

Liberal pluralists emphasise the media's autonomy from the rest of society. According to the social control point of view, however, power is not so equitably distributed. Some groups rule over others to further their own interests. The institutions of public and private ownership reveal that the media are not autonomous from other sectors of society. Rather, the influence of commercialism shows that they are organised by an unequal distribution of economic and political power.

When we relate the media to their wider social context, we must treat them as businesses which stay afloat because they make a dollar. In New Zealand, newspapers are privately owned, while broadcasting is divided between private and public ownership. All, however, are constrained by commercial imperatives. The media must be treated as commodity-selling businesses because they depend on advertising dollars. Public broadcasting may get a licence fee, but this covers only a small percentage of running costs.[3] Like newspapers, television and radio live off advertising. They must be attractive to advertisers; they have to deliver audiences to whom advertisers want to sell something. Much of what goes on in the media is therefore influenced by commercial considerations. Moreover, during the last 30 or so years, New Zealand mass communications have become increasingly commercialised.

Historically, newspaper owners have not always been preoccupied with the search for profits. Until the late 1800s the press was primarily concerned with campaigning on particular political issues. But the commercial motive increased in prominence around the turn of the century and has remained so ever since. Moreover, since the 1960s the pattern of press ownership has changed dramatically. The number of independently owned newspapers has declined. The most common pattern is now that of 'group newspapers' run by large corporations. Consequently, the scope of competition has drastically narrowed. Two companies, Wilson and Horton Ltd and Independent Newspapers Ltd, now monopolise the newspaper market in this country. This trend has been accompanied by the growing involvement of foreign capital. Independent Newspapers Ltd, for example, is half-owned by the multinational media tycoon, Rupert Murdoch.

Over recent years, then, the powers of private property have been significantly concentrated in the New Zealand press. Newspaper companies have been transformed by the increasing dominance of commercial motives (Day, 1990; McGregor, 1992). The same can be said even more emphatically of broadcast media. Public ownership has always figured prominently in New Zealand radio and television. From the 1930s the state became the monopoly broadcaster, driving all private operators from the field. Broadcasting was not so much a matter of profiting from market demand as of providing a 'public service' to meet the needs of citizens. It is important to remember, however, that most of the revenue for these state-owned media came by way of advertising dollars. Radio and television were not completely immunised from commercial motives. This compromise between public and private property proved unstable and resulted in recurrent conflict. Over the last 30 or so years, it has broken down, so that commercial motives are now ascendant.

Private capital made a 'piratical' entrance in the form of Radio Hauraki in 1966. Since then, its scope has rapidly expanded. This has been made easier by government policies of deregulation and privatisation, aimed at increasing the role of competition in broadcasting. The late 1980s were watershed years. The Ministry of Commerce was established and placed in charge of broadcasting policy. Frequencies were sold by auction to the highest bidder, leading to a meteoric expansion in the number of privately-owned radio stations. The franchise for a third television channel was sold to a private operator, whose major current owners are Canwest and Westpac. 'Pay TV' appeared in 1990 with the initiation of Sky satellite transmission. The increased presence of overseas companies has been made easier by the 1991 Broadcasting Amendment Act, which abolished all restrictions on foreign ownership.

Increasing commercialism has also been a marked feature of the state-owned media. In 1988, Television New Zealand and Radio New Zealand were set up as

'State Owned Enterprises', required by law to have a commercial orientation. RNZ has since endured protracted financial difficulties. The National Government has recently ordered the privatisation of its commercial stations. TVNZ, on the other hand, has made the SOE transition much more effectively, although with a sharp reduction in staff levels. It is now a diversified corporation consisting of stand-alone 'profit centres' and subsidiary companies. Along with a number of North American and Canadian companies, TVNZ is a substantial owner (24 per cent) of Clear Communications Ltd, Telecom's major competitor. It is directly involved in 'pay TV' through its 16 per cent shareholding in Sky Network Television Ltd (whose majority shareholder is a North American consortium). Moreover, TVNZ is developing local services in Fiji and Western Samoa. In 1992 it became an independent satellite operator, providing programmes to the Cook Islands, Nauru, Nuie, Vanuatu and other Pacific islands. It recently joined a consortium (including North American, Singapore and Hong Kong-based companies) to establish Asia Business News, a satellite channel for South East Asia. TVNZ has also entered into numerous co-production deals with overseas media companies, including U.S. cable operators and NHK of Japan.

Deregulation and privatisation have increased the role of market demand in New Zealand broadcasting. Government policies, however, have also maintained some commitment to public controls and priorities. The 1989 Broadcasting Act, for example, set up two new organisations, the Broadcasting Standards Authority and the Broadcasting Commission. The BSA hears complaints and applies sanctions. It produces an expanding set of *Codes of Broadcasting Practice for Radio and Television*. It has also commissioned research (notably on television violence and alcohol advertising). The Broadcasting Commission, now called New Zealand On Air, administers the public broadcasting fee. NZOA is charged 'to reflect and develop New Zealand identity and culture' by promoting local content programming in general, and minority group and Maori programming in particular. Its support is most evident in the expansion of Maori radio and in the emergence of a Maori news service, Mana Maori Media. These significant developments, of course, are not solely due to actions by NZOA.

Commercialism, then, has not meant abandoning all public controls. Government policies have promoted social as well as market objectives. As the Ministry of Women's Affairs (1988) has suggested, the new broadcasting system attempts both to allow the market to operate and to maintain a public 'safety net' to ensure that important but unprofitable responsibilities are not forgotten. New Zealand broadcasting remains a mixed system, a compromise between private and public property. Market concerns, however, are still on the advance. In 1993, for example, the BSA lost control of broadcast advertising, with its powers passing to the industry-run Advertising Standards Authority. NZOA often attempts to meet its objectives in a way that satisfies commercial interests as well, such as by helping fund production of the 'Shortland Street' soap opera. It allocates small amounts of money compared to the advertising dollar and has no control of programming decisions.

In general, media commercialism is on the rise, in broadcasting just as in print. Both cases, moreover, show that profit motives have brought large, multinational corporations into the field. These developments have resulted from and generated considerable debate. Though the debate has covered numerous issues, it has focused on questions about the appropriate form of media ownership. Those in favour of public property argue that the media have responsibilities which are neglected by profit-seeking markets. Their opponents, however, claim that the market can be relied upon to organise mass communication. If there is an audience of sufficient size, then the media will address their concerns (Bailey, 1986). The debate goes on. Just how compatible are public and private ownership of the media? Can their objectives be reconciled? What is the right 'mix' of commercialism and public service? Does the current system achieve this? The various conflicts and debates that have accompanied media commercialisation suggest otherwise.

There has been recurrent conflict over newspaper 'advertorials'. 'Advertorial' refers to the structuring of news and editorial comment to attract advertising dollars. As the press depends on these dollars, there is considerable pressure to produce news which in effect sponsors advertising interests. Readers, however, are not informed that the article they have just read was written and placed to support the advertisements that accompany it. Many journalists have complained about the spread of this practice. In mid-1993, for example, the New Zealand Journalists and Graphic Process Union lodged a complaint with the Press Council on behalf of its members at the *Christchurch Press*, focusing on the placing of a brewery banner over the sports coverage. The Union's national secretary complained that editors were increasingly surrendering the control of news columns to advertising managers. This was the third approach to the Press Council on this issue. While the Council noted the spread of this practice, as before it rejected the complaint. Advertorials blur the line between news and advertising and so threaten the professional standards of journalists. They have proved a source of conflict which, given the Press Council's inaction, can be expected to continue in the future.[4]

In general, however, the debate over media commercialism has centred more on broadcasting than print. This is not surprising, since newspapers have been organised by profit motives for a much longer time. The broadcasting debate has covered a number of different issues. The 1991 Broadcasting Amendment Act allowing 100 per cent foreign ownership, for example, prompted heated controversy. Many were unhappy when Sky outbid TVNZ for television rights to the 1991 All Black games in South Africa. The volume of advertising on TVNZ has provoked often vocal public displeasure. This extended to the controversial (and subsequently abandoned) practice of 'trimming' programmes like the BBC's 'Blackadder' to create more room for advertisements.

Debates over the impact of commercialism on broadcasting have highlighted three major concerns. First, it has been argued that markets promote programming with the widest possible appeal and so fail to cater for what are numerically minority interests. Maori have been particularly active on this count, and have lodged as yet unresolved claims upon broadcasting resources under the terms of the Treaty of Waitangi. Many Maori are striving to carve out an autonomous system that meets needs unaddressed by both the old public service and the emerging commercial order. Second, and on a related theme, in an increasingly international marketplace, New Zealanders as a whole are themselves a small group. Commercially driven broadcasters, it has been argued, rely on imports of relatively cheap, foreign programming and so fail to address specifically local concerns.[5] Finally, some have claimed that commercialism privileges entertainment and so has lead to a deterioration in television news. TVNZ, for example, cut back its news services by replacing the previous four regional bulletins with the national magazine show, 'Holmes'. There has been recurrent controversy over TVNZ's 6 p.m. news. It has been repeatedly criticised from the public service point of view by the former BCNZ Director, Ian Cross. But it has also been attacked by the libertarian broadcaster, Lindsay Perigo, who left TVNZ making widely publicised charges that it was 'braindead'. Such criticisms are buttressed by Atkinson's (1992) research, which found that between 1985 and 1992 the average news items became shorter and hence covered issues in less depth. Moreover, Atkinson reports that the political content of TVNZ's news declined, having been replaced by much greater concern with crime, sports, disasters and 'human interest' stories.

These various media debates reflect widespread concerns of the New Zealand public and are by no means over. The trends emerging in broadcasting are already well advanced overseas. As in this country, deregulation and developments in telecommunications have often been heralded as a 'revolution' which will allow individuals freedom of choice. Unfortunately, the reality is otherwise. Overseas' experience shows that the new market-oriented media perform badly when it comes to quality, equity and access. What begins as a promise of unlimited choice quickly fades as media ownership is concentrated into a few hands seeking to profit from large markets. As Farnsworth (1988: 469) argues:

> ... [the] structure of media markets leads advertising to restrict the range and quality of programming possibilities. In addition, advertising in tandem with consistent trends to conglomeration and concentration, deters new entrants to the market unless they already have resources.

A deregulated market of private media properties fails to sustain competition and limits access to communication resources (see also Farnsworth, 1990). The 'free' market does not live up to expectations and needs to be regulated if it is to function in a socially equitable way.

It should not be taken from these conclusions that the easy answer lies with a return to traditional public service broadcasting. This would not be possible even if it were wholly desirable. In the coming years, direct satellite broadcasting will rapidly expand in New Zealand. Using a small receiving dish, people will be able to receive a multitude of programmes from around the world, regardless of what the government of the day might want. Mass communications are increasingly in the hands of multinational corporations. They provide a global culture. This global media falls largely outside the control of any one country and its elected representatives. Any proposals for retaining nationally-based, public service broadcasting must acknowledge this development. However, the notion that private property alone should organise mass communication does not go uncontested. The search for an appropriate mix of private and public ownership remains high on the agenda. This search is sustained by widespread scepticism about the ability of commercial media to deliver the cultural diversity which underpins democratic politics.

Conclusion

This chapter has sought to contribute to the formation of media studies by outlining a sociological approach. A wide range of issues has been considered. We have examined how media representations make sense of the world, the role played by audiences and the institutions of property ownership. Throughout, we have argued that the sociological approach emphasises the wider social context. Studies of the media must consider the various ways they are embedded in New Zealand society. A theory of the media must be a theory of society. Accordingly, mass communications can be understood only by being situated within widespread conflicts over the distribution of power.

In emphasising a sociological point of view, we recognise that there are competing priorities about the appropriate orientation of media studies as it emerges in this country. However, as the chapter introduction noted, New Zealand media studies is in an unruly state. Focusing on the wider social context can help to organise the field of study.

The mass media are characterised by rapid change and considerable uncertainty. The same can be said of New Zealand at large. Over the last few decades, New Zealand has been riven by conflict and doubt, by intense questioning and considerable change. Questions about the identity of the various peoples who collectively inhabit these islands dominate public life. It is no longer clear just who the people who live together here are. How are they to culturally and politically represent themselves to each other? Radically new government policies have intensified the prevailing sense of uncertainty. Post-1984 governments advanced policies of deregulation and privatisation on many different fronts. This commercialisation of formerly public domains has been the occasion of acute conflict in New Zealand society. Mass communications have been caught up in these processes. This is not surprising since, as socially organised communications, they are a central feature of our collective life.

Debates about the media have focused on many different and specific issues. In general, though, they are one part of this much wider controversy about the relationship between commercial and public objectives. This is the social context to which the media debate belongs. The somewhat haphazard and disorganised state of media studies matches the rapid expansion, uncertainty and controversy of the New Zealand media themselves. The two are tied together. Struggle over the definition of media studies maps onto struggle over what the media should be. And conflicts about what the media should be are ultimately conflicts about what sort of society New Zealand should be.

Notes

1. See the discussions of news and gender-neutral language by Leitch and McGregor in Olsson (1992: 174-190). On the troubled relationship between the media and women's sport in general, see Ferkins (1993).
2. Such arguments have surrounded the Censorship Bill which was before Parliament in 1993. Similar thoughts inspired the private member's Bill on television violence which was introduced by Tirakatene-Sullivan. Frequently, these concerns focus on the young who are felt to be particularly vulnerable to manipulation. They are often worked up as extensive 'moral panics' about the media's baleful influence on society (see Shuker, 1989; Shuker and Openshaw, 1990).
3. The licence fee (1993) of $110 is the lowest of all OECD nations. In 1989 it amounted to only 5.3 per cent of public broadcasting revenue.
4. On the *Christchurch Press* case, see the paper of the New Zealand Journalists and Graphic Process Union, *The Word* (June/July 1993). For further material on advertorials, see Wilton (1992).
5. Research has shown that the proportion of New Zealand-produced television declined following the onset of commercialism in the 1980s (Lealand, 1991). Opponents to this trend have advocated the use of quotas to ensure the broadcasting of a certain amount of local programming (Maharey, 1992; Pickering and Shuker, 1993). As yet, they have achieved no notable successes. On the general relationship between broadcasting and New Zealand national identity, see Farnsworth (1990).

Further Reading

Barrett, D., 1985, *Media Sociology*, London, Tavistock.
Comrie, M. and McGregor, J. (eds), 1992, *Whose News?* Palmerston North, Dunmore Press.
Curran, J. and Gurevitch, M. (eds), 1991, *Mass Media and Society*, London, Edward Arnold.
Lealand, G., 1988, *A Foreign Egg In Our Nest? American Popular Culture in New Zealand*, Wellington, Victoria University Press.
Leitch, S., 1990, *News Talk*, Palmerston North, Dunmore Press.
Lusted, D. (ed.), 1991, *The Media Studies Book: A Guide for Teachers*, London, Routledge.
Royal Commission of Inquiry, 1986, *Broadcasting and Related Telecommunications in New Zealand*, Wellington, Government Printer.
Spoonley, P. and Hirsh, W. (eds), 1990, *Between the Lines. Racism and the New Zealand Media*, Auckland, Heinemann Reed.

14 Crime, Deviance and Punishment

John Pratt

In June 1992 the number of crimes reported to the police in New Zealand was 537,295 – its highest ever level. In 1993 the daily average prison population reached 4,500, – or 133 per 10,000 of the total population – its highest ever level. But not only are reported crime and imprisonment levels at their peak in this country; they are also extremely high by international standards (for example, the state of Victoria in Australia has a level of imprisonment around half that of New Zealand). Why then should the figures on crime and imprisonment be so high for this country? To answer such questions we must:

(i) identify and examine the specific features of crime patterns in New Zealand at present;
(ii) and then look at why New Zealand favours the imprisonment of its offenders.

Common Sense and the Crime Figures

The way in which crime became a feature of the 1987 election in this country provides a good case study here. Crime tends to feature regularly in commonsense conversation, usually based on inaccurate, distorted or partial sources of knowledge (e.g. newspaper reports or television programmes) or personal experiences from which, however unpleasant or unfortunate they might have been, it is not possible to generalise out as evidence of 'the crime problem at large'. Such interests are likely to be stimulated by media interest in *particular* crimes from time to time (e.g. gang rape, murder), and in the publicity given to *deviant* behaviour (not itself criminal) but which, nonetheless, seems different from normal standards and is likely to give alarm to supposedly non-deviant 'ordinary people'. In the party political broadcasts prior to the election, National tried to capture the feeling of threat and menace that both deviant and criminal behaviour posed: three 'skinhead' types, armed with clubs, were pictured on the prowl down a dimly lit street. The menace conveyed by their *deviant identity* was sufficient; they did not need to actually break the law and become criminals to achieve this (see Pratt and Treacher, 1988).

Equally, media interest in crime frequently comes alive with the quarterly publication of the 'crime figures' by the Department of Justice, that is, crimes that have been reported to the police and recorded as such by them. These are usually taken as important indicators of the level of crime in society. If they show an increase, then this is taken to mean that the real level of crime is rising. Thus, the number of crimes reported to the police stood at 200,937 in 1972; at the 1992 level (see above), the figures indicate that over a period of 20 years, crime has become nearly three times as prevalent as it used to be. The crime figures in themselves are likely to cause alarmist headlines ('Urban Terrorism Possibility Raised', reported the *Evening Post,* 16 September 1986, on the strength of rising figures for violent crime) and provide ammunition for politicians aiming to speak on behalf of 'ordinary New Zealanders'. In the 1986 parliamentary debate on law and order, it was claimed that:

> ... serious crime has increased by twenty per cent ... . Last year there were 61 murders, which was a 110 per cent increase. More than one New Zealand citizen is killed every week by violent crime ... the message must be put across that all the young thugs, the youngsters some of them as young as 12 years old, cannot ignore the justice system and get away with it (Jim Bolger, MP, National Party, *New Zealand Hansard*, 1986: 1032).

More specifically, the crime problem was posed as being one of a:

> ... gang problem and a Maori crime problem ... the elderly of the country are too scared to go out ... 8.9 per cent of the population is Maori, yet last year ... 43 per cent of all sexual offences, 41 per cent of all violent offences, 30 per cent of all burglaries and 43 per cent of all wilful damage offences were committed by Maori (Norman Jones, MP, National Party, *New Zealand Hansard*, 1986: 1035).

Such comments illustrate the *presumed* reliability of the statistics. And reliance on them leads to assumptions that crime is committed in the main by certain sections of the population – here Maori and young people – and that deviance, not just law-breaking, is a major problem.

Yet the foundation of these comments – the crime figures themselves – is highly problematic and open to question. First of all, the figures represent only a fraction (perhaps as little as 10 per cent) of all crime that is committed. Many forms of criminal behaviour, such as white-collar and corporate crime, do not get reported or are not even treated as 'criminal' by the respective law enforcement agencies (this vast area of unresearched crime is usually referred to as the 'dark figure'). Second, the accuracy of the crime figures may be distorted by bias. Research from overseas suggests that the police may be more likely to press charges against young working-class offenders than their middle class-counterparts (Gill, 1976).

Third, the findings of self-report and 'victim surveys'[1] indicate that crime is much more ubiquitous than the impression given by the crime statistics. Indications are that most people have broken the law on numerous occasions but have never been prosecuted or even been spoken to by the police. On the other hand, it now appears that working-class persons commit more crimes of a serious nature (see West *et al.*, 1974). It may be that middle-class offenders begin their criminal careers later on in life, at work rather than in adolescence, where they may experience a different crime pattern, such as tax fraud and other forms of occupational crime.

If such factors highlight the unreliable foundations of commonsense talk about crime, we are also likely to find major problems and inconsistencies in the nature of the response we should make to it. Let us return again to the 1987 election. For National, the solution was more police, tougher sentencing and, *inter alia*, a crackdown on 'young violent offenders who seem almost to get a pat on the head, as they are sent back into society and told to be good', the aim being 'to have the streets, the suburbs and the cities of New Zealand safe for New Zealanders' (Jim Bolger, *New Zealand Hansard*, 1986: 1032). Good political rhetoric and lots of commonsense appeal, no doubt.

However, it is a moot point whether the streets of New Zealand have ever been 'safe for New Zealanders' or that there was ever some 'golden age' when the behaviour of young people was exemplary. In 1960, for example, it was reported that:

> ...conduct at some popular holiday results, especially on the part of young people and during the main holiday season, has come into prominence over the last few years. This year more complaints than ever were received about disorder, rowdyism, hooliganism and general lowering of standards of conduct ... (Police Department Annual Report, 1960: 10).

There are reports from the last century that complain about the behaviour of young people. Shuker (1987) refers to the Hawke's Bay *Herald* in 1880 reporting that 'young hopefuls fill their mouth full of sulphur, and by setting it alight, terrify timid pedestrians on a dark night' (see also Pratt, 1988a: 117).

Furthermore, National's responses have already been tried – in the United Kingdom – and with disastrous results:

> ... expenditure on law and order had increased by almost 40 per cent in real terms since 1979.... The police force had been expanded by 13,000 since 1979, bringing the total number of officers to 159,000 and 4,000 extra civilian staff had been taken on to reduce the time spent by uniformed police on paperwork. Police pay had been increased by 96 per cent between May 1979 and September 1984. The Police and Criminal Evidence Act of 1984 had given the courts much more extensive and flexible sentencing powers. Hundreds more young people in trouble with the law were being sent to the refurbished, and highly militarised regimes in detention centres, for the infamous 'short, sharp shock' and, in the meantime, the daily adult prison population had increased, by May 1986, to nearly 55,000 (an increase of 11,500 or 20.9 per cent in the seven years of the Thatcher Government). Nearly a dozen new penal institutions had been opened (out of 16 that were planned) to create more places for these new convict populations (Taylor, 1987).

Despite all this, recorded crime has actually doubled from around 2.5 million crimes known to the police in 1978 to around five million in 1992. So much for commonsense responses and solutions! But, returning to New Zealand, Labour's response was also inadequate. Basically, this frequently took the form of denying the reality of crime: 'the chances of being run over by a car are greater than being injured in a criminal attack' (Palmer, 1987). This may be so when the crime figures are applied across the country as a whole. Yet the flaws in this argument are well-illustrated by reference to the findings of the 'British Crime Survey':

> ... the chances of being mugged in London are, on the basis of the official statistics, 1 in 2,000 per year. But then he goes on to point out that in certain areas this is at least 1 in 1,000 or quite possibly 1 in 500. And, if you take into account the dark figure of unreported crime, you would arrive at a figure of perhaps 1 in 200 in certain areas. Now this is not an insubstantial figure ... (Lea and Young, 1984: 25).

By the same token, we could say that the chances of being the victim of a criminal are considerably higher in some parts of New Zealand than others. For people living in those areas, usually working-class people, or other vulnerable sections of the community such as the elderly who will also have most to lose from crime, criminal behaviour really is a problem.

This review has indicated some of the shortcomings of the commonsense responses to crime. The criminal statistics are blithely accepted as fact or are written off altogether. There is no sense of history, no clear analysis of why crime may or may not be increasing, and at times, the separate categories of crime and deviance are conflated to try and sustain one point of view or another on the 'crime problem'.

Explaining Crime

To begin to explain crime, rather than simply perpetuate some of the myths about it, we must turn to sociological theory where there are a range of approaches to the study of crime and deviance, providing different interpretations of these phenomena. The theories are not without fault, nor does it seem likely that we will ever arrive at some perfect explanation of crime and deviance.

The range of theories (they are by no means exhaustive) we will consider are as follows:

1. Positivism.
2. Strain Theory.
3. Radical Deviancy Theory.
4. Neo-Marxism.
5. New Right.
6. Left Realism.
7. Maori Criminology.

All of these theories in their various ways have made substantial inroads into or provide significant critiques of the existing system of criminal justice.

New Zealand's criminal justice system effectively dates from the Treaty of Waitangi. However, it was not until later in the nineteenth century, with the centralisation of government in particular, that an essentially European system of criminal justice of today came into existence, a system which included adversarial proceedings (initially), fixed and certain punishments, backed up by a system of administrators which from 1880 began to publish the criminal statistics (see Pratt, 1992).

Of the theories we will consider, it must be recognised that positivism (from around 1880) and strain theory (from the 1930s) were the most predominant modes of thought, and most influential, up to 1970. As will be apparent, there has been much wider debate and analysis since then, culminating in a range of new theoretical frameworks.

1. Positivism

The crucial feature of positivism has been its insistence that human behaviour – or, more specifically criminal and deviant behaviour – can be studied and understood using the same methods and principles of natural science. In the same way that we would study plants or animals (e.g. under laboratory conditions), it was believed that we could study criminals to find out what special features they might have, what it was about them that made them different from supposedly 'normal' people. The Italian Count Lombroso (1911) was the first such *criminologist,* in the sense that he began to study criminals. Up to this point, there had been no reason for any such study: the only point of issue in any criminal inquiry had been whether or not an individual had broken the law. Now the positivist's began to ask *why* that person should have broken the law.

The work of Lombroso and others helped to establish a particular tradition in criminological thought which has continued for much of this century: the belief that criminals are different from normal people, whether this be manifested in physical stigmata, body-types, personality features, chromosome make-up or family background and the like. In such ways, criminals have come to be seen not just as different from 'normal people' but *deficient* by comparison. By isolating such deficiencies, it is thought possible to:

(a) discover the causes of crime (the Holy Grail of most positivists) and
(b) provide remedies or rehabilitation to alleviate such problems.

In this way, the tradition of penal rehabilitation owes its existence to the positivists. In the extreme forms of positivism, criminal behaviour was understood to be nothing more than a form of illness and should be treated as such by criminological experts such as psychiatrists, probation officers and so on, who would be able to unravel the 'special features' of the individual criminal and suggest forms of punishment designed to provide treatment for them. In other words, positivists have always argued that punishment should fit the criminal rather than the crime.

Positivists have usually been ambivalent regarding the accuracy of the criminal statistics. On the one hand, they acknowledge that they *are* likely to be accurate statements of criminal behaviour, collected and compiled by experts, and they have been used to provide hard evidence of *criminal types.* On the other hand, their interest in behavioural problems goes much further than that which contravenes the law. Law breaking may go hand in hand with other behaviour that breaches social norms, and is likely to stem from the same malfunctions in any given individual. As such, positivists are interested in *deviance as a whole,* not just criminal behaviour. Crime becomes just one form of deviance.

Clearly, such arguments are useful to politicians and policy-makers who have an interest in preserving the status quo. There is no consideration of all the crimes missing from the criminal statistics, particularly white-collar and corporate crime. Not only that, but by the implication that criminals are sick, no consideration need be given to social influences (such as unemployment and poverty). Instead, the problem is located firmly in the lap of the individuals concerned. Nor is it necessary to consider the 'meaning' of crime – it can just be written off as sickness. Yet crime might be the result of a form of rebellion, as in the Bastion Point land occupation, or it may be a form of behaviour such as petty theft that almost all adolescents have some brief experience of.

Some positivists would also infer from the racial dimension to the crime figures that there is a strong connection between race and crime (see the earlier comments of Norman Jones, MP and the comments of the Minister of Police in early 1993 regarding what he saw as the Maori 'propensity' to commit crime). In the New Zealand context, this view would take the form that there is something inherent in being Maori – rather than the criminogenic social conditions that many of them experience – that makes some Maori 'crime prone' (cf. Eysenck, 1968). I will return to the matter of crime and 'race' at various times in this chapter and illustrate the way in which different theoretical approaches provide a critique of such assertions.

2. Strain Theory

For much of this century, the main counterweight to positivism was to be found in what is known as strain theory. Perhaps its greatest significance has been that, in contrast to positivism, it has always argued that crime is *socially* rather than individually induced. Its main architect has been Robert Merton (1938), writing in the U.S.A. at a time of high migration from rural to urban America, high immigration and the apparent break-up of the old social order, as evidenced by an increase in the crime rate.

Merton suggested that in stable and relatively low-crime societies, there was a balance between cultural goals and social structure, i.e. 'getting on' in life on the one hand, and on the other, the legitimate means to achieve this, such as doing well at school, getting a job. In such a society, most individuals will be well integrated. If they make the most of the means to do well, they reap the harvest of the 'ends'. However, *malintegration* and social problems (including crime) occur when this equilibrium is no longer in balance, when there is a disproportionate emphasis on ends without the means to achieve them. For example, when many people experience 'blocked opportunities' as they find that despite doing all that is requested of them at school or college, there are no jobs for them at the end of their training.

The new economic orthodoxy of Western society – free market economics – which is now being practised in New Zealand as in many other countries, would seem to provide the classic example of these circumstances. In deregulated economies, there is more emphasis than ever before on entrepreneurial skills, getting to the top and so on. Mass unemployment (around 150,000 at present in New Zealand) has made this an impossible goal for large sections of the population.

It might be thought that this is a particularly appropriate crime theory for the 1990s: it makes sense of crimes such as vandalism or burning schools which can no longer offer any material reward for the students' attendance and good behaviour; it would seem to explain why young men might be keen to join the gangs, given that they are denied legitimate opportunities to 'get on' as a result of unemployment. The New Zealand crime figures would seem to illustrate the shift from a previously homogeneous and stable society to one that is becoming increasingly fragmented and unstable:

> A generation ago New Zealand proudly had one of the lowest crime rates in the world. In the 66 years between 1878 and 1954 reported crime increased by 263 per cent. In the 29 years since 1956, crime has increased 476 per cent to 435,640 reported offences for the 1985 calendar year (Police Department Annual Report, 1986: 3).

This theory and some of its derivatives[2] have played an important part in generating penal reform. Alongside their long-term objectives of making the structures of society more egalitarian and ensuring that all have equal opportunity, strain theorists would argue that the punishment of offenders must be constructive and useful. They would favour, for example, such New Zealand provisions as community service. This is intended to give clients a sense of value and worth; harsh penalties will only alienate them further.

There are, though, problems with strain theory. It might be thought that it could provide an explanation of white-collar crime. However, Merton himself believed that crime was concentrated primarily amongst the lower classes. Furthermore, it may well be that entrepreneurial success is now a prominent feature of the *dominant* culture in New Zealand as elsewhere, but there are other cultural values. Working-class culture would put class solidarity before individualism; Maori culture rejects individualism in favour of the wellbeing of the Maori people as a whole. Similarly, many women's groups would be opposed to the dominant cultural values and would place much greater emphasis on gender solidarity. The point is that Merton's consensus (the breakdown of which is seen as the cause of crime) may simply not be shared by large groups of the population, in which case there must be other causes of crime.

In addition, strain theory may explain some of the migratory and economic causes of crime, but it does not capture the cultural and ethnic factors specific to New Zealand. Applying strain theory to the urban drift of the Maori in the post-war period misses the sense of *cultural* alienation then in existence as the result of a century of colonialism. To reverse this, it may not be sufficient to provide more opportunities for deprived people in order to facilitate their integration into mainstream society. More fundamental structural change may be necessary (see Jackson, 1988, and later in this chapter).

But against this, it could also be argued, in Durkheimian fashion, that, given the static and stagnant nature of New Zealand society between 1975 and 1984, the social change we have seen since was both necessary and inevitable. If this produces anomic conditions, leading to higher crime rates, this is a consequence not of the changes themselves but of the unhealthy state to which New Zealand society had degenerated by 1984.

3. Radical Deviancy Theory

So far, the origins of criminal and deviant behaviour have been explained in terms of individual (positivism) and social (strain theory) disorganisation. New deviancy theory, itself the product of late 1960s radical sociology, presented an important departure from these positions (although in itself it has undergone considerable modification over a comparatively brief time).

Its starting point was that *there was no such thing* as crime itself, only that which society, or powerful people in society, so labelled as crime (Becker, 1963). Thus, if some of the New Zealand drug laws were repealed, there would be no such thing as 'being a drug offender' and a significant proportion of those labelled as criminal would disappear. As such, the new deviancy theorists were initially interested in the *process of labelling* (by the police, judiciary and others) rather than crime itself. Once the label of 'criminal' had been imposed in the form of a conviction, prison record, etc., this was then seen as limiting the range of behaviour available to the person so labelled, with the effect that their future conduct would be drastically reshaped.

More generally, this perspective raised important questions regarding the role of the mass media in generating public concern about crime problems, and then, by the news coverage continuing to feed such concerns to the effect that the initial problem came to be *amplified* out of all proportion to its reality. One of the best studies in this tradition in New Zealand – indeed, one of the very few studies of New Zealand gangs – is that of Kelsey and Young (1980). They claimed that the 'gang crisis' of 1979 was to a large extent manufactured by the media:

> Gangs were singled out as a special problem, and became a widely publicised issue of major public concern, sometimes to the point of almost monopolising the news media coverage. They came to be seen as one of New Zealand's most pressing social problems, and were certainly considered the country's most threatening kind of criminal problem until drugs took the limelight later in the year. Gangs were discussed almost solely in terms of their criminality. Gang members

became symbols of irrational, anti-social and violent behaviour. They represented a threat to the very roots of society; a threat which was made all the more potent by their supposed exploitation for political ends by radical 'revolutionary' groups. Their offending became linked, at times even fused, with other social issues causing concern – violence in general, assaults on police, drugs, black activism and racial discontent, and the problems of the 'idle unemployed' whose numbers were steadily increasing. One type of challenge to society became merged with other forms of discontent, and added even further to the scale of the problem. Predictions of future chaos, anarchy or violent upheaval, based on overseas experiences, ensured that society would respond with urgent hard-line action. Once this *artificial picture had been created, the actual frequency or seriousness of gang offending became unimportant* (Kelsey and Young, 1980: 135 – emphasis added).

What gave new deviancy theory its radical edge was its insistence that behaviour which could be labelled criminal occurred right across society and yet the official crime figures produce a very different picture of the class distribution of crime. For the new deviancy theorists, this discrepancy was the product of police and courtroom bias against working-class people, while the 'crimes of the powerful' were likely to be ignored (Pearce, 1976).

For the first time in the sociology of crime and deviance, *social reaction* is considered, particularly in relation to the generation of public concern about criminal and deviant behaviour. The policy implications are fairly obvious: leave people alone, decriminalise wherever possible in such a way as to avoid imposing 'labels' which only make the problem worse.

However, one of the main problems with this strand of new deviancy theory is that far too much emphasis was given to social reaction at the expense of the initial act of deviance, which can be extremely mundane (car theft or shoplifting) or horrifically unpleasant (gang rape). Much empirical work focused on so-called deviance such as drug taking, nudism and stripping (Young, 1973; Douglas, 1970). While the reality of crime and its consequences was ignored, the criminal was seen as a kind of working-class hero, the innocent victim of the bias of criminal justice professionals, even if the wider social structure which determined their role was likely to be ignored.

4. Neo-Marxism and the New Criminology

It was this latter concern that led some criminologists into a new Marxist approach to crime and deviance (see Taylor, Walton and Young, 1973). Marx himself did not have much to say about crime, other than putting forward a *demoralisation* thesis.

That is, in capitalist society, the labour of the urban proletariat is exploited by the bourgeoisie. At the bottom of the social structure, there existed a *lumpenproletariat* left out of the mainstream of society altogether, through unemployment, mental illness or whatever, who were left to fend for themselves. This exigency inevitably manifested itself in crime, particularly theft, street crime, prostitution, etc. It also brought such people into regular contact with the police.

From this somewhat rudimentary analysis, neo-Marxists sought to adapt nineteenth century Marxism to the social conditions of the 1970s. The classic text of this genre is Hall *et al.* (1978). Here, there is a heavy reliance on the Italian writer Gramsci's (1971) interpretation of Marx, which is then applied to the British 'law and order crisis' in the 1970s. The argument of Hall *et al.* is that in the post-war period, social tensions were (temporarily) resolved by the reforms of that period – greater pensions, increased access to education, the provision of a national health service, etc.

The working class felt that it too had a place in the framework of modern capitalist society. However, the successive economic crises from the late 1960s inevitably began to eat into the erstwhile consensus that had been established. The onset of mass unemployment created a new lumpenproletariat. The young black working class, in particular, saw that there was no place for them in British society, and crime and deviant behaviour (e.g. 'mugging', drug-dealing) became some of the few options available to them 'to get by'. Meanwhile, the response of the state was to orchestrate a sustained law and order campaign against these offenders, promising 'tougher action' and more police.

For Marxists, it was not the issue of crime and deviance that was of interest. This was the inevitable and logical response of alienated youth. In contrast, it was the way in which 'law and order' became functional to the state in maintaining ruling-class power and privilege. A tough penal policy would act as a deterrent to those who did not conform. Meanwhile, those who are sent to prison – mainly working-class youths for minor property crime – are seen as a major threat to the social order, deflecting attention away from other more serious but unreported forms of crime (e.g. tax fraud). For Marxists this is a feature of the prison's *success*. It operates as an important form of control over troublemakers and deters others by being tough on law and order. The state gives the appearance of protecting the interests of society as a whole. In reality, it only protects those of the ruling class.

There are, though, empirical problems here. Most Western governments in the 1980s have been keen to shift the focus of punishment *away* from the prison and into community-based sanctions. New Zealand has been no exception (Pratt, 1987a). Furthermore, crime and deviance are given rather simplistic economic motives, which does not explain such criminal behaviour as rape and child abuse. In addition, New Zealand experienced youth cultural forms and styles such as the Teddy Boys from the late 1950s. For Marxists, this is seen as an expression of alienation from the economic and class structure (Hall and Jefferson, 1976). Yet, New Zealand at this time had the third highest standard of living in the world, unemployment was virtually zero, and there was not the rigid class structure of British society. Above all, the main problem with the 'New Criminology' is that the impact and seriousness of crime is minimised if it is considered at all. It is in relation to this issue that the sociology of crime and deviance has taken a fundamentally different route in the 1980s. Crime and its consequences have been 'put back on the agenda'.

5. The New Right

Much of the responsibility for this can be attributed to the emergence from the late 1970s of a 'New Right' criminology (mainly in Britain and North America). As distinct from 'Old Right' political traditions of a commitment to the welfare state and a role for government in the management of the economy (exemplified by the Muldoon administration in New Zealand between 1975-84), the New Right have a commitment to free market economics, privatisation, and a minimalist role for the state.

In these respects, crime and other social problems of the 1970s and 1980s (e.g. drug-taking, disruption in schools) have been important to the New Right theorists. Such matters are seen not as the product of too little commitment to welfare programmes by government (the usual liberal/left approach) but *too much*. The post-war welfare state is seen as the cause of the problem. As affluence has increased during the period, so have 'authority' and 'traditional' values declined. Without such props crime has risen, as evidenced by the criminal statistics. Morgan (1978), as with other New Right theorists, seems to have implicit faith in these and other social indicators. She claims that poverty and unemployment are no excuse or explanation for modern crime problems. These factors were worse in the 1930s when crime rates were much lower. Accordingly, the 'causes of crime' are located in individuals or sections of the community, particularly the young who have been brought up to think that they can act with impunity given the liberal penal policies of the welfare area. Wilson (1975: 69), in an extract which also shows the simplistic and populist message of the New Right, claims that:

> ... if you were to ask a taxi driver, hotel clerk or news vendor in London, they would explain the increase in violent crime, especially robbery, by the presence of West Indians.

Strangely, there is no consensus on the Right regarding the punishment of those, such as the above, who are seen as responsible for modern crime problems. Van den Haag (1973) supports the death penalty. Wilson seems to have turned towards resocialising offenders through behaviour modification programmes. Morgan favours

Classicist-type punishments – fixed, certain and efficient (e.g. community service and restitution for acts of vandalism). *All are against* liberal penal policy and the involvement of social work organisations in the penal system.

In New Zealand there has as yet been no attempt to formulate a New Right criminology, that is, an analysis which sees crime as the product of post-war welfare state policies, although Upton (1987) provides a more general New Right social policy. However, attempts to formulate such a criminology would have to address the unusual political circumstances of New Zealand where a Labour Government between 1984 and 1990, pursued a right-wing economic programme, whereas National, as a legacy of the Muldoon era, seems split between Old and New Right factions. Thus, despite closely following Mrs Thatcher's successful use of the law and order issue in the 1979 British election, National failed when it attempted to imitate it in 1987:

> ... the political conjuncture in 1987, while containing many of the [1979 British] elements did not reproduce the formula *in toto*. The crisis of hegemony was inherited by Labour when it came to power in 1984: this was the end product of nine years of National Government wherein state intervention had been pushed to the limits of this political paradigm. Furthermore, there seemed to be no clear alternative to 'Rogernomics', aside from its impact, sometimes favourable, sometimes unfavourable, on individual citizens (Pratt and Treacher, 1988: 264).

This is not to say that this theoretical contribution is unimportant in our understanding of crime problems in New Zealand. As was evident in the quotation from Norman Jones earlier, there is a tendency in most societies to single out particular groups as being criminogenic. In this respect New Zealand demonstrates a history of tolerance towards groups of people thought to be 'different' (see Pratt, 1991a). Yet the social dimension that underlies criminal acts and the producing of criminal statistics is rarely considered by the Right. Nor does the history of social and penal policy in the last two decades – here or elsewhere – lend itself to the view that governments became 'soft on crime' during this period.

Furthermore, the attempts to attribute criminal behaviour as being the fault of, say, Maori, is certainly racist in its consequences if not in its intent, the consequences being that this will become a self-fulfilling prophecy. If it is popularly believed that criminals can be identified by their 'race', then this has obvious implications for police and prosecution policies. Notwithstanding such criticisms, the New Right have reminded us that crime for many people *is* a serious problem. It is simply not enough to dismiss crime as the consequences of labelling or the product of capitalism.

6. Left Realism

Cognisant of such matters and aware, often through self-critique, of some of the shortcomings of the New Criminology, Left Realists (e.g. Lea and Young, 1984; Young and Matthews, 1987; Kinsey et al., 1986)[3] have attempted to turn law and order into an issue for the Left. Their arguments are:

(a) Crime really is a problem affecting mainly working-class people. It is they who are most hurt by crime. Little wonder that in the past they have voted for the Right who have at least promised to do something about it (with the Left usually remaining silent).

(b) Today's social conditions (e.g. unemployment, poverty) are criminogenic but criminal behaviour is an individualistic response to such dilemmas. It ensures that political energies that might have been able to change society are channelled into maintaining its inertia.

(c) We must take crime control seriously: radical criminology must be much more policy oriented. The above writers have thus proposed a number of strategies including the minimum use of prisons, crime prevention programmes and the democratic accountability of the police.

(d) We must be realistic about crime problems *in the 1990s*. This is a critique of the liberal position which takes the view that there always has and always will be crime in society – today's concerns are thus nothing more than a 'moral panic'. In contrast, Realists argue that crime patterns *inevitably* change. Given the social conditions of New Zealand in the 1980s and the established link between unemployment and crime, there would seem every reason to think that crime may indeed be increasing at present, whether this takes the form of directly related economic crime, or social protest (e.g. school vandalism), or more indirectly linked criminal behaviour, such as aggression at home or drunkenness.

Most significantly of all, Left Realism has abandoned the libertarianism and the Utopian socialism which informed radical criminology in the 1970s. Indeed, it seems to be moving towards a recognition that a fundamental prerequisite of social life in the late twentieth century is *security*.

What would a Left Realist approach look like in New Zealand? First, it would be essential to address the reality of crime. Too often in recent years, the Left, apart from women's organisations and feminist criminologists such as Smart (1977) and Heidensohn (1985), have been silent on such matters as rape, domestic violence and child abuse. Clearly, criminal justice resources must give much more security to potential victims of these crimes, in just the same way that white-collar crime (the left's traditional *bête noire* here) needs to be targeted, albeit using different resources and strategies. Policing must adapt to the new crime patterns and concerns of the 1980s. In such respects, the Ford Report (1986) is an important step forward: this heralded a major policy shift in the police approach to domestic violence. It is now treated as an arrestable offence rather than a quarrel to be quickly patched up and forgotten about by investigating officers.

Perhaps one of the main problems with Realism is that it is by no means certain that 'the community' *does* favour democratisation of the police and other aspects of the criminal justice system. Rather more to the point, it seems likely that most people would simply prefer the police and others to get on with their job, only more effectively and efficiently than has been the case in recent years. Some of the strongest criticisms of Realism have come from erstwhile colleagues on the Left, particularly over the issue of ethnicity and crime. For the Realists, black crime is both a reality and a problem:

> ... the notion that increasing youth unemployment, coupled with a high young population in the black community, and the effects of a massive, well-documented racial discrimination and the denial of legitimate opportunity, did *not* result in a rising rate of real offences is hardly credible. If these sorts of deprivation are not crucial factors leading to increasing crime rates then what are? (Lea and Young, 1984: 167-8).

Against this, it has been argued that 'the key to understanding the disproportionate number of black people in the official criminal statistics could be found in the practices of the [police] both bureaucratically and on the street ...' (Sim, 1982: 59). The implication of such criticisms of the Left Realists is that black crime is just a fabrication.

7. Maori Criminology

The fierce debate between these two positions on the left leads us to a consideration of Maori criminology, which attempts:

> ... to provide some insight into the complex questions of why some Maori men become criminal offenders and how the criminal justice process responds to them. It approaches the topic from within a Maori conceptual framework and seeks to explain Maori perception of the causes and consequences of criminal offending (Jackson, 1988: 17).

Jackson addresses the issue of ethnicity and crime in New Zealand as follows. First, there *is* a problem of Maori crime, particularly violence by Maori men to women. At the same time, the incidence and problem of Maori offending is likely to be considerably exaggerated and distorted by the 'institutional racism' which he sees as pervading the whole criminal justice system. At each stage of the criminal justice decision-making process, Maori will be unfairly treated. For example, the system itself helps to reproduce the problem of Maori crime by using police definitions of the ethnicity of offenders rather than self-identification, leading, it is claimed, to an over-representation of Maori in the crime figures. This then confirms the beliefs of police and politicians that Maori are responsible for most of the country's crime problems, leading to greater concentration on Maori offenders, etc.

Nonetheless, such people *do* exist, and from his interviews and discussions, Jackson (1988: 61) suggests that:

> ... the Maori offender is mainly a young urban dweller who is part of a family which has been in the city and separated from tribal ties for less than three generations. The family structure is nuclear and is headed by two adults, either married or in a de facto relationship. In a substantial minority of cases, the family is headed by a solo parent because of the death, separation, or divorce, of the other partner. A small minority of male parents have had some degree of criminal involvement as have a substantial number of siblings.
>
> The majority of the families are economically supported by both partners although there is a marked history of parental unemployment. The parents' jobs tend to be in 'unskilled', labouring, or seasonal work. The family home was most often rented, although a substantial minority were under mortgage with the Maori Affairs Department or Housing Corporation. The families clearly fell within the lower socio-economic levels of society.
>
> The children often witnessed heavy drinking by one or both parents in the home, or were aware of regular hotel drinking. The families were subjected to periods of violence by the male parent against his partner or the children, often coincident with heavy drinking. A disturbing number of children also knew of the sexual abuse of sisters or nieces (Jackson, 1988: 61).

He further mentions their lack of education and an ignorance of Maori culture and language. He presents the same kind of profile as Farrington and his positivistic colleagues, and the same kind of profile that Merton would have favoured in describing the fate of second generation North American immigrants. What is very different, though, is Jackson's *explanation* of this profile. Against the individual deficiency and under-socialisation of positivism, and against the social disorganisation of strain theory, he links Maori offending with the low socio-economic status of Maori people and the destruction of Maori *culture* in the aftermath of the Treaty of Waitangi. The economic base of Maori society was removed by land confiscation. Denied the power and wealth that comes from land ownership, they could have little influence on the law-making process (see Pratt, 1991b, 1992). At the same time, their own system of justice and punishment was replaced by an imported replica of the Anglo-Welsh system. Even though there are strong similarities in the behaviours prohibited in both systems, the *process* of justice is very different. In the Maori justice system, the purpose of criminal proceedings was to restore a sense of balance between victim, offender and their respective families. In the European adversarial system, the Crown takes over from the victim, who is left out of the matter altogether.

For Jackson, such factors have produced cultural deprivation and denigration. These same forces that have destroyed Maori culture, induce Maori crime. To counter this, he proposes a twofold strategy. First, there should be economic and social reforms which ensure that Maori and Pakeha do become equal partners in the wealth and prosperity of New Zealand. Second, since the existing criminal justice system is seen as *institutionally* racist, there is little point in trying to reform it. Instead, he argues for the introduction of a Maori criminal justice system which will run parallel to that which already exists:

> The aim of a Maori system would not be to simply transplant the Pakeha organisation into a Maori context, but to develop a structural framework which reflects the imperatives of Maori law and the processes it developed for maintaining order. The runanga concept, consisting of selected people rather like the committees envisaged under the reform of the Maori Community Development Act, would be one obvious structure. The idea of a panel rather than an individual is important as it would stress the community responsibility to remedy wrongs committed against it. However, unlike the proposed committees under that Act, runanga would have power and authority to hear and determine all cases involving offenders and victims who identify as Maori. The attribution of guilt or innocence and the determination of reparation or other sanction, would be within its jurisdiction. If a victim was non-Maori, or an institution as distinct from a person, jurisdiction would be varied in the sense that the victim would have the right to have the matter heard within the Maori system or referred to Pakeha courts (Jackson, 1988: 277).

These proposals were quickly dismissed by leading politicians in both main parties, even though it is clear that the important *juvenile* justice legislation of 1989 (Children, Young Persons and Their Families Act) is modelled at least in part, on principles of Maori justice (see Maxwell and Morris, 1993). At the same time, there clearly *would be* enormous difficulties in trying to implement a second justice system. Would Maori as a whole welcome such a development? In one of the few studies of the process of criminal justice in New Zealand (albeit the juvenile justice system), Morris and Young (1987) claimed that Maori juveniles and their parents strongly resented references to tribal affiliations, Maoridom and so on. Like their Pakeha counterparts, they wanted their cases to be dealt with as quickly as possible and wanted their punishment to be fair. Such expectations are no doubt derived from 150 years of colonisation.

Furthermore, although it is *stated* that the criminal justice system is institutionally racist, little evidence is produced in support of this claim other than that the defendants did not understand what was happening, legal aid lawyers were not very interested in their cases, etc. But it is not something that is unique to the Maori defendant caught up in the New Zealand criminal justice system and does not in itself prove that this system is 'institutionally racist'.

Perhaps a more viable way forward would be to implement reforms that open up the existing criminal justice system to Maori influences and practices. Such matters aside, we must also be careful not to be over-deterministic about Maori crime – blaming it all on 'colonialism' in the same way that the new criminologist blamed it on 'capitalism'.

The range of theories that we have considered provides us with different explanations of the phenomenon of crime. Furthermore, depending on which theory we choose or are sympathetic to, they provide us with competing views on the validity and reliability of the criminal statistics, a range of appropriate sanctions, and the motivation underlying offending patterns.

The Reality of Crime Today

Whatever sociological theory we choose, it is inevitable that there will continue to be Maori and Pakeha criminals in New Zealand, and it also seems certain that crime and law and order will remain high on the political agenda. I would like to conclude this section by giving some thought to the reality and extent of current crime problems in New Zealand (the data for our respective theories). Let us return again to the issue of crime figures. Clearly, we have to approach them with caution in view of the various shortcomings in their collation that we referred to earlier. Nonetheless, I think we can still draw certain conclusions from them. The first of these relates to the *general* level of offending in this country. In 1964 the rate per 1,000 mean population of crimes reported to the police was 45.58; in 1974 it had increased to 71.09; on the basis of the 1992 crime figures, it stands at around 140 (with an overall population of 3.5 million). Can it be said that police recording practices and the eagerness to report crime by the public have changed so dramatically as to account for such differences? I think not, and in which case we would have to say these figures *are* a reflection of a general increase in crime. This is borne out when we consider offences where there is little room for ambiguity in the way which the police record these crimes. Reported murders, for example, rose from 27 in 1977 to 72 in 1992. Furthermore, there is a strong likelihood that some offences are consistently reported to the police because of the requirements of insurance claims. For example, total burglaries rose from 43,705 in 1977 to 77,941 in 1988, and would seem to indicate a *real* increase in such crime.

Second, unemployment may account for some forms of property crime (and thus be partly related to the rise in burglaries) but it can hardly account for the growth of white-collar crime, amongst the most unreported of all types of offending behaviour. Indeed, participation in this form of activity is dependent on being in work. It may, though, be another feature of the same economic climate. There seems no doubt at all that economic deregulation, and the ethics of 'making a fast buck' associated with this, has lent itself to further increases in their form of criminal activity: for example, insider trading on the stockmarket and GST fraud. The extent of revenue that is lost to the government in this way is difficult to estimate, but it is likely to far exceed all other types of property crime. One example from Britain puts the matter in perspective. In 1975 it was calculated that £11,000 million was lost each year in income tax fraud; property lost to burglary and robbery amounted to £80 million per year; £4 million was lost to social welfare fraud (Pearce, 1976). As has been evident in New Zealand in recent years, the Serious Fraud Office seems particularly under-resourced to deal with the complexities of this matter (see Newbold, 1992) despite the fact that its investigations and prosecutions have revealed crimes involving hundreds of millions of dollars.

Furthermore, there is evidence (see Grabrosky *et al.*, 1987) that there is growing public concern about white-collar and corporate crime and also breaches of environmental laws and health and safety at work. Street crime and property crime is *not* the only dimension to the law and order issue. If this points to a need for considerably more policing of this area of law-breaking, it would also seem to make very little sense to fill our prisons with white-collar rather than working-class offenders as a response. Rather than bringing prosecution procedures here into line with those usually in operation for property crime, perhaps it would be more appropriate to apply the procedures for dealing with white-collar crime – warnings, mediation, civil action, negotiation and so on – to a wider area of the criminal law (see Braithwaite, 1991).

Third, let us consider the issue of violent and sexual crime, since it is these areas of law-breaking that cause greatest public concern, as well as provoking the greatest interest from the media and politicians. The crime figures indicate significant increases in both areas: in 1982, 18,621 violent offences had been reported to the police; in 1992, there were 29,120. In 1982, 2,953 sexual offences were reported to the police; in 1992 the figure was 4,263. Aside from the usual caution with which we must treat statistics, there are additional matters to take into account here. First, there is no doubt that the new police response to domestic violence *has* increased the number of incidents being recorded as such. Domestic violence *per se,* then, may not have increased. It is just that more is now being reported and recorded. Furthermore, it is certain that changes in public attitudes leading to a greater willingness to report criminal behaviour has contributed to marked increases in some recorded offences. Child abuse is an example. Again, it does not mean that such behaviour has actually increased. Indeed, the greater willingness to report could be interpreted as evidence of our increasing civilisation and concern for ensuring high standards of child care and protection, rather than our increasing depravity.

Finally, a further comment on street violence and public crime to try and put New Zealand's problems in an international perspective. It is quite understandable that many people take fright at the appearance of gang members, are outraged by the reports of some aspects of their behaviour and by the very existence of gang 'fortresses'. At the same time, there is not the perpetual threat of violence and disorder in the streets that there is in Britain as the result of soccer friction. Gang violence in New Zealand does not carry the same menace as it does in the United States – in 1987 there were 174 gang-related murders in the city of Los Angeles alone.[4] In addition, such forms of public crime are only a fragment of the overall problem of violence in this country. It has been estimated that 80 per cent of all violent offending takes place within the home (Roper, 1987: 95). Again, an important issue for future research would seem to be to analyse the nature of *private life* in New Zealand and the form of social relations that are experienced there – irrespective of what politicians say they will do to make the 'streets, suburbs and cities' safe for New Zealanders.

Punishment and the Persistent Prison

As stated at the outset, New Zealand's prison population is now at its highest ever level. In addition, this country is second only to the United States in Western societies in relation to its rate of imprisonment. Why should this be so? Why should the prison be so persistent and so over-used in a country such as New Zealand? Evidence that the modern prison does not reform criminals but only pushes them into more criminality has been around for 150 years now (Foucault, 1977). At the same time, it costs between $24,000 and $60,000 per year to keep a person locked up in prison in New Zealand, depending on their security classification – an enormous waste of human and financial resources. So why the reliance on this sanction?

First, it seems clear that New Zealand has a deeply ingrained and very unforgiving culture of punishment. Elsewhere (Pratt, 1992), I have attempted to show how the nature of colonisation of this country had the effect of valorising such virtues as functionality, utility and hard work. New Zealand was to be a 'perfect society' – a Britain of the South Pacific but without any of the home country's social problems. Such values may be worthy in their own right, but they also made this new society very intolerant and exclusionary, always quick to penalise those who did not fit or conform to its norms in one way or another. Hence, the 1860s and 1870s saw the introduction of severe laws and sanctions against fairly trivial misdemeanours such as vagrancy and prostitution (Pratt, 1992: 99-109). Furthermore, at a time when resources were scarce, it was convenient to dump society's casualties in run-down prisons and simply forget about them. Why should the virtuous, worthy and hard-working settlers – those helping to build up New Zealand – have to provide sustenance or assistance for those who would not pull their weight? This culture of punishment still has a very strong hold on the way we punish today. This includes the reliance on the prison as a convenient dumping ground, and the anger at any thought of providing options for those breaking the law (for example, through job placement or training facilities). In 1991 the Minister of Police was outraged when he heard that prisoners were being fed chicken at Mount Crawford Prison, Wellington, even though it was subsequently revealed that it was infected with salmonella.

Second, the location of most prisons today – hidden away in the country or remote suburbs – again helps to ensure that its unwanted inmates are kept out of sight and away from the public at large. The physical disappearance of the prison this century can be seen here and in most other Western countries as a part of a much longer historical trend going back several hundred years. As Spierenberg (1984) has shown, from around the early fourteenth century to the beginning of the nineteenth, the infliction of legal punishment in Europe gradually became an altogether more 'civilised' affair than had previously been the case. In the early modern period, punishment was likely to involve the infliction of at least discomfort to the bodies of offenders, at worst, excruciating pain – and in full view of the public at large. It might involve maiming, flogging or execution; or humiliation, through putting the offender on the ducking stool or in the stocks or pillory. The public would come along to watch – here are the origins of many local public holidays in Britain – and often to participate. Nor, in the cases of execution, need the punishment just end with the death of the offender: the body might be further mutilated and then put on public display (see Foucault, 1977: 1-4).

Nonetheless, the extravagant spectacle that made up legal punishment in those days began to diminish in two ways. First, the infliction of bodily pain became steadily more restricted. Even at the start of this period, it was not supposed to be administered gratuitously, but had an order and protocol to it, as Langbein (1976) indicates. Or such punishment might simply be delivered in a symbolic fashion: for example, the executioner's sword could just be waved over an offender's head in cases where it was thought that this was sufficient penalty. Thus, in the nineteenth century, punishment to the body began to be replaced by imprisonment. And the distaste for physical punishment has not ended here. Corporal punishment in schools has largely disappeared, and in Sweden it is even prohibited for parents to physically chastise their children.

The growth of imprisonment in the nineteenth century – and the subsequent relocation of prisons in this century – thus continue this tradition of having the spectacle of punishment hidden away. The removal of prisons from public view in Wellington in the early twentieth century provides a good example of this trend. Initially, the capital had two prisons – one on the Terrace, and the other built on Mount Cook, dominating the entire city landscape. Opposition to the presence of the Terrace Gaol had begun in the late 1870s when the area became an affluent residential area for civil servants working in the nearby Parliament Buildings (Hamer, 1990). In 1983 it was suggested that, 'it is impossible to avoid pointing out the deplorable mistake made by the Government in setting down a convict establishment in the centre of this city ... It is objectionable from every point of view – objectionable as opposed to all good taste or proprietary in placing a criminal lazar-house on the finest site in the whole town, where a public building dedicated to some noble or benevolent purpose should stand as the cynosure to the public eye' (NZPD, 1883: 205). Equally, its intended replacement, Mount Cook, had had to be left 'lying idle' because of 'local agitation' against any housing of prisoners amongst that community' (Report of the Inspector of Prisons, 1900: 3). The death knell of the Terrace Gaol was finally sounded in 1924 when it was reported that '[this prison] has been obsolete for some years past, and fully ten years past the site upon which it stands was promised to the Wellington Education Board for school purposes' (Report of the Under-Secretary for Prisons, 1925: 5). And around the same time, Mount Cook prison was replaced by Mount Crawford, hidden away around the bays.

What also seems clear is that a good part of the impetus for this privatisation of punishment came from the public, not government. The secrecy that this has since produced may well suit governments now – it can hide the reality and inhumanity of prison and so on – but the fact remains that this initial development seemed to be what the public wanted. The sight of convicts and even of prisons themselves had become distasteful and offensive to public mores. These same sentiments would seem to have important consequences for the determination of the nature and form that punishment takes today. For example, governments may well wish to open after-care hostels or 'half-way' houses, whether this be for economic (wanting to provide a cheap alternative to prison) or humanitarian reasons (wanting to reintegrate former prisoners into society in this way). But these initiatives are likely to be vote losers and will make politicians think very carefully about pursuing them. Any such plans will almost certainly be met by waves of protest from the communities which have been chosen to house them. Local citizens will prefer not to have to live alongside formally designated and known ex-prisoners. If they are to be reintegrated, do not involve us in the process.

The prison continues to play a useful function in modern society, despite its deleterious effects on its inmates. Surely its main purpose is not so much to do something for its inmates, but to remind the rest of us – those outside the walls – what is likely to happen to us if we step out of line. By and large, the pains of imprisonment today are not caused by the hideous physical suffering and the torture that characterised punishment in the pre-nineteenth century period; instead, they are caused by the remorseless decay of the human spirit that prison life engenders. If prisons are no longer as physically dominant as they used to be, they remain fearful spectres that haunt the *weltanschauung* of Western society. They remind most of us in New Zealand that crime is something that we had best have nothing to do with. Irrespective of social and economic conditions in this country today, most of us have too much to lose.

Notes

1. These have been used quite extensively in the United Kingdom and the United States of America. The findings of the first crime survey undertaken in New Zealand, conducted by staff at the Institute of Criminology, Victoria University, are being analysed.
2. See, for example, ecological theories of crime, Rex and Moore, 1967; differential association, Sutherland and Cressey, 1966; and sub-cultural theories, Cohen, 1956.
3. See Pratt (1987b) for a more detailed analysis and adaptation of Left Realism for New Zealand.
4. See *Dominion*, 26 August 1988. Some of this concluding section is based on Pratt (1988b).

Further Reading

Braithwaite, J., 1991, *Crime, Shame and Reintegration*, Cambridge, Cambridge University Press.
Garland, D., 1990, *Punishment in Modern Society*, Oxford, Oxford University Press.

Heidensohn, F., 1985, *Women and Crime*, London, Macmillan.
Maxwell, G. and Morris, A., 1993, *Families, Victims and Culture: Youth Justice in New Zealand*, Wellington, Department of Social Welfare.
Pratt, J., 1992, *Punishment in a Perfect Society,* Wellington, Victoria University Press.
Young, J. and Matthews, R., 1987, *Controlling Crime,* London, Sage.

15 Work

Terry Austrin

What we call work is a matter of cultural convention. For example, massaging a body, taking money over a counter, cutting meat, feeding a child and cooking are all specific tasks which are embedded in wider networks of collective activity. In those cases in which the networks of collective activity involve an employment relationship, and what we conventionally call a job, there is no doubt that the tasks can be understood as 'work'. However, where the forms of collective activity do not involve an employment relationship, and are unpaid, the labelling of the tasks as 'work' is ambiguous. This ambiguity arises because, until recently, the term work was generally reserved for paid activities.

This ambiguity in the classification of what is covered by the term 'work' has been central to the establishment of a new agenda for the sociology of work. The establishment of this agenda has involved replacing the term work by the more general term 'activities', and acknowledging that: first, unpaid activities in the household and the community are as important as subjects of study as paid activities; second, the division between paid and unpaid activities, which used to be referred to as a division between public and private, has been socially constituted through specific struggles involving states and other collective actors such as employers' associations, trade unions, women's organisations and households; third, new forms of organising activities as work always involve processes of either redrawing the boundaries of existing networks of collective activity or, alternatively, establishing new networks.

The incorporation of these three concerns over the way in which the boundaries of activities are socially constructed and negotiated has required sociologists to define what they mean when they refer to work as activities. Richard Brown has suggested that we should understand work in the following way:

> ... any physical or mental activities which transform material into a more useful form, provide or distribute goods and services to oneself

or others, and/or increase or improve human knowledge and understanding of the world (Brown, 1985: 262).

Brown's definition of work fulfils the criteria of being free of ethnic, gender and sexual bias but at the same time it is passive and gives the impression that activities are fixed. In this chapter I will accept Brown's definition, but will stress that activities are more fluid than fixed. In writing about activities as work, I will be referring to bundles of tasks and the different processes by which these tasks are negotiated and renegotiated through collective activity. The bundles of tasks that I can refer to in this chapter are limited by word restrictions but in practice, for the sociologist of work, the boundaries of research are continually expanding and changing. This expanding agenda arises from the sociological practice of undermining conventionally understood boundaries between activities. The sociology of work is guilty of this practice and as a result it is not possible to draw a boundary around it. Brown's definition, you will notice, makes no reference to whether activities are paid or unpaid.

The acceptance of ambiguity and the refusal to draw boundaries around the sociology of work makes this area of study open and exciting. Sociologists of work are interested in activities which may, or may not, be registered formally as 'jobs' through a legal framework. They may, for example, be activities which are not legally prescribed, but are constituted informally through the complex social relations of marriage, family or community networks. Of course, what is legal in one society may be illegal in another, and the explanation of such differences makes comparative study important for the sociologist. Just as significantly, the attention of the sociologist is also directed to the shifting boundaries within societies between informal activities and more formal and legal employment. For example, many activities that were once considered as unpaid community or caring work have recently entered into the sphere of paid employment. Similarly, what are generally considered paid activities can take the form of unpaid or voluntary activity in the community. The sociologist of work, then, is involved in a discussion of how different activities, paid and unpaid, fit together (Becker, 1982).

The Braverman Debate

If the study of work in sociology is currently structured around the ambiguous and shifting boundaries within and between paid and unpaid activities, what requires explanation is how this branch of sociology came to be that way and what it means for researching work in New Zealand? My explanation will begin with Harry Braverman and the publication in 1974 of his book, *Labour and Monopoly Capital*. I am not alone in choosing this arbitrary date and this particular book. Many British sociologists would do the same (Nichols, 1978; Littler, 1982), but it is doubtful that an American sociologist would choose the same starting point. I make this comment because what you will read in this chapter will be inevitably spiced with my own journey through research and the texts, written mainly by British and American authors, that I have found useful along the way. The explanation presented does not pretend to be the definitive argument or map for tracking down how sociologists reached their new agenda but rather a plausible argument which will allow me to establish how we can use sociological analysis to understand the New Zealand examples that I will present. My concern is not to follow the arguments presented in British and American material but rather to use them as appropriate, or otherwise, for dealing with New Zealand circumstances.

Braverman's book was sub-titled *The Degradation of Work in the Twentieth Century*. If it had been published today, there is no doubt that the sub-title would have made it clear that he was dealing with paid work, but 20 years ago this was not part of the way we thought about work. In 1974 Braverman was concerned with a system of managerial control called Taylorism. His contribution to the study of work was to equate this system of management with general tendencies in the capitalist organisation of work. According to Braverman, the removal of managerial reliance upon workers' knowledge was the central logic of the historical development of paid work in capitalist societies. The development of Taylorism – a set of managerial practices developed at the turn of the twentieth century and named after their author, Frederic Winslow Taylor – represented the codification of this logic into a management 'science'. Braverman referred to this logic as a process of deskilling, and in doing so opened up a large-scale controversy over trends in the organisation of work.

Braverman argued that the development of capitalist societies involved the rearrangement of paid collective activities through a process of fragmenting skills. This process was carried out not for efficiency reasons, as argued by Taylor, but to achieve increased output from a cheaper, more manageable, less skilled workforce. In the management-dominated world that Braverman conjured up, technology was not neutral but a social construction designed to further management control. Technology was, therefore, as much a part of the control systems of management as the formal rules and disciplinary procedures governing paid activity. Further, with the spread of the use of information technology into white collar and professional work, all, without exception, would be subject to deskilling.

Braverman's thesis of deskilling was to be supplemented by analysis which began to concentrate upon managerial strategies. By the end of the 1970s, Friedman (1977), Littler (1982) and Edwards (1979) had produced important work in this area. The conceptualisation of Fordism (Sabel, 1982) as a dominant managerial strategy in crisis was also part of this new agenda. Fordism is the term used to link together the system of mass production work with the organisation of mass consumer markets (Aglietta, 1981). Henry Ford, from whom the system takes its name, introduced the first assembly line in manufacturing into his Michigan plant in 1913. The plant made only one product – the Model T Ford – thereby allowing standardised machine tools designed for a maximum simplicity of operation. The idea of Fordism, following Braverman, is not that we are dealing simply with technology – the assembly line – but rather with a new social order of mass production and mass consumption which expanded worldwide. Ford, and his main competitor General Motors, set up plants in Britain, Germany and Japan and the system of work spread from the car to the whiteware industry. It provided high-volume standardised production through a specific type of assembly-line technology which, following Taylor, not only deskilled work but enhanced managerial control over it. Fordism, then, is a system of work. The term Fordist characterises the societies based on it.

This analysis of Fordist work practices and Fordist societies was to be coupled with the grand historical projection of Braverman's thesis to produce a simple formula combining large-scale manufacturing and deskilling as fate. For sociologists of work in both Britain and America, the attraction of the formula was that it integrated arguments concerning the development of capitalist societies and class analysis with arguments concerning work and technology. This attraction took different forms. Inevitably, there were those who endorsed Braverman's conclusions concerning the thesis of deskilling but there were also those who accepted that he had asked some interesting questions and, in doing so, had inadvertently established a new research agenda. It produced a sociological corrective involving the undoing of the deskilling formula, and a subsequent debate over Fordism which eventually led to a new comparative and historical sociology of work. This new sociology of work is particularly useful for our understanding of the contingent and specific characteristics of the organisation of paid activities in New Zealand, a society in which large-scale manufacturing is conspicuously absent. In what follows, I will draw upon this new sociology to interpret the ways in which paid activities have been, and currently are, organised in selected labour markets.

Deskilling and Labour Markets

It is argued that Ford took his idea of the assembly line from the Chicago slaughterhouses in which animals were disassembled section by section on a moving line. This type of disassembly line was introduced into the New Zealand meat industry in 1932-33. The way in which it was introduced has been used to illustrate a Braverman approach to the question of work and by extension an example of Fordism in New Zealand:

> When in 1932-33 the meat workers went on strike to protect themselves from threatened pay cuts, management, who in some works had

previously stored 'chain' machinery in anticipation, quickly set up the new system. The solo butchers were replaced by a 'chain' – a slow-moving mechanical conveyor from which the carcass dangled, and which pulled it past a line of workers, each of whom completed his own operation upon it until, between them, they had done all the work of the solo man. Head, hoofs, liver, entrails, heart, tongue, hide and other organs were stuffed into appropriate containers and chutes and taken to other departments for further processing. It was like a car assembly line in reverse – if you like, a disassembly line (Inkson and Cammock, 1988: 70).

The transformation of the process of butchering involved in the introduction of the chain also transformed the workers employed in the process. Unemployed, non-union workers were recruited to the new line. These men lacked both the knowledge of the traditional solo butchers and their union strength. Their pay was reduced to as little as 40 per cent of the solo butchers.

In this classic example of the introduction of new technology, a Braverman type of analysis links technology and a specific system of managerial control with the reduction of the power of the skilled craft union. The strike that took place over a six-month period, although initially concerned with a wage claim, eventually became bound up with the introduction of the new system of work design and work practices of the disassembly line. Viewing the strike in these terms, it is not difficult to see how, under the influence of Braverman, the sociology of work became a debate concerning a managerial project of deskilling.

What is missing from this account, and from similar types of analysis which concentrate on the management and workers as actors at the point of production, is a recognition of the role of wider collective networks in which these different actors were embedded. If, for example, we consider how the union was organised, we find that what was at stake for the butchers was a transition from a craft union-regulated labour market to an industrial union-regulated labour market. The butchers' craft unions had originally regulated a craft labour market operating between New Zealand and Australia. Union regulation of this Australasian labour market allowed butchers to follow the killing season between the two countries. The decision of the meat companies to introduce the disassembly line did not change the pattern of the killing seasons. On the contrary, their investment in what was then new technology was constrained by the requirement to continue with seasonal work, but at the same time they no longer relied on travelling skilled solo butchers. In this context, if unionism was to survive, it was required to develop new controls over the regulation of a new local labour market. This was achieved through establishing a form of local union organisation resting on claims to seniority in local firms rather than on occupational skill that could be carried between firms (Austrin and Curtis, 1992;

Curtis, 1992). In 1959 these local claims were consolidated in the first national award ever won by the newly established and first ever national meat workers' union. This transformation in regulation of the labour market was socially organised through collective activity.

The same exercise can be carried out with reference to the relevance of the Fordist thesis to an analysis of the development of work organisation in the meat industry. Two observations can be made. First, the New Zealand meat industry may have employed Taylorist work practices, but again this emphasis on the point of production obscures the way that, in addition to the union, the industry was, and still is, regulated through collective and interlocked networks of farmers, meat companies and a state-sponsored Meat Producers' Board. It is the struggle between these different actors over the complex forms of state licensing and distribution that is critical for the organisation of work on the slaughterboard and in the follow-on departments. For example, the Meat Producers' Board has historically operated to defend farmers' interests by keeping out large-scale multinational ownership of the meat industry. In doing so, it has facilitated the retention of both small-scale and dispersed meat companies and independent family farming. Thus, the classic feature of Fordism, the vertically integrated company organised to control supplies of raw materials to subordinate suppliers and distribute final product, has never operated in the New Zealand meat industry. This leads to the conclusion that it is unrealistic to think of New Zealand as representative of a Fordist type of society.

The second observation is linked to the first and concerns the fact that the agenda represented by both the Fordist thesis and Braverman does not allow us to grasp the significance of how new forms of work organisation are actually produced. For example, both companies and unions in New Zealand have always been subject to extensive state regulation and, in the case of primary producing industries such as meat, this remains the case despite the degree of economic deregulation that has recently taken place. The continuity of this state regulation reminds us that economic institutions are always embedded in political contexts. This argument concerning political contexts also encompasses the fact that the discontinuity in the organisation of union regulated labour markets has occurred as a result of the introduction of the Employment Contracts Act in 1991. In the meat industry this means that what is important for contemporary forms of work organisation is the combination of these continuities and discontinuities in regulation and the process of working through the possibilities opened up by this new combination. To date, this process has resulted in an extensive and decentralised renegotiation of work organisation in both the old-style freezing works and the new meat processing plants (Austrin and Curtis, 1993). Reveley (1992) has presented a similar argument with reference to the waterfront industry in New Zealand.

New Technology, Gender and Health

Braverman's emphasis on deskilling and control was also to run into difficulties when dealing with the newer, more flexible technologies based upon the computer. A study of the introduction of computerised technology into the New Zealand printing industry by Hill and Gidlow (1988) provides us with three further qualifications that need to be made to the deskilling thesis. First, the introduction of new computer technology into the printing industry in the late 1970s had variable effects upon the male workforce. It involved both the upgrading of skills – compositors and linotype operators being trained as computer personnel – as well as deskilling. Second, the introduction of new technology involved negotiation with the printers' union. The printers' union, like the butchers' unions before the introduction of the disassembly line, was a significant regulatory agency operating in a craft labour market. It was not surprising, therefore, that negotiations with the union resulted in the printers establishing their right to be retrained in the new technologies.

These qualifications, involving upskilling and negotiation, require us to recognise that skill is socially negotiated. The authors' third qualification further strengthens this claim. The technological changes were, they argue, bound up with important gender divisions within the workforce. The new technology required computer keyboard skills and the male printers were trained in the new skills by female typing teachers from the local polytechnic. At the same time, women who worked in the clerical side of the industry were prevented from being retrained. This was the significance of the negotiated agreement won by the union. The agreement ensured both the continuity of male work and segregated job structures in the industry.

Printing provides a classic example of how gender-based work organisation is in the process of being challenged and renegotiated. Traditional printing had been claimed as a male practice but the introduction of computer technology challenged this claim by drawing a distinction between the male craft practices of hot mechanical printing and the new 'female' keyboarding activities. Zuboff (1988) has introduced the body into this debate on technology by arguing that the shift from craft practices to computer-mediated work involves a shifting of activities into the abstract domain of information. This shift lifts knowledge entirely out of the body's domain. In Hill and Gidlow's (1988) example, the male printers were able to defend their historical claim to printing work and to capture what they had formerly considered to be 'women's work'. The same process of negotiation and appropriation by men occurred in the American (Reskin, 1988), British (Cockburn, 1983), and Australian printing industries (Reed, 1988). In every case, however, printers experienced the changeover to an information-based system as a threat to their masculinity.

This printing example makes it clear that an understanding of paid activities involves much more than simply discussing management-worker relations.

Understood as collective activity, the analysis of paid activity involves a recognition of a process of constant struggle over both the divisions of labour and gender. In their account of the introduction of new technology, Hill and Gidlow (1988) emphasise these points and further qualify Braverman's deskilling thesis by drawing upon the idea of how skills are not given but socially constructed. This type of analysis has roots in the study of work made by the Chicago School (Hughes, 1958). The significant contribution of this school was an emphasis placed upon the informal and negotiated character of work activity. Salaman (1986) has referred to this informal process through the metaphor of 'shadow structures'. These structures are:

> ... for those who live within them, the source of work identity, work knowledge, work morality and significant relationships. As such they are a basis for resistance, opposition, distraction, incorporation (Salaman, 1986: 112).

By deploying Salaman's concept of 'shadow structures', we can argue that, in the case of male printers, the mobilisation of an informal organisational politics enabled them to enforce a continuation of the formal gender-segregated job structures. We could, however, also go beyond Salaman and argue that the distinction or boundary between formal and informal worlds is not helpful and that what the action of the male printers makes clear is that the resource of gender identity is not part of a shadow structure or a separate lived-in world, but actually directly constituted through the organisation of work. This second interpretation overcomes the dualism of both formal and informal organisation that was so characteristic of earlier sociologies of work. It is also consistent with a new sociology of work in which gender and sexuality have become important topics (Pringle, 1991).

These observations concerning gender, skill and the way in which labour markets are regulated are also pertinent to an analysis of developments in the service sector. For example, the financial services sector has been a major growth area in the employment of women. At the same time, the industries which make up this sector have been transformed through the introduction of computerisation and, more recently, as a result of the deregulation of the finance sector (Austrin, 1992). This transformation has involved the renegotiation of the boundaries between the different industries of banking, insurance and retailing. On the union side, the amalgamation between the banking and insurance workers' unions, and the inclusion of former clerical workers union members who worked in the finance sector, has produced a new and much larger single finance union. Following the changes in state legislation that eroded the union regulation of labour markets by abolishing industry-based national awards, this new union attempts to regulate the labour market through company contracts.

A gender-based historical analysis of just how this current position was realised illustrates the significance of viewing work activities as negotiated processes. Women were first drawn into the industries of banking and insurance in the immediate post-war period. As with printing, these industries were constituted as male preserves. They were also different from printing in so far as they were constituted as male-career hierarchies or, in a different language, firm internal labour markets. In this context, the introduction of women into the industries was regulated by management introducing marriage bars requiring women to leave their employment on marriage. These bars preserving male careers remained in operation until the late 1960s.

This use of marriage bars and the arrangement of a gendered form of work organisation may be seen as similar to the exclusionary practices of the printers. Over time, however, the process of feminising work was to lead to the reverse of the printing example. Beginning in the 1970s, women in banking not only organised to change their own male-dominated union but also began struggling to open up the male-dominated career structures of their employers' internal labour markets to women. As a result, what was then the Bank Officers' Union began to consistently monitor gender discrimination. Questions of skill and deskilling were integral to this monitoring process. In those financial service institutions where the new finance union still retains a presence, this monitoring practice remains central. The new union has also been able to obtain negotiating rights over the extensive programmes of work redesign which, following the deregulation of the finance sector, have facilitated the introduction of retailing practices into the sector (Austrin, 1992; 1994a; 1994b).

The central place of gender in the new sociology of work has also generated research on the very important issue of sexual harassment (Mackinnon, 1979). This research, involving an analysis of the renegotiation of what can and cannot be spoken of and what can and cannot be done, or got away with, has been constituted as a new area of sexuality in work (Hearn *et al.*, 1989). Linked to gender but with reference to the body, the issues of health and accidents have become more central.

Work shapes and misshapes the human body in different ways. The muscles are shaped in work. So too are the stress reactions, for industries have their own characteristic diseases and accidents which mutilate and deform the human body. These are easily recognised in manual industries. In the meat industry, men and women in the cutting rooms suffer from repetitive strain injury. In the printing industry – in the hot metal days – burns, lead poisoning and deafness took their toll on employees.

The new computer-mediated work associated with the 'clean' information technology in the service sector requires different uses of the body. These also take their toll. For example, the constant use of the computer screen can impair vision, and constant use of the fingers by operators involved in data entry can lead to repetitive strain injury. A woman explains what is involved in the latter case:

> First of all it feels like pins and needles in your fingers, then an ache, a considerable ache in your wrist, then the pain starts to go up your arm. I found it was very difficult to grasp anything and I couldn't move my arms upwards. I lost the sense of power in my fingers and hands. If you don't do anything about it, it gets worse. It can go through three stages in a matter of days to a point where you are actually incapable of using your hands ... rehabilitation can take months.

These are important but under-researched issues in the sociology of work (Nichols, 1975; Willis, 1986; Dwyer, 1991). They also qualify Zuboff's claims concerning the removal of the body from work in the age of the smart machine.

Flexibility, Gender and Labour Markets

Beechey and Perkins (1987) argue that one type of activity, part-time work, is the most common type of employment relationship regulating women's paid activities in Britain. Further, they argue that women's paid activities are increasingly being constructed as part-time work. This development has also occurred in New Zealand. In 1987, 70.2 per cent of all part-time paid employees were women (RCSP, 1988, II: 502). However, as with skills, the increasing use of part-time work does not automatically relate to developments in the economy or the uses of particular technologies. Comparative evidence concerning women's participation in the paid labour market reveals radical differences between countries. David and Starzen (1992), for example, attribute the differences in the pattern of gender inequalities between Britain and France to the organisation of state taxation policies. Again, as in the case of the meat industry example referred to above, we are required to recognise that the organisation of work is embedded in particular political contexts.

The social organisation of paid part-time work has definite consequences for women in New Zealand. The majority of such jobs are found in service industries and occupations. They are usually located at the bottom of the occupational ladder and generally segregated from men's work. Women are more likely to be locked into a 'job career' – passing from one job to another – than to experience promotion in a single career. These jobs are likely to be classified as less skilled, and the women in them do not generally benefit from sick pay, maternity pay, paid holidays or superannuation. These disadvantages are supplemented by the fact that part-time work is generally intensive. Women are hired for the busy period; in banks and supermarkets, they work the rush hours. Intensity and disadvantage are combined in the new version of part-time work – zero-hours contracts. In this type of arrangement, the person concerned is hired only for the hours needed. There are no guaranteed hours and therefore no guaranteed payment. In this context, increases in paid part-time activities can be accompanied by decreases in the number of hours actually worked. Pringle (1993) reveals how these developments characterise developments in New Zealand retailing since the introduction of the Employment Contracts Act.

This discussion of part-time work and the embedding of gender divisions introduces the idea that different types of work and differently 'qualified' workers are found in different types of labour markets (see Paul Spoonley's chapter). Beechey and Perkins (1987) argue that women are generally located in a secondary labour market, whereas men have, until recently anyway, always been located in a primary labour market. This argument is based upon a distinction between types of labour market which is also at the centre of what is referred to as the 'flexibility' or post-Fordism debate (Piore and Sabel, 1984). This debate is linked to the organisation of modern firms, new technology and Japanese work practices (Moore, 1987; Dore, 1992).

Flexibility, or freeing up the labour market (as it is referred to in the New Zealand media), involves the restructuring of both the organisational forms and the traditional social relationships within paid employment. It involves employers renegotiating their own employment arrangements by redrawing the boundaries of the contracts they offer, the times at which work will be performed, the content of the jobs and the payment systems they use. These social arrangements, which were 'cemented' into the understandings people had of their work, have been modified throughout New Zealand to produce what are claimed to be more flexible organisations and workforces.

Sociological analysis of this process of redrawing the boundaries of firms and contracts has concentrated on either describing new network or hybrid forms of organisation (Powell, 1987; Austrin, 1994b) or, alternatively, has emphasised the break-up of existing, hierarchically organised labour markets. The most popular account by Atkinson (1986) emphasises the latter. Atkinson (1986) has identified two different types of flexibility: numerical and functional. Numerical flexibility is concerned primarily with the boundaries of the contract and times of work. It involves the adjustment of the workforce to the fluctuating workloads of firms. The increasing use of part-time work is a good example of this process. So too is the use of short-term contract work and youth employment. In these cases the employer is not generally bound by long-term obligations over and above the wage paid. It should be noted, however, that this type of flexibility is not new. It has always been a characteristic of the informal arrangements of the hotel and restaurant trades. Similarly, work in the agricultural sector in New Zealand and, as noted above, in the meat industry, has always been seasonal and therefore organised in this way. Atkinson (1986) argues that these types of arrangements are becoming a general feature of all work, regardless of sector.

Functional flexibility is concerned with the internal organisation of the job content of those employed. It involves elements of what was described in the printing industry as re-skilling. Instead of the worker carrying out one detailed task, as in the Taylorist system, the worker is expected to display a set of competencies across a wider range of tasks. This type of flexibility has been facilitated by new technology but is also characteristic of workplaces that still operate with labour-intensive work practices. Involvement in a wide range of tasks makes the worker not only more useful to the employer but also able to respond to market changes. In this way, ideas about job boundaries are broken down and workers are required to know and shift between a number of different tasks.

These flexible practices are central to the Japanese system of work organisation and can also be found operating in many New Zealand workplaces. For example, in the service sector, the selling of insurance has, in some parts of the industry, shifted to a flexible model. Where this model operates, insurance is sold by customer service officers who work with their own personal on-line computers. The officers have keyboard skills, knowledge of the insurance product and authorisation to complete the sale. The transactions which they process take place at branch office level but are recorded immediately at the head office of the company. Where processing information takes this form, the officers are not only combining what were formerly three entirely distinct areas of activity – clerical, administrative and supervisory – but they are also using a type of technology that no longer requires them to be based in their employers' offices. Similar changes are also in process throughout the finance sector. The long-term implications are for the expansion of home-working through computer link-ups (Hakim, 1988; Armstrong, 1992).

Atkinson (1986) identifies a further feature of modern work which he calls distancing. This is an alternative to companies organising their own flexibility. In this case, companies contract out to other organisations to supply workers. Sub-contracting work as traditionally used in the construction industry is the major example of this type of arrangement (Austrin, 1979). This method of organising work has now spread throughout both private industry and the state sector. The growth of specialised consultancy firms operating in communications, finance and social welfare is one part of it; cleaning and catering by contract is another (Bernstein, 1988). Another version of this contractual model is franchising.

Following Atkinson, it has been argued that the overall result of these changes in employment practices has been to produce three differently qualified groups of workers operating in three distinctly different types of labour market. The core workers, those employees carrying out essential activities within the firm or enterprise, tend to be full-time, multi-tasked and permanent. The printing example of Hill and Gidlow would fit this description. As 'core' workers, printers work in the primary labour market. The second category, the peripheral workers, carry out routine and mechanical activities. They are more likely to be female or members of ethnic minorities and employed on a part-time or temporary basis. Their skills are readily available in the labour market. The third category, termed external workers, are the contract workers. They are drawn from either a third, highly specialised professional, or occupational labour market or again from a secondary labour market. There is much disagreement in the contemporary sociology of work as to whether this model signals an extension of traditional labour market arrangements or whether it marks a break into a qualitatively different type of work and organisation (Hyman, 1988; Pollert, 1989). The dispersal of managerial power involved in these new types of arrangements has also given rise to a further debate on new forms of control involving computer surveillance and human resource management practices (Knights, 1989; Austrin, 1994a). I would also add that such models have a tendency to displace the analysis of the complexity of how paid activities are actually 'strung' together.

The Household and the Informal Economy

The literature in this area has been concerned with both the character of unpaid household work and how the boundaries between women's and men's paid and unpaid activities are linked. It is connected directly with the previous discussion of the gendered segregation of the labour market.

In the New Zealand context, the case of the rural sector can be used to illustrate the issues in this debate. The 1981 Census recorded four different categories of worker in the rural sector. There were 91,321 working owners, leaseholders and sharemilkers, 28,014 employees, 8,570 casual employees and 31,270 unpaid family members (RCSP, 1988, II: 503). What is of interest here is the category listed as 'unpaid family members'. This category is listed because production in the rural sector is to a large extent still based upon the household.

Household production in the rural sector reveals in a very clear way the mechanisms that link paid male labour to unpaid female labour in the household. 'I was that extra person, the wife', is how one woman, who was part of a 'married couple' team, who worked on dairy farms in the 1970s, described it. The 'wife' was a condition of her husband's employment. 'Married couples' received a rudimentary home, a side of mutton a week, sometimes some land to run sheep and grow vegetables and a weekly wage paid to the man. Part of that wage – a minimal part – was paid for the wife's activities. This usually involved cooking and washing the clothes for farm boys and shearers. In this employment relationship, unpaid household activities of the 'wife' were provided for her husband, but the same activities were paid for when they involved looking after the needs of other men or boys.

To work as a 'married couple' was to work in a personal, open-ended paternalistic employment relationship. Within this relationship, the 'married couple' were set apart from the employer but at the same time they were obligated to work at any hour. 'The only thing specific was the time off, a weekend every three weeks.' The paternal arrangement, in which work and living overlapped, also meant that tasks could be added at short notice. The 'wife', for example, was expected to 'muck in', to 'throw an eye over the paddock', to know and practice some animal husbandry ('you had to know which end was which and what to do in an emergency'), round-up the cows for milking, feed the extra men employed during the year and so on. She was, as was her husband, expected to do whatever the farmer required.

The 'wife' was absolutely essential to the organisation of activities on the farm, yet she did not receive a separate wage. She was paid a minimal amount for specific duties and the rest was classed as 'helping out'. This arrangement was possible because her activities were viewed as an extension of the unpaid activities provided for her husband. The 'duties' performed for others in the wage relationship were the same as those for her husband. Both were carried out in the household. As a result, they were not classed as 'work' in the same way as her husband's. This was her 'lot' in life.

This case of the 'married couple' may seem extreme, but it is illustrative of a gendered division of labour which, although organised as paid male work and unpaid female 'housework', was at the same time extremely flexible. Organising this flexibility was the responsibility of the woman. Her domestic activity involved extensive production – in the form of sheep and vegetables – for the family's consumption. If today this feature of production for consumption has lessened, it is still nevertheless the case that work in the household remains productive and, more significantly, is now open to dispute over the shares which household members contribute. Christine Delphy (1984: 90) uses the term domestic work and defines it as 'all the work done unpaid for others within the confines of the household or the family'. For Delphy, domestic work as unpaid activity, like all forms of activity, is defined by the social relations that organise it. The marriage relation is one set of social relations, amongst others. Another would be the family responsibility involved in the care of elderly parents (Finch and Mason, 1993).

Mackintosh (1988) has proposed that it is the marriage relation and women's position in the household that forces them into a subordinate position within paid activities. Other feminists (Walby, 1987) argue that the relation is the reverse. In Walby's account, women were excluded from paid activities and this exclusion explains their subordination in the household. Either way, the current question addressed is how the marriage relation – which has historically linked the performance of domestic activity to the status of being a housewife – operates to constitute the household in contemporary society.

The discussion of unpaid activities and the 'married couple' in the rural sector has raised the issue of self-provisioning households. According to Pahl (1988: 470), self-provisioning involves 'work in and around the household by household members or the reciprocal exchange of labour between one household and another'.

This type of activity includes domestic activity but also goes beyond it to include all household transactions conducted outside paid regular employment. It includes the self-provisioning made possible not just by the activity of the 'wife' but also with the assistance of new domestic technologies such as freezers, power tools and computers (Gershuny, 1983). It also includes the exchange of goods and services within community networks (Pahl, 1984).

These household and network support activities have always been present and have always featured prominently in accounts of rural life. Only recently, however, and in the context of unemployment, have sociologists 'discovered' them in the urban environment. In New Zealand, where households have traditionally kept vegetable gardens and undertaken extensive do-it-yourself maintenance on homes, this type of informal economy has always been widespread. The extent and significance of it has not been assessed but activities in this sector, as much as paid activities, mark New Zealand out as a different society from, for example, Britain.

In the new sociology of work, other forms of 'invisible' activities which also escape the official statistics on production and employment are also considered. These range from moonlighting – holding a second job but paying no tax on earnings – through to involvement in organised crime. Such illegal activities require extensive network arrangements to carry them through and sociologists of work argue that, together with household activities, these illegal activities must also be taken into consideration in order to understand the social division of labour of both regions and countries (Grossman, 1985; Mingione, 1988).

Conclusion

In this account of the new sociology of work, I have traced its origins from Braverman's thesis of deskilling through to the current concerns of sociologists writing in the area. I have argued that, following criticisms of Braverman's deskilling thesis, sociologists have returned to the idea of work as activities which are socially constructed and negotiated through active processes of co-operation and conflict (Strauss, 1978). In the case of paid activities, these processes have involved a continual renegotiation of the organisation of labour markets. This renegotiation has been concerned with the boundaries of paid work, firms, industries and unions (Powell and Di Maggio, 1992). I have also stressed and provided examples of the way in which the renegotiation of gender and sexual identities is inseparable from these processes. (The same argument applies to ethnic identities). The new sociology of work does not therefore marginalise paid activity. Paid activity – whatever its nature – has been and remains a central resource for assembling identities. It is also the case that the organisation of paid activity in the factory remains central to explaining economic development (Lazonick, 1990). Similarly, I have argued that the inclusion of the gendered arrangements of households within the sociology of work is a recognition of the significance of the redrawing of the boundaries between paid and unpaid activity.

One possible future for the sociology of work lies in integrating the different ways in which the boundaries between the different activities have already been, and are currently, in the process of being redrawn. In Britain, a new research agenda concerned with the forms of interdependence established between paid work in the formal economy and unpaid work in the informal or household economy has been proposed (Roberts *et al.*, 1985). Sociologists in America have also proposed what they refer to as a new economic sociology (Granovetter and Swedberg, 1992). These new sociologies are concerned with the plurality and diversity of networks of collective activity. As an agenda for research, they offer an exciting future by focusing on new ways of understanding developments in paid and unpaid activities in New Zealand. As new sociologies, they contribute towards resituating the study of work as fundamental to sociological enquiry.

Further Reading

Granovetter, M. and Swedberg, R., 1992, *The Sociology of Economic Life*, San Francisco, Westview Press.
Grint, K., 1991, *The Sociology of Work: An Introduction,* Oxford, Blackwell.
Pahl, R.E., 1988, *On Work,* Oxford, Basil Blackwell.
Roberts, B. *et al.*, 1985, *New Approaches to Economic Life: Economic Restructuring, Unemployment and the Social Division of Labour*, Manchester, Manchester University Press.
Salaman, G., 1987, *Working,* London, Tavistock.
Thompson, P., 1983, *The Nature of Work: An Introduction to Debates on the Labour Process,* London, Macmillan.
Willis, E. (ed.), 1988, *Technology and the Labour Process: Australasian Case Studies,* Sydney, Allen and Unwin.

16 Leisure and Recreation

Bob Gidlow, Harvey Perkins, Grant Cushman, Clare Simpson

Introduction

Popular notions of leisure focus on pleasure, fun and enjoyment by oneself, or with friends and family in a variety of settings. Unlike the serious business of work, leisure has an atmosphere of frivolity about it. This is one reason why social scientists have spent more effort studying work than leisure. Since 1950, however, a growing social scientific interest in leisure has emerged in Europe, North America, Australia and, more recently, New Zealand (Perkins and Cushman, 1993). Our purpose in this chapter is to introduce several important issues for the sociology of leisure (Gidlow, 1993).

Historical Overview

In this section, our focus is on the historical development of European leisure patterns in New Zealand. There are two reasons for this focus. First, there is a lack of documented research on the leisure patterns of Maori[1] and the various non-British immigrant groups in New Zealand (Perkins and Gidlow, 1991). Second, uncertainty exists about the meaning and significance of Western concepts such as 'leisure' for Maori, Pacific Islands and other non-European ethnic groups (McGregor and McMath, 1993).

Current trends in Pakeha leisure are traceable to colonial origins (Watson, 1993). As society changed[2] in response to wider social, economic, and technological developments, leisure patterns both reflected and reinforced such changes. By the 1860s, pioneering New Zealanders had established a variety of settlements, ranging from the transient, almost exclusively male, 'canvas' communities, to the newly settled but planned communities of Dunedin, Christchurch, Nelson, New Plymouth and Wellington. The 'canvas' communities were tough, isolated and boisterous places, where men filled their leisure with drinking, gambling and other, disreputable, pleasures (Eldred-Grigg, 1984; Crawford, 1987).

In the planned settlements, the more puritan members of the middle class sought to control the 'disreputable' pleasures of the 'idle' poor and the less respectable working class. They disliked the prevalence of prostitution and the high level of alcohol consumption (Eldred-Grigg, 1982). Religious groups sought to have Sunday sports fixtures abolished by making public playing fields unavailable. They also opposed the operation of public transport on Sundays (Collins and Lineham, 1993).

During the initial years of European settlement, away from the frontier communities leisure was predominantly family-centred, particularly in middle-class and respectable working-class families (Sinclair, 1960; Simpson, 1962). In this early period, before leisure became more organised and commercialised, families and communities created their own recreation using whatever resources were available (Barker, 1873; Woodhouse, 1988). Churches frequently provided a social and spiritual focus for the community (Eldred-Grigg, 1982; Collins and Lineham, 1993). Hotels, too, served as social centres, although they drew upon a different section of the community and offered different pastimes.

Communities commonly came together to celebrate festivals and anniversaries. At the first Otago Anniversary Sports in 1849, for example, a few hundred pioneers gathered to give thanks that they had survived a year of settlement. They drank English beer, watched some athletic contests, bet on the horse races and enjoyed their first official holiday (McLintock, 1949). Eldred-Grigg (1982) paints a fascinating portrait of colonial Canterbury at play. Carnival Week, for example, was a great annual holiday, reaching a climax on Cup Day and Derby Day. Ten thousand people gathered at Riccarton Racecourse on Cup Day in 1875. Similarly, over the summer of 1872-3, the citizens of Christchurch had the opportunity to attend 129 performances of professional theatre, 33 of opera, several chamber music concerts and appearances by solo artists. Handel concerts drew large crowds, as in 1872 when special trains from Kaiapoi and Lyttelton carried at least 1600 people to attend a performance (Eldred-Grigg, 1982).

Later in the century, the wonders of New Zealand's natural environment began to be commercially exploited for their tourist potential (Perkins et al., 1993). By the beginning of the 1880s for example, Queenstown and the Lake Wakatipu region of Central Otago had established a reputation for outstanding, rugged beauty. As access routes to the region were improved, so visitor numbers increased. By July 1878, improved rail links considerably speeded the journey between Dunedin and Queenstown. By 1885, yachts and pleasure boats could be hired on Lake Wakatipu, and tramping routes were clearly marked by signs (Temple, 1980).

Team spirit or group solidarity was at the foundation of pioneer survival, and this was reflected in the early popularity of competitive team sports. These sports were largely male preserves during most of the nineteenth century. Women did other things (Lynch and Simpson, 1993). Moral standards, social conventions and etiquette, combined with dress and fashion codes, severely restricted the readiness of, and opportunity for, women to participate in active recreation.

There were also class distinctions in leisure patterns. Cricket was predominantly a gentleman's game.[3] Middle-class men played at athletics and, with women, joined their 'betters' for games of tennis. Male members of the working class found their pleasures in prize-fighting, cock-baiting and in pub-related activities (games of chance, cards, billiards and snooker). For men, rugby was a sport which most quickly cut across class lines. Yet, in so doing, it entrenched a particular set of gender relationships which has continued in the rugby world, almost unchanged, to this day (Fougere, 1989; Cameron, 1993). Hampered by social expectations and constraints, women's sport developed more slowly, gaining momentum during the 1890s and 1900s. Tennis and hockey were considered most appropriate for females. However, some women cyclists succeeded in highlighting the benefits of healthy physical activity and the need for more sensible and liberating clothing (Simpson, 1993).

As the century progressed, the continued growth of urban populations created a secure market for commercial suppliers of popular entertainment. The respectable and cultured classes had shown their willingness to pay for artistic and musical performances at an early stage of colonial settlement. However, it was the widespread popularity of the music hall and vaudeville which gave New Zealand's first true leisure entrepreneurs their origins. The influence of some of these entrepreneurs (e.g. John Fuller) continued well into the twentieth century. They established theatres for music hall and other 'live' forms of entertainment which later became the first cinemas. These introduced a new age of commercial colonialism which linked New Zealand to the U.S.A. whilst still maintaining cultural links with Britain.

From the 1920s onwards, American business practices strongly influenced New Zealand. A gradual cultural change accompanied this commercial dominance as American tastes in music and fashion replaced diverse home-grown cultural forms. This process was reinforced by the close links forged between New Zealand and the U.S.A. during the Second World War. Twenty-thousand U.S. troops were stationed in New Zealand (Dunstall, 1992: 525) and many other U.S. forces from the Pacific theatre came here for 'Rest and Recreation'. Despite the impact of the cinema, much leisure was still home-based. The radio and the gramophone carried the growing cultural uniformity of leisure practice into most homes. They were the true foundation of the modern leisure-goods industry. The advent of television in 1960 also reinforced patterns of home-centred leisure by undermining the popularity of cinema.

Changes in transport technology modified leisure participation away from the home. Bicycles were widely available by the turn of the century and cycling was a popular form of recreation, particularly among young people. Improvements in public transport made it possible for people of all ages and fitness levels to move about freely. The seaside became a major weekend attraction in summertime (Eldred-Grigg, 1982).

The motorcar revolutionised post-war New Zealand. It changed urban form by encouraging the spread of suburbia (see David Thorns' chapter). It also supported the development of a new type of travel accommodation – motels – and helped the development of domestic and in-bound tourism. Further, it provided a venue for recreational sex and a focus of popular music for a growing youth culture and it became an important leisure object for males. Weekend rituals of car-grooming spawned a related industry catering to the demand for waxes, polishes and accessories.

Besides the growing commercialisation of leisure, the twentieth century also brought greater public sector involvement in leisure management. In the initial period of European settlement, central government limited its direct involvement in leisure to the establishment of national parks (Devlin, 1993). Thereafter, until the election of the first Labour Government, central governments hardly concerned themselves with leisure. They simply regulated a wide range of 'morally suspect' leisure activities (e.g. alcohol, gambling and prostitution). Local government involvement was hardly more active, although it was responsible for the establishment of botanic gardens, parks, libraries, swimming pools, community halls, museums and similar facilities.

In 1936 the Hon. W.E. Parry, the Minister of Internal Affairs, argued for a more positive central government role in leisure and recreation provision. As the Physical Welfare and Recreation Bill passed through the House in 1937, Parry declared that 'good physical and mental health should be the foundation of a good life, besides making the individual profitable to the nation to which he [sic] belongs. Physical fitness gives confidence; its absence weakens the moral fibre of the nation' (Stothart, 1978).

The government established a National Council of Sport and a Physical Welfare and Recreation Branch in the Department of Internal Affairs. In 1939 National Fitness and Recreation Weeks began, and were reminiscent of the 'Have a Go' campaigns of more recent years. The Physical Welfare and Recreation Branch had a wide brief to educate the public about leisure, to raise standards of health and fitness, to encourage active participation and to provide training courses (Stothart, 1978).

The Second World War and its aftermath led to a redirection of national priorities and severely interrupted the development of plans under the Act. The defeat of Labour in 1949 brought to office a National Government which let the Physical Welfare and Recreation Branch die a quiet death. National did not support a governmental role in leisure and recreation and was concerned about state interference in the affairs of national sporting bodies.

The third Labour Government set up a Ministry and Council for Recreation and Sport in 1973. This was a time when local governments were beginning to take a more active interest in community recreation development. The Ministry and Council often funded local initiatives and helped to speed change in this area. In 1984 the fourth Labour Government objected to the duplication of functions of the Ministry and the Council. It passed the Recreation and Sport Act 1987 and established the Hillary Commission for Recreation and Sport. In 1991 a National Government amended the 1987 Act to replace recreation by a narrower perspective on leisure which emphasises fitness and physical activity. The Hillary Commission is now responsible for 'sport, fitness and leisure'. Laidler and Cushman (1993:8) and Perkins *et al.* (1993:178) suggest that this is a return to the ethos of the Physical Welfare and Recreation Act 1937, since '... most non-physical and 'non-serious' leisure pursuits are seen by the Minister [John Banks] as falling outside the purview of the legislation'.

In the next section, we examine contemporary patterns of leisure participation in New Zealand, particularly from the 1970s onwards (Laidler and Cushman, 1993).

Leisure Participation Patterns

A popular conception of New Zealanders at leisure includes health, physical fitness and high levels of involvement in organised sport. They are thought to consume healthy foods and to participate in regular exercise in an invigorating climate. Is this an accurate description? What are the patterns of leisure participation of New Zealanders? What factors influence leisure choices and satisfactions, and what are the barriers to leisure participation?

Before we begin to answer these questions, we need to be aware that research into leisure participation is fraught with difficulties. First, researchers define 'leisure' in different ways. Second, it is not possible to make firm predictions about leisure participation. Many leisure activities and experiences are 'fads', and have short, intense and unpredictable life spans. Methodological problems add to the difficulty of prediction. Present research methodology makes it difficult to distinguish between the effects of population change and changing tastes and preferences on variations in leisure patterns.

A third set of problems arises when we try to interpret patterns of leisure choices and satisfactions. Leisure participation and demand are dependent on a host of changing social and economic factors. These include: personality; gender; family and peer group; age; life cycle stage; educational attainment; socio-economic background; residential history; experience in childhood; ethnicity; influence of the media; the content of school curricula; and value positions and changes in the allocation of time to work and leisure (Cushman, 1983; 1986).

The predominant research instrument in the analysis of leisure has been the leisure participation survey. The forerunners of these surveys in New Zealand were regional and local recreation studies (e.g. Larkin, 1968; Palmerston North City

Council, 1969; Auckland Regional Authority, 1971). Jorgensen (1974) reviewed these studies and concluded that the bulk of this research was descriptive, superficial and displayed several methodological shortcomings. Jorgensen also noted a general tendency for New Zealand leisure research to overlook non-sporting forms of leisure, particularly social forms of leisure such as entertaining and 'being with friends' (Robb and Howorth, 1977). The emphasis on sport and outdoor recreation in the early surveys was not surprising as the initiative and resources for the research came from government agencies with a primary involvement in policy problems concerned with these two forms of leisure.

A national recreation survey – known as the New Zealand National Recreation Survey – was conducted in the mid-1970s. This survey informed policy-makers and planners for the first time of New Zealanders' diverse range of leisure activities. Most importantly, the study highlighted the minority status of many leisure activities, including vigorous sport and the 'high' arts, which the government was promoting.

Table 16.1 shows the levels of participation in the most popular twenty-three leisure activities in New Zealand. The figures present patterns similar to those in surveys conducted in Canada (Zuzanek, 1979), Britain (Veal, 1984) and Australia (Department of Arts, Sport, the Environment, Tourism and Territories, 1988) in which home-based and social activities are much more popular than sport and cultural events. The researchers deliberately excluded television-watching and sex from the list of activities in the questionnaire and they omitted pub-going through an oversight (Tait, 1984).

The data (see Table 16.1) dispel the popular image of New Zealanders as favouring vigorous and active outdoor activities and sport. They support the conclusion that most leisure activities are essentially minority activities. For example, less than 14 per cent of the respondents shared 191 out of the 216 leisure activities listed in the survey. A striking characteristic of the study was the concentration of leisure activities in and around the home.

Leisure participation patterns change over time. Some time-series data on patterns of leisure behaviour have resulted from the Hillary Commission's recent *Life in New Zealand* survey. Unlike the earlier national survey, which used an interviewer-administered questionnaire, this survey employed a self-administered questionnaire to measure leisure participation patterns and activity categories. While the two surveys have points of comparison, establishing trends and changes with any confidence requires a standardised approach to surveying. The surveys contain enough similarities, however, to provide a macroscopic view of changing leisure patterns in New Zealand.

An initial examination of the survey data (Tables 16.1 and 16.2) suggests that there is a large measure of stability in results over the fifteen to sixteen-year period. The recent data confirm the attraction of home-based and physically undemanding interests.[4] The surveys provide some support for the stereotypical view of New

Table 16.1
Involvement Level in Specific Activities, 1974-75

Activity	Men %	Men Rank	Women %	Women Rank	Total %	Total Rank
Reading	35	2	53	2=	44	1
Gardening	37	1	44	5	40	2
Listening to records	33	4=	39	6	36	3
Swimming	34	3	36	7=	35	4
Cooking, baking	-	-	49	4	29	5=
Visiting or entertaining friends	22	11=	36	7=	29	5=
Sewing	-	-	55	1	28	7
Knitting	-	-	53	2=	28	7=
Watching sport	33	4=	21	15=	27	9
Picnics, barbecues and hangis	22	11=	30	9	26	10
Dining out	21	13	28	10	25	11
Cinema, theatre	19	14=	25	12	22	12
Music	17	20=	24	13	20	13=
Fishing - saltwater	30	7=	-	-	20	13=
Rugby Union	33	4=	-	-	20	13=
Walking	-	-	26	11	20	13=
House maintenance	27	9	-	-	19	17=
Driving	19	14=	19	19=	19	17=
Travelling	17	20=	21	15=	19	17=
Cards	18	17=	20	18	19	17=
Billiards, snooker, pool	30	7=	-	-	18	21=
Religion	-	-	22	14	18	21=
Visiting parks, gardens, zoos	-	-	21	15=	18	21=

Other activities ranked in the top 23 activities for men were vehicle maintenance (24%), woodwork (19%), cricket (18%), soccer (18%) and boating (16%) and for women crochet (19%).21=

Source: Tait, D., 1984, New Zealand Recreation Survey 1974-75, (Sample size: 4,011).

Zealand women being more interested in home-based activity and social interaction than men. For the majority of both sexes, and especially for women, visiting and being visited play a part in weekly life. Both surveys show that the pub and outdoor sports are still predominantly male preserves in New Zealand, although this is less apparent in 1989-90 than in 1974-75 (Cushman and Laidler, 1990; Lynch and Simpson, 1993).

While national leisure surveys provide useful benchmark data on leisure participation, they offer only a very generalised and preliminary understanding of

Table 16.2
Favourite Leisure Activities 1989-90

Activity	Men %	Men Rank	Women %	Women Rank	Total %	Total Rank
Reading	39	2	56	1	48	1
Television/video	47	1	37	3	42	2
Visiting friends/family	24	4	45	2	35	3
Listening to music	31	3	32	5	32	4
Gardening	23	5	33	4	28	5
Walking	17	7=	27	6	22	6
Arts and crafts	7	16	24	7	16	7
Playing with children	15	10	16	8	15	8=
Organised sport	19	6	11	11=	15	8=
Relaxed/doing nothing	14	11=	12	10	13	10=
Dining out	11	14	14	9	13	10=
Driving for leisure	14	11=	11	11=	12	12
Watching sport	17	7=	6	15=	11	13=
Informal sport	16	9	7	14	11	13=
Beach/river	9	15	11	11=	10	15=
Pub/clubs	14	11=	6	15=	10	15=

Source: Cushman, G. and A. Laidler *et al.*, 1991, Life in New Zealand Survey: Leisure, Volume IV, (Sample Size: 4,373)

leisure participation, motivation and satisfaction. To interpret how and why patterns of leisure participation develop, overseas researchers (e.g. Stebbins, n.d.; Brandenburg *et al.*, 1982; Woodward *et al.*, 1988) have used qualitative methods.

Qualitative researchers interpret the *meanings* respondents ascribe to leisure. They do this by studying the day-to-day activities which make up the respondents' way of life or lifestyle. This approach might counter Roberts' (1978) disappointment that 'orthodox' recreation research '... tells us little about the interrelationships between recreation, the rest of leisure and the rest of life' (Glyptis, 1981). This problem could be overcome by using qualitative methods in culturally sensitive ways to interpret the leisure experiences and activities of specific groups, for example, women, the elderly, Maori and other Polynesian people, and people with disabilities.

A Particular Form of Leisure: Sport

In the last section, we noted that New Zealanders often treat 'recreation' and 'sport' synonymously, as though sport is the only form of recreation practised (Cameron, 1993). At one level, it is difficult to understand the cultural dominance of sport and its symbols. As indicated earlier, information from leisure participation surveys shows the diversity of New Zealanders' recreational involvements and the numerically minor nature of sporting participation. In other ways, the dominance of sport is easier to understand. This is partly due to the international successes of New Zealand sportsmen and women which has helped to give New Zealand a worldwide identity as a sporting nation. In the 1970s and 1980s the commercial exploitation of sport by sponsors and the mass media – particularly television – gave sport and its sponsors a high public profile in many Western societies including New Zealand (see, e.g. Moore, 1990). The state and its agencies have encouraged sports education and sports participation because of the assumed personal, community and national benefits of sport. Many New Zealanders see sport as a 'good thing'. They believe that healthy bodies make for healthy minds, and that teamwork and co-operation on the playing field have wider, community implications, such that sectional interests are submerged by national accomplishments, such as 'Going for Gold'.

Sporting prowess, epitomised by the Silver Fern on the All Blacks' jersey, has undoubtedly been a major source of national identity and pride in a young country which has lacked more conventional measures of worldly importance. In Victorian England, team sports – particularly rugby – were valued in public schools (private schools in New Zealand) for their character-forming qualities and for teaching leadership skills to the children of the élite. However, in colonial New Zealand, such sports initially supported egalitarian values associated with male mateship (McCrone, 1988).

Sport has evolved from a colonial pastime with an informal style of organisation and a heavy emphasis on the socialising and recreational benefits of participation, to highly structured and competitively-organised activities. The transformation of sport reflects wider social, economic, political and demographic processes associated with New Zealand's development as an industrial producer of agricultural commodities.

Certain controlling institutions dominate the sporting scene (Simpson, 1983; Cameron, 1993), and they display the same administrative tendencies – notably bureaucratisation (Thompson, 1969; 1975) – which are normally associated with industrial and state organisations. Moreover, a dominant leisure organisation such as the New Zealand Rugby Football Union has close links with economic and political élites (Simpson, 1983). This renders suspect any researcher's decision to treat leisure as somehow distinct from mainstream institutions in New Zealand.

During the 1970s and 1980s, academics, politicians and some sportsmen and women began to question long-held beliefs about the benefits of sport. One school of criticism developed in response to New Zealand's continuing rugby ties with South Africa. Its adherents questioned the morality of sporting links with a nation which officially discriminated against the bulk of its inhabitants, and the right of one sporting organisation to put at risk the futures of other sportsmen and women by defying Commonwealth (and much domestic) opinion (Thompson, 1969; 1975; Whannel, 1983). A second school of criticism developed as part of the women's movement in New Zealand. Its members disliked differences in sporting participation of men and women (as this reflected social mores governing 'feminine' pastimes), the 'superiority' of men's sports (as reflected in mass media coverage) and the wider social implications of the masculine values commonly portrayed and encouraged by 'male' sports – aggressiveness, competitiveness and domination (Cameron, 1993). There is also some evidence, albeit anecdotal, that some New Zealand men are rejecting these values and the sporting activities which support them.

The sociology of sport – a newcomer to sociology – has expanded almost exponentially in the 1980s outside New Zealand, particularly in relation to women and sport. In New Zealand, the sociology of sport is in its infancy, although some authors, not all sociologists, have made some significant contributions to the analysis of the sociological (Cameron, 1993), political (Thompson, 1969, 1975), and 'cultural' aspects (Fougere, 1989; Phillips, 1987) of sport. Though we still lack basic descriptive data on sporting participation, some of the issues related to women and sport have been explored (Jones, 1981; Lynch and Simpson, 1993; Cameron, 1993). Other researchers have studied the ways that commercial imperatives of television have led to high media profiles for four sporting codes (cricket, rugby – union and league – and netball), three of them 'male', while rendering other codes partly or completely invisible (Ferkins, 1992; O'Leary, 1984). The invisibility of women's sport is not, however, limited to the electronic media (McGregor and Melville, 1992).

Interpretations of the Nature and Role of Leisure

While research on participation in sport and other forms of leisure provides important information, we have to theoretically interpret that information if we are to understand leisure in a more substantial way (Gidlow, 1993; Parkin, 1993; Perkins, 1993). We will introduce those interpretations which highlight and define key sociological perspectives. In doing so, we are entering an arena of theoretical conflict (Rojek, 1985) between three major perspectives or paradigms: those of 'pluralists', 'neo-Marxists' or 'class domination' theorists, and feminists. We will consider each in turn.

'Pluralism' is a concept from political science, relating to the arrangement of power in Western political democracies. Leisure pluralists believe that the characteristics of leisure behaviour – including the diversity of leisure interests, the weakening impact of social class influences on leisure participation and the sovereignty of the consumer – reflect the *power* of individuals, as leisure actors or consumers, to express their preference, and the *responsiveness* of institutions to these preferences.

Leisure pluralists invoke several arguments to support their case. The first emphasises the diversity of leisure interests. Since the Second World War, and particularly since the mid-1960s, the types of leisure opportunities available to the public have expanded rapidly. Social, economic and demographic trends have encouraged leisure consumers to try new activities, and leisure suppliers to provide such activities. For example, increased disposable income has made it possible for ordinary people to enter leisure markets as consumers of leisure goods. A reduction in family size has left families and family members less tied to child-rearing tasks and with potentially more time available for leisure.

Changing gender roles have increased women's participation in the workforce and in a wider variety of leisure activities (Lynch and Simpson, 1993). A recent upsurge of interest in maintaining a healthy lifestyle and being physically fit has led to increased participation in activities such as jogging, aerobics, jazzercise, running, cycling and swimming.

The second argument used by the leisure pluralists is that family and friendship networks (Kelly, 1983; Roberts, 1981) and lifestyle and status (Veal, 1989) rather than social classes, are the contexts within which leisure socialisation takes place and in which much leisure behaviour is practised. Many popular forms of recreation and leisure – such as television viewing, newspaper reading and movie-going – are general 'lifestyle' activities, not class activities.

Moreover, according to Young and Willmott (cited in Clarke and Critcher, 1985: 22), a process of 'stratified diffusion' is at work. Leisure activities which began as the prerogative of upper-class groups (e.g. skiing and motorcar ownership) gradually became available to other groups. For the pluralists, these examples point to the 'democratisation' of leisure – to the fact that people are no longer prevented by income, values or by the closure strategies of other groups from making real choices in leisure markets (Roberts, cited in Clarke and Critcher, 1985: 38).

The third argument used by leisure pluralists is that the consumer, not the supplier, has the power in leisure markets. Suppliers respond to, and try to predict, changes in consumer demand but are unable to dictate leisure 'choices'. As Roberts (1981) points out, since the leisure market relies largely on disposable income, it is fickle and unpredictable, involving high risks and resulting in a significant rate of failure for those suppliers who venture into it.

Pluralist definitions of the role of leisure focus on freely chosen participation in enjoyable activities. Leisure '... serves a plurality of ends, such as restoring and recreating energies for the task ahead, diverting attention from burdensome cares, raising consciousness or mind expansion, ... (and) keeping people off the streets' (Andrew, 1981: 151). From the pluralist perspective, therefore, leisure contributes to the physical and mental health of individuals and the well-being of society.

Turning now to the second theoretical perspective or paradigm, neo-Marxist theorists of leisure hold that while Marx did not *directly* address the issue of leisure, his explanation of the emergence and persistence of capitalist society has implications for *all* aspects of society, including leisure (Rojek, 1985: 4). Rojek (1985) and Clark and Critcher (1985), British writers in the neo-Marxist tradition, take issue with the pluralists on several grounds. First, when pluralists note the declining importance of class in leisure behaviour, they are expressing a superficial understanding of social class and employing definitions of class which are methodologically convenient but not theoretically reasoned. Marxists define a class by its relationship to other classes in its productive role – by what it does, not by opinion polls as to the prestige or status of occupational groups. Moreover, classes are not distinct 'entities', which are independent of other variables such as family, religion, gender, occupation and education. These groups and institutions are the embodiments of class values and constraints, and the transmitters of class cultures – of values, attitudes, expectations and aspirations. Thus, for example, from a neo-Marxist perspective, 'class' and 'family' are not alternative, discrete, explanatory variables.

Nor, according to the neo-Marxists, should we always expect to find *direct* correlations between class and types of leisure participation (Clarke and Critcher, 1985), for class cultures change with time and incorporate new experiences. For example, capitalism encourages the democratisation of leisure and hence the participation of the working class – not simply the middle and upper classes – in leisure markets as consumers of videos, compact disc recorders, packaged holidays, home-brewing kits and other goods and services. Class culture mediates and informs such leisure consumption experiences (working-class tastes in reading and music, and types of holiday pleasures, for example, may not suit the middle class). But these experiences also change class culture. Leisure consumption comes to be taken for granted as a regular and legitimate part of working-class life, and leisure experiences can provide new knowledge and insights and contribute to attitudinal change.

Second, neo-Marxists argue that pluralists ignore the dynamics and tendencies of capitalist production when they discuss the diversity of peoples' leisure interests (Rojek, 1985). In the capitalist mode of production, leisure 'manufacturers' and suppliers, like other capitalists, seek to increase profitability and reduce risk-taking by forming cartels and monopolies; involving foreign capital and multi-national organisations; standardising, packaging and marketing 'unique' experiences such as New Zealand's scenic wonders; manipulating consumer 'choice' through 'image' and 'brand' marketing; and by attempting to turn 'luxuries' (e.g. alcohol) into necessities, to increase the predictability of demand.

These tendencies are already well advanced in those industries which supply mass leisure markets, so that 'choices' are becoming increasingly restricted. Cigarette manufacturing, newspaper production, the brewing industry and cinema chains in New Zealand are each dominated by one or two large companies. Some of these are partly or wholly foreign-owned and some are New Zealand-owned, with their own offshore commercial investments. Local, 'independent', producers, such as small brewers, often emerge to fill *niche* markets, and provide greater choice for consumers but their existence testifies to the overall market dominance of a few large companies, such as the two brewing 'giants'.

Third, neo-Marxists believe that pluralists fail to pay sufficient attention to the structured inequalities in society which influence leisure 'choices'. People do not enter the leisure market as consumers with equal capital. Some consumers enjoy greater 'sovereignty' than others because they have higher levels of disposable income. Yachting, polo and skiing, winter holidays abroad, the acquisition of artistic products and craftware, etc., are not viable choices for many New Zealanders. Many 'middle' New Zealand families can no longer afford to enjoy expensive leisure activities and lifestyles because of the cost of supporting their children through tertiary education. Cultural capital, too, is unevenly distributed (Bourdieu, 1977). In schools, for example, a 'hidden' curriculum prepares children from different social class and ethnic backgrounds for different social destinations and hence 'choices' in work (Bowles, 1976) and in leisure (see Roy Nash's chapter).

Fourth, neo-Marxists point out that pluralism is a perspective on *power,* not a coherent theory of *society* in which leisure-related behaviour can be sited (Clarke and Critcher, 1985). Moreover, important historical questions about the evolution of leisure and recreational practices remain unanswered by a theoretical and research emphasis which remains in the present. By comparison, Marxism offers a theory of society which is historically grounded in the dynamics of class struggle, and can therefore provide a valuable interpretation of the rise of leisure forms. For example, reading is a mass leisure activity in Western societies, and the novel figures prominently in peoples' reading tastes, but the novel is a comparatively recent invention. It dates from the early capitalist period when it satisfied the tastes of a new group of readers: the families, and particularly the unmarried daughters, of the new men of industry and commerce (Fiedler, 1960). The early novels – for example, those of Samuel Richardson – were heavily instructional and their plots mirrored the struggles of the bourgeoisie for political, and not simply economic, ascendency.

From the neo-Marxist perspective, leisure in capitalist societies does not, as the pluralists would have it, lie at the centre of a largely harmonious, integrated society. The role of leisure is to reproduce capitalist society in its present inequitable forms. Thinking of leisure only in terms of pleasure and individual development is an example of false consciousness. While members of the working class have maintained a partial cultural identity separate from the dominant capitalist class, much of their leisure behaviour is constrained and directed by the logic of capitalist production primarily concerned with profit generation. An example is rugby league, which, through skilful marketing, sponsorship[5] and media linkages, has generated a large following among working-class New Zealanders of various ethnic backgrounds, but which is quite ruthless in its treatment of players who do not 'perform'.

While neo-Marxists offer a critical theory of society, it is not critical enough for some. Radical feminists set the study of leisure in the context of women's oppression and gender relations. They wish to change positively the social position of women (Deem, 1986). *Patriarchy*, the existence of social structural forces which produce and reproduce the dominance of men over women, is the central issue in the radical feminist analysis of society and leisure.

For feminists, leisure can only be understood within the context of women's lives (Wearing and Wearing, 1988). Many feminist leisure writers have sympathy with the neo-Marxist position on leisure (Cameron, 1993) but believe that the unwillingness of neo-Marxism to fully accept that women are oppressed primarily by gender relations and patriarchy, rather than by class, is a major flaw. Feminists point out that the leisure participation of most women is severely constrained by their subordinate position in society. Women, therefore, do not experience 'leisure', if by that concept we mean freely chosen participation in enjoyable activities. Deem (1986) discusses the constraints on women's opportunities to enjoy freely chosen leisure. The problem for women is that 'men see leisure as a right; women do not and are not encouraged by men so to do. To the extent that women do engage in leisure, they do so in ways which are largely determined by men and on terms inferior to those enjoyed by men' (Deem, 1986: 13; Henderson *et al.*, 1989; Dempsey, 1991).

This array of perspectives supports Rojek's contention that the meaning of leisure occupies 'contested theoretical space'. 'Writers representing different paradigms disagree fundamentally about what leisure signifies, how it has developed, and why it should be studied' (Rojek, 1985: 6). Given the different sets of assumptions of the theorists considered here, it is most unlikely that a theoretical unity in the sociology of leisure will emerge, although structuration theory (Giddens, 1984) and other 'postmodern' approaches, offer some possibility of a *rapprochement* between certain perspectives previously considered distinct (for further discussion, see Perkins, 1993: 125-127).

Leisure and Social Policy

Leisure has only recently become a significant social policy issue in New Zealand. The reason for its past neglect is that leisure was for many years viewed as individually-chosen and subject to voluntary authority (Lane, 1978). Unlike education, health and employment which have lain at the core of social policy debates, leisure has been associated with private desires and not the public interest.

Central and local government interest in leisure issues first gained strength with the inception of national parks and local government reserves departments in the nineteenth century (Stothart, 1980; Perkins *et al.*, 1993). Since the economic depression of the 1930s, social policy-makers have displayed a marked increase of interest in managing leisure and associated resources. Recently, as well as concerning themselves with the immediate issues of service delivery and technical land use matters, practitioners and academics have discussed the role of leisure in social policy. Unemployment, and other social problems with leisure implications (e.g. inadequate health and fitness; recreational drugs), have acted as catalysts to change views about leisure and leisure policy. As a result, '... leisure now gives rise to questions of values and responsibility; it is no longer a matter merely of technical problem-solving, physical resource management, nuisance control and conflict resolution over land' (Cushman and Laidler, 1988: 509). Leisure is now established in the network of social services in New Zealand, and confirmed by statute (see earlier discussion). Leisure has also become an important area of economic activity – most obviously in the tourism field – with important implications for government action (Community Services Institute, 1985; Hillary Commission, 1993).

Western governments accept, to varying degrees, several roles in leisure policy. The directions taken by these leisure policies are generally based on the principles of equity, universality, diversity, conservation, co-ordination and promotion (Cushman, 1983; Cushman and Laidler, 1988). Underlying these principles is the idea that leisure is a fundamental right of all citizens. New Zealand's leisure policies have been based on the notion that leisure has personal and social benefits, has an important role in social services, and is an economically significant industry. In specific terms, New Zealand's central and local governments have attempted to improve the nation's health and fitness, and promoted '... social activity organised for social ends, especially if those ends are compatible with political objectives and strategies for problem-solving (as with the 'problems' of the unemployed and 'youth-at-risk')' (Cushman and Laidler, 1988: 510).

Since 1984, as the New Zealand government has attempted to reduce its welfare commitments, leisure has been increasingly left to the commercial and voluntary sectors. Consequently, rather than support recreation as a common (universal) good, government is more inclined to view recreation as welfare (as an antidote to social problems of political urgency, such as unemployment) and to offer 'safety nets' for disadvantaged groups (Coalter, 1986). Coalter (1989) argues that in Britain there are increasing tensions between ideologies of the market and those of welfare and that the challenge of contemporary leisure policy is to find the 'middle way'. This tension is evident in New Zealand and is unlikely to weaken while the present social and economic policy environment continues (Perkins, 1992).

Conclusion

In this chapter we have examined some issues relating to the sociology of leisure. In doing so, we have highlighted the following themes: the growing commercialisation of leisure; increasing government involvement in leisure and the tensions which presently exist between 'recreation-as-welfare' policies and 'market-driven' leisure policies; the questioning of the deeply held values that underpin sport and sporting prowess in New Zealand; and the theoretical polemic that exists in the sociology of leisure.

As we researched and wrote this chapter, another theme emerged that we have only briefly alluded to in the main body of the text: that is, the limited knowledge we have of the sociology, history and social geography of New Zealand leisure among ethnic groups other than those of Northern European origin. Some historically-important patterns of leisure and recreation *have* become more apparent. These are due partly to a growing interest in the history of Aotearoa/New Zealand, but mainly to the drive and determination of groups and individuals to render visible what has previously been invisible. In particular, in the year 1993 which marks the centenary of women's suffrage, it is appropriate that the historical contribution of women to leisure and recreation, and the pastimes, sports and activities of women, are being increasingly documented (see, e.g. Coney, 1986; Macdonald *et al.*, 1991; Brookes *et al.*, 1993). Nevertheless, in many sections of this paper, we have relied on British and North American literature for guidance. This was particularly the case for the leisure theory section. At best, this material is only suggestive of the nature of leisure in New Zealand.

The lack of systematic studies of leisure from a social science perspective partly reflects the state of social science in New Zealand (Perkins and Gidlow, 1991). The number of social scientists is limited, and the history of social science research in this country is a brief one. In sociology, for example, most sub-disciplines, not simply leisure sociology, are characterised by a paucity of knowledge, by an absence of historical continuity and the lack of a critical mass of researchers. Also, few social scientists in New Zealand can devote themselves full-time to research. Moreover, New Zealand government and research funding agencies have allocated little funding for leisure research and seem to regard it as a low priority. The exception to this has been the funds allocated to outdoor recreation and tourism research over the last twenty years.

These explanations are too simple, however. While, for example, sociology might be a comparatively new discipline in New Zealand, departments of history and geography have been established in New Zealand universities for many years. Yet leisure has never been an important focus of their research programmes. The exception to this is the occasional individual who has specialised in leisure related issues (e.g. Pearce, 1987). Furthermore, in allocating grants and determining research priorities, funding agencies are influenced by the demands of would-be researchers. Hitherto, leisure-related issues have not figured highly in researchers' proposals. The conclusion that social scientists have not taken leisure seriously as a field of research is inescapable. When sociologists, historians and geographers have written about leisure in New Zealand, they have often done so as adjuncts to other substantive interests. It is mainly for this reason that writers like ourselves have had to glean what we can from a disparate and fragmented literature.

We suggest that the social science community in New Zealand would benefit from some critical self-questioning of its neglect of leisure research and explanation. The field of leisure and the interconnections between leisure and other key social processes are worthy of sustained attention. To take just one illustration, leisure is an area of spending, investment and employment that is of considerable and growing importance (Cushman and Laidler, 1988: 514; Hillary Commission, 1993). Tourism, for example, became New Zealand's second largest foreign exchange earner in 1984 (Community Services Institute, 1985). The Hillary Commission (1993: 4, 64) estimates that the total economic impact of sport and physical leisure is $1,648m per year or $4.5m per day, while tourism contributed 5.2 per cent of G.D.P. in 1989 and generated 69,000 full-time jobs. Economic trends in leisure and recreation have important sociological implications: the 'commodification' of leisure forms; the commercial domination of mass leisure markets by 'large', and often multinational, capital; the 'capture' of state agencies by commercial interests; the exploitation and trivialisation of Maori culture; status competition by means of conspicuous leisure consumption; inequalities of access to commercially-provided leisure goods and services, etc. Implications such as these make the study of leisure anything but frivolous or incidental. It is time for social scientists in New Zealand to take leisure seriously. This includes not just high-profile sports and dollar-earning tourism but also the informal, unstructured and spontaneous types of leisure which are significant to all New Zealanders on a daily basis.

Notes

1. A recent addition to our knowledge of one aspect of leisure among Maori people, physical activity, is provided by a study of the Tainui people (Rewi, 1992).
2. See Watson (1993) for a useful periodisation of the history of leisure, recreation and tourism in New Zealand.
3. The first cricket pitches in Christchurch's Hagley Park were established in 1867 (Barnett et al., 1963:22).
4. Such data call into question the 1991 Sport, Fitness and Leisure Amendment Bill, and the changed emphasis of the Hillary Commission referred to earlier. The most popular leisure pastimes of New Zealanders include 'activities' in which physical exertion plays only a small or secondary part.
5. Hyde (1993: 106) estimates that Lion Breweries spends approximately $6m per year on sponsorship of rugby league in New Zealand and, through Lion Nathan subsidiaries, in Australia.

Further Reading

Clarke, J. and Critcher, C., 1985, *The Devil Makes Work: Leisure in Capitalist Britain*, Chicago, University of Illinois Press.
Henderson, K., 1989, *A Leisure of One's Own: A Feminist Perspective on Women's Leisure*, State College, Pennsylvania, Venture.
Kelly, J., 1982, *Leisure*, Englewood Cliffs, Prentice-Hall.
Perkins, H. C., and Cushman, G. (eds), 1993, *Leisure, Recreation and Tourism*, Auckland, Longman Paul.
Perkins, H. C. et al., 1993, 'Recreation and Tourism', in P. Ali Memon and H. C. Perkins (eds), *Environmental Planning in New Zealand*, Palmerston North, Dunmore Press.

17 Art and Ideology

Peter Beatson

Introduction

Art is never innocent. It is always caught up in the economic, political, social and cultural struggles of its time. This is because the stories it narrates and the images it constructs are consciously or unconsciously charged with ideology.

Ideology is the manipulation of language and other sign systems to falsify or conceal a group's drive for wealth, power or prestige. It presents one-sided definitions of reality as though they were indisputable, self-evident truths. Some ideologies are dominant, shoring up the vested interests of ruling groups. Others are oppositional, attempting to deconstruct the dominant ideology and replace it with alternative versions of the world which are more favourable to those currently excluded from power.

An ideology which has dominated many people's minds for several generations is termed a 'meta-narrative' or alternatively a 'master narrative'. A meta-narrative tells an epic, all-encompassing story about the history of an ethnic group, a church, a social category, a nation or even the entire world. A master narrative claims to give a total and faithful explanation of why things are the way they are and how they got that way. It purports to account for the smallest detail of everyday life but at the same time it is underpinned by some ultimate principle such as the will of God, the laws of evolution, the destiny of the master 'race' or the superiority of one sex over the other.

Although they themselves are not necessarily aware of it, artists frequently contribute to the construction, preservation and dissemination of meta-narratives. On the other hand, those belonging to groups who have been excluded, exploited or oppressed by reigning master narratives can use their art as weapons in the struggle to overthrow them and substitute new, more congenial ones. In New Zealand, the artistic monologue has been conducted mainly from the point of view of middle-class, male Pakeha. Their master narrative has pushed the working class, women, non-Pakeha and other dispossessed or minority groups into the margins of society. It has trivialised, stereotyped, demeaned or at the very least ignored them.

This chapter will show how over the last 20 years or so the monologue has been interrupted. Maori, women and spokespeople for other under-privileged groups have, in the arts as elsewhere, raised their voices against the master narrative. They have begun to construct new ideological stories of their own which place them, rather than white, middle-class men, at the centre of the stage. They have introduced into the arts new images, new themes, new issues and new ways of interpreting our history and the place of the excluded or oppressed in that history. In the national culture of the 1990s there is a plurality of voices, giving alternative versions of the truth. In the following pages, we shall introduce some of the main speakers and explore their versions of reality.

John Bevan Ford
Te Hono - the Connections LXVII
coloured inks on paper 1986

Maori Art

Before the Pakeha came to Aotearoa, it was the Maori who controlled the master narrative of these islands, a narrative which the arts had a central role in constructing. In traditional Maori society, arts such as carving, chant, weaving and oratory were as integral a part of the activities of everyday life as were planting, fishing, building canoes or preparing for war. Art was also blended inextricably with the religious ceremonies which surrounded such activities. Art, life and religion made one indissoluble totality.

This art and the values it embodied became marginalised and trivialised in national life as economic, political and cultural power passed into the hands of European settlers. Missionaries tried to suppress elements of indigenous culture which they regarded as pagan, barbaric or obscene. For other Pakeha, Maori art was simply picturesque or exotic local colour, something with which to entertain tourists. In its most grisly form, the European taste for native curios manifested itself in the trade in preserved tattooed heads which flourished during the early years of contact. When Maori artefacts were not displayed for the titillation of jaded foreign appetites, they tended to be stored away in museums as dead momentoes to a 'race' which was itself assumed to be dying.

At the same time that Maori art was being devalued, Pakeha painters, writers and film makers created images of Maori people which reduced them to the level of objects to be looked at with detached interest or amusement by white settlers. The richness and complexity of Maori society was simplified to a number of superficial stereotypes. Some of these appeared to be reasonably sympathetic, with men depicted as chivalrous if bloodthirsty warriors, or as dignified, gentlemanly chiefs (as in the paintings of C.F. Goldie), and young women depicted as romantic heroines (as in Rudall Hayward's film *Rewi's Last Stand*). Even here, the reality of the Maori was being falsified to conform to European notions of the noble savage and the barebreasted, dusky maiden. More insultingly, Maori adults tended to be shown as lazy, feckless, immoral, irrational and clownish. Maori children were diminished to the status of cute, big-eyed 'piccaninnies'.

In spite of the misrepresentation of Maori people and their culture by Pakeha artists, Maori art managed to stay alive during the period from the Land Wars in the 1860s to the Maori renaissance of the 1960s. In some areas the indigenous tradition was even given new life and direction by contact with European technology and art forms. Tools such as steel saws and chisels, for instance, allowed the art of the whare whakairo (carved meeting house) to flourish as never before, while European paint and illustrations gave rise in the hands of young Maori artists to new forms of pictorial decoration of these houses. A folk art was born which blended Maori and European elements (Taylor, 1988). Similarly, in the domain of music, European tunes and harmonies were adapted and blended with Maori words, dance and chant to become the basis of the cross-cultural form called waiata-a-ringa. Thus for a hundred years, artists in meeting houses and cultural clubs kept traditional art precariously alive and at the same time experimented with the possibilities opened up by contact with European culture (Walker 1990: 188-191).

Over the last quarter of a century, Maori people have increasingly challenged the dominance of the Pakeha master narrative. They have claimed back the rights to land, resources and political autonomy that were guaranteed by the Treaty of Waitangi. At the same time, they have worked to restore Maori language and culture to a central position in national life, insisting that the Maori interpretation of the world and the Maori version of New Zealand history should stand on equal terms to those of the Pakeha. The art of the Maori renaissance has played a significant role in this challenge to Pakeha ideology. Maori artists are constructing an alternative version of reality to that created by Pakeha artists, a version in which the Maori occupy the foreground.

In the visual arts, the tide began to turn in the 1950s and 1960s. Under the guidance of educationist Gordon Tovey, Maori arts and crafts were introduced into schools. A group of Maori trained in European art forms was drawn into the educational system to aid in teaching Maori culture. In the process, they themselves rediscovered their Maori cultural traditions which in many cases they had lost. Artists such as Cliff Whiting, Paratene Matchitt, John Ford, Buck Nin, Fred Graham and Selwyn Muru formed the nucleus of a revival in the visual arts and crafts. They were linked to the past by their contact with older traditional master carvers like Pine Taiapa but they were also skilled and knowledgable in European styles.

The group grew as artists such as Robyn Kahukiwa, Shona Rapira Davies, Kura Rewiri-Thorsen, Emare Karaka and Bob Jahnke came on the scene. Between them, they created a body of work which affirmed the centrality of Maori cultural identity in this country. This affirmation was greatly strengthened by the *Te Maori* exhibition of traditional taonga which toured the U.S.A. then New Zealand in the mid-1980s and which provided a focal point for the renewed sense of pride in mana Maori (Mead, 1984; O'Biso, 1987). Partly inspired by *Te Maori*, there has since been a wave of exhibitions of contemporary Maori art including *Karanga Karanga*, *Kohia Ko Taikaka Anake*, *Whatu Aho Rua*, *Choice* and the *Te Koanga* series.

The visual arts were soon joined by literature. In the mid-1960s, there had been only one major Maori writer in English, the poet Hone Tuwhare. In the first half of the 1970s, the short story writers and novelists Patricia Grace and Witi Ihimaera began publishing. They used their writing to draw into national consciousness the warmth and humanity of Maori communities in the rural hinterland. They gave voice and substance to a section of the New Zealand population who, until then, had been largely unheard by and were invisible to many Pakeha (Beatson, 1989; Melbourne, 1990).

The number of Maori writers was swelled throughout the 1970s and 1980s by people such as Rori Habib, Bruce Stewart, Bub Bridger and Apirana Taylor. The general reading public were given a chance to sample the work of these writers in the 1982 anthology, *Into the World of Light,* which contained extracts from 39 writers (Ihimaera and Long, 1982). Maori literature then achieved international fame when Keri Hulme's novel, *the bone people,* received the prestigious British Booker Prize in 1985. The full breadth of the new tradition of Maori literature can be seen in the five volumes of the *Te Ao Marama* anthology which Witi Ihimaera began publishing in 1992.

By the 1980s, Maori music had also added its voice to the chorus. Maori singers, composers and instrumentalists have played an important part in the popular music scene for decades, starting with Ruru Karaitiana's 'Blue Smoke', our first homegrown pop song, and climaxing with a tear-jerking rendering of 'Tukua Ahau' by Howard Morrison at the opening of the Commonwealth Games. Until the 1980s, however, they had mainly been entertainers and had not used their art for social or political ends. Over the last ten years, musicians such as Herbs, Dread Beat & Blood, Mahinarangi Tocker, Aotearoa, Moana and the Moa Hunters and Upper Hutt Posse have borrowed the styles, forms and idioms of overseas 'black' music like reggae, soul, rap and dance, weaving these together with Maori words and themes to create a form of music which speaks both with the voice of young Maori and of oppressed people everywhere.

Another art form blending the Maori and European to emerge in the 1970s and 1980s was theatre (Potiki, 1991). Drama and dance groups such as *Maranga Mai, Te Ohu Whakaari, Te Ika a Maui Players, Te Ara Hou* and *Taio* took the message of the Maori renaissance onto the stage and also into prisons, hospitals and marae with collectively created works.

At the same time, a small but growing number of plays by individual Maori playwrights such as Harry Dansey (*Te Raukura: The Feathers of the Albatross,* 1974), Hone Tuwhare (*In the Wilderness Without a Hat,* 1976), Rori Habib (*Death of the Land,* 1976), Apirana Taylor (*Kohunga,* 1986), John Broughton (*Michael James Manaia,* 1991) and Riwia Brown (*Roimata,* 1988) were being produced, either live or on television. A small but important landmark in Maori drama was the publication in 1991 of *He Reo Hou: 5 Plays by Maori Playwrights,* the first book of Maori plays. At the same time that Maori playwrights were beginning to infiltrate local theatre, New Zealand audiences were also growing familiar with an increasing number of Maori actors and entertainers such as George Henare, Billy T. James, Lani Tupu, Rawiri Paratene, Rima Te Wiata and, above all, Nancy Brunning and Temuera Morrison, two of the *Shortland Street* megastars.

Finally, in the latter part of the 1980s, a breakthrough was made into the field of feature films with Barry Barclay's *Ngati* and *Te Rua* and Merata Mita's *Mauri.* These directors adapted the Western techniques of cinema to the community-centred values of the Maori. Their aim was to work alongside the people they filmed and to explore their emotions and culture from the inside. This is in contrast to the approach of Pakeha film-makers who frequently tend to rush in, grab images and rush off again, subordinating their subjects to the dictates of the camera, the script and Western notions of time and efficiency (Barclay, 1990; Mita, 1992).

Having noted these developments, however, it is important not to exaggerate the Maori conquest of the mass media. There was a major disappointment for Maoridom in the 1980s when it lost its bid to gain the new third channel on television. Maori programmes like *Waka Huia* and *Marae* continued to occupy off-peak cathode ghettoes on Sunday morning. Furthermore, it was difficult for musicians with a Maori message, particularly if they used te reo Maori, to get played on commercial radio. Unlike the indigenous people of Wales, those of Aotearoa received little representation in the mainstream electronic media of their own country. The tide only began to turn in the early 1990s with the establishment of a growing number of iwi-based radio stations which promoted Maori culture at the grassroots level. There were also some up-market FM stations such as Auckland's Mai-FM which played dance and rap for Maori teenagers and gave aspirant announcers, producers and engineers hands-on experience (Walker, 1990: 268-273).

In the preceding discussion, we have focused on the ways in which the colonised people of Aotearoa have interrupted the cultural monologue of the white colonisers by infiltrating their art forms and turning them to the ends of the tangata whenua. Maori have progressively appropriated the European arts of painting, literature, music, theatre and film, staking out a space within mainstream national art for their own narratives and images.

At the same time, there has been an equally important resurgence of specifically Maori art. If one side of the Maori renaissance has involved the capture of European forms, the other has seen a new flowering of traditional ones and the continuing evolution of new folk art such as waiata-a-ringa. This renewed sense of past identity is found in individuals such as master carvers Lyonel Grant and Paki Harrison, weavers Pute Rari and Te Aue Davis, composers Pita Sharples and Ngapo Wehi and of cultural groups like Te Waka Huia and Te Roopu Manutaki. The strength of these revitalised traditions can be seen in the size of the audiences which attend the Aotearoa Maori Festival. Perhaps even more significant for the future is the growing size of the Maori and Pacific Island Cultural Festival for Auckland secondary school students. This began in 1976 at Hillary College with four schools competing. In 1993 Nga Tapuwae hosted around 120,000 people for a festival in which 142 school cultural clubs participated.

Most importantly, new generations of young Maori fluent in te reo are now passing through kohanga reo and entering a growing number of kura kaupapa. The vacuum in relevant Maori education is being replaced by a system devised by and for the tangata whenua. This has three major implications for indigenous art. First, pupils and teachers are hungry for educational resources. Writers and composers of material in the Maori language like Hirini Melbourne are urgently needed to keep pace with swelling market demand. Second, this newly literate and culturally aware generation will later provide an informed adult audience for Maori work. Finally, from their midst will emerge in the twenty-first century a host of creative artists far out-numbering those who have already fought to put the indigenous art of Aotearoa back on the map.

In 1973 a handful of Maori had met at Te Kaha to form an artists' association called Nga Puna Waihanga. At that time, very few Maori artists were known in mainstream New Zealand culture. In 1993 Te Kaha overflowed with more than 800 members of the association celebrating its twentieth anniversary. In the intervening years, Maori art had stepped out of the shadows and taken its place prominently in the centre of the stage.

What do they tell us? A number of strongly felt central themes and images are shared by artists working in all media. They can be summed up in the three words: mamae (pain), riri (anger) and tumanako (hope). At one level, Maori art is a sustained cry of pain for the loss and mutilation inflicted upon the people by the Pakeha. The anguished sense that traditional Maori society has been torn apart appears in many painful images. Witi Ihimaera's short story 'The Whale' in *Pounamu, Pounamu* (1972), for instance, ends with a stranded but still living whale being ripped and eaten by gulls, a clear reference to the fate of Maori communities in the modern world. This pain is, on the one hand, caused by the disintegration of traditional family life and values. Poem after poem, story after story mourn the derelict marae, the loneliness of deserted kuia and koroua, the passing away of the Maori language and the devaluing of old customs. Much Maori art is an elegy for the slow death of the rural Maori world.

On the other hand, Maori artists record the pain of their people adrift in the Pakeha cities. They show the moral disintegration and emotional confusion or torment of those who left the rural hinterland sometimes to look for European education, sometimes to find work and sometimes just to get their kicks in the big smoke. Many Maori have been scarred by their move from home into the city. Maori art portrays their scars. Most poignantly, it reveals the psychic dislocation of young people who have lost their Maori identity but who cannot or do not wish to merge into the Pakeha world.

Sometimes a strong moralistic tone can be felt in portrayals of degenerate city Maori. This is expressed most fiercely in Alan Duff's 1990 novel *Once Were Warriors*, a remorseless indictment of what the author perceives to be the fecklessness, drunkenness, emotional shallowness, violence and squalor endemic in much working-class Maori family life. Unlike most Maori authors, Duff does not blame Maori deprivation on the Pakeha but on the irresponsibility of Maori themselves. Putting questions of blame to one side, however, his writing reinforces the theme of social mutilation found elsewhere in Maori writing and given its most powerful expression in Ihimaera's image of a living whale being ripped apart by gulls.

Duff's novel is exceptional in that he sees Maoridom's wounds as self-inflicted and that his anger is aimed at Maori, not Pakeha. In most Maori art, the anger is directed outwards at the Pakeha system which is held responsible for Maori suffering. It is anger over the betrayal of Treaty promises, anger over the loss of land, anger over racial insults to the Maori both collectively and as individuals. There is also a very strong vein of anger aroused by the way in which the Maori have become the victims of the police, the law courts and the prison system. The art of the early Maori renaissance recorded the wounds of Maoridom. The later art has begun to denounce those who inflicted the wounds.

As part of this denunciation, Maori artists have started re-telling the story of Aotearoa from their own perspective. They retrace the history of race relations since the first contact, visiting sites of past conflict and bringing them back to life from a new point of view. Historical heroes of the nineteenth century who resisted the white settlers are enshrined in the new literature. Harry Dansey's play *Te Raukura*, for instance, traces the story of Maori struggles against settler invasion from the start of the Hauhau movement in the early 1860s through to the destruction of Parihaka and the arrest of Te Whiti in 1881. In Witi Ihimaera's novel, *The Matriarch*, a detailed account of the career of Te Kooti is given which explains his 'atrocities' as legitimate tactics in a war of resistance against British invaders. The same spirit of defiant resistance can be heard in the words of Rewi Maniapoto during the siege at Orakau as recounted by Rori Habib (Ihimaera and Long, 1982: 102-103):

> And still the invaders come
> Their numbers seem limitless.
> . . . .
> Yet through the ordeal, the sinking morale
> These words still able to be uttered.
> 'Friend, this is the word of the Maori.
> Ka whawhai tonu, ake, ake, ake.'
> We will fight for ever and ever and ever.

The struggles of more recent history have also been drawn on as a source of inspiration by contemporary writers. Events such as the Land March, the occupation of Bastion Point, the Raglan golf course dispute and the 1981 Springbok tour have been retold in novels, plays, poems and films, giving new significance to those words spoken at Orakau: 'We shall fight for ever'.

As well as interrupting the monologue of Pakeha history with their own account of the New Zealand story, Maori artists have spoken up against the master narrative of the Christian religion which the European brought to Aotearoa. European missionaries and settlers dismissed traditional Maori religion as pagan superstition. The gods and supernatural beings of the Maori world were pushed into the margins of national consciousness to be replaced by 'the one true God' of the newcomers. This suppression of Maori religion had important political significance. It was part of a wider ideological attempt to convince Maori that their world view was not real and that they should therefore abandon their sense of identity in favour of the 'truth' as taught by the Europeans.

As part of their renewed political resistance, Maori artists have breathed fresh life into their own traditional beliefs. Ancient gods and goddesses such as Tane Mahuta, Hine-titama, Hine-ahu-one and Hine-nui-te-Po have again come to life in their paintings, words and carvings, as has the supernatural aura of everyday life found in dreams, omens, sacred talismans and ghosts. Of all such spiritual beings, the most powerful to find their way into modern Maori art are Papatuanuku, the Earth Mother, symbol of the deep bond between the Maori and their land, and Tumatauenga, God of War, symbolising the new political militancy of Maori.

The revival of the old gods brings us to our third theme, namely hope for a new and better world for Maori in the future, summed up in the often-used term 'te ao marama' – the world of light. The hope is frequently embodied in the resurrection of the whare whakairo. This building, which is at the very heart of Maori social and cultural life, combines the roles of art gallery, church, parliament, guest house, history book and symbol of tribal mana. In its very form, it is a living whakapapa since it is created as the body of a famous ancestor. It combines and balances all traditional Maori art forms of both men and women.

The whare whakairo provides contemporary Maori artists with a strong unifying symbol for the sense of renewed identity, vitality and hope of the Maori. It appears constantly in paintings, novels, poems and plays. The action of Witi Ihimaera's *The Matriarch*, for instance, revolves around and is constantly drawn back to his ancestral house Rongopai. The building and re-building of the meeting house provides the main thread of continuity in Patricia Grace's *Potiki*, and the hope for a new and better life with which Keri Hulme's *the bone people* ends is once again expressed through the image of a new communal house.

For over a hundred years Pakeha artists constructed a master narrative about New Zealand society in which the material interests and the ideological world view of British settlers were assumed to be the only normal and natural ones. The Maori became strangers in their own land. During that time they continued to practise their own traditional arts but these made very little political impact upon the dominant Pakeha system. Over the last 30 years or so, however, Maori have mounted a challenge to this Pakeha monologue. They have started to construct an alternative version of the history of Aotearoa in which they, rather than the Pakeha, are the subjects. They have woven together traditional art forms and images with the new ones introduced by European settlers to create works which are both traditional and modern, both Maori and Pakeha. In doing so, they are making an important contribution to the revival of Maori identity; asserting unequivocally that in the twenty-first century, the Maori voice should be heard in this country on equal terms with that of the Pakeha.

Women's Art

We shall begin the second strand of our narrative with a paradox. Female creative artists and performers such as the writer Katherine Mansfield, painter Frances Hodgkins, singer Kiri Te Kanawa, organist Gillian Weir, novelist Keri Hulme and film director Jane Campion have been in the forefront of internationally celebrated New Zealanders throughout this century. Moreover, women tend to go to concerts and exhibitions and to study art-related subjects at school and university in greater numbers than do men (Scott *et al.,* 1987).

Yet in the past, women in this country have been heavily under-represented amongst those deemed to be 'serious' artists. Fewer women than men have had their work bought by public galleries, shown on television, published in journals and anthologies or performed on stage. This is the paradox. Nobody could doubt the artistic ability of those women who have made it to the top in the arts, and women in general are more interested in art than men. Yet the official tradition of New Zealand art is dominated by male artists.

A few statistics from the art world reveal the bias. There have been virtually no women conductors of the New Zealand Symphony Orchestra. Of those involved in the light music industry who appear in John Dix's *Stranded in Paradise,* just eight per cent are women. In the 1987 Sonic Circus, which explicitly set out to bring together all our major composers of classical music, only 24 per cent were women. Under one-third of the articles in the first 50 numbers of *Art New Zealand* were about women. Thirty-two per cent of the playwrights listed in the 1988 Playmarket *Directory of New Zealand Plays & Playwrights* were women. Only 40 per cent of the poets in the 1985 *Penguin Book of New Zealand Verse* were women.

Men have out-numbered women in the permanent collections of painting and sculpture held in our public art galleries. A 1983 survey by Jo Seton of the gender division of labour in New Zealand feature films showed that women were either totally absent or massively under-represented in top positions such as director, producer, editor and cinematographer but over-represented in roles traditionally allocated to women such as wardrobe or make-up (Seton, 1983). Since Seton wrote her article, a number of feature films have been directed or produced by women using female crews, but New Zealand cinema remains a predominantly male preserve.

Art and Ideology   281

Jacqueline Fahey
Family Quarrelling
oil 1986

A number of social factors have acted together to discriminate against women practising the arts. On the one hand, cultural gatekeepers such as the directors of art galleries, editors of magazines and anthologies, producers and promoters in the entertainment industry, teachers and scholars have tended to filter women out of the mainstream tradition of 'named' artists. On the other hand, domestic family pressures have made it more difficult for women to aspire to the career of artist in the first place. The exception is where the arts in question can be seen to have a practical or decorative use around the home, as do knitting, weaving or embroidery. Such typically 'women's work', however, has usually been trivialised by the male gatekeepers just mentioned.

Women have also tended to be stereotyped when they appear as subjects in art created by men. Cultural forms such as novels, films, paintings and plays construct images of society which give the illusion of being accurate, honest and gender-neutral reflections of social reality. Male artists, however, frequently construct that reality from their own point of view. Men's interests, activities, values and desires dominate, with the result that the patriarchal perspective comes to be accepted, even by many women, as the only right and normal way of seeing things (Davis *et al.*, 1983).

Women are often pushed to one side to make room for central male figures. When the spotlight does fall on them, they are depicted in a limited number of stock roles. They are typically portrayed as subverters or opponents of the values, aspirations and friendships of masculine characters. On the one hand, they disrupt the male ethos by introducing a dangerous element of eroticism and therefore sexual competition or anarchic desire into the male world. On the other hand, they are often represented as narrow-minded, oppressively conformist and intellectually limited wives or mothers. In this latter role, they embody the conservative world of the puritanical and spiritually desiccated petty bourgeoisie which cramps the potential of more adventurous, free-booting men.

There have always been a few courageous women artists who have defied the conventional male perspective. These were often isolated individuals who made little headway in their own time but are now adopted as role models or 'cultural mothers' by many women. Since the mid-1970s, however, female artists, teachers and scholars have been fighting a collective battle to break down the patriarchal bias and to construct a more central place for women in our culture. To achieve this, they have adopted a three-fold strategy.

The first component of the female artistic renaissance of the last 20 years has been the rediscovery and re-evaluation of a tradition of female art in New Zealand. Art history has been revised by female scholars to include a line of those cultural mothers mentioned above. Anne Kirker's *New Zealand Women Artists* (1986), for instance, tells the story of New Zealand art from a female perspective, surveying the achievement of women artists, many of whom had been passed over by male art historians. Editors such as Heather Roberts in *Where Did She Come From?* (1989) and Lydia Wevers in *Happy Endings* (1987) have performed a similar salvage operation on New Zealand women writers in their surveys and anthologies of women's writing.

Women artists have also helped celebrate the life and work of their cultural foremothers. They have found strength and inspiration in the work of older painters such as Lois White, Evelyn Page, Rita Angus and Olivia Spencer Bower, or writers such as Robyn Hyde and Jean Devanny. Katherine Mansfield has been a particular focal point for both scholars and artists. Composer Gillian Whitehead and poet Fleur Adcock, for instance, collaborated on the production of *Out of This Nettle Danger*, which set extracts of Mansfield's writing to music, while in her one-woman play, *The Case of Katherine Mansfield*, Cathy Downes wove together passages from the writer's letters, journals and stories in a dramatic portrait of her complex personality.

After this rediscovery of the past, the second prong of the feminist movement in art has been the creation of supportive women's networks, collectives and art spaces in the present. Women who had often lived in suburban isolation and who had not fully tapped their own creativity were encouraged to come together, to support one another, to explore their artistic potential and to promote cultural forms and ideological perspectives which challenge patriarchal assumptions about what art should do and what it should say.

For instance, in 1976 a Spiral collective began publishing women's art, literature and criticism. *Broadsheet*, another feminist collective publication, has supported women's arts since the early 1970s. A Women's Gallery was established in Wellington between 1980 and 1984 to provide a cultural space in which women's work could be exhibited and discussed. All women theatre groups have toured the country with plays and revues such as Renee's *What Did You Do in the War, Mummy?* and the comedy collective *Hen's Teeth*. Women musicians such as the Topp Twins, Jan Hellriegel, Shona Laing and Jenny Morris have challenged the male hegemony in rock and pop music. In the 1980s a number of anthologies of contemporary women's poetry and short stories appeared, many published by the New Women's Press founded by Wendy Harrex in 1982 to promote women's work (Dann, 1985).

The third strategy of the women's art movement has been to introduce new subject matter into their work, subject matter previously regarded as too trivial, too personal or too sexually explicit to be treated by 'serious' art (Evans *et al.*, 1988). Beginning with the premise that 'the personal is political', women have constructed their new art from the intimate details of this personal experience. They have focused on the worlds of domesticity and motherhood. They have portrayed female sexuality including pregnancy, childbirth and the menstrual cycle as experienced by women, in contrast to the voyeuristic representations of female eroticism created by men. They explore the play of inner emotions as recounted in diaries, and they depict the subtleties, nuances and fluctuations of inter-personal relationships between family members or female friends.

As well as chronicling this immediate, everyday world of feminine experience, radical feminist artists, such as Juliet Batten and Bronwynne Cornish, also push beyond it into wider themes. They resurrect cultural archetypes of the female essence as personalised in ancient goddesses of the earth and the moon. Going deeper, their art uncovers the basic underlying rhythms and cycles of the life process itself, rhythms and cycles which are claimed as essentially female. Starting with the apparently trivial details of domestic life, the art of radical feminists concludes by affirming an essential connection between female biology, female spirituality and the deep groundswell of the universe.

Not all feminists, however, accept the idea of women's essential difference and superiority. Among women artists, as among feminists in general, there is an ongoing debate about the exact nature of the difference between women and men. The 'essentialist' position of radical feminists outlined above can be contrasted with three other major perspectives.

Liberal feminist artists, such as Gretchen Albrecht, maintain there is no such thing as a distinctively female aesthetic. Art transcends gender. They simply want to be accepted by the mainstream art establishment on equal terms with men. Another approach, which can be termed 'poststructuralist' or 'postmodernist', also attacks the belief in a fundamental female essence to be discovered and expressed in goddesses, natural cycles, moon dances, images of women's genitalia and the like. Poststructuralists such as Merylyn Tweedie reject sex in favour of signs. They explore the way identity is constructed through signifying practices and they subvert semiological metanarratives by scrambling habitual codes of representation. Postmodernism replaces gynocentrism with polymorphic perversity (Barrie, 1986; Barrie, 1987).

Yet another perspective can be found in the work of Maori women artists. In some cases, as with Rangimarie Hetet, they work with traditional materials such as flax, and in ancestral forms such as tukutuku. In other cases, as with Merata Mita and Robyn Kahukiwa, they use European art forms. Either way, their work constructs a specifically female Maori identity, which differs from those of men (both Pakeha and Maori) and Pakeha women. Until recently, the voice of Maori women had little success in making itself heard against the predominantly Pakeha and predominantly male monologues. The appearance on the scene of powerful Maori women artists reflects the beginnings of a breakdown of dominant ideologies and their replacement by a plurality of identities, images and voices.

The new subject matter of women's art can be viewed either negatively or positively – or as a tension between positive and negative. Women's experience of domesticity, sexuality and relationships is seen negatively when these are not in the control of women themselves. Much contemporary female art constructs such negative images of women trapped in and mutilated by a male-dominated world. Women are often depicted as imprisoned and imperilled by their own bodies, as shown by the many stories set in hospitals. They are portrayed as victims of men, subjected at one extreme to the violence of rape and incest, subjected at the other pole to the frustration and boredom aroused by male pomposity and self-centredness.

They are victims, too, of their suburban homes and their children. Domesticity becomes a grey, neurotic purgatory or even a nightmare which drives its victims into the hell of full-blown psychosis. Finally, female characters are not infrequently victimised by other women, even their mothers, who have been so conditioned by traditional attitudes that they have become allies of patriarchal structures. Feminist art is as frank about exposing women's complicity in male oppression as it is about unmasking men's deficiencies.

All these aspects of the female condition can be converted from negative to positive when women regain control of themselves and their environment. Where this has happened, women's art celebrates the fulfilment and creativity of personal life and human relationships. The home, children, other women, sexuality and even friendships with men are portrayed as sources of pleasure and growth for those who have discovered their own identity and worth.

The subject of women's art then can be either imprisonment and mutilation or release and celebration. Since life is never totally black nor white, the best women's art is constructed around the tensions and ambiguities of a world in which the same person, object or experience can be both destructive and creative, imprisoning and liberating. Such ambiguity, such blending of the positive and negative, is found above all in images of motherhood. Of all the themes in contemporary women's art, this is the one which is most central because it is central in the lives of so many women. It is also the one in which the tension between personal destruction and personal fulfilment is at its most acute.

The women's art movement experienced a strong surge of vitality during the 1993 celebrations of the centennial of women's suffrage. The Suffrage Centennial Year Trust spent nearly $4 million to sponsor around 50 books, ten film and TV productions, four videos, seven festivals, four memorials and a wide range of art exhibitions, theatrical productions and musical projects. Specific works included the Women's Suffrage Mural, the film *Dream Weavers* and the exhibitions *Alter/Image*, *Journey Without Maps*, *No-Man's-Land* and *New Zealand Women Artists 1840-1993*.

The progress which women have made since the mid-1970s could be judged by the fact that in 1993 most of the key positions in arts institutions were held by female executives. The directors of the Museum of New Zealand, the Film Commission and New Zealand On Air were women, as were the chairperson of the Arts Council, the manager of its strategic Arts Development Unit and the film and video censors. Women had still not attained parity with men in many areas of economic, political and social life, but by the mid-1990s it was no longer possible to claim that they were invisible in the mainstream of our national artistic culture.

The Community Arts Movement

Phill Rooke, *Avondale Community Mural.* 1991

> It is our belief that creativity is central to humanity and that the means of creative expression is every person's right. However, social and economic conditions in late twentieth century society adversely affect this right. Many groups of people have limited access to resources that other sectors in society take for granted. We believe it is our work to ensure the fair and just distribution of cultural resources so that the means of communicating ideas, stories and other aspects of people's life experiences is truly democratic.
> (Community Art Workers Network Iritekura Statement)

We shall group our third category of oppositional artists under the broad umbrella term 'community art'. This is part of a wider social movement to empower dispossessed, oppressed or marginalised people at the grassroots level. Its main target is the élitist high art which is practised and appreciated by the educated middle and upper classes and which receives the lion's share of Arts Council funding.

Community artists' primary concern is not with pursuing aesthetic excellence or thematic complexity but with the social function their art serves. Resolutely anti-élitist, they attack bastions of high art like the opera house, art museum and symphony orchestra. Their aim is not to turn out icons of pure art but rather to use art-making as part of a wider strategy for improving the world. They contrast the concepts of participation, local autonomy and cultural democracy with the opposed practice of artistic 'diffusion'. The diffusion model of artistic distribution is akin to the 'trickle down' theory of economics which claims that if the wealthy are encouraged to accumulate financial capital, some will eventually percolate down and benefit the working classes. In art, the trickle-down or diffusion approach bases artistic policy upon the promotion of high professional standards amongst an artistic élite. This top tier of aesthetic experts is to create paintings, symphonies, ballets, literature and films which will be diffused throughout society to edify passive, non-artistic consumers. The community arts perspective rejects this notion of excellence by the few in favour of participation by the many. It holds that arts policies should serve not the narrow doctrine of art-for-art's-sake but a more general social policy through which the quality of life for all is enhanced.

Commitment to this wider cause is sometimes expressed by rejecting the terms 'art' and 'artist' altogether in favour of the more general concepts 'culture' and 'cultural worker'. By culture is meant the entire mental world view of a group and all its external manifestations. A people's culture comprises their tastes, manners, attitudes and life style, their moral codes, religion, stores of knowledge, beliefs and artefacts. Above all, culture contains a group's sense of a common history, identity, future destiny and the language through which these are represented. It provides stories and symbols that allow people to make sense of the world and their place in it.

Arts activists are feral rather than domestic animals, working out in the social wilds where other species of artists seldom venture. They abandon environments constructed specifically for the creation or distribution of the arts like galleries, theatres and television studios. They operate instead in the sites where people live or work, encouraging participation in those who through institutionalisation, cultural deprivation, age, disability or poverty are cut off from mainstream art.

In taking art to the people, community artists not only find themselves in unusual places but are also obliged to deal with authority figures not normally encountered by artists working in other fields. They have to negotiate for funds, for access or for co-operation with city councillors, officials in the Justice, Health or Social Welfare Departments, with prison superintendents and wardens, with trade unionists, charge nurses, psychiatric workers, superintendents of homes for the mentally or physically disabled and with school principals.

These gatekeepers have their own institutional roles to play, professional protocols to observe and administrative problems to solve. Finding money for arts projects, arranging access to factories and prisons or monitoring the impact of role playing upon anti-social teenagers are not high on their list of priorities. A great deal of time and energy must be spent by community artists in diplomacy to break down resistance, gain confidence and ensure ongoing co-operation. All this is a far remove from the world of art dealers, publishers, broadcasters or studio managers with whom other artists interact.

The variety of art workers within the present category covers a wide spectrum, from those who simply want to take the rough edges off contemporary social life to those who are dedicated to the overthrow of the whole system. At the soft end of the spectrum are occupational or art therapists, educationists and the like whose main goals are participation, education, amelioration or healing. Their object is not to change the wider society but to make life more meaningful, or at least slightly more bearable, for those whom it has neglected or crushed.

In the softest of all cases, art is simply used to bring a little colour and interest into otherwise drab and monotonous lives by painting bright murals on sterile hospital walls or encouraging the institutionalised disabled to dance, sing or make kites. More seriously, the arts have been employed within the educational system – notably but not uniquely in Rudolf Steiner schools – as an ally of special education for handicapped or disturbed children. They are also increasingly used as a form of adult occupational therapy, psychotherapy or rehabilitation, helping people to develop motor or social skills, gain greater self-knowledge, construct a sense of identity and communicate with others. In these roles, the arts reintegrate shattered personalities and build bridges by which patients or prison inmates can cross from enclosed institutions to open society.

Artists have on occasions been mobilised in the cause of public health or safety crusades, their aesthetic skills contributing to the promotion of causes like safe sex, road safety and the war on tobacco. In conjunction with old temporary employment schemes like PEP or more recent ones like Access and Maccess, the arts have also been used to help combat unemployment. For instance, there has been a proliferation of courses on bone carving for young Maori aimed at helping them set up as self-employed, small-scale businesspeople feeding the tourist market.

Although the art workers we are discussing may direct their attention to single issues, such as AIDS or unemployment, their work is frequently based upon a wider philosophy of community development.The Treaty of Waitangi is a major plank in this community-oriented philosophy. It is felt that particular attention should be given to Maori culture both because it is the unique indigenous heritage of Aotearoa and also because Maori people figure largely in the ranks of the economically, politically and socially dispossessed. But while respecting Maoritanga, the community arts movement also works towards both biculturalism and multiculturalism. The arts are used on the one hand to strengthen each ethnic group's own sense of cultural identity and on the other to forge bonds between diverse ethnic groups. This, at least, is the philosophy. In practice, the causes of Maori sovereignty, biculturalism and multiculturalism frequently pull in contradictory directions which are not easy for art to reconcile.

Although not all community art workers belong to it, there is a Community Arts Network in this country that was created to put into practice and act as the advocate for the philosophy of cultural democracy. Formed in 1986 and issuing a manifesto the following year, the loosely structured network has outposts in a number of cities, each with its own philosophical orientation, institutional setting and style of action.

The main emphasis up to this point has been on education or healing in one form or another. Yet although painting murals in hospitals, teaching prisoners bone carving or encouraging psychiatric patients to perform psychodramas may soften the lives of victims, they do nothing about the social system which creates these victims. Moving along the spectrum from soft to tough action, community artists begin to elide into political activists.

For artistic militants, the focus is not so much on the socially deprived or marginalised themselves as on the dominant economic, political, social and cultural forces which have divided society into winners and losers. They are no longer therapists but propagandists for whom art is just one weapon in an arsenal which also contains marches, strikes, political lobbying or even revolutionary mass action. Theirs is a rough, tough, ephemeral art, thrown up in the heat of the moment, brandished fiercely then thrown aside again. It is the art of cartoons, banners, t-shirts, posters, chants and street theatre at whose heart is the one word – protest.

Protest art first came on the scene in conjunction with industrial action, with times of acute economic deprivation like the Depression and with the doctrines of class struggle preached by old style socialism. Its targets were the bosses, the cops, right-wing politicians, working-class scabs and the capitalist system of production, distribution and exchange. After the defeat of the militant unions in the great watersiders' dispute of 1951, the sting was largely taken out of traditional class politics. Although industrial struggles and their accompanying art continued unabated, hard-line socialism was replaced in the public arena by a variety of social movements with other agendas and new forms of protest art.

One major strand in the new politics of protest was the peace/environmental movement which opposed both nuclear-based militarism and the rape of the planet in the name of industrial development. As we have already seen, the feminist movement generated a second strand of artistic political activism from the 1970s, a decade which was also a turning-point in Maori cultural politics. The other major social movement to raise its voice emerged from arguably the most oppressed and victimised of all groups in New Zealand society – the gay community. The gay world has a thriving artistic culture of its own which used to be kept invisible from mainstream society for fear of victimisation. It came out of the closet during the homosexual law reform debate of 1984-86 during which, under assault from the authoritarian right, male and female homosexuals took to the streets with the same arsenal of protest art that has been used by unionists, socialists, feminists and Maori.

A number of these movements, ranging from old-fashioned communism to recent Maori activism, united in the anti-tour demonstrations of 1981. As well as creating deep divisions and strange alliances, the protests generated a great deal of oppositional art – from ephemeral chants, posters and graffiti to the full-length film *Patu!*. The socially explosive nature of such art is suggested by the fact that *Patu!* was not given wide public exposure until many years after the events, and that members of the New Zealand Symphony Orchestra threatened to walk out of a 1987 performance of Chris Cree Brown's *Black and White*, a musical evocation of the 1981 conflicts.

The early work of the Wellington Media Collective brought together many strands of political activism. Its members had first-hand experience of working with various facets of the British and West European New Left movement in the 1970s, returning home to establish the Media Collective in 1978. Its underlying philosophy was 'prefiguring socialism', that is, preparing the ground at the grassroots level for a change in social consciousness that would eventually lead to the destruction of capitalism, racism and sexism. The strategy they employed in pursuit of this long-term goal was to assist a wide range of social groups prepare graphic material, such as posters, banners, t-shirts and cartoons, to put across their message succinctly and effectively.

The people we have drawn together under the general heading 'community artist' are so disparate in their backgrounds, their activities, their goals and the contexts in which they work that it is useful to emphasise the common threads. Community artists are not interested in aesthetic excellence as an end in itself, nor are they in the art game for fun, for personal mana or to maximise sales of cultural commodities. Their work is collectivist rather than individualist. They avoid the established sites and channels of artistic creation and distribution, taking art to the people rather than expecting the people to come to temples of high art.

Conclusion

This chapter has surveyed the attempts by three social movements in New Zealand to disrupt the master narrative of Pakeha, middle-class males. It has shown that art-making does not take place in a social and political void. Although the arts can give enjoyment in and for themselves, they are also ideological weapons with which competing groups attempt to defend themselves or overpower their opponents.

Women and Maori artists have by the 1990s come close to achieving their goal. Largely excluded from the official tradition of New Zealand art up to the 1970s, their work is now taken seriously by the mainstream art establishment. In other social areas, they have come nowhere near achieving parity with men and with Pakeha, but at least culturally they have succeeded in stopping the flow of the monologue. Less visibly, the community arts movement works away at street level to empower the dispossessed and oppose oppressive social structures. The art scene in New Zealand in the 1990s is vastly different from that of 20 years ago. There is a new sense of strength and direction, a host of new images and themes. Monologue has been replaced by a plurality of speaking voices, each with its own story to tell.

Further Reading

Barclay, B., 1990, *Our Own Image*, Auckland, Longman Paul.
Batten, J., 1989, 'Art and Identity', in D. Novitz and B. Willmott (eds), *Culture and Identity in New Zealand*, Wellington, GP Books.
Beatson, P., 1989, *The Healing Tongue: Themes in Contemporary Maori Literature*, Palmerston North, Sociology Department, Massey University.
Dann, C., 1985, 'Creativity', in C. Dann (ed.), *Up From Under: Women and Liberation in New Zealand*, Wellington, Allen and Unwin/Port Nicholson Press.
Evans, M. et al. (eds), 1988, *A Women's Picture Book: 25 Women Artists of Aotearoa*, Wellington, GP Books.
Ihimaera, W. and Long, D.S., 1982, 'Contemporary Maori Writing: a Context', in W. Ihimaera and D.S. Long (eds), *Into the World of Light,* Auckland, Heinemann.
Kedgley, S., 1989, *Our Own Country: Leading New Zealand Women Writers Talk About Their Writing and Their Lives*, Auckland, Penguin.
Kirker, A., 1986, *New Zealand Women Artists*, Auckland, Reed Methuen.
O'Biso, C., 1987, *First Light*, Auckland, Heinemann.

18 Religion

Michael Hill

Religion in contemporary New Zealand continues to be a somewhat minority interest among sociologists. In part, this reflects the policy orientation of much of New Zealand sociology since religion has not played a major institutional role in political activity in this society. The contrast with Australia is immediately evident, especially in the willingness of the churches there to intervene in political debate. In New Zealand, religious sorties in the political arena are muted and sporadic. It is in part because of the significant institutional presence of religion in Australia that its study by sociologists is more comprehensively developed (see, for example, Black, 1991).

By contrast, the number of sociologists studying religion in New Zealand is small, though recent research has surveyed a range of aspects of the area, including the comparison with coutries such as Australia and Canada (Hill and Zwaga, 1989a). To this can be added the inter-disciplinary contributions of research in religious studies, history and anthropology, which cumulatively provide a fuller survey of the place of religion in New Zealand society: an excellent overview is provided in the essay which prefaces the findings of the 1985 New Zealand Values Study (Webster and Perry, 1989). In addition, the role of fundamentalist Christian groups in moral crusades, such as that over homosexual law reform, together with their involvement in a broader spectrum of right-wing political activity, has enhanced the visibility of – and research interest in – religion in recent years (Jesson et al., 1988; Spoonley, 1987). This visibility is likely to be enhanced by the part which Christian fundamentalists have played in the stimulation of moral panics, especially that over alleged satanism (Hill and Barnett, 1994). Finally, in terms of the secularisation debate, religion in New Zealand has attracted some interest. Even among researchers who in general accept the assessment of New Zealand as a society in which religion has maintained a low social profile, attention has been paid to the origin and implications of this situation (Hill and Zwaga, 1989b), as well as to the vitality of sectarian and cultic expressions of religiosity (Hill, 1985; 1987b; 1992; 1993).

In providing a general sociological introduction to the influence of religion in New Zealand, there is a similar theme in the following assessments:

> In social terms a religion can be seen to have two particularly important functions – to express in a ritual and symbolic way the identity of the community it serves, and to validate and perpetuate a system of morality. In neither of these activities is the Christian Church in New Zealand very effective (Jackson and Harré, 1969: 131-132).

> Tangible evidences of religion in New Zealand are unspectacular enough to be taken for granted most of the time. We have no holy cities, and few sacred shrines. Every traveller up and down the country sets foot, at some time or other, in a vaguely 'historic' church. But, for the most part, places and buildings with religious uses, whether they be churchyards or maraes, temples or Kingdom Halls, chapels or New Life Centres, get little attention from the daily passer-by. Like the buildings containing government departments, we only know which is which and what they stand for if we happen to have done some business with them ourselves. Otherwise religious buildings signify nothing much to us, empty and closed as they generally appear to be (Colless and Donovan, 1985: 9-10).

Rather more eloquent testimony to the low social profile of religion in New Zealand is given by the frequency with which reference to religion is completely absent from historical and sociological assessments. While Keith Sinclair could encapsulate the religion of New Zealanders as 'simple materialism' in his 1969 history, it is omitted in the 1980 edition, and there is no reference to religion in his 1986 work on national identity (Sinclair, 1969; 1980; 1986).

Such appraisals provide a background to the present treatment of religion in New Zealand. This chapter will first evaluate historical trends, asking the question, was there ever a 'golden age' of religiosity in this society? Then consideration is given to the remarkable series of Maori prophetic and millennial movements which emerged in the early years of European contact, ran in successive waves throughout the nineteenth and early twentieth centuries, and can still be identified today. Contemporary patterns of religious belief and activity are assessed in terms of the sociological concept of secularisation, suggesting that a process of gradual but persistent decline in mainstream Christianity has accompanied a selective growth in sectarian and cultic groups. In conclusion, current developments within religion in New Zealand are analysed from the perspective of the increased polarisation between a resilient, activist core of Christian fundamentalism on the one hand and a diffuse, individualistic 'cult of humanity' on the other.

Historical Trends

Sociological accounts of change in Western religion are frequently placed in a context of secularisation. Variously defined, the concept of secularisation signifies a decline in religion or a weakening of its public role, implying that at some time in the past religion had played a more central social role: the Victorian period has been identified as one such 'golden age' (Hill, 1987a: 232-234). It is valuable to examine the extent to which nineteenth century New Zealand showed high rates of religiosity as measured by such indicators as religious adherence and church attendance. There is clear disagreement on what the evidence reveals.

On the one hand, several writers have quoted with approval the assessment of André Siegfried in the last decade of the nineteenth century that: 'No tradition has remained so strong in New Zealand as the religious one' (McLeod, 1968: 160; Mol, 1972: 365). Whether Siegfried's evaluation may have been influenced by his own minority (French) Protestant background and his admiration for the individualistic goals of the Protestant entrepreneurial ethic as realised in a New Zealand environment, must also be considered (Siegfried, 1982: xxix-xxxi). Evidence is certainly apparent in accounts of life in a New Zealand community, at about the same time as Siegfried made his visit, of the more central *social* role played by the church: 'Many of the communal leisure events in the district focused on the school and the church, and these buildings served as multi-functional centres for social intermixing' (Pearson, 1980: 23).

On the other hand, the evidence on levels of religious practice points to lower levels of church attendance in New Zealand than in England from an early stage of migration. Sinclair reports that in Auckland in the late 1840s, 'only a quarter or less of the population attended church - rather less than in England' (Sinclair, 1969: 105). Jackson summarises his detailed analysis of churchgoing in nineteenth century New Zealand by suggesting that 'the churchgoing of New Zealanders was mediocre by the standards of the British at home' (Jackson, 1983: 51) and offers five reasons why this should have occurred. First, churchgoing in Britain was more characteristic of those in higher social classes and they comprised a low proportion of migrants to New Zealand. Second, place of origin within Britain was associated with different levels of church attendance and patterns thus established may well have been perpetuated after migration. Third, greater social homogeneity in New Zealand weakened religious belonging by removing one of the sources of religio-political allegiance and identity which in Britain served to heighten religious commitment. Fourth, the process of migration and resettlement weakened the practice of churchgoing by detaching it from a familiar lifestyle. Fifth, geographical mobility within New Zealand weakened both the social ties within each congregation and the social pressures encouraging regular attendance (Jackson, 1983: 54-55).

Further evidence on the level of religious activity in the late Victorian period is provided by the New Zealand Census which, between 1874 and 1926, attempted to estimate religious attendance in different denominations on an average Sunday. Although attendance criteria were not strictly defined by Census enumerators so that the figures illustrate broad trends only, there are interesting patterns in the distribution of 'nominalism' – those who stated an adherence to a particular denomination without attending a place of worship (Table 18.1).

Table 18.1
'Usual Attenders' as a Percentage of Census Adherents,
Selected Denominations, New Zealand, 1889-91

Denomination	%
Church of England	15
Presbyterian	29
Methodist	56
Roman Catholic	35
Congregational	55
Baptist	34

Source: Jackson, 1983: 57

As will be seen when contemporary patterns of religious belief and practice are analysed, the stark 'golden age' decline scenario is less appropriate to New Zealand than a picture of gradual disengagement from religious involvement, with a large percentage of the population having always been prepared to adopt a nominal religious label while being otherwise inactive.

In brief, the historical situation can be described as follows. Despite some early attempts to transplant various Christian denominations to New Zealand on a regional basis – the Church of England in Canterbury, the Free Church of Scotland in Otago, vestiges of which can still be found in regional patterns of religious adherence – no denomination managed to establish claims to monopoly, and from the mid-nineteenth century there was an acceptance of pluralism and a secular stance on the part of the state (Breward, 1967; Wood, 1975). While a majority of the population adopted some form of denominational label, nominalism was evident in the considerably lower proportions who engaged in regular religious activity. It is important to retain this background, both as an antidote to discussions of secularisation which incorporate a 'decline and fall' diagnosis, and in evaluating the claims of moral entrepreneurs who tend to mythologise the Victorian past.

Maori Religious Movements

One of the main sources of dynamism in nineteenth century New Zealand religion can be found in the contact and interchange between the beliefs and practices of the indigenous Maori population and those of the European missionaries and settlers. A remarkable sequence of prophetic and millennial movements spanning a whole century of contact can be traced – it is too extensive and variegated to be adequately summarised here – which had the following interrelated features, many of them characteristic of millennial movements in other Third World and colonial settings (Lanternari, 1965; Wilson, 1973). First is the process of syncretism, whereby the traditional beliefs and practices of the Maori were substantially modified in response to Christian missionary activity to provide a new amalgam. In particular, the interpretation of the Maori as Hurai (Jews), and the belief that they represented one of the 'lost tribes of Israel', gave them an ethnic identity which could find legitimation in the Judaeo-Christian, Mormon, and more recently, Rastafarian belief systems that were introduced. A related feature was the frequent emergence of Maori religious movements around a charismatic prophet: such prophets tended to pursue a 'charismatic career' (Berger, 1963), beginning with a traditional status in Maori society (often as minor chief or tohunga) and radicalising their message on the model of the Hebrew prophets. The expectation of an imminent millennium is often associated with large-scale disasters such as military defeats and epidemics (Barkun, 1974), and these are clearly evident in the Maori movements. Considerable debate has centred on the extent to which movements of radical protest oscillate between the opposite poles of political activism and religious pacifism (Hill, 1987a: 205-16). While these categories are somewhat arbitrary, there is evidence among the Maori movements of successive and sometimes parallel phases of aggression and withdrawal. Scott (1992) uses a Gramscian theoretical framework to show how Maori prophets used religion as a counter ideology on which to base counter-hegemonic movements of a millennial kind.

Bearing in mind these features, the chronology of some of the major prophetic and millennial breakthroughs can be traced. The identification of the Maori with the Jews was initially made by Christian missionaries such as Samuel Marsden, who in 1819 wrote: 'I am inclined to think that [the Maori] have sprung from some dispersed Jews, at some period or other from their religious Superstitions and Customs ... ' (quoted in Binney, 1966: 325). Shortly afterwards, in the disrupted social environment of Northland, the movement associated with Papahurihia ('one who works wonders') or Te Atua Wera ('the hot/fiery god') arose. Combining chiefly status – of the Rangihoua area of the Bay of Islands (Elsmore, 1989: 37) – and the traditional ventriloquism and whistling techniques of the tohunga with elements of biblical prophecy and symbolism, Te Atua Wera adopted the serpent of Genesis as god and proclaimed his converts Hurai (Jews). In this way, they forged an identity which marked them off from the Christian missionaries and their followers, and eagerly awaited the resurrection of the dead and the ushering in of a promised new world. Increasingly, the prophet took on the role of war-priest, being consulted before battle by Hone Heke, and as his status increased, he adopted more closely the traditional role of tohunga. It was for later prophets to achieve a radical charismatic breakthrough.

The 'lost tribe' motif, which emerged both from a combination of syncretism between traditional Maori culture and beliefs and the introduction of biblical beliefs – especially those of the Old Testament with its prophetic, tribal emphasis – and from the disruption of the indigenous social structure, was important in providing two-way plausibility. On the one hand, it explained the depressed situation of the Maori as part of the divine fate of Israel as God's 'suffering servant'; on the other, it promised them future hope as a 'chosen people'. As well as being traceable in prophetic movements which arose in the first quarter of the twentieth century, it has its counterpart in the Mormon belief in a dark-skinned tribe of Labanites who suffer this 'curse' until by their own moral regeneration they become 'exceeding fair and delightsome'; and in the more recent growth of Rastafarianism, where the equivalent belief in a Babylonian 'enslavement' followed by a 'return to Ethiopia' again lends plausibility to a perceived situation of ethnic oppression.

The New Zealand Wars of the 1860s, initiated by disputes between Maori and settlers over sovereignty, land ownership, and then later by large-scale government confiscation of land, saw the emergence of a new prophetic movement, Pai Marire ('good and peaceful'), known also by settlers by its more notorious name, Hauhau. Its leader, Te Ua Haumene, had been educated by Wesleyan missionaries as well as learning the arts of the tohunga, and had been a teacher in Taranaki for some years. While accounts of the early emergence of his movement disagree, they include reference to the miraculous intervention of angels and to his generally peaceful reputation. Some of the militant aspects of Hauhau may owe their origin to the assistants he selected and the emissaries he sent to other tribes. In all events, this movement illustrates better than most the pacifist and militarist poles of the millennial response. The ritual of Pai Marire included chanting which incorporated words in Maori together with others taken from Christian worship and British military drill, again illustrating the syncretic nature of the movement; and Te Ua pointed to parallels between the situation of the Maori and that of the Israelites. The Hauhau movement developed in a militant direction and was directly involved in the New Zealand Wars as well as stimulating internecine conflict among some tribes (Belich, 1988: 205), but the pacifist aspect of Pai Marire appears to have persisted alongside this tendency, leading one observer to describe the movement as comprising 'two canoes – one full of wrath, the other of peaceful propaganda' (Elsmore, 1989: 197). Pai Marire involvement in the Maori King movement also shows the merging of political and religious goals.

A defeated group of Hauhau prisoners was deported to the Chatham Islands. Among them (though not himself a Hauhau member) was Te Kooti. Educated in a mission station, he laid the basis for a new religious movement, Ringatu, during his imprisonment. The syncretic nature of Maori prophetic movements was evident in the parallel drawn between Te Kooti and Moses, as well as in the identification of the Maori with the Children of Israel (Elsmore, 1989: 228-229). The prophet established his charismatic credentials by a dramatic escape from captivity, and after returning on board a captured ship to Poverty Bay, he spent some time as a guerrilla leader engaging in several battles with government forces (Belich, 1988: 216-234) before settling into a more peaceable life and being pardoned by the government.

His prediction that another prophet would soon appear was influential in establishing the charismatic claim of Rua Kenana Hepetika, who emerged as a prophetic figure in the early years of this century (Webster, 1979: 158). He already had an established reputation as a faith healer, and he built his movement on a reinterpretation of the beliefs and practices of Ringatu. He organised his followers – who were known as Iharaira, or Israelites – into an Old Testament-based theocracy at Maungapohatu. The movement contained a strong millennial element, anticipating the expulsion of the Europeans and the return of New Zealand to the Maori.

Worsley (1968: 254-256) has noted the tendency of Third World and nativistic groups to become politicised in their later stages of development, and this appears to characterise the last of the major Maori prophetic movements, Ratana. This religious group has had a substantial involvement in New Zealand political life (it maintained a monopoly over the four Maori parliamentary seats until very recently) and its ties with the New Zealand Labour Party were strong for many years. The Ratana Church was founded in 1925 by Tahupotiki Wiremu Ratana, himself a faith healer and the nephew of a Maori prophetess. In the process of syncretism, it can be seen to have incorporated a larger component of Judaeo-Christian beliefs than earlier prophetic movements such as Ringatu, but in common with some of the earlier movements it showed the influence of a region – in this case South Taranaki – which had enjoyed substantial Maori autonomy in the nineteenth century (Belich, 1988: 307-308).

Contemporary Religious Patterns

New Zealand shares with other Western societies the tendency of a large majority of the population to adopt a religious label. Around 75 per cent of the population in 1991 stated a religious profession: in 1991 the comparable Australian figure was 75 per cent (Bentley *et al.*, 1993: 1975). The percentage adherence to selected religious professions over a 35-year period is given in Table 18.2.

A notable feature of changing patterns of adherence has been the steady erosion of respondents listing one of the four mainline religious groups – Anglican, Presbyterian, Roman Catholic and Methodist. In 1921 these four categories accounted for 93 per cent of the population, while in 1991 this proportion was reduced to 57 per cent. Furthermore, in the latest census figures, 20 per cent reported no religious adherence, a figure almost as large as that of the Anglicans. Evidence of the decline in mainline adherence is also given by the increased use of the 'Christian' label

Table 18.2
Percentage Adherence to Selected Religious Professions, 1956-1991

	1956	1966	1976	1986	1991
Total NZ Population	2,174,062	2,676,919	3,103,263	3,263,283	3,373,926
% adherence:					
Anglican	35.9	33.7	29.3	24.3	21.7
Presbyterian	22.3	21.8	18.2	18.0	16.0
No religion	0.6	1.2	3.2	16.4	19.8
Roman Catholic	14.3	15.9	15.3	15.2	14.8
Object to state	8.0	7.9	14.0	7.5	7.5
Methodist	7.4	7.0	5.5	4.7	4.1
Baptist	1.6	1.7	1.6	2.1	2.1
Not specified	0.8	0.7	1.1	1.8	1.8
Christian*	0.4	0.8	1.7	1.3	2.3
Ratana	0.9	1.0	1.1	1.2	1.4
Latter Day Saints	0.1	1.0	1.2	1.1	1.4
Brethren	1.0	0.9	0.8	0.6	0.6
Salvation Army	0.6	0.7	0.7	0.5	0.6
Jehovah's Witness	0.2	0.3	0.4	0.5	0.6
Pentecostal*	-	-	0.2	0.5	0.6
Assemblies of God	-	0.1	0.2	0.4	0.5
Seventh Day Adventist	0.3	0.4	0.4	0.4	0.4
Ringatu	0.2	0.2	0.2	0.2	0.2
Hindu	0.1	0.2	0.2	0.2	0.5
Buddhist	-	-	0.1	0.2	0.4
Lutheran	0.2	0.2	0.2	0.2	0.1
Agnostic	0.1	0.2	0.5	0.1	-
Protestant*	2.2	1.7	1.0	0.1	-
Churches of Christ	0.5	0.4	0.3	0.1	-
Congregational	0.3	0.4	0.2	0.1	-
Hebrew Congregations	0.2	0.2	0.1	0.1	-
Atheist	0.1	0.2	0.5	-	-
All other religions	1.2	1.3	1.7	2.1	2.6
	100.0	100.0	100.0	100.0	100.0

* No other designation.
** Figures may not total 100% due to rounding.

Source: New Zealand Census of Population and Dwellings, 'Religious Professions'.

which now ranks higher than the percentage specifying Baptist as their denominational allegiance. Other notable gainers in recent censuses have been the ethinically-based religions Hindu and Buddhust, influenced principally by migration from Asia and the Pacific, together with a range of small sectarian groups such as

Pentecostals and Jehovah's Witnesses. Caution should be exercised in comparing 1981 and 1986 figures because in 1986 there was a change in question format (from write-in to precoded): not only did this result in a large growth in the 'No religion' category and a marked decline in the 'Object' numbers, but 'Agnostic' categories were decimated. There was also a 1.5 per cent rise in the percentage of Presbyterian adherants between 1981 and 1986 which led to some speculation about a reversal in the secularisation process. A more likely interpretation is that in 1986, respondents no longer had to spell 'Presbyterian'; a smaller phenomenon has been noticed in Australia (Bentley *et al.*, 1992: 176-177).

A comparison of 1986 Census data with that of the 1985 New Zealand Values Study sample provides a broad picture of the main categories of religious identification in contemporary New Zealand. Table 18.3 summarises this material.

Table 18.3
Religious Adherence of Values Study Sample and 1986 Census,
15 years and over

	1985 Values Study Sample %	1986 New Zealand Census %
Anglican	28.3	25.8
Presbyterian	19.4	19.4
Roman Catholic	14.2	15.2
Methodist	4.3	5.1
Baptist	2.9	2.1
Other	9.6	9.9
No religion/Object	21.3	22.5
Total	N=1,952	N=2,431,488

Source: Webster and Perry, 1989

Accompanying the gradual decline in mainline adherence shown above, there has been an overall contraction in the 'core' membership of the four main religious professions as measured by statistical criteria employed by the groups themselves. 'Core' membership – which has declined in three of the four denominations listed – can be seen as the converse of nominalism which has proportionately increased (see Table 18.4).

Significantly, the 'core' percentages correspond quite closely to the levels of weekly adult church attendance found in several surveys in the early 1980s: three surveys established a weekly adult attendance rate of 15 or 16 per cent of the overall

Table 18.4*
'Core' Membership of Mainline Denominations, 1971 and 1981

	1971 %	1981 %
Anglican	18	19
Presbyterian	22	18
Roman Catholic	42	35
Methodist	24	19

* Explanation: Christmas communicants (Anglican) or communicant members (Presbyterian and Methodist) as percentage of Census adherence aged 15+; Roman Catholic mass count (all dioceses, 1971, Wellington and Palmerston North 1984) as percentage of total Census Catholic population in the equivalent areas.

population aged 15+ (Social Indicators Survey, 1984; AGB: McNair, 1982; Heylen Research Centre, 1986).

The frequency of church attendance increases with age and the lowest rate of attendance is concentrated in the 20-29 year old group. The latter age group is strongly associated with religious non-alignment, so that those claiming to be Atheist or Agnostic are predominantly from this age category (Hill and Zwaga, 1989b). Recent Census data also show a characteristic ageing social profile in the mainline Protestant denominations, a situation which contrasts with that of the earlier years of this century when adherents to these denominations had a broadly similar age composition to that of the New Zealand population as a whole. A similar 'ageing' pattern is evident in Australia and Canada (Hill and Zwaga, 1989a). Roman Catholic adherence has a more 'youthful' age profile but this feature is even more prominent in the case of Mormons and Jehovah's Witnesses. Since these two groups have shown rapid increases over the past three decades (see Table 18.2), at least part of the explanation for this must be given in terms of the importance of demographic factors in understanding church growth (Hoge and Roozen, 1979).

The overall picture, then, is of a relatively high level of 'religious encasement' (Bibby, 1985) – in that a majority of the population claims adherence to one of the main Christian denominations – coupled with high rates of nominalism. Research is also available which shows to what extent Census respondents retain or change their religious adherence. An intercensal consistency survey compared a sample of 1981 Census returns with 1976 returns completed by the same matched individuals (Nolan et al., 1986); this comparison was made before the change in the question format and is thus not influenced by extraneous variables. The study found that no fewer than 26 per cent of the sample changed their religious affiliation over that five-year period, and Table 18.5 shows the degree of encasement among mainline denominations contrasted with the volatility of those categories of adherence or non-alignment which contained the largest proportions of young adults. This suggests that a 'generational' interpretation is appropriate in the case of religious switchers, with most of the realignment occurring in the 20-29-year-old group.

Table 18.5
Percentage of 1976 Census Sample Still Retaining the Same Religious Label in 1981

	%
Roman Catholic	86
Ratana	84
Anglican	82
Presbyterian	80
Mormon	73
Methodist	72
Other religions	67
Baptist	66
Atheist/Agnostic	50
No religious adherence	49
Christian (n. o. d.)	48
Object to state	48
Not specified	26

Source: Computed from Nolan et al., 1986: 64

Religious Polarisation: Christian Fundamentalism and Religious Individualism

With the numerical decline in and ageing membership of mainline Christian denominations, contemporary New Zealand religion has increasingly polarised into, on the one hand, a visible and vocal fundamentalist core and, on the other, a fluid and proliferating variety of individualistic cultic groups. The latter have often been referred to collectively as part of the New Age movement. The fundamentalist core has been strengthened since the 1970s by the growth of Pentecostalism and the neo-charismatic movement, both in increased adherence to sectarian groups of this type and in changes within the mainline denominations. One explanation of this growth is that as the less committed adherents of the larger denominations cease to be active participants, the remaining core participants become increasingly aware of themselves as a cognitive minority which is able to engage in less conventional forms of religious activity. Another explanation would suggest that fundamentalism is an expression of status politics by sections of the old petty-bourgeoisie in response to a perceived decline in their socio-economic situation. Thus, fundamentalist groups and conservative churches are a small constituency within a larger 'moral right' movement (Spoonley, 1987: 234-37). Because such groups instil high levels of commitment in their members and have a more clearly crystallised set of beliefs than those of the mainline churches, they are likely to prove resilient in the face of secularisation, although they are equally likely to remain small and to be relatively unsuccessful in recruiting outsiders (Bibby, 1978).

A major campaign has been waged by the Christian Right in New Zealand to reclaim what they see as the lost ground of traditional morality. To do this, they have mobilised the rhetoric of civil religion in their moral crusade against such issues as the liberalisation of the law on homosexuality and other emancipatory movements including feminism, educational reform and the Maori revival. Under the slogan *For God, for Family, for Country,* they have politicised their own form of conservative Christianity and have sought to persuade a wider segment of the population that these represent the core values of New Zealanders. Although the moral right is both vocal and visible – having a number of sympathisers among conservative politicians – they have not succeeded in capturing a wide base of popular support. An important reason for this lack of success is the absence in New Zealand of a kind of civil religion which sociologists have identified in societies like the United States (Hill and Zwaga, 1987). Because New Zealand religion has a low social profile and because the society in general lacks a consensual mythology of nationhood, the Christian Right has not been able to establish the cultural resonance needed for the widespread acceptance of these symbols.

More recently, Christian fundamentalists have been active in introducing to New Zealand a moral panic which began in the United States in 1980 and spread to Britain in the later half of the 1980s. In 1991 the first claims were made in Christchurch about the existence of satanic ritual abuse, and these were given prominent coverage in the media. The details of this moral panic are considered elsewhere (Richardson *et al.,* 1991; Jenkins, 1992; Hill, 1992a; Hill and Barnett, 1994) but can be briefly summarised here. Fundamentalists believe that the world has entered the 'end time' before the second coming of Christ and that, in accordance with predictions in the Book of Revelations, the forces of evil are particularly strong. Accounts by alleged 'survivors' of satanic ritual abuse began to appear in the United States in 1980 and soon focused on allegations of sexual abuse in childcare centres; these were consonant with the fundamentalist goal of the re-domestication of American mothers. A variety of counsellors, therapists, social workers, talk-show hosts and police officials became associated with the ritual abuse scenario and it rapidly escalated to the proportions of a major moral panic. Its spread to Britain a few years later resulted in a series of dawn raids on homes to remove children allegedly involved in abuse by networks of satanists and culminated in the Orkneys fiasco, which led to a judicial and government inquiry.

Allegations of satanism arrived in New Zealand direct from the United States. In August 1991 a Christian sexual abuse therapist from the States spoke in Christchurch about satanic ritual abuse of children and its links with multi-personality disorder (*Press*, 27 August, 1991). At about the same time, a Ritual Abuse Workshop was presented at a Family Violence Prevention Conference in Christchurch by two social workers representing the DSW-funded Ritual Action Group (*FVPCC*, 1991; see volume 1:5; volume 2: 5-24). Their presentation revealed a degree of cross-fertilisation between American anti-cult and anti-satanic literature and claimed that as in the United States 'ritual abuse occurs without parents knowing, at pre-schools, day-care centres, churches, summer camps, and at the hands of baby sitters and neighbours, it is likely to be so here in this country'. The claims were predominantly featured in newspapers (*Dominion Sunday Times*, 1 September 1991; *Star*, 1 September 1991; *Sunday News*, 3 November 1991) along with the allegations of a child pornography network in Christchurch. The police inquiry into the Christchurch civic crèche, which began within three months of the first satanic claims, was demonstrably linked with the first moral panic and, at one stage, a parent had sought to enlist the help of an American author on alleged ritual abuse (*Press*, 4 December 1992). The Christian fundamentalist connection was later confirmed in a controversial television interview in which the detective inspector in charge of the inquiry made the statement: 'Really what I'm saying is that I actually believe in a God who will not be mocked. And currently I believe that this country is actually now starting to reap the harvest of liberalism and of compromise and of double standards' (*Dominion*, 16 June 1993).

New Zealand's 'cultic milieu' (Campbell, 1972) – the individualistic, free-floating market of 'New Age', human potential and therapeutic groups – has recently attracted the attention of sociologists of religion in North America and Europe. It has been argued that, on a statistical basis, New Zealand has one of the highest rates of Indian and Eastern cults, Scientology practitioners and Hare Krishna centres in Western societies (Stark and Bainbridge, 1985). Although the empirical evidence for this claim is somewhat dubious, a valid argument could be made for the fact that the pluralistic religious situation and absence of any established or dominant Christian church has encouraged the proliferation of smaller, frequently innovative groups. Furthermore, the 'simple materialism' which has been seen as New Zealand's characteristic form of religion, can be found in the world-affirming, market-oriented stance of many of these groups (Hill, 1993).

An individualistic religious style in complex modern societies was foreseen by Durkheim who labelled it 'the cult of humanity' (Hill, 1992). He thought that as societies became larger, more densely populated and differentiated, individual differences between members would increase to the point where the only thing they had in common was their shared humanity. In such a situation, he maintained, human personality would be elevated to a supreme position and would take on a religious character. There would be a variety of groups within the overall 'cult of humanity', variegated according to the different occupations and lifestyles of their members, but they would have in common the pursuit of an idealised human personality, and this would lead to tolerance between groups of each others' goals. At the same time, the groups would take a positive attitude towards the world and would incorporate scientific ideas in their belief systems.

Durkheim's prediction is appropriate to a range of religious and quasi-religious groups and practices in New Zealand. An area of particular vitality in contemporary New Zealand is that of alternative or complementary therapies which 'appear to function as religions for many adherents – providing cosmologies, rituals, a language for the interpretation of the believers' worlds, a social context for belief and practice and a group of fellow believers' (McGuire, 1985: 275). Such therapies have been the subject of a Health Department report (Leibrich et al., 1987), and the approach taken by many of them emphasises themes such as idealised human personality, inner potential, the empowering of clients and the use of alternative scientific techniques. Tolerance towards other groups in the cultic milieu is shown by the characteristic approach of 'mixing and matching' therapies and by the simultaneous adoption of a range of therapeutic techniques.

Another group which has been active in New Zealand is Transcendental Meditation (TM). Its 1978 'Ideal Wellington Campaign' was an attempt to recruit one per cent of the city's population into TM meditation techniques. Based on the theory of the 'Maharishi Effect', this level of meditation would trigger a series of positive social variables including less crime, sickness and accidents. TM bases its claim to effectiveness on the release of inner potential, and presents the results of its techniques in a scientific idiom, incorporating a range of graphs, charts and tables. Its individualism is evident in the practice of meditation, which can be performed by adepts in isolation for 15 to 20-minute daily sessions. The world-affirming nature of TM is apparent in its claim to be able to assist adepts in making career progress and even in reversing the ageing process (Posner, 1985: 101-102).

Perhaps the best-known indigenous growth in the 'cult of humanity' is Centrepoint, the Auckland community based on the guru, Bert Potter. During 1992 this group was the subject of considerable controversy and its founder was sentenced to seven years imprisonment on sexual abuse charges (*Press*, 28 November, 1992). The Centrepoint community – now increasingly controlled by its female members (*Sunday Times*, 13 December 1992) – has adopted an eclectic variety of therapies including Gestalt, Transactional Analysis and Hypnotherapy and, in addition, has found sources in Eastern religion, for instance Rajneesh, Buddhism and Hinduism. Personal growth – the idealised human personality of Durkheim's prediction – is evident in the empowering motif of the workshops offered by the community

(Oakes, 1986), and while the group maintains a communal lifestyle, many of its clients come into contact with it on an individualistic basis. The appeal of the type of therapeutic techniques found at Centrepoint is strong in New Zealand, and an excellent argument could be made for the potential of groups based on them to increase in number as a counterbalance to the conservatism of fundamentalist sects and denominations; indeed, the growth of the 'Rainbow Network' in Auckland confirms this prediction. Significantly, members of the latter are strongly opposed to the 'New Age Movement', condemning it as satanic and a repository of humanistic atheism (*Challenge Weekly*, 1988). No clearer indication could be given of the polarisation which now exists in the religious sphere in New Zealand.

Conclusion

Since the 1960s, sociologists of religion, faced with the irresistible theme of the secularisation of modern societies, have tended to see themselves as being in the unenviable position of observing and recording the alleged demise of their subject matter. Perhaps in attempting to counter fears of such anticipated intellectual redundancy, some sociologists (Turner, 1983; Thompson, 1986) have proposed ideology rather than religion as the main unit of analysis. While not disputing the notion that religious beliefs and practices belong to a wider cultural and ideological spectrum within which people make sense of their everyday life, this chapter has shown that both the resilience and the selective growth of religion in societies such as New Zealand warrants the analysis of religion *per se* instead of encapsulating it within an inclusive category of ideology. The sociological study of religion for the forseeable future is likely to interact most fruitfully with the sociology of deviance.

Returning to the theme of secularisation, this chapter has shown that the New Zealand religious situation has been characterised by a dynamic interplay between Western Christianity and, first, a sequence of Maori religious movements, then, more recently, the cultic milieu which offers an eclectic range of cosmologies as an alternative to mainline Christian nominalism. The latter is congruent with the secular emphasis within New Zealand society which, officially defined from an early stage, finds its contemporary expression in those who increasingly refrain from religious adherence. It is against this secular environment that more conservative Christian groups have restated a fundamentalist form of Christianity. While Christian fundamentalists may have a significant influence as moral entrepreneurs, it is unlikely that the Christian Right will be successful in promoting its version of a mythological Christian past among a wider segment of the population, the reason being that New Zealand lacks the kind of diffuse religious legitimation which underpins civil religion, as occurs in the United States. New Zealand's past, as well as its present, contains a large measure of secularity.

Further Reading

Barker, E., 1989, *New Religious Movements: A Practical Introduction*, London, H.M.S.O.
Barker, E., Beckford J.A. and Dobbelaere K. (eds), 1993, *Secularization, Rationalism, and Sectarianism: Essays in Honour of Bryan R. Wilson*, Oxford, Clarendon Press.
Beckford, J.A., 1989, *Religion and Advanced Industrial Society*, London, Unwin Hyman.
Colless, B. and Donovan, P. (eds), 1985, *Religion in New Zealand Society* (Second Edition), Palmerston North, Dunmore Press.
Hill, M. , 1987, *A Sociology of Religion*, Aldershot, Avebury/Gower.
Hill, M. and Barnett, J., 1994, 'Religion and Deviance' in P. Green (ed.), *Studies in New Zealand Social Problems* (Second Edition), Palmerston North, Dunmore Press.
Hill, M. and Zwaga, W. , 1990, 'Religion and Deviance', in P. Green (ed.), *Studies in New Zealand Social Problems,* Palmerston North, Dunmore Press.
McGuire, M. B., 1987, *Religion: The Social Context* (Second Edition), Belmont, California, Wadsworth.
Wilson, B. (ed.), 1992, *Religion: Contemporary Issues. The All Souls Seminars in the Sociology of Religion*, London, Bellew Publishing.

19 Population

Arvind Zodgekar

The study of population has had a changing profile in recent years. There is a growing awareness that population change is not something that happens in the abstract. Population events (births, death and migration) are a regular occurrence in the lives of individuals, families and societies. All these events are surrounded by particular personal, social and societal circumstances and, as a consequence, personal and social meanings are attached to them. In order to fully understand the nature of human society, one needs to recognise the role played by the population process in the dynamic of social life.

The fundamental characteristics of population (size, distribution and composition) are the result of a recurrent and cumulative process of population events. This process[1] shapes the form and content of social structure. In turn, the individual and personal aspects of population characteristics are conditioned and affected by the power of social forces (Goldscheider, 1971).

The population process and population growth can be studied in a variety of ways. One perspective, the formal demographic approach, views population events as a purely self-contained process within which population size and structure emerge from relationships between demographic variables. The study of population is reduced to a description of the cumulative patterned relationship between levels of births, deaths and migration. However, such an approach seldom provides an insight into the social scientific questions associated with the reasons for population growth, trends and patterns. This kind of analysis of population process is incomplete because it does not reflect on the issues which ultimately affect population growth and its structure (e.g. natural resources, economic growth and the social system). A further perspective, which we can call the analytical approach, argues that population growth acts as an independent variable in changes to the economy or in society.

The recognition of the relevance of population studies among social scientists in general, and sociologists in particular, for understanding New Zealand society has been a slow and also very recent process. Most of the early work was done by geographers and this is reflected in the demography produced. However, during the past few decades we have witnessed a period of considerable vitality in cross-disciplinary teaching and research in demography in this country. There has been a growth in the numbers of demographically minded people both in academia and policy circles in New Zealand. This has resulted in the more widespread teaching of demography in New Zealand universities, which in turn has contributed tremendously towards the recognition of demography as a relevant social science. A further and very necessary step is for population studies to be integrated into the teaching of all social science disciplines, as well as planning, law, public administration and business studies (Johnston, 1982). The continuation of such a development should result in an increase of qualified demographers and experts. This in turn should result in better analysis and an understanding of demographic material. Beyond academia, we have also seen the growth in interested parties that have become involved in population matters – ranging from single individuals, to government departments, politicians, media and policy-makers. A feature of the general expansion of interest in demography has been the emergence of professional bodies, working parties and policy groups. In particular, the New Zealand Demographic Society, Department of Statistics and Population Monitoring Group of the New Zealand Planning Council have played an important role in bringing the subject to prominence.

All these activities have increased the understanding of New Zealand's demography, and created a new awareness of the importance of population trends in social and economic planning. The report of the Task Force on Economic and Social Planning (1976) claimed that 'population' is one of the key base variables for planning and policy-making and that understanding the dynamics and implications of population change was therefore crucial to any consideration of New Zealand's future.

In spite of this interest in the 1970s and 1980s, the situation in terms of population policy is not encouraging in the immediate future. A good number of politicians acknowledge that population factors are important but no more than one or two appear to understand why or how this should be so (Heenan, 1979). Thus, in the early 1990s, there is no evidence of the development of a population policy for New Zealand. Likewise, there has been a failure to consider whether population trends and changes have contributed to major social and economic change in New Zealand (Bane, 1980).

The following sections of this chapter will examine the major changes in New Zealand's population growth and structure since World War II. Specific attention is paid to ageing, fertility and international migration, and the relationship of these changes to social and economic conditions.

Population Change Since 1945

In comparison with many Western countries, New Zealand's population is small. It did not reach one million until the beginning of the twentieth century. Then it took another fifty years to reach its second million. The third million, by comparison, was reached within the next twenty years. Despite the continuous growth in population, there has been considerable fluctuations in the growth rate over the last hundred years.

The post-World War II years have witnessed significant changes in the growth pattern and structure of the New Zealand population. As one can see in Table 19.1, trends in natural increase (excess births over deaths) and net external migration (difference between arrivals and departures) have contributed unevenly to the overall

Table 19.1
Intercensal Increase in New Zealand Population 1951-1991

Census Year	Population	Intercensal Numerical Change	Change Per cent	Average Annual %
1951	1,939,472			
1956	2,174,062	234,590	12.10	2.31
1961	2,414,984	240,922	11.08	2.12
1966	2,676,919	261,935	10.85	2.11
1971	2,862,635	185,712	6.94	1.35
1976	3,129,383	266,752	9.32	1.80
1981	3,175,737	46,354	1.48	0.29
1986	3,307,084	131,347	4.14	0.82
1991	3,434,950	127,866	3.87	0.76

Components of Population Increase in New Zealand

Period (Calendar Year)	Natural Increase	Net Migration	Population Increase Attributed to:	
			Natural Increase	Net Migration
1951-55	169,004	69,015	71.00	29.00
1956-60	197,210	43,942	81.78	18.22
1961-65	205,164	70,196	74.51	25.49
1966-70	187,297	6,455	96.67	3.33
1971-75	179,580	116,917	60.57	39.43
1976-80	134,965	- 98,800	373.22	- 273.22
1981-85	125,109	9,687	92.81	7.19
1986-90	148,426	-21,709	117.13	-17.13

Source: Census of Population and Dwellings 1951-1991. Population and Migration, Department of Statistics Vital Statistics, Department of Statistics.

growth of New Zealand's population. These trends indicate a steady decline in natural increase and a wide fluctuation in net external migration. In fact, it is these changes in net external migration which have caused considerable demographic disruption to the growth of New Zealand's population. The major fluctuations observed in the growth rate are largely the result of the levels and direction of the external migration balance. Figure 19.1 gives a clear picture of the various components of population growth and their relative importance. Natural increase has played a consistent role in New Zealand's population growth. Its contribution gradually increased during the post-war baby-boom period (1945-61).

Figure 19.1
Components of Population Change, 1961-1986

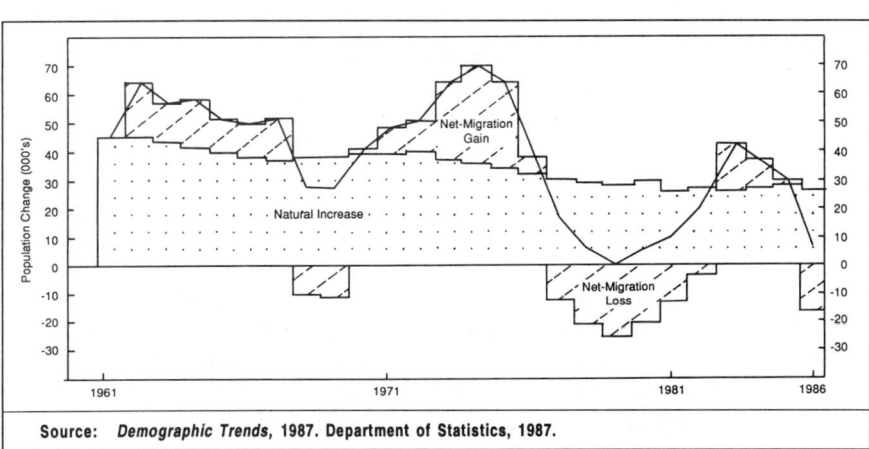

Source: *Demographic Trends*, 1987. Department of Statistics, 1987.

Since the early 1960s, the rate of natural increase has stabilised, with New Zealand's population growth experiencing a gradual fall until 1991. Natural increase figures clearly reflect the two phases of fertility change experienced in New Zealand. The nature and pattern of fertility changes experienced are discussed in detail in a later section of this chapter. Even though mortality has been continuously declining in New Zealand since the late nineteenth century, its impact on population growth in recent times has been insignificant.

The impact of net external migration, while sometimes dramatic, has been more short-term in its effect. Up until the mid-1960s, external migration has always contributed positively to population growth. Since the late 1960s, however, both extreme lower and higher rates of net external migration have been experienced in New Zealand. These levels had a marked influence on the percentage contributions of the various components of population growth and overall rates of growth during the periods concerned. Such fluctuations in external migration very clearly coincided with the economic cycles which were experienced in New Zealand during these periods. The decline in net migration during 1966-70 was the result of a recession in the economy. This was followed by an upturn of net migration gains during 1971-75 in response to the economic boom. The subsequent downturn in the economy has kept the net migration at a lower level.

The post-World War II trends of New Zealand's population growth clearly indicate that since the mid-1970s it has slowed down considerably. Thus, even without the migration factor, New Zealand's population would now be growing at a rate considerably below one-half of that prevailing in the early 1960s (Kuzmicich, 1988).

Any discussion of New Zealand's population growth would be incomplete without reflecting on the growth of the Maori population. The Maori population has been characterised by a significantly different demographic history to that of Pakeha. It has been estimated that at the time of initial European contact in 1769, there were somewhere between 125,000 and 175,000 Maori in New Zealand (Department of Statistics, 1988). Since that period, disease and warfare have resulted in high levels of mortality and an overall decline in numbers (Pool, 1977). By the late nineteenth century, the total Maori population numbered little more than 40,000 (Neville and O'Neill, 1979).

The twentieth century has witnessed a resurgence in Maori population growth, particularly after World War II. This is largely the result of a steady reduction in the Maori mortality rate, coupled with the maintenance of a traditionally high fertility level. The decline in mortality is the result of an improved standard of living, better health facilities for Maori and the eradication of endemic diseases (Papp, 1985). The peak growth rate of 4.4 per cent per annum was experienced by the Maori population during the early 1960s, but since then there has been a steady decline in the population growth rate. Currently, the Maori population is experiencing a growth rate of around 1.2 per cent per annum. This decline in the growth rate is the result of a fertility transition which the Maori population has experienced since the early 1960s.

International migration did not emerge as a significant factor influencing the growth of the Maori population until the 1970s. Over the last two decades, there has been a significant movement of young Maori overseas, particularly to Australia and the United Kingdom (Department of Statistics, 1988). The effect of the higher growth rate of the Maori population has been to increase its share of New Zealand's population from 6.0 per cent in 1951 to 12.0 per cent (of Maori descent) in 1986. A Maori descent population ranging from 650,000 to 700,000 in 2011 appears possible with upper limits of 750,000, representing perhaps 19 per cent of the total New Zealand population (Pool and Pole, 1987: 33). This is expected to have considerable implications for government policies.

The Changing Age Structure and Ageing of the New Zealand Population

New Zealand is experiencing a maturing population which is characteristic of most economically developed countries. Advances in medicine, health and social welfare have combined to extend the life expectancies of the whole population. At the same time, birth rates have declined. The effect of declining fertility has seen a decreasing proportion of people in the younger age group and an increasing proportion in the 60+ age group.

These structural changes have resulted in a steady rise in the median age of the population in recent years. In 1971 the median age of the population was 25.6 years compared with 30.4 years in 1987. These structural changes are going to have a profound effect on the structures and functions of the family, economic policies, health, education and welfare services, as well as government policy and practice.

In Table 19.2, various indices of ageing and dependency ratios are presented to indicate the nature of ageing and the consequent extent of the dependency burden. In the post-World War II period, the aged have formed a stable fraction of the total population at around 13-14 per cent, and the projection to the end of this century indicates that the proportion of old people will increase only minimally. This has led some people to conclude that an increase in old-age dependency is of limited policy concern. In my opinion, this is not the case, because the percentage of the population beyond age sixty is not the appropriate index. The index of ageing presented in Table 19.2 reflects a more accurate picture. It contrasts the two ends of the life cycle. By comparing the number of people aged 60+ with those under 15, we are able to establish the extent to which the population as a whole is ageing. This index also reflects the long-term interaction of changing fertility and mortality patterns on age structure. The information contained in this indicator of age structure is crucial when forecasting fundamental changes in our institutional structure. The steady increase in the index from 1961 to the 1991 census, and in the future projected population of New Zealand, indicates that the aged will rapidly increase their dominance in relation to the young. This trend will have a great effect on social and economic structures which will mean an increasing amount and proportion of national income will have to be allocated for superannuation benefits, geriatric health care and other social services for the elderly.

One needs to look beyond old-age dependency. Koopman-Boyden (1986) notes that such economic dependency ratios may be only one of the social implications of the increasing dependency ratio of the elderly. Elderly people can be dependent in many other ways and on many other people. Most of the physical and social support is usually provided by the family. Yet dependence on the family, and particularly on middle-aged women who are doing unpaid caring work, is not measured in any of the dependency ratios (Koopman-Boyden, 1986). The supply of such unpaid women

Table 19.2
Percentage Distribution, Dependency Ratios and Index of Ageing 1951 – 2031

	Under 15	Percentage 15-59	60+ (Old)	80+ (Old-old)	Old Dependence 60+ 15-59	Two Generation Geriatrics 80+ 60-64	Index of ageing 60+ 0-14
1951	29.4	57.3	13.2	1.1	23.0	28	44.8
1956	31.5	55.9	12.6	1.3	22.6	37	40.2
1961	33.1	54.7	12.1	1.5	22.3	42	36.9
1966	32.6	55.4	12.0	1.5	21.7	41	36.9
1971	31.8	55.7	12.5	1.6	22.5	39	39.6
1976	29.7	57.3	13.0	1.5	22.7	38	43.8
1981	26.9	59.2	13.9	1.7	23.5	42	51.6
1986	24.6	60.7	14.7	2.0	24.2	46	59.8
1991	23.2	61.4	15.4	2.3	25.1	55	66.4
2001	23.9	60.2	15.9	3.0	26.4	75	67.8
2011	21.4	60.1	18.5	3.7	30.8	68	89.5
2021	19.0	58.9	22.2	4.0	37.7	69	121.9
2031	19.0	55.7	25.3	5.4	45.4	92	140.0

Source: New Zealand Census of Population and Dwellings 1951-91. Projection of Future Population was supplied by Department of Statistics (Base Year 1991)

workers will become scarce with the increasing participation of women in the paid workforce. Future government policy will need to consider the problem of dependency beyond direct government expenditure on superannuation.

The projected increase in the elderly population, particularly in the number of 'old-old' (80+), is also likely to have significant implications for the financing, organisation and utilisation of health care resources (see Koopman-Boyden, 1986).

Demographic analysis reveals that old age is not a problem simply in terms of the number beyond age sixty, there are also social structural considerations (Zodgekar, 1980a). The distribution of population beyond age sixty by sex clearly illustrates a predominance of females. This is because women live longer. Another characteristic of old age which is of significance from the social adjustment point of view is marital status. Loss of a marriage partner occurs much more frequently among elderly women than among elderly men. Hence, there are the attendant problems of loneliness, inadequate means of support and the readjustment in living arrangements that typically accompany widowhood during old age. These considerations are going to become more significant in the future.

The number of living generations in families is another important facet of demographic change. The number of living 'generations' in families has been undergoing a gradual change in past decades due to mortality decline. The anticipated future rate of mortality decline will also have an effect on the age of the generations. The increased life expectancy and increase in the number of elderly in many households has resulted in what has been called a two-generation 'geriatric family'. The emergence of two generations of older people will cause changes in the mutual support network among family members. In other words, there is an increased probability that people will enter old age and still have surviving parents.

The significance of the aged as a grouping within the population lies not just in the proportion who have reached a certain age, but in issues of status and role. Old age in Western societies is characterised by the loss of a series of significant roles by elderly individuals. Society should work more towards providing a number of optional role resources with which the individual can enter old age to allow men and women in this group to better withstand the demoralising effects of exit. At the present time, little attention has been given to the effects of role exits. More research should be geared towards understanding the problem of social adjustment among the aged.

In modern Western society, older people have less voice and authority, especially when society places a high value on youth and vitality. But this is likely to change in the future. As they become a larger and larger proportion of the population, older people will acquire more political influence. There is already a campaign in New Zealand to amalgamate senior citizens' groups under a Grey Power banner. This group has been modelled on America's Grey Power organisation (*Dominion*, 27/9/89).

Apart from ageing, the New Zealand population has also experienced a considerable ripple in its age structure by the entrance of different sized birth cohorts. The passage of cohorts of different sizes through the age structure has profound implications for planning because of the fact that needs and demands vary from age to age. Pool (1988), for example, has demonstrated the passage of the very large baby-boom cohort through time, and describes how cohort size will affect consumer demand patterns and the need for services in New Zealand.

Fertility Trends

Levels of fertility in New Zealand since the Second World War have experienced rapid changes. These fertility changes have been the result of major shifts in patterns of family formation. Two major trends in fertility may be distinguished in the post-World War II period. The first is the post-war rise in fertility resulting in a baby-boom period. During this period, New Zealand's crude birth rate continued to rise until 1961. The high birth rate during the 1940s was due, first, to a large proportion of females bearing children and, second, to an increase in individual fertility. However, the major contributing factor to the increased fertility rates during the 1940s and 1950s lay in the younger generation's adoption of an almost universal marriage pattern. Another important factor, which contributed to the rise in fertility, is the timing and spacing of births within marriage. Thus, in post-war New Zealand, two groups of marriage cohorts, an older and younger group, were procreating simultaneously to produce the so-called baby-boom (Zodgekar, 1980b).

The older group were those couples married during the Depression years and who, as a consequence of the economic recession, had deferred parenthood or, having limited their family size, quickly resumed reproduction in the more affluent post-war economic climate. The younger group were couples who had married during the war or soon after. In contrast to their elders, the younger couples began their families earlier and compressed their family building into a shorter time span. The various demographic analyses concerning this rise have pointed to major changes in marriage and childbearing patterns, with a particularly strong tendency towards younger and more universal marriage, early onset of childbearing, a shortening of birth intervals and fewer childless and one-child marriages (O'Neill, 1979; Sceates, 1985; Khawaja, 1985).

The second major change in fertility in New Zealand started in the early 1960s. There has been a steady fall in the crude birth rate during this period due to a marked decline in fertility. Again, the timing of births was a crucial factor. The fertility decline of the 1960s was partly due to the fact that the babies that might have once been expected to have been born in this decade had instead been born during the 1950s. The women who were born between 1925 and 1940 had extraordinarily high fertility in their younger ages but followed this with lower than average fertility as they aged. A further change in the timing of births took place as this giant cohort of baby-boom women started entering their reproductive years in the early 1960s. Because of its larger size, the cohort had been expected to generate another baby-boom. Instead, the baby-boom cohort has produced fertility patterns that patently changed from those of their parents:

> It does appear that the unique economic and social climate experienced by the baby-boom cohort engendered expectations of marriage and parenthood that deviated from those of their parents. The baby-boom cohort did not have their children as quickly as their parents. They postponed marriage and family production, pushing births back in timing and deepening the trough of the 'baby bust' (Zodgekar and McClellan, 1986: 208).

These timing factors – the delay in marriage and the delay in childbearing are the crucial factors in understanding the fertility behaviour of the baby-boom generation.

The average age of brides at first marriage also increased from 21.19 in 1971 to 24.03 in 1985. A substantial decline in the proportion of females currently married has been experienced in every five-year age group under 45 years of age during 1971-85. These changes indicate a decided move away from earlier marriage and an increase in marital dissolution in New Zealand. Clearly then, a large proportion of fertility decline can be attributed to a growing proportion of females either not marrying, delaying marriage or to an increase in marital dissolution.

Another important factor in the decline of period (annual) fertility at this time was the deferment of childbearing within marriage, particularly that of the first birth. The various statistics on birth and fertility measures point out that there has been a tendency among the baby-boom generation to abandon early childbearing in marriage (Zodgekar and McClellan, 1986). In the main, most demographic analyses have suggested that the fertility behaviour of recent cohorts is characterised by delayed childbearing and increased childlessness. The interesting question then is why has the baby-boom birth cohort delayed having children and opted to have fewer of them?

The improved status of women over the last two decades has undoubtedly had a major impact upon the baby-boom birth cohort's fertility behaviour. This generation is the first to come of age with aspirations that usually extend beyond that of motherhood and domesticity. Major social changes affecting the fertility of baby-boom women are undoubtedly related to their high levels of education and their participation in the paid labour force. These two factors have had a major influence in the raising of female consciousness.

Another form of behaviour unique to the baby-boom generation was that of residential lifestyle. Baby-boom women spent a considerable amount of their young adulthood years in non-familial residences (either they lived on their own or shared non-familial residences) compared to their mothers and, as a consequence, developed new values and norms.

There has been very little done in the way of social surveys in New Zealand to investigate the various issues and attitudes involved in the fertility decision. Some local surveys (SROW, 1984; Dawson, 1984) have explained deferred parenthood as being primarily due to one or more of the following reasons: financial considerations, career aspirations and preferred lifestyles.

It is apparent that the fertility behaviour of the baby-boom generation has been, to a large extent, shaped by the shift in women's perceptions of themselves and their role in New Zealand society. The view that a woman's place is in the home has been increasingly challenged (Select Committee on Women's Rights, 1975: 11).

The socio-structural changes which New Zealand has experienced since the 1960s are important from a life-course perspective. They determine the amount of time spent in the non-mother state – a time that is critical with respect to getting education, establishing a career, accumulating wealth, pursuing personal interests and to the maturation process in general. All of these issues and attitudes have influenced the fertility behaviour of New Zealand women and will continue to do so in the future (Zodgekar and McClellan, 1986: 215).

Trends in Ex-Nuptial Fertility

In the process of the fertility change, another important issue which has emerged is the substantial increase in ex-nuptial fertility. In 1962 only 8 per cent of total births were registered as ex-nuptial. By 1991, ex-nuptial births accounted for nearly 35 per cent of the total births. The steady rise in the proportion of births which are ex-nuptial is, in part, a corollary of the larger drop in nuptial births and, in part, the result of a shift in societal values relating to marriage and reproduction. The movement in the ex-nuptial birth rate, which relates ex-nuptial births in any year to unmarried women aged 15-49 years, does not fully support the steep rise in extra-marital fertility (Khawaja, 1985: 168).

A closer look at the data in Table 19.3 indicates a high proportion of these births are to mothers under the age of 25. The ex-nuptial rates for women in their teens and early twenties saw an upsurge whereas the ex-nuptial rates for older women did not (Khawaja, 1985: 168). Such a high proportion and incidence of ex-nuptial fertility to teenagers and young females could be attributed to the lack of sex education and knowledge, and access to contraceptives, for this segment of our society. This is largely because of the legal and social constraints imposed on single females of these ages by society. This aspect of the fertility behaviour of our society certainly warrants the development of policies and programmes through which the teenager and young unmarried segment of our population could be better educated and prepared for their fertility planning.

One further factor which has undoubtedly played a role in the rise in ex-nuptial births is the growth in numbers of de facto partnerships. Whereas the majority of ex-nuptial births prior to 1970 are likely to have been to women living without a partner, in recent times it appears that many are to women living with partners (Department of Statistics, 1987).

It is important to point out that there is a high incidence of ex-nuptial births among Maori women, especially young Maori women. In 1985 almost two-thirds of all Maori births were classified as ex-nuptial, and one-third of these were to women under 20 years of age. The relatively high incidence of ex-nuptial births among the Maori population reflects in part the fact that customary marriages are not recognised as formal marriages in New Zealand and hence the ex-nuptial classification is based purely on a culturally specific view of marriage (Population Monitoring Group, 1985). The status of these children in Maori society may be rather different from that of their counterparts in other cultures.

Table 19.3
Measures and Indices of Ex-Nuptial Fertility

Year	Ex-Nuptial Births as a Percentage of All Births		Ex-Nuptial Birth Rate[1] Under Age	Percentage of Ex-Nuptial Births
	<20	<25		
1962	8.06	17.7	31.9	66.6
1966	11.56	21.3	41.4	75.6
1971	13.93	25.0	41.6	76.0
1976	17.40	23.7	44.3	73.9
1986	26.95	29.0	28.5	66.5
1991	35.69	34.8	20.9	57.9

[1] Ex-nuptial births per thousand not married women aged 10-49.
Source: Computed from Vital Statistics, Department of Statistics.

Maori Fertility Transition

The discussion of fertility levels and patterns would not be complete without reflecting on the Maori fertility transition. This transition has been very different to that of the non-Maori because of the maintenance of a distinct cultural identity, the emphasis on large family norms and the retention of tribal, kinship and familial associations.

As far as can be calculated, it appears that Maori fertility was high and remained high up until 1961. This level was around 45 births per thousand of the Maori population. Since 1961 the Maori population has experienced a decisive downward trend in its fertility level (Zodgekar, 1975; Khawaja and Rolleston, 1975; Khawaja, 1985). The 1985 level of the crude birth rate (22.0 births per thousand of population) is half the level of 1961. The age pattern of fertility decline suggests that it has followed the 'classical pattern' of a slower rate of decline among younger women and a relatively high rate of decline among the older women (Zodgekar, 1975; Khawaja, 1985).

It is very difficult to pinpoint the factors which have caused such a dramatic decline in Maori fertility since the early 1960s. Various studies (Zodgekar, 1975; Khawaja and Rolleston, 1975) have discussed the role of education, urbanisation, improved survivorship and other demographic and socio-economic circumstances in this fertility transition. Perhaps the most influential factor has been the rapid urbanisation of Maori in the post-World War II period. In the past there were traditional sanctions which encouraged high fertility among those Maori living in rural isolation, but this tradition is being broken down by the process of urbanisation and increasing contacts, both in formal and informal situations, with Pakeha culture. This contact with Western norms led to the greater dissemination of knowledge about contraception and consequent reductions in family size. A continuous decline in Maori fertility level since the early 1960s has progressively brought Maori fertility much closer to the non-Maori fertility level.

International Migration

International migration has been a major feature of New Zealand's history and is an important factor influencing almost all aspects of social life. Particular areas affected include: the growth and composition of the population, the size, composition and skills of the labour force, and the demand for, and provision of, various services.

The last few decades have witnessed some major and unprecedented changes in migration levels and patterns in New Zealand. Since 1945 the rates of migration have increased dramatically and there have been significant shifts in the direction of migration balances (see Figure 19.1). These fluctuations in international migration during the post-World War II period were prompted by the introduction and refinement of immigration policies. External migration was also affected by economic and political conditions, both in New Zealand and in traditional source countries. As a result, a sharp drop in net migration was experienced during the economic recession of 1968-69 followed by the heaviest period of gain in net immigration during the early 1970s. Since the mid-1970s, the downturn in the economy, coupled with government measures to reduce the inflow of immigrants, has resulted in a period of heavy net emigration.

Since 1945, net immigration has been a relatively small component (around 15 per cent) of New Zealand's population growth (Department of Statistics, 1988). In spite of this, it has made a positive contribution to economic development and the expansion of the labour-force in New Zealand. At times, it has been viewed as a labour force phenomenon. The real significance of immigration during these years arose from its concentration in the younger working age groups (Zodgekar, 1985; Farmer, 1985).

Another notable feature of the migration flow since 1945 has been the decrease in the preponderance of immigrants coming from the British Isles. In recent times, Pacific Islands Polynesian and trans-Tasman migration have been a visible element of international migration to New Zealand (Farmer, 1979). As a consequence of the growing volume of trans-Tasman migration, there are now quite sizeable communities of New Zealanders in Australia and, to a lesser extent, Australians in New Zealand. The possibilities of higher real incomes and more varied opportunities in Australia have been responsible for attracting more New Zealanders to Australia in the past, whereas the increased migration of Polynesians to New Zealand is more in response to a labour shortage in New Zealand and a perceived labour surplus in Pacific countries. The expanding New Zealand economy in the 1960s and early 1970s created the necessary conditions for an extensive population movement between the Pacific Islands and New Zealand. A substantial proportion of this movement was short-term, but it still resulted in a net gain of population from Pacific societies to New Zealand. Many of these immigrants entered New Zealand on temporary work permits, or visitor's permits, but remained in New Zealand beyond the granted period. This resulted in a sizeable number (nearly 10,400 to 12,000) of overstayers (Farmer, 1979: 38). The presence of overstayers only became an issue with the onset of the 1970s recession. This resulted in attempts to deport illegal immigrants, which in turn caused bitterness. Government was forced to seek new solutions to the problem.

During the last few decades the international migration statistics of New Zealand reflect the fact that New Zealand-born are migrating. New Zealand-born emigrants leaving the country permanently or long-term has been an important characteristic of migration, although there has also been an increase of New Zealand-born immigrants returning permanently (Farmer, 1985: 73). This pattern contrasts with past trends when the majority of international movements was accounted for by the foreign-born.

The growth in refugee immigration to New Zealand over the last two decades has been another factor in adding to the diversity of immigrant groups in the post-World War II period. The numbers involved are still very small in comparison with the total migration flows to and from New Zealand. It is estimated that Indo-Chinese people comprise around 0.2 per cent of New Zealand's total population (Department of Statistics, 1988: 106).

Since the end of World War II, New Zealand's international migration has been marked by greater ethnic and geographic diversity. This is reflected in the changing proportion of foreign-born and the ethnic origin distribution of New Zealand's population. The percentage of the European/Pakeha population in New Zealand has declined from 93.3 per cent in 1945 to 86.8 per cent in 1981. There has been a steady growth of Maori, Pacific Island Polynesian and other ethnic groups. The April 1987 Immigration Bill abolished national origin as a criteria in immigration selection. This has widened the range of people and countries from which occupational immigrants can be selected and could result in some diversification in the ethnic composition of immigrant flows.

Immigration has always played an important and sometimes a dominant role in New Zealand. Its influence has varied with time and circumstances but there can be no doubt that the collective influence of successive waves of immigrants has been considerable. Migrants and their New Zealand-born children have contributed to population growth and drawn on diverse origins, thus contributing significantly to the emergence of a multicultural society. In spite of the important role played by immigrants, New Zealand's immigration policy in the past has been ad hoc in nature and at times reactionary. Hence, most of the policy and changes in policy have been geared more towards selection criteria rather than recognising the role and importance of migration to the future of New Zealand's population and economic growth and social development.

Conclusion

The post-World War II years have witnessed significant changes in the growth pattern and structure of the New Zealand population. The two main changes, with major consequences for population growth and its structure, have been the dramatic fluctuations in international migration and a significant change in the level of fertility. As a consequence of these changes, the relative importance of natural increase and net external migration as components of population growth have varied significantly. The changing levels and composition of immigration and emigration have resulted in a greater diversity in origin and ethnic diversity in New Zealand's population. In particular, the growth of the Polynesian population in New Zealand has been noticeable during this period.

The New Zealand population also underwent rapid changes in its levels of fertility. This resulted in an increase in population growth during the post-war baby-boom era, but since 1961 fertility has been continuously declining and has reached replacement, or just below replacement, level. During the same period, and for the first time, the traditionally high Maori fertility level has undergone an accelerated decrease.

Some of these changes in levels of fertility have resulted from major shifts in patterns of family formation over the decades from 1930 to the present. During this period we have seen a movement from relatively late parenthood in the Depression and war years, through the young parenting of the baby boom, to today's pattern of delayed childbearing.

The effect of declining fertility has been a decreasing proportion of people in the younger age group and an increasing proportion in the 60+ age group. These structural changes are going to be of considerable significance for the immediate and future planning of policy in New Zealand.

Post-war demographic changes have now been well documented in New Zealand. They have resulted in a greater awareness and understanding of the demographic process. Unfortunately, the lack of demographic studies beyond the use of official statistics is very evident. A more complete understanding of the complex reality of the social and economic world and demographic changes can only be achieved by primary research which is focused on specific aspects of the demographic process.

Note

1. Population Process – There are two basic processes in every population system – the number of people who enter, and the number of people who leave that population. Entering and exiting thus entail three elements of population system: fertility, mortality and migration. In addition, the following factors are often included as integral elements of a population system: (1) population structure, i.e. age and sex distribution; (2) population composition, i.e. wide range of socio-demographic characteristics of population, including marital status, income, ethnicity, education, occupation etc.; (3) population distribution, i.e., the spread and location of population over a given territory. Population structure, composition and distribution provide the beginning clues for analysing the determinants and consequences of mortality, fertility and migration; as such, we shall treat these factors as part of the social context of population analysis.

Further Reading

Crothers, C. and Bedford, R. (eds), 1988, *The Business of Population,* Wellington, New Zealand Demographic Society.
Department of Statistics, 1988, 'The People of New Zealand', in The Royal Commission on Social Policy, *The April Report, New Zealand Today,* Volume I, Wellington, RCSP.
ESCAP, 1985, *Population of New Zealand,* Country Monography Series No.12, New York, United Nations.
New Zealand Planning Council and Population Association of New Zealand, 1992, *Population Change and Social and Economic Policy in the 1990s,* New Zealand, Planning Council and Population Association of New Zealand.
Trlin, A. and Spoonley, P. (eds), 1986, *New Zealand and International Migration, A Digest and Bibliography, No.1,* Palmerston North, Department of Sociology, Massey University.
Trlin, A. and Spoonley, P. (eds), 1992, *New Zealand and International Migration, A Digest and Bibliography, No.2,* Palmerston North, Department of Sociology, Massey University.

List of Contributors

Nicola Armstrong is a Lecturer in the Sociology Department, Massey University. She is currently engaged in research concerning home-based work in New Zealand and teaches in the areas of the sociology of gender and work, feminist theory and research. Her latest publications include *Women and Work: Directions and Strategies for the 1990s* (edited with Celia Briar and Keren Brooking) and "Homeworking and Gender Relations" in *The Gender Factor* (S. Olssen – ed.).

Terry Austrin is a Senior Lecturer in sociology at the University of Canterbury. Before coming to New Zealand in 1987, he taught at universities in Britain and the USA. He is currently carrying out research into the changing structures of work organisation in the finance and meat industries.

Peter Beatson is a Senior Lecturer in Sociology at Massey University. He teaches courses on New Zealand society, the New Zealand arts and disability. His main research is in the New Zealand arts, and on the sociology of blindness.

Ian Carter has been Professor and Head of the Sociology Department, Auckland University, since 1982. His interests include rural sociology, social history and sociology of literature. Major books are *Farm Life in Northeast Scotland* (1979) and *Ancient Cultures of Conceit: British University Fiction in the Postwar Years* (1990).

Grant Cushman is Professor and Head of the Department of Parks, Recreation and Tourism, Lincoln University. He teaches leisure theory and recreation policy and his research interests include leisure and public/social policy, leisure participation research, urban studies and urban management. He is co-editor, with Harvey Perkins, of *Leisure, Recreation and Tourism* (1993).

Geoff Fougere is a Senior Lecturer in Sociology at Canterbury University. Among other topics, he has written extensively on health care in New Zealand and has served as an advisor to central government and other organisations on health policy.

Bob Gidlow is Senior Lecturer in the Department of Parks, Recreation and Tourism, Lincoln University, where he teaches leisure theory, social theory and recreational and leisure studies. His present research interests include the study of leisure-work and leisure-family connections.

Michael Hill is Professor of Sociology at Victoria University, Wellington, having previously taught at the London School of Economics. He has published extensively on the sociology of religion, most recently in books edited by, or for, Bryan Wilson, and is currently writing on nation-building, citizenship and religion in Singapore.

Steve Maharey is the Member of Parliament for Palmerston North. Previously, he was a Senior Lecturer in the Department of Sociology, Massey University. He has written extensively on the media.

Roy Nash is an Associate Professor in the Department of Cultural and Policy Studies in Education at Massey University. He is co-editor with John Codd and Richard Harker of *Political Issues in New Zealand Education* and author of *Succeeding Generations: Family Resources and Access to Education in New Zealand*.

Rosemary Du Plessis is a Senior Lecturer in Sociology at the University of Canterbury. She jointly edited *Feminist Voices: Women's Studies Texts for Aotearoa/New Zealand* and teaches courses on body politics and the sociology of gender. Her published work focuses on state policy and women's employment.

David Pearson, Reader in Sociology at Victoria University, Wellington, is one of the original editors of *New Zealand: Sociological Perspectives* (1982). His most recent publications include *A Dream Deferred: The Origins of Ethnic Conflict in New Zealand* (1990) and *Nga Take: Ethnic Relations and Racism in Aotearoa/New Zealand* (1991).

Harvey Perkins is a geographer and Senior Lecturer in the Department of Parks, Recreation and Tourism, Lincoln University. His research and teaching interests lie in the areas of social geography of the city and of leisure, urban planning and qualitative social research methods.

John Pratt is a Senior Lecturer in the Institute of Criminology at Victoria University of Wellington. His research includes the sociology of punishment and aboriginal justice issues. His most recent publication is *Punishment in a Perfect Society: The New Zealand Penal System* (1840-1939). He is currently working on a sociological history of laws relating to dangerous offenders.

Clare Simpson lectures in community development and women and recreation at Lincoln University. Currently, her main research projects focus on an examination of competing definitions of 'femininity' in nineteenth century New Zealand using women and cycling as a frame of reference, and a study of women's outdoor recreation in New Zealand. Clare's recent publications include an annotated bibliography of women and recreation research in New Zelaldnd, biographical 'vignettes' on nineteenth century women cyclists, and papers discussing gender issues for recreation research.

Ian Shirley is Professor of Social Policy and Social Work at Massey University, and Director of the Social Policy Research Centre. He is the author of *Planning for Community* (1979), editor of *Development Tracks* (1982), co-editor of *New Zealand: Sociological Perspectives* (1982) and *In the Public Interest: Health, Work and Housing in New Zealand* (1984). He is an overseas consultant to the Editorial Board of the *Journal of Social Policy* (Cambridge).

Paul Spoonley is an Associate Professor in Sociology and the Associate Dean, Social Sciences, at Massey University's Albany campus. He is the author of *Racism and Ethnicity* (1993) and co-editor of *Nga Take. Ethnic Relations and Racism in Aotearoa/New Zealand* (1991) and *Between the Lines. Racism and the New Zealand Media* (1990). His current research includes economic participation and iwi development (*Mahi Awatea*, 1993) and the politics of culture and ethnicity.

David Swain is Associate Professor in the Department of Sociology and Social Anthropology at the University of Waikato. His research and publications are in the areas of family sociology, family law and social services. Publications include *Childcare in New Zealand: People, Programmes, Politics* (1988) with Anne Smith, articles in family law and family sociology journals, and publications in Estonia!

David Thorns is a Reader in the Department of Sociology at the University of Canterbury. His current research explores the effects of economic restructuring upon urban regions, labour markets, local lifestyles and the development of local consciousness and urban social movements. He is the co-author of *Social Theory and the Australian City* and the author of *Fragmenting Societies?* (1992).

Jack Vowles is a Senior Lecturer in Politics at the University of Waikato. He was previously a lecturer at the University of Auckland. His research interests are currently in New Zealand politics. More specifically, he is interested in the comparative politics of capitalist democracies, with particular attention to electoral behaviours, explaining public policy outcomes, and the organisation of interests.

Brennon Wood is a Sociology Lecturer at Massey University. His interests centre on political and cultural theory, with reference to the mass media in particular. Current research focuses on the reshaping of broadcasting in postwar New Zealand.

Chris Wilkes is Professor of Sociology at Lewis and Clark College in Portland, Oregon. His research interests centre on sociological epistemology and theory, social class and the area of state analysis. He has recently completed two manuscripts – *Reinventing Class*, which is an account of class formation and class structure in New Zealand, and with Mike O'Brien *The Tragedy of the Market* (1993) .

Arvind Zodgekar is a Senior Lecturer in the Department of Sociology and Social Work, Victoria University of Wellington. He has a wide-ranging interest in social demography and is completing a major study of British migrants. Recent publications include (with V. McClellan) 'Fertility of the Babyboom Generation: The New Zealand Experience, in the *New Zealand Population Review,* and 'Immigrants in the 1981 Census', in A. Trlin and P. Spoonley (eds), *New Zealand and International Migration.*

Bibliography

Abbott A., 1986, 'Jurisdictional Conflicts: A New Approach to the Development of the Legal Professions', *American Bar Foundation Research Journal*, xx: 187-224.
Abercrombie, N., Hill, S. and Turner, B.S., 1984, *The Penguin Dictionary of Sociology*, Harmondsworth, Penguin.
Advisory Committee on Legal Services, 1985, *In Search of Justice*, Wellington, Department of Justice.
Advisory Council of Educational Planning, 1974, *Directions for Educational Development*, Wellington, Government Printer.
AGB McNair, 1982, 'Frequency of Church Attendance', (personal communication).
Aglietta, M., 1981, *A Theory of Capitalist Regulation: the US Experience*, London, New Left Books.
Aimer, E.P., 1989a, 'The Changing Party System', in H. Gold (ed.), *New Zealand Politics in Perspective*, (Second Edition), Auckland, Longman Paul.
Aimer, E.P., 1989b, 'Travelling Together: Party Identification and Voting in the New Zealand General Election of 1987', *Electoral Studies,* 8(2):131-142.
Alford, R., 1975, *Health Care Politics*, Chicago, University of Chicago Press.
Anderson, B., l983, *Imagined Communities*, London, Verso.
Andrew, E., 1981, *Closing the Iron Cage: The Scientific Management of Work and Leisure,* Montreal, Black Rose Books.
Aries, P., 1960, *Centuries of Childhood*, Harmondsworth, Penguin.
Armstrong, N., 1992, 'Sweatshop or Sanctuary? Home Working and Gender Relations', *Women and Work Conference: Decisions and Strategies for the 1990's*, Conference Proceedings, Palmerston North, Department of Sociology.
Armstrong, N. (1989), '"The Hand That Rocks The Cradle Can Rock the Boat": Feminism, Monetarism and the Role of the State', *Women's Studies Conference Papers, 1989*, Christchurch, Women's Studies Association.

Armstrong, P., Glyn, A. and Harrison, J., 1984, *Capitalism Since World War II*, London, Fontana.

Arnold, R., 1981, *The Farthest Promised Land*, Wellington, Victoria University Press/Price Milburn.

Atkinson, J., 1986, 'Employment Flexibility and Internal and External Labour Markets', in R. Dahrendorf *et al.* (eds), *New Forms of Work and Activity*, Luxembourg, Office for Official Publications of the European Communities.

Auckland Regional Authority, 1971, *Recreation Patterns in Auckland*, Auckland, Auckland Regional Authority.

Austrin, T., 1980, 'The "Lump" in the UK Construction Industry', in T. Nichols (ed.), *Capital and Labour*, Glasgow, Fontana.

Austrin, T., 1991, 'Flexibility, Surveillance and Hype: The Transformation of Work in New Zealand Financial Retailing', *Work, Employment and Society*, 5 (2): 201-221.

Austrin, T., 1992, 'Electronic Texts and Retailing: The Transformation of Work in the Finance Sector', in J. Deeks and N. Perry (eds), *Controlling Interests: Business, Government and Society in New Zealand*, Auckland, Auckland University Press.

Austrin, T., 1994a, 'Positioning Resistance and Resisting Position: Human Resource Management and the Politics of Appraisal and Grievance Hearings', in J. Jermier *et al.* (eds), *Power and Resistance in Organisations*, New York, Routledge.

Austrin, T., 1994b, 'Bringing the Consumer In: Sales Networks in Retail Banking in New Zealand', D. Knights, and T. Tinker (eds), *Financial Services and Social Relations*, Oxford, Blackwell.

Austrin, T. and Beynon, H., 1980, *Global Outpost. The Working Class Experience of Big Business in the North East of England*, Working paper, Durham, University of Durham.

Austrin, T. and Curtis, B., 1992, 'The Politics of Just In Time Systems: The Case of Meat Processing in New Zealand', Paper presented at the 10th International Labour Process Conference, Birmingham, England.

Austrin, T. and Curtis, B., 1993, 'The Fortex Way: Accountability and Co-operation', Report prepared for the Institute of Social Research and Development, Christchurch.

Awatere, D., 1984, *Maori Sovereignty*, Auckland, Broadsheet Publications.

Bae, S.K., 1991, 'Contextual Effects on Voting Behaviour in New Zealand: Electorate and Regional Efects in the 1987 and 1990 Elections', M.Phil thesis, University of Waikato.

Bailey, D.C., 1985, 'Changing Channels: An Analysis of the People and Forces Shaping the Development of New Zealand Broadcasting', M.A. thesis, Massey University.

Bane, M.J., 1975, 'Economic Justice: Controversies and Policies', in D.M. Levine and M.J. Bane (eds), *The 'Inequality' Controversy: Schooling and Distributive Justice,* New York, Basis Books.

Bane, M.J. and Masnick, G., 1980, *The Nation's Families 1960-1990,* Cambridge, Joint Centre for Urban Studies of MIT and Harvard University.

Banton, M., 1977, *The Idea of Race,* London, Tavistock.

Barclay, B., 1988, 'The Control of One's Own Image', *Illusions,* 8:8-14.

Baritz, L., 1960, *The Servants of Power,* New York, Wiley.

Barkun, M., 1974, *Disaster and the Millennium,* New Haven, Yale University Press.

Barnett, R. and Newton, P., 1977, 'Intra-urban Disparities in the Provision of Primary Health Care: an Examination of Three New Zealand Urban Areas', *Australian and New Zealand Journal of Sociology,* 13(1):60-8.

Barratt, D., 1986, *Media Sociology,* London, Tavistock.

Barrington, J.M. and Beaglehole, T.B., 1974, *Maori Schools in a Changing Society: an Historical Review,* Wellington, NZCER.

Barrington, R. and Gray, A., 1981, *The Smith Women: 100 New Zealand Women Talk About Their Lives,* Wellington, A.H. and A.W. Reed.

Bart, P., 1971, 'Sexism and Social Science', *Journal of Marriage and the Family,* 33(4):734-745.

Bassett, G., 1984, 'Screen-play and Real Play: Manufacturing Sport on Television', *Sites,* 9:3-31.

Batten, J., 1989, 'Art and Identity', in D. Novitz and B. Willmott (eds), *Culture and Identity in New Zealand,* Wellington, GP Books.

Baudelot, C. and Estable, R., 1981, 'France's Capitalistic Schools', in C.C. Lemert (ed.), *French Sociology: Rupture and Renewal Since 1968,* New York, University of Columbia Press.

Bean, C.S., 1982, 'From Confusion to Confusion: the 1981 General Election in New Zealand', *Politics,* 17(2):108-120.

Bean, C., 1984, 'A Comparative Study of Electoral Behaviour in Australia and New Zealand', Ph.D. thesis, Australian National University.

Bean, C., 1988, 'Class and Party in the Anglo-American Democracies: the Case of New Zealand in Perspective', *British Journal of Political Science,* 18:303-321.

Bean, C., 1990, 'New Zealand', in M.N. Franklin, T.T. Mackie and H. Valen (eds), *Electoral Change: Responses to Evolving Social and Attitudinal Structures in Fifteen Countries* (forthcoming).

Bean, C.S., 1991, 'Regional Variations in Political Party Support in Australia and New Zealand', *Australian Journal of Politics and History,* 37.

Beatson, P., 1989, *The Healing Tongue: Themes in Contemporary Maori Literature,* Palmerston North, Department of Sociology, Massey University.

Becker, H., 1982, *Art Worlds*, Berkeley, University of California Press.
Becker, H., 1983, *Outsiders: Studies in the Sociology of Deviance*, New York, Free Press.
Bedford, R., 1980, *Rural Population Change: a Bibliography*, Christchurch, Canterbury University, Department of Geography.
Bedford, R., 1988, 'International Migration in the South Pacific System', Paper to Seminar on International Migration Systems, Processes and Policies, Malaysia.
Bedggood, D., 1980, *Rich and Poor in New Zealand*, Auckland, Allen and Unwin.
Bedggood, D. and Bedggood, J., 1988, 'What's Behind the Picot Report?', *Access*, 7:67-72.
Beeby, C.E., 1966, *The Quality of Education in Developing Countries*, Cambridge, Mass., Cambridge University Press.
Beechey, V., 1982, 'The Sexual Division of Labour and the Labour Process a Critical Assessment of Braverman', in S. Wood (ed.), *The Degradation of Work?*, London, Hutchinson.
Beechey, V. and Perkins, T., 1987, *A Matter of Hours: Women, Part-time Work and the Labour Market*, London, Polity Press.
Belich, J., 1986, *The New Zealand Wars and the Victorian Interpretation of Racial Conflict*, Auckland, Auckland University Press.
Belich, J., 1988, *The New Zealand Wars and the Victorian Interpretation of Racial Conflict*, Auckland, Penguin.
Bell, C., 1983, 'The Working Unemployed: Job-Creation in Northland', M.A. thesis, Auckland University.
Bell, C. and Adair, V., 1985, *Women and Change: A Study of New Zealand Women*, Wellington, National Council of Women.
Bell, C. and Newby, H., 1971, *Community Studies*, London, Allen and Unwin.
Bell, D., 1973, *The Coming of Post-Industrial Society*, London, Heinemann.
Belshaw, H., 1933, 'Agricultural Labour in New Zealand', *International Labour Review*, 28:26-45.
Bentley, P., Blombery, T. and Hughes, P.J. (eds), 1992, *A Yearbook for Australian Churches 1993*, Brunswick East, Vic., Christian Research Association.
Benton, R., 1987, *How Fair is N.Z. Education? Part 2: Fairness in Maori Education*, Wellington, NZCER.
Berger, P.L., 1963, 'Charisma and Religious Innovation: The Social Location of Israelite Prophecy', *American Sociological Review*, 28(6):940-950.
Berger, P.L., 1966, *Invitation to Sociology: a Humanistic Perspective*, Harmondsworth, Penguin.
Berger, P.L., 1963, 'Charisma and Religious Innovation: the Social Location of Israelite Prophecy', *American Sociology Review*, 28(6): 940-950.
Bernard, J.S., 1973, *The Future of Marriage*, London, Souvenir.

Bernstein, B., 1977, *Class, Codes and Control*, Volume 3, London, Routledge and Kegan Paul.
Bernstein, D., 1988, 'The Sub-contracting of Cleaning Work in Israel: a Case in the Casualisation of Labour', in R. Pahl (ed.), *On Work*, Oxford, Basil Blackwell.
Beveridge, W., 1942, *Social Insurance and Allied Services*, (Beveridge Report), London, HMSO.
Beynon, H., 1982, *Born to Work*, London, Pluto.
Beynon, H., 1984, *Working for Ford*, Harmondsworth, Penguin.
Bibby, R.W., 1978, 'Why Conservative Churches *Really* Are Growing: Kelley Revisited', *Journal for the Scientific Study of Religion*, 17(2):129-137.
Bibby, R.W., 1985, 'Religious Encasement in Canada: an Argument for Protestant and Catholic Entrenchment', *Social Compass*, 32(2-3):287-303.
Binney, J., 1966, 'Papahurihia: Some Thoughts on Interpretation', *Journal of the Polynesian Society*, 75(3):321-331.
Bisseret, N., 1979, *Education, Class Language and Ideology*, London, Routledge and Kegan Paul.
Bittman, M., 1991, *Juggling Time: How Australian Families Use Time*, Canberra, Office of the Status of Women, Department of the Prime Minister and Cabinet.
Black, A.W. (ed.), 1991, *Religion in Australia: Sociological Perspectives*, Sydney, Allen and Unwin.
Blackburn, P., Combs, R. and Green, L., 1985, *Technology, Economic Growth and the Labour Process*, London, Macmillan.
Blackburn, R.M. and Mann, M., 1979, *The Working Class in the Labour Market*, London, Macmillan.
Blais, A. and Carty, R.K., 1990, 'Does Proportional Representation Foster Voter Turnout?', *European Journal of Political Research* 18(2):167-182.
Blaxall, M. and Reagan, B. (eds), 1976, *Women and the Workplace*, Chicago, Chicago University Press.
Bollard, A. and Buckle, R. (eds), 1987, *Economic Liberalisation in New Zealand*, Wellington, Allen and Unwin.
Bonney B. and Wilson, H., 1983, *Australia's Commercial Media*, London, MacMillan.
Boston, J. and Holland, M. (eds), 1987, *The Fourth Labour Government: Radical Politics in New Zealand*, Auckland, Oxford University Press.
Boudon, R., 1974, *Education, Opportunity and Social Inequality*, New York, Wiley.
Bourdieu, P., 1971, 'Intellectual Field and Creative Project', in M. Young (ed.) *Knowledge and Control*, London, Collier-Macmillan.
Bourdieu, P., 1974, 'The School as a Conservative Force', in J. Eggleston (ed.), *Contemporary Research in the Sociology of Education*, London, Methuen.
Bourdieu, P., 1977, 'Cultural Reproduction and Social Reproduction', in J. Karabel

and A.H. Halsey (eds), *Power and Ideology in Education,* New York, Oxford University Press.

Bowles, S., 1976, 'Unequal Education and the Reproduction of the Social Division of Labour', in R. Dale *et al.* (eds), *Schooling and Capitalism: A Sociological Reader,* London, Routledge and Kegan Paul.

Bowles, S. and Gintis, H., 1976, *Schooling in Capitalist America,* London, Routledge and Kegan Paul.

Braithwaite, J., 1982, 'Paradoxes of Class Bias in Criminological Research', in H. Pepinkey (ed.), *Rethinking Criminology,* Beverly Hills, Sage.

Brandenburg, J. *et al.,* 1982, 'A Conceptual Model of How People Adopt Recreation Activities', *Journal of Leisure Studies,* 1:263-276.

Braverman, H., 1974, *Labor and Monopoly Capital: The Degradation of Work in the Twentieth Century,* London, Monthly Review Press.

Breward, I., 1967, *Godless Schools,* Christchurch, Presbyterian Bookroom.

Briggs, A., 1961, 'The Welfare State in Historical Perspective', *European Journal of Sociology,* 2:221-258.

Briggs, A., 1965, The Welfare State in Historical Perspective, in M. Zald (ed.), *Social Welfare Institutions,* New York, John Wiley and Sons.

Brittan, A., 1989, *Masculinity and Power,* Oxford, Basil Blackwell.

Brittan, A and Maynard, M., 1984, *Sexism, Racism and Oppression,* Oxford, Basil Blackwell.

Britton, S., Le Heron, R. and Pawson, E., 1992, *Changing Places in New Zealand,* Christchurch, New Zealand, Geographical Society.

Britton S. and Le Heron, R., 1987, 'Regions and Restructuring in New Zealand: Issues and Questions in the 1980s', *New Zealand Geographer,* 43(3):129-139.

Brod, H., 1987, *The Making of Masculinities,* Boston, Allen and Unwin.

Broderick, C.B., 1971, 'Beyond the Five Conceptual Frameworks: a Decade of Development in Family Theory', *Journal of Marriage and the Family,* 33:139-159.

Brown, R., 1976, 'Women As Employees: Some Comments on Research in Industrial Sociology', in D. Barker and S. Allen (eds), *Sexual Divisions and Society: Process and Change,* London, Tavistock Publications.

Brown, R., 1985, 'Work: Past Present and Future', in K. Thompson (ed.), *Work, Employment and Unemployment: Perspectives on Work and Society,* London, Open University Press.

Burawoy, M., 1979, *Manufacturing Consent: Changes in the Labour Process Under Monopoly Capitalism,* Chicago, Chicago University Press.

Burch, W.R., 1969, 'The Nature of Community', in J. Forster (ed.), *Social Process in New Zealand,* Auckland, Longman Paul.

Burgess, E. and Bogue, D. (eds), 1964, *Contributions to Urban Sociology,* Chicago, University of Chicago Press.

Burr, W.R. et al. (eds), 1979, *Contemporary Theories About The Family: Volume 1 Research-based Theories, Volume 2, General Theories/Theoretical Orientations*, New York, Free Press.

Burton, C., 1985, *Subordination: Feminism and Social Theory*, Sydney, George Allen and Unwin.

Business Roundtable, 1987, *Fiscal Strategy: The Next Stages*, Auckland, Business Roundtable.

Cameron, J., 1984, 'Why Have Children? A Study of Method and Meaning in Value-of-Children Research', M.A. thesis, University of Canterbury.

Cameron, J., 1985, 'Conceptualising "Family": An Epistemological Concern for Fertility Researchers', *New Zealand Population Review*, 11(1):17-18.

Cameron, J., 1986, 'Transition to the No-child "Family": Cultural Constraints in the New Zealand Context', *New Zealand Population Review*, 12(1):4-17.

Campbell, C., 1972, 'The Cult, the Cultic Milieu and Secularization', in M. Hill (ed.), *A Sociological Yearbook of Religion in Britain – 5*, London, SCM Press.

Campbell, W.J., 1957, *Hydrotown*, Dunedin, University of Otago.

Carrigan, T., Connell, B. and Lee, J., 1985, 'Toward a New Sociology of Masculinity', *Theory and Society*, 14(5).

Carson, W., 1989, 'Occupational Health and Safety: A Political Economy Perspective', *Labour & Industry*, 2(2):301-316.

Carter, I., 1979, *Farm Life in North-East Scotland, 1840-1914: the Poor Man's Country*, Edinburgh, John Donald.

Carter, I., 1986, 'Most Important Industry: How the New Zealand State Got Interested in Rural Women, 1930-1944', *New Zealand Journal of History*, 20:27-43.

Carter, I., 1988, 'A Failed Graft: Rural Sociology in New Zealand', *Journal of Rural Studies*, 4: 215-222.

Carter, I. and Perry, N., 1987, 'Rembrandt in Gumboots: Images of Rural Life in New Zealand Television Advertisments', in J. Phillips (ed.), *Te Whenua Te Iwi: the Land and the People*, Wellington, Allen and Unwin.

Cartwright, S., 1988, *The Report of the Cervical Cancer Inquiry Committee of Inquiry*, Auckland, Government Printer.

Castles, F.G. and McKinlay, R., 1979, 'Public Welfare Provision, Scandinavia and the Sheer Futility of the Sociological Approach to Politics', *European Journal of Political Research*, 9.

Castles, F.G., 1985, *The Working Class and Welfare: Reflections on the Political Development of the Welfare State in Australia and New Zealand, 1890-1980*, Wellington, Allen and Unwin.

Castles, F.G., 1987, 'Thirty Wasted Years: Australian Social Security Development 1950-1980 in Comparative Perspective', *Politics*, 22:67-74.

Castells, M., 1976, 'Is There an Urban Sociology?', in C. Pickvance (ed.), *Urban Sociology. Critical Essays*, London, Tavistock.

Castells, M., 1977, *The Urban Question,* London, Edward Arnold.
Castells, M., 1983, *The City and the Grassroots,* London, Edward Arnold.
Castell, M. (ed.), 1985, *High Technology, Space and Society,* Beverly Hills, Sage.
Castells, M., 1989, *The Information City,* London, Basil Blackwell.
Castles, S., Booth, H. and Wallace, T., 1984, *Here for Good: Western Europe's New Ethnic Minorities,* London, Pluto Press.
Castles, S. and Kozack, G., 1973, *Immigrant Workers and Class Structure in Western Europe,* London, Oxford University Press.
Cave, S., 1989, 'Complaints', *New Zealand Listener,* 8 July: 29.
Caygill, D., 1988, *Health, A Prescription for Change,* Wellington, Government Printer.
Caygill, D., 1989, *Securing Economic Recovery,* Budget Speech, Wellington, Government Printer, 27 July.
Challenge Weekly, 1988, Supplement, 7 October.
Chapman, R.M., 1962, 'The General Result', in R.M. Chapman, W.K. Jackson and A.V. Mitchell (eds), *New Zealand Politics in Action: the 1960 General Election,* London, Oxford University Press.
Chapman, R.M., 1963, 'The Response to Labour and the Question of Parallelism of Opinion, 1928-1960', in R.M. Chapman and K. Sinclair (eds), *Studies of a Small Democracy,* Auckland, Longman Paul.
Chapman, R.M., 1969, *The Political Science 1919-1931,* Auckland, Heinemann.
Chapple, D.L., l976, *Tokoroa,* Auckland, Longman Paul.
Chetwynd, S.J., 1988, 'Satisfaction and Dissatisfactions with Public and Private Hospitals', *New Zealand Medical Journal,* 101:563-566.
Chetwynd, S.J., 1989, 'Trends in Private Medical Insurance Ownership: Lessons for the Public Sector', *New Zealand Medical Journal,* 102:107-109.
Chetwynd J., Fougere G., Salter D. and Hunter W., 1984, 'Private Medical Insurance in New Zealand: Issues of Membership and Growth', *New Zealand Medical Journal,* 96:1052-5.
Child, J., 1985, 'Managerial Strategies, New Technology and the Labour Process', in D. Knights, *et al.* (eds), *Job Design: Critical Perspectives on the Labour Process,* Aldershot, Gower.
Clarke, J. and Critcher, C., 1985, *The Devil Makes Work: Leisure in Capitalist Britain,* Chicago, University of Illinois Press.
Cloke, P., 1983, 'Policy Responses to Rural Depopulation and Repopulation: Contrasts Between New Zealand and the United Kingdom', *New Zealand Agricultural Science,* 17:231-236.
Coalter, F., 1986, *Rationale for Public Sector Investment in Leisure,* London, Sports Council and the Economic and Social Research Council.
Cockburn, C., 1983, *Brothers: Male Dominance and Technological Change,* London, Pluto Press.

Cockburn, C., 1985, *Machinery of Dominance: Women, Men and Technological Know-how,* London, Pluto Press.
Cocker, A., 1989, 'The Business of Broadcasting', *New Zealand Listener,* 15 April: 14, 39, 42, 47.
Codd, J., Gordon, L. and Harker, R., 1988, 'Educational Administration and the Role of the State: Devolution and Control', *Proceedings of the First NZCER Conference on Educational Policy,* Wellington, NZCER.
Cohen, A., 1956, *Delinquent Boys,* Chicago, Free Press.
Cohen, A.P. (ed.), 1982, *Belonging – Identity and Social Organisation in British Rural Cultures,* Manchester, Manchester University Press.
Cohen, A.P., 1985, *The Symbolic Construction of Community,* London, Ellis Horwood and Tavistock.
Cohen, R., 1987, *The New Helots,* Farnborough, Avebury.
Colgan, A. and McGregor, J., 1981, *Sexual Secrets: the New Zealand Report on Love and Marriage,* Wellington, Alister Taylor.
Colless, B. and Donovan, P. (eds), 1985, *Religion in New Zealand Society,* (Second Edition), Palmerston North, Dunmore Press.
Commission of Inquiry, 1971, *Housing in New Zealand,* Wellington, Government Printer.
Community Services Institute, 1985, *Recreation and Government in New Zealand,* Wellington, Ministry of Recreation and Sport.
Congalton, A., 1966, 'Methodology of Research into Occupational Prestige', *Australian and New Zealand Journal of Sociology,* 1: 121-129.
Connell, R.W., 1983, *Which Way is Up?: Essays on Class, Sex and Culture,* Sydney, Allen and Unwin.
Connell, R.W., 1987, *Gender and Power,* Sydney, Allen and Unwin.
Connell, R.W., 1991, 'Live Fast and Die Young: the Construction of Masculinity Among Young Working Class Men on the Margin of the Labour Market', *Australian and New Zealand Journal of Sociology,* 27(2): 141-171.
Cook, (May) H., 1985a, 'The Contradictions of Post-War Reconstruction; The Aspirations and Realities of a Post-War Generation of Wives and Mothers', in H. Haines (ed.), *Women's Studies Conference Papers '84,* Auckland, Women's Studies Association.
Cook, (May) H., 1985b, 'Images and Illusions: 1950s Wife and Mother', *NZ Women's Studies Journal,* 1(2):86-92.
Cook, (May) H., 1986, '"The Lady Juggler": Workers, Wives, Mothers and Managers', *Women's Studies Conference Papers '85,* Auckland, Women's Studies Association.
Coriot, B., 1980, 'The Restructuring of the Assembly Line: a New Economy of Time and Control', *Capital and Class,* 11:34-43.
Cox, S. (ed.), 1987, *Public and Private Worlds: Women in Contemporary New*

Zealand, Wellington, Allen and Unwin and Port Nicholson Press.
Craig, W., 1989, 'Women, Unpaid Work and the Welfare State', *Women's Studies Association Conference Papers, 1989*, Christchurch, Women's Studies Association.
Craig, W., 1992, 'The Politics of Caring', in C. Briar, R. Munford and M. Nash (eds), *State and Economy in New Zealand*, Auckland, Oxford University Press.
Crompton, R. and Jones, G., 1984, *White Collar Proletariat: Gender and Deskilling in the Workplace*, London, Macmillan.
Crothers, C. and Loveridge, A., 1986, 'Aspects of the New Zealand Agricultural Labour Force, 1971-1975', unpublished paper, Auckland, Auckland University Department of Sociology.
Crothers, C. and Macpherson, C., 1984, 'Selected Demographic and Social Characteristics of the Forestry and Logging Workforces', Auckland, Auckland University, Department of Sociology, Working Papers in Comparative Sociology 14.
Culyer, A., 1973, *The Economics of Social Policy*, London, Martin Robertson.
Currie Report, 1962, *Report of the Commission on Education in New Zealand*, Wellington, Department of Education.
Curtis, B., 1993, 'Product Markets and Labour Markets: The Paradox of Flexibility in the Export Meat Industry', in P.S. Morrison (ed.), *Labour and Employment and Work in New Zealand*, Wellington: Department of Geography.
Cushman, G., 1983, *Towards a Recreation Policy for Victoria: A Discussion Paper*, Melbourne, Victorian Government Printing Office.
Cushman, G. and Laidler, A., 1988, 'Recreation, Leisure and Social Policy', *Report of the Royal Commission on Social Policy*, Volume IX, Wellington, Royal Commission on Social Policy.
Dahl, R., 1961, *Who Governs?*, New Haven, Yale University Press
Dahrendorf, R. et al., 1986, *New Forms of Work and Activity*, Luxembourg, Office for Official Publications of the European Communities.
Daley, C., 1991, 'Taradale Meets the Ideal Society', *New Zealand Journal of History*, 25(2): 129-46.
Dann, C., 1982, 'The Game is Over', *Broadsheet*, March.
Dann, C., 1985, *Up From Under: Women and Liberation in New Zealand 1970-1985*, Wellington, Allen and Unwin and Port Nicholson Press.
David, M-G. and Starzec, C., 1992, 'Women and Part Time Work: France and Great Britain Compared', in N. Fobre et al. (eds), *Issues in Contemporary Economics*, New York, New York University Press.
Davis, J.F., 1980, 'Capitalist Agricultural Development and the Exploitation of the Propertied Labourer', in F.H. Buttel and H. Newby (eds), *The Rural Sociology of the Advanced Societies*, London, Croom Helm.
Davidson, J.M., 1981, 'The Polynesian Foundation', in W.H. Oliver and B.R. Williams

(eds), *The Oxford History of New Zealand*, Wellington, Oxford University Press.

Davis, P., 1981, *Health and Health Care in New Zealand*, Auckland, Longman Paul.

Davis, P., 1988, 'Objective Measures of Social Wellbeing', in Royal Commission on Social Policy, *The April Report*, Volume III(1), Wellington, Royal Commission on Social Policy.

Davis, S. *et al.*, 1983, 'She Through He', *Alternative Cinema*, Summer 1983-84:5-7.

Dawson, L., 1984, 'Why Aren't We Making Babies Any More?', *More*, September: 35-46.

De Jong, P., 1986, 'Looking Forward To Saturday': A Social History of Rugby in a Small New Zealand Town, M.A. thesis, Massey University.

De Jong, P., 1987, 'The Old Rugby Grows on You', *Sites*, 14:35-56.

De Jong, P., 1991, *Saturday's Warriors: The Building of a Rugby Stronghold*, Palmerston North, Department of Sociology, Massey University.

Deeks, J., and Perry, N., 1992, *Controlling Interests: Business, the State, and Society in New Zealand*, Auckland, Auckland University Press.

Deem, R., 1986, *All Work and No Play? The Sociology of Women and Leisure*, Milton Keynes, Open University Press.

Deem, R. and Salaman, G. (eds), 1985, *Work, Culture and Society*, London, Open University Press.

Denoon, D., 1983, *Settler Capitalism: the Dynamics of Dependent Development in the Southern Hemisphere*, Oxford, Oxford University Press.

Department of Arts, Sport, the Environment, Tourism and Territories, 1988, *Physical Activity Levels of Australians*, Canberra, Australian Government Publishing Service.

Department of Statistics, 1987, *Demographic Trends*, Wellington, Department of Statistics.

Department of Statistics, 1988, 'The People of New Zealand', *The April Report, New Zealand Today*, Volume I, Wellington, Royal Commission on Social Policy.

Department of Statistics, 1989, *Profiles of New Zealanders Number 3: Families and Households*, Wellington, Department of Statistics.

Department of Statistics, 1992, *New Zealanders At Home*, Wellington, Department of Statistics.

Department of Statistics, 1993, *Demographic Trends 1992*, Wellington, Department of Statistics

Department of Statistics and Ministry of Women's Affairs, 1990, *Women in New Zealand*, Department of Statistics, Wellington.

Ditch, J., 1987, 'The Undeserving Poor: Unemployed People, Then and Now', in M. Loney *et al.* (eds), *The State of the Market*, London, Sage.

Doeringer, P. and Piore, M.J., 1971, *Internal Labor Markets and Manpower Analysis*, Lexington, Mass., D.C. Heath.

Dohse, K., Jurgens, V. and Malsch, T., 1985, 'From "Fordism" to "Toyotism"? The Social Organisation of the Labour Process in the Japanese Automobile Industry', *Politics and Society*, 14(2):115-146.

Doig, W.T., 1940, *A Survey of the Standards of Life of New Zealand Dairy Farmers*, Wellington, Department of Scientific and Industrial Research Bulletin 75.

Donley, J., 1986, *Save the Midwife*, Auckland, New Women's Press.

Donnison, D. and Ungerson, C., 1982, *Housing Policy*, London, Penguin.

Dore, R., 1977, *The Diploma Disease: Educational Qualifications and Development*, London, Allen and Unwin.

Dore, R., 1992, 'Goodwill and the Spirit of Market Capitalism', in M. Granovetter and R. Swedberg (eds), *The Sociology of Economic Life*, San Fransisco, Westview Press.

Douglas, J. (ed.), 1970, *Understanding Everyday Life*, London, Routledge and Kegan Paul.

Douglas, R. and Callen, L., 1987, *Toward Prosperity: People and Politics in the 1980s*, Auckland, David Bateman.

Doyal, L., 1979, *The Political Economy of Health*, London, Pluto Press.

Du Plessis, R., 1992, 'Women, Politics and the State', in B. Roper and C. Rudd (eds), *State and Economy in New Zealand*, Auckland, Oxford University Press.

Duffin, J.M., 1984, *Growing Up Fostered: Four Young People Present an Indepth View of How it Feels to be 'Nobody's Child'*, Wellington, Department of Social Welfare.

Duncan, S. and Goodwin, M., 1988, *The Local State: An Uneven Development*, Oxford, Polity Press.

Dunleavy, P., 1980, *Urban Political Analysis. The Politics of Collective Consumption*, London, Macmillan.

Dunleavy, P., 1981, 'Alternative Theories of Liberal Democratic Politics: The Pluralist – Marxist Debate in the 1980s', in D. Potter *et al.* (eds), *Society and the Social Sciences: An Introduction*, London, Routledge and Kegan Paul and Open University Press.

Dunleavy, P., 1981, 'Perspectives on Urban Studies', in A. Blowers *et al.* (eds), *Urban Change and Conflict*, Milton Keynes, Open University Press.

Dunleavy, P. and Husbands, C., 1985, *British Democracy at the Crossroads*, London, Allen and Unwin.

Dupuis A., 1989, 'Consumption Sectors', M.A. thesis, University of Canterbury.

Durie, M., 1989, 'The Treaty of Waitangi Perspectives for Social Policy', in I. Kawharu (ed.), *Waitangi: Maori and Pakeha Perspectives of the Treaty of Waitangi*, Auckland, Oxford University Press.

Dutton, B., 1986, *The Media*, London, Longman.

Dwyer, T., 1991, *Life and Death at Work: Industrial Accidents as a Case of Socially Produced Error*, New York, Plenum Press.

Easton, B., 1986, *Wages and the Poor*, Wellington, Allen and Unwin.

Easton, B., 1987, 'Agriculture in New Zealand Economy', in L.T. Wallace and R. Lattimore (eds), *Rural New Zealand: What Next?*, Christchurch, Lincoln College Agribusiness and Economics Research Unit, Discussion Paper 109.

Easton, B. (ed.), 1989, *The Making of Rogernomics*, Auckland, Auckland University Press.

Easton, B., 1993. Poverty and Families: Priority or Piety? A paper in the 'Issues for Families Workshop', sponsored by Barnardos and Birthright, Wellington.

Edwards, R.C., 1979, *Contested Terrain: The Transformation of the Workplace in the Twentieth Century*, London, Heinemann.

Edwards, B., 1993, 'Bureaucracy Remains But Many Jobs Lost', *Evening Post*, June 10: 5.

Edwards, M., 1990, *Mihipeka: Early Years*, Auckland, Penguin.

Edwards, M., 1992, *Mihipeka: Time of Turmoil*, Auckland, Penguin.

Eldred-Grigg, S., 1980, *A Southern Gentry*, Wellington, Reed.

Eldred-Grigg, S., 1982, *A New History of Canterbury*, Dunedin, McIndoe.

Eldred-Grigg, S., 1984, *Pleasures of the Flesh: Sex and Drugs in Colonial New Zealand, 1840-1915*, Wellington, Reed.

Eldred-Grigg, S., 1988, '*Oracles and Miracles*, Working Class Novel, Okay?', *Sites*, 16:111-120.

Elias, N., 1974, 'Towards a Theory of Communities', in C. Bell and H. Newby (eds), *The Sociology of Community*, London, Frank Cass.

Elling, R., 1986, *The Struggle for Workers Health*, New York, Baywood Publishing Co.

Elliott, R., 1981, 'The Private Sector Option', in D. Salter (ed.), *Health Planning and Resource Allocation*, Wellington, Wellington Clinical School of Medicine.

Else, A., 1992, 'To Market and Home Again: Gender and the New Right', in R. Du Plessis *et al.* (eds), *Feminist Voices: Women's Studies Texts for Aotearoa/New Zealand*, Auckland, Oxford University Press.

Elsmore, B., 1989, *Mana from Heaven. A Century of Maori Prophets in New Zealand*, Tauranga, Moana Press.

Engels, F., 1971, *The Condition of the Working Class in England*, London, Granada Publishing.

Engels, F., 1975, 'The Condition of the Working Class in England', in Karl Marx and F. Engels, *Collected Works*, New York, International Publishers.

Esland, G. and Salaman, G. (eds), 1975, *People and Work*, London, Open University Press.

Esping-Anderson, G. and Korpi, W., 1984, 'Social Policy as Class Politics in Post-War Capitalism: Scandinavia, Austria and Germany', in J. Goldthorpe (ed.),

Order and Conflict in Contemporary Capitalism, Oxford, Clarendon Press.
Evans, E.J., 1983, *The Forging of the Modern State,* Harlow, Longman.
Evans, M. et al. (eds), 1988, *A Women's Picture Book: 25 Women Artists of Aotearoa,* Wellington, GP Books.
Evans, P., Ruesschmeyer, D. and Skocpol, T., 1985, *Bringing the State Back In,* Cambridge, Cambridge University Press.
Eysenck, H., 1968, *Crime and Personality,* London, Paladin.
Fairburn, M., 1985, 'Why Did the New Zealand Labour Party Fail to Win Office Until 1935?', *Political Science* 37(2):101-124.
Fairburn, M., 1989, *The Ideal Society and its Enemies,* Auckland, Auckland University Press.
Fairweather, J., 1982, 'Land, State and Agricultural Capitalism in New Zealand: a Study of Change from Estate to Small Farm Production', Ph.D. dissertation, University of Missouri-Columbia.
Faris, R., 1967, *Chicago Sociology 1920-32,* San Fransisco, Chandler.
Farmer, R.S.J., 1979, 'International Migration', in R.J.W. Neville and C.J. O'Neill (eds), *The Population of New Zealand: Interdisciplinary Perspectives,* Auckland, Longman Paul.
Farmer, R.S.J., 1980, 'External Migration Issues in New Zealand', *New Zealand Population Review,* 6(1):12-23.
Farnsworth, J., 1984, 'Media Studies in Britain: Some Lessons for New Zealand' *Sites,* 9:52-55.
Farnsworth, J., 1988, 'Social Policy and the Media in New Zealand', *Report of the Royal Commission on Social Policy,* Volume IV, Wellington, Royal Commission on Social Policy, April:455-480.
Farrington, D. et al., 1980, 'Unemployment, School Leaving and Crime', *British Journal of Criminology,* 26:335-356.
Farrington, D., 1980, 'Truancy, Delinquency, the Home and the School', L. Hersov and I. Berg (eds), *Out of School,* Chichester, John Wiley and Sons.
Farrington, D., Ohlin, L. and Wilson, J., 1986, *Understanding and Controlling Crime,* New York, Springer-Verlag.
Fergusson, D.M., Horwood, L.J. and Shannon, F., 1984, 'A Proportional Hazards Model of Family Breakdown', *Journal of Marriage and the Family,* 46(3):539-549.
Fergusson, D.M., Horwood, L.J. and Shannon, F., 1985, 'A Survival Analysis of Childhood Family History', *Journal of Marriage and the Family,* 47(2):287-295.
Fergusson, D.M., Horwood, L.J., Kershaw, K.L. and Shannon, F., 1986, 'Factors Associated with Reports of Wife Assault in New Zealand', *Journal of Marriage and the Family,* 48(2):407-412.

Fielder, L., 1960, *Love and Death in the American Novel*, New York, Criterian Books.
Finch, J. and Mason, J., 1993, *Negotiating Family Responsibility*, London, Routledge.
Fleras, A., 1989, '"Inverting the Bureaucratic Pyramid": Reconciling Aboriginality and Bureaucracy in New Zealand', *Human Organization*, 48(3):214-225.
Flora, P. and Heidenheimer, A. (eds), 1987, *The Development of Welfare States in Europe and America*, New Brunswick, Transaction Books.
Ford, G., 1986, *Research Project on Domestic Disputes*, Wellington, New Zealand Police National Headquarters.
Forster, J. (ed.), (1969), *Social Process in New Zealand*, Auckland, Longman Paul.
Fougere, G.M., 1974, 'Exit, Voice and the Decay of the Welfare State Provision of Hospital Care', Christchurch, M.A. thesis, University of Canterbury.
Fougere, G.M., 1978, 'Undoing the Welfare State: the Case of Hospital Care', in S. Levine (ed.), *Politics in New Zealand*, Sydney, George Allen and Unwin.
Fougere, G.M., 1984, 'From Market to Welfare State? State Intervention and Medical Care Delivery', in C. Wilkes and I. Shirley (eds), *In the Public Interest*, Auckland, Benton Ross.
Fougere, G.M., 1987, 'Government Sponsored Services: Their Capacity to Enhance Income', Paper given at New Zealand Planning Council Conference, July, Wellington.
Fougere, G.M., 1989, 'Sport, Culture and Identity: The Case of Rugby Football', in D. Novitz and B. Willmott (eds), *Culture and Identity in New Zealand*, Wellington, Government Print.
Fox, A., 1980, 'The Meaning of Work', in G. Esland and G. Salaman (eds), *The Politics of Work and Occupations*, London, Open University Press.
Fox, B., 1980, 'Being Different', M.A. thesis, Auckland University.
Franklin, H., 1969, 'The Village and the Bush', in J. Forster (ed.), *Social Process in New Zealand*, Auckland, Longman Paul.
Franklin, H., 1978, *Trade, Growth and Anxiety*, Wellington, Methuen.
Fraser, D., 1973, *The Evolution of the British Welfare State*, London, Macmillan.
Fraser, R. (ed.), 1968, *Work*, 2 Volumes, Harmondsworth, Penguin.
Freidson, E., 1970, *Profession of Medicine, a Study of the Sociology of Applied Knowledge*, New York, Harper Row.
French, M., 1985, *Beyond Power: Women, Men and Morals*, London, Cape.
Friedland, W.H., Barton, A.E. and Thomas, R.J., 1981, *Manufacturing Green Gold*, Cambridge, Cambridge University Press.
Friedman, A.L., 1977, *Industry and Labour: Class Struggle at Work and Monopoly Capitalism*, London, Macmillan..
Friedman, M., 1962, *Capitalism and Freedom*, Chicago, Chicago University Press.

Friedmann, H., 1980, 'Household Production and the National Economy: Concepts for the Analysis of Agrarian Formations', *Journal of Peasant Studies,* 7.
Furniss, N. and Tilton, T., 1977, *The Case for the Welfare State,* Bloomington, Indiana University Press.
FVPCC (Family Violence Prevention Co-ordinating Committee), 1991, *Family Violence: Prevention in the 1990s.* 1-6 September, Christchurch, New Zealand. Conference Proceedings, Two Volumes, Wellington, FVPCC.
Galbraith, J., 1973, *Economics and the Public Purpose,* Boston, Houghton Mifflin.
Gamble, A., 1981, *An Introduction to Modern Social and Political Thought,* London, Macmillan.
Gamble, A., 1988, *The Free Economy and the Strong State: The Politics of Thatcherism,* London, Macmillan.
Game, A. and Pringle, R., 1983, *Gender at Work,* Sydney, Allen and Unwin.
George, V. and Wilding, P., 1976, *Ideology and Social Welfare,* London, Routledge and Kegan Paul.
George, V. and Wilding, P., 1984, *The Impact of Social Policy,* London, Routledge and Kegan Paul.
Gershuny, J.I., 1983, *Social Innovation and the Division of Labour,* Oxford, Oxford University Press.
Giddens, A., 1984, *The Social Construction of Society,* Cambridge, Polity Press.
Gill, H. and Gill, T., 1975, 'New Zealand Rural Society – a Framework for Study', *New Zealand Agricultural Science,* 9:60-68.
Gill, O., 1976, *Luke Street,* London, Macmillan.
Gill, T., Koopman-Boyden, P., Parr, A. and Willmott, W.E., 1975, *The Rural Women of New Zealand: a National Survey,* Christchurch, Canterbury University, Department of Sociology.
Gilling, M., 1988, 'The Family', Royal Commission on Social Policy, *The April Report,* Wellington, Royal Commission on Social Policy.
Gilroy, P., 1987, *There Ain't No Black in the Union Jack,* London, Hutchinson.
Glenny, A. and Perkins, R., 1987, 'Television and Advertising: The Art of Selling' *Illusions*:3-14.
Glyptis, S., 1981, 'Leisure Lifestyles', *Regional Studies,* 15(5):311-326.
Gold, H., 1989, 'Party and Society in 1987', in H. Gold, (ed.), *New Zealand Politics in Perspective,* 2nd ed., Auckland, Longman Paul.
Goldscheider, C., 1971, *Population, Modernization and Social Structure,* Boston, Little, Brown and Company.
Goldthorpe, J. et al., 1980, *Social Mobility and Class Structure in Modern Britain,* Oxford, Clarendon.
Goldthorpe, J. (ed.), 1984, *Order and Conflict in Contemporary Capitalism: Studies in the Political Economy of Western European Nations,* Oxford, Clarendon Press.

Goldthorpe, J.H. and Hope, K., 1974, *The Social Grading of Occupations*, Oxford, Clarendon.
Goldthorpe, J.H. *et al.*,1980, *Social Mobility and Class Structure in Modern Britain*, Oxford, Clarendon.
Goode, W.J., 1963, *World Revolution and Family Patterns*, New York, Free Press of Glencoe.
Goodman, D., Sorj, B. and Wilkinson, J., 1987, *From Farming to Biotechnology*, Oxford, Blackwell.
Gorz, A., 1983, *Farewell to the Working Class*, Glasgow, Fontana.
Gough, I., 1979, *The Political Economy of the Welfare State,* London, Macmillan.
Gough, I., 1989, 'De-Commodification in Social Policy', an unpublished paper, Department of Social Policy and Social Work, Massey University.
Gould, A., 1988, *Conflict and Control in Welfare Policy: The Swedish Experience*, London, Longman.
Grace, V., 1989, 'The Marketing of Empowerment and the Construction of the Health Consumer: a Critique of Health Promotion in New Zealand', Ph.D. thesis, Canterbury University.
Graetz, B., 1988, 'The Reproduction of Privilege in Australian Education', *British Journal of Sociology,* 39(3): 358-376.
Gramsci, A., 1971, *Selections from the Prison Notebooks,* London, Lawrence and Wishart.
Gramsci, A., 1985, *Selections from Cultural Writings,* London, Lawrence and Wishart.
Granovetter, M. and Swedberg, R. (eds), 1992, *The Sociology of Economic Life,* San Francisco, Westview Press.
Granovetter M. and Tilly C., 1988, 'Inequality and Labour Processes', in N. Smelser (ed.), *Handbook of Sociology,* Beverly Hills, Sage.
Gray, A., 1983, *The Jones Men: 100 New Zealand Men Talk About Their Lives,* Wellington, A.H. and A.W. Reed.
Gray, J., McPherson, A.F. and Raffe, D., 1983, *Reconstructions of Secondary Education: Myth, and Practice Since the War,* London, Routledge and Kegan Paul.
Gray, M., 1987, 'Trends and Problems in Rural Social Services Delivery', in J. Fairweather (ed.), *Proceedings of the Rural Economy and Society Study Group Symposium on Rural Research Needs,* Christchurch, Lincoln College Agribusiness and Economics Research Unit, Discussion Paper 113.
Greenland, H., 1984, 'Ethnicity as Ideology: The Critique of Pakeha Society', in P. Spoonley *et al.* (eds), *Tauiwi. Racism and Ethnicity in New Zealand,* Palmerston North, Dunmore Press.
Grigg, R., 1987, 'A Woman Farmer's Perspective', in L.T. Wallace and R. Lattimore (eds), *Rural New Zealand: What Next?* Christchurch, Lincoln College

Agribusiness and Economics Research Unit, Discussion Paper 109.
Grossman, G., 1985, 'The Second Economy of the USSR', in C.R. Littler (ed.), *The Experience of Work,* New York, St Martins Press.
Guille, H., 1981, 'Land, Labour or Capital: Industrial Relations in New Zealand Agriculture', *Journal of Industrial Relations,* 23:139-162.
Gurevitch, M. *et al.* (eds), 1981, *Culture, Society and the Media,* London, Methuen.
Gustafson, B., 1976, *Social Change and Party Reorganisation: the New Zealand Labour Party Since 1945,* London, Sage.
Gustafson, B., 1986, *The First Fifty Years: A History of the New Zealand National Party,* Auckland, Reed Methuen.
Gustafson, B., 1989, 'The Labour Party', in H. Gold, (ed.), *New Zealand Politics in Perspective,* 2nd ed., Auckland, Longman Paul.
Habermas, J., 1975, *Legitimation Crisis,* Boston, Beacon Press.
Haigh, D. and Gavin, D., 1977, *Social Planning for New Community in Auckland,* Auckland, Auckland Regional Authority.
Haines, H., 1983, *Violence on Television: A Report on the Mental Health Foundation's Media Watch Survey,* Auckland, New Zealand Mental Health Foundation.
Hakim, C., 1988, 'Homeworking in Britain', in R. Pahl (ed.), *On Work,* Oxford, Basil Blackwell.
Hall, R.R., Thorns, D.C. and Willmott, W.E., 1983, *Community Formation and Change,* Working Paper No 3, Department of Sociology, University of Canterbury.
Hall, R.R., l987, *Te Kohurau: Continuity and Change in a New Zealand Rural District,* Christchurch, Department of Sociology, University of Canterbury.
Hall, R.R., Thorns, D.C. and Willmott, W.H., 1984, 'Community, Class, and Kinship – Bases For Collective Action Within Localities', *Environment and Planning D: Society and Space,* 2:201-15.
Hall, S. *et al.,* 1978, *Policing the Crisis,* London, Macmillan.
Hall, S., 1980, 'Encoding and Decoding', in S. Hall *et al.* (eds), *Culture Media and Language,* London, Hutchinson.
Hall, S. and Held, D., 1989, 'Left and Rights', *Marxism Today,* June:16-23.
Hall, S. and Jefferson, T. (eds), 1976, *Resistance Through Rituals,* London, Hutchinson.
Hall, R.R., Thorns, D.C. and Willmott, W.H., 1984, 'Community, Class, and Kinship – Bases For Collective Action Within Localities', *Environment and Planning D: Society and Space,* 2:201-15.
Halsey, A.H., Heath, A.F. and Ridge, J.M., 1980, *Origins and Destinations: Family, Class and Education in Modern Britain,* Oxford, Oxford University Press.
Ham, C. and Hill, M., 1984, *The Policy Process in the Modern Capitalist State,* Brighton, Wheatsheaf.

Hamer, D., 1979, 'Towns in Nineteenth-Century New Zealand', *New Zealand Journal of History,* 13(1):5-24.
Hamer, D., 1988, *The New Zealand Liberals,* Auckland, Auckland University Press.
Hamilton, C.M., 1981, *Marriage As A Trade,* London, Women's Press, [originally published 1909].
Harastzi, M., 1977, *Worker in a Worker's State,* Harmondsworth, Penguin.
Harding, A., 1983, 'An Introduction to the Social Wage', *Social Society Journal,* Canberra, Australian Government Publishing Service, December:13-21.
Harloe, M., 1980, 'The Recommodification of Housing', in M. Harloe and E. Lebas (eds), *City, Class and Capital,* London, Edward Arnold.
Harloe, M. and Paris, C., 1984, 'The Decollectivisation of Consumption', in I. Szelenyi (ed.), *Cities in Recession,* Beverly Hills, Sage.
Harris, G.T., 1980, *A Socio-Economic Study of Farm Workers and Farm Managers,* Christchurch, Lincoln College Agricultural Economics Research Unit, Research Report 115.
Hart, N., 1986, 'Inequalities in Health: The Individual versus the Environment', *J.R. Statist. Soc. A.,* 149(3):228-246.
Hartmann, H., 1987, 'The Unhappy Marriage of Marxism and Feminism: Towards A More Progressive Union', in L. Sargent (ed.), *Women and Revolution,* London, South End Press.
Harvey, D., 1973, *Social Justice and the City,* London, Edward Arnold.
Harvey, D., 1985, *Conciousness and the Urban Experience,* Oxford, Basil Blackwell.
Harvey, D., 1985, *The Urbanisation of Capital,* Oxford, Basil Blackwell.
Harvey, D., 1989, *The Condition of Post Modernity,* London, Basil Blackwell.
Hatch, E., 1992, *Respectable Lives. Social Standing in Rural New Zealand,* Berkeley, California University Press.
Hay, I., 1989, *The Caring Commodity. The Provision of Health Care in New Zealand,* Auckland, Oxford University Press.
Hayek, F., 1949, *Individualsim and Economic Order,* London, Routledge Kegan Paul.
Hayek, F., 1960, *The Constitution of Liberty,* London, Routlege and Kegan Paul.
Haythornthwaite, D., 1983, 'The Sociology of Landholding on the Former Cheviot Hills Estate, 1893-1980', M.A. thesis, Canterbury University.
Hearn, J. et al., 1989, *The Sexuality of Organisation,* London, Sage.
Heath, A., Jowell, R. and Curtice, J., 1983, *How Britain Votes,* Oxford, Pergamon.
Hedley, M., 1985, 'Mutual Aid Between Farm Households: New Zealand and Canada', *Sociologia Ruralis,* 25:26-39.
Hedley, M., 1988, 'The Peasant Within: Agrarian Life in New Zealand and Canada', *Canadian Journal of Sociology and Anthropology,* 25:67-83.
Heenan, L.D.B., 1979, 'Population', *Pacific Viewpoint,* 20(2):95-102.

Henderson, J. and Castells, M., 1987, *Global Restructuring and Territorial Development,* New York, Sage.

Heylen Research Centre, 1986, *New Zealand Values Study* (personal communication).

Hicks, A.H. and Swank, D.H., 1992, 'Politics, Institutions, and Welfare Spending in Industrialized Democracies, 1960-82', *American Political Science Review* 86(3):658-674.

Higgins, J., 1981, *States of Welfare,* Oxford, Basil Blackwell.

Hill, M., 1985, 'The Sectarian Contribution. The Decline of Church-Based Religiosity and the Rise of Sectarianism', in B. Colless and P. Donovan (eds), *Religion in New Zealand Society,* (Second Edition), Palmerston North, Dunmore Press.

Hill, M., 1987a, *A Sociology of Religion,* (reprint) Aldershot, Gower and Avebury.

Hill, M., 1987b, 'The Cult of Humanity and the Secret Religion of the Educated Classes', *New Zealand Sociology,* 2(2):112-127.

Hill, M., 1992a, Review Articles: 'The Satanism Scare', *Religion Today,* 7(2).

Hill, M., 1992b, 'The New Zealand's Cultic Milieu: Individualism and the Logic of Consumerism', in B. Wilson (ed.), *Religion: Contemporary Issues. The All Souls Seminars in the Sociology of Religion,* London, Bellew Publishing.

Hill, M., 1993, 'Ennobled Savages: New Zealand's Manipulationist Milieu', in E. Baker, J.A. Beckford, and K. Dobbelaere (eds), *Secularisation, Rationalism, and Sectarianism: Essays in Honour of Bryan R. Wilson,* Oxford, Clarendon Press.

Hill, M. and Barnett, J., 1994, 'Religion and Deviance' in P. Green (ed.), *Studies in New Zealand Social Problems* (Second Edition), Palmerston North, Dunmore Press.

Hill, M. and Zwaga, W., 1987, 'Civil and Civic: Engineering a National Religious Consensus', *New Zealand Sociology,* 2(1):25-35.

Hill, M. and Zwaga, W., 1989a, 'Religion in New Zealand: Change and Comparison', J.A. Beckford and T. Luckmann (eds), *The Changing Face of Religion,* London, Sage.

Hill, M. and Zwaga, W., 1989b, 'The "Nones" Story: A Comparative Analysis of Religious Nonalignment', *New Zealand Sociology,* 4(2).

Hill, R., 1984, 'From Hot Metal to Cold Type: New Technology in the Newspaper Industry', *New Zealand Journal of Industrial Relations,* 9(3):161-175.

Hill, R.M., 1984b, 'Gender, Skill and Technological Change: The Linotype Operator and the VDT', in H. Haines (ed.), *Women's Studies Conference Papers '83,* Auckland, Women's Studies Association.

Hill, R. and B. Gidlow, 1988, *From Hot Metal to Cold Type: Negotiating Technological Change in the New Zealand Newspaper Industry,* Wellington, DSIR Publishing.

Hill, R., 1989, '"The men make it seem like a secret society..." The Struggle for Control over 'Direct Inputting' of Classified Advertising in the New Zealand

Newspaper Industry', *New Zealand Journal of Industrial Relations*, 14: 267-278.

Hill, R.M. and R. Novitz, 1985, 'Class, Gender and Technological Change', A paper presented at the annual conference of the New Zealand Sociological Association, University of Waikato, December 1985.

Hill, S., 1982, *Competition and Control at Work*, London, Heinemann.

Hirschman, A.O., 1970, *Exit, Voice and Loyalty: Responses to Decline in Firms, Organizations and States*, Cambridge Mass, Harvard University Press.

Hoch, P., 1979, *White Hero, Black Beast: Racism, Sexism and the Mask of Masculinity*, London, Pluto Press.

Hoge, D.R. and Roozen, D.A., 1979, *Understanding Church Growth and Decline 1950-1978*, New York, The Pilgrim Press.

Hohepa, P.W., 1964, *A Maori Community in Northland*, Wellington, Reed.

Holman, T.B. and Burr, W.R., 1980, 'Beyond the Beyond: the Growth of Family Theories in the 1970s', *Journal of Marriage and the Family*, 41:729-741.

Holt, J., 1986, *Compulsory Arbitration in New Zealand: the First Forty Years*, Auckland, Auckland University Press.

Holt, J., 1986, *Compulsory Arbitration in New Zealand: the First Forty Years*, Auckland, Auckland University Press.

Horsfield, A., 1988, *Women in the Economy: A Research Report on the Economic Position of Women in New Zealand*, Wellington, Ministry of Women's Affairs.

Horsfield, A. and M. Evans, 1988, *Maori Women in the Economy: A Preliminary Review of the Economic Position of Maori Women in New Zealand*, Wellington, Ministry of Women's Affairs.

Hospital and Related Services Taskforce, 1988, *Unshackling the Hospitals*, Wellington, Government Printer.

Hughes, D. and Lauder, H. 1988, 'School Certificate and the Logic of Educational Decision-Making: Selection or Control', *New Zealand Sociology*, 3(2):97-115.

Hughes, E.C., 1959, *Men and Their Work*, New York, Free Press.

Hyman, R., 1988, 'Flexible Specialisation: Miracle or Myth?', in R. Hyman and W. Streeck (eds), *New Technology and Industrial Relations*, Oxford, Basil Blackwell.

Ihimaera, W. and Long, D.S., 1982, 'Contemporary Maori Writing: A Context', in W. Ihimaera and D.S. Long (eds), *Into the World of Light*, Auckland, Heinemann.

Illich, I., 1971, *Deschooling Society*, Harmondsworth, Penguin.

Inkson, J.H.K., 1977, 'The Man on the Dis-assembly Line: New Zealand Freezing Workers', *Australian and New Zealand Journal of Sociology*, 13(1):2-11.

Inkson, K. and Cammock, P., 1988, 'The Meat-freezing Industry in New Zealand', in E. Willis (ed.), *Technology and the Labour Process*, Sydney, Allen and Unwin.

Irwin, K., 1992, 'Towards Theories of Maori Feminisms', in R. Du Plessis, P. Bunkle, K. Irwin, A. Laurie, S. Middleton (eds), *Feminist Voices: Women's*

Studies Texts for Aotearoa/New Zealand, Auckland, Oxford University Press.
Jackson, H., 1983, 'Churchgoing in Nineteenth-Century New Zealand', *New Zealand Journal of History*, 17(1):43-59.
Jackson, K. and Harre, J., 1967, *New Zealand*, London, Thames and Hudson.
Jackson, M., 1988, *The Maori and the Criminal Justice System, Part 2*, Wellington, Department of Justice.
Jacoby, E.G., 1947, 'Rural Sociology in New Zealand', *Transactions of the Royal Society of New Zealand*, 77:331-5.
Jagger, A. and Rothenberg, P., 1984, *Feminist Frameworks: Alternative Theoretical Accounts of the Relations Between Women and Men*, (Second Edition), New York, McGraw Hill.
Jahoda, M., 1982, *Work, Employment and Unemployment: A Social Psychological Analysis*, Cambridge, Cambridge University Press.
James, B., 1979, *A Report to the Kawerau Community*, Hamilton, University of Waikato.
James, B., 1982, 'Family', in P. Spoonley, D. Pearson and I. Shirley (eds), *New Zealand: Sociological Perspectives*, Palmerston North, Dunmore Press.
James, B., 1985, 'Mill Wives: A Study of Gender Relations, Family and Work in a Single-industry Town', D.Phil. thesis, Waikato University.
James, B., 1986, 'Taking Gender into Account: Feminist and Sociological Issues in Social Research', *New Zealand Sociology*, 1(1):18-33.
James, B., 1987, 'Millworkers' Wives', in S. Cox (ed.), *Public and Private Worlds.*, Wellington, Allen and Unwin and Port Nicholson Press.
James, B. and Saville-Smith, K., 1989, *Gender, Culture and Power: Challenging New Zealand's Gendered Culture*, Auckland, Oxford University Press.
James, C., 1987, 'The Revolution Revisited', in A. von Tunzelmann and J. Johnston (eds), *Responding to the Revolution: Careers, Culture and Casualties*, New Zealand Institute of Public Administration, Wellington, Government Printer.
James, C., 1988, 'Warning Signs for a Divided Labour', *National Business Review*, March 31.
Jesson, B., 1987, *Behind the Mirror Glass*, Auckland, Penguin.
Jesson, B., 1989, *Fragments of Labour*, Auckland, Penguin.
Jesson, B., Ryan, A. and Spoonley, P., 1988, *Revival of the Right. New Zealand Politics in the 1980s*, Auckland, Heinemann Reed.
Jessop, B. et al., 1984, 'Authoritarian Populism, Two Nature and Thatcherism', *New Left Review*, 147:32-60.
Jessop, B., 1986, *Thatcher's England*, Seminar at Massey University, 2 September.
Jessop, B., 1989, 'Thatcherism: The British Road to Post-Fordism', mimeo.
Johnston, J., 1982, 'Population', in P. Spoonley, D. Pearson, and I. Shirley (eds), *New Zealand: Sociological Perspectives,* Palmerston North, Dunmore Press.
Johnston, R.J., 1971, *Urban Residential Patterns*. London, G. Bell.

Johnston, R.J. (ed.), 1973, *Urbanisation in New Zealand*, Wellington, Reed.
Johnston R.J., 1973a, 'New Zealand's Urban System in the Late 1960s', in R.J. Johnston (ed.), *Urbanisation in New Zealand*, Wellington, Reed.
Johnston R.J., 1973b, 'Neighbourhood Patterns Within Urban Areas', in R.J. Johnston (ed.), *Urbanisation in New Zealand*, Wellington, Reed.
Johnston, R., 1992, 'Electoral Geography', in Holland, M. (ed.), *Electoral Behaviour in New Zealand*, Auckland, Oxford University Press.
Jones, D., 1981, 'The National Projects Scheme, 1975-1980: Applications and Funding of Selected Women's, Men's and Mixed Sports', M.A. (Applied) thesis, Victoria University of Wellington.
Jones, F.L. and Davies. P.M., 1986, *Models of Society*, Sydney, Croom Helm.
Jones, T., 1975, *A Hard Won Freedom: Alternative Communities in New Zealand*, Auckland, Hodder and Stoughton.
Jones, A., 1991, *"At School I've Got a Chance" Culture/Privilege: Pacific Islands and Pakeha Girls at School*, Palmerston North, Dunmore Press.
Jordan, B., 1987, *Rethinking Welfare*, Oxford, Basil Blackwell.
Jorgensen, M., 1974, *Recreation and Leisure: A Bibliography and Review of the New Zealand Literature*, Wellington, Ministry of Works and Development.
Joyce, P. (ed.), 1987, *The Historical Meanings of Work*, Cambridge, Cambridge University Press.
Julian, R., 1989, 'Women: How Significant a Force?' in H. Gold (ed.), *New Zealand Politics in Perspective*, (Second Edition), Auckland, Longman Paul.
Kaim-Caudle, 1973, *Comparative Social Policy and Social Security: A Ten-Country Study*, London, Martin Robertson.
Kaplan, P.F., no date, *Social Aspects of Productivity: Hill-Country Sheep-Beef Farms in the Mangamahu Valley*, Palmerston North, Massey University Department of Sociology.
Kawharu, I.H. (ed.), 1975, *Conflict and Compromise*, Wellington, Reed.
Kawharu, I.H., 1977, *Maori Land Tenure*, Oxford, Oxford University Press.
Kawharu, H. (ed.), 1989, *Waitangi. Maori and Pakeha Perspectives of the Treaty of Waitangi*, Auckland, Oxford University Press.
Kayll, J., 1905, *A Plea for the Criminal*, Invercargill, W. Smith.
Kedgley, S., 1985, *The Sexual Wilderness: Men and Women in New Zealand*, Auckland, Reed Methuen.
Kedgley, S., 1989, *Our Own Country: Leading New Zealand Women Writers Talk About Their Writing and Their Lives*, Auckland, Penguin.
Kelly, J., 1983, *Leisure Identities and Interactions*, London, Allen and Unwin.
Kelsey, J., 1988, 'Free Market "Rogernomics" and Maori Rights Under the Treaty of Waitangi – An Irresolvable Contradiction', Paper to Australian Law and Society Conference, Melbourne.
Kelsey, J. and Young, W., 1980, *The Gangs as Moral Panic*, Wellington, Victoria

University of Wellington, Institute of Criminology.

Keohane, N.A., Rosaldo, M.Z. and Gelpi, B.C. (eds), 1982, *Feminist Theory: A Critique of Ideology*, Brighton, Harvester.

Kernot, B., 1972, *People of the Four Winds*, Wellington, Hicks Smith and Sons.

Keynes, J., 1926, *The End of Laissez-Faire*, London, Hogarth.

Keynes, J., 1936, *The General Theory of Employment, Interest and Money*, London, Macmillan.

Khawaja, M., 1985, 'Trends and Differentials in Fertility', in ESCAP, Population Division (eds), *Population of New Zealand*, Country Monograph Series No. 12, New York, United Nations.

Khawaja, M. and Rolleston, W., 1975, 'A Note on the Transition in Maori Fertility in New Zealand', Paper presented at the Conference of the Sociological Association of Australia and New Zealand, Hamilton.

Kilmartin, L. and Thorns, D.C., 1978, *Cities Unlimited*, Sydney, Allen and Unwin.

Kilmartin, L., Thorns, D.C. and Burke, T., 1985, *Social Theory and the Australian City*, Sydney, Allen and Unwin.

King, D., 1987, *The New Right: Politics, Markets and Citizenship*, London, Macmillan.

King, M., 1985, *Being Pakeha*, Auckland, Hodder and Stoughton.

King, M. (ed.), 1988, *One of the Boys?: Changing Views of Masculinity in New Zealand*, Auckland, Heinemann.

King, M. (ed.), 1990, *Pakeha. The Quest for Identity*, Auckland, Penguin.

Kinsey, R. *et al.*, 1986, *Losing the Fight Against Crime*, Oxford, Basil Blackwell.

Kirker, A., 1986, *New Zealand Women Artists*, Auckland, Reed Methuen.

Klein, R. and O'Higgins, M. (eds), 1985, *The Future of Welfare*, Oxford, Basil Blackwell.

Knights, D. and Sturdy, A., 1989, 'New Technology and the Self Disciplined Worker in Insurance', in J. McNeill, *et al.* (eds), *Deciphering Science and Technology*, London: Macmillan.

Knights, D. *et al.* (eds), 1985, *Job Redesign: Critical Perspectives on the Labour Process*, Aldershot, Gower.

Koopman-Boyden, P.G., 1986, 'Population Ageing in New Zealand: Some Characteristics and Policy Implications', *New Zealand Population Review*, 12(2):92-106.

Koopman-Boyden, P.G. and Abbott, M., 1985, 'Expectations for Household Task Allocation and Actual Task Allocation: a New Zealand Study', *Journal of Marriage and the Family*, 47(1):211-219.

Koopman-Boyden, P. and C. Scott., 1984, *The Family and Government Policy in New Zealand*, Sydney, Allen and Unwin.

Korpi, W., 1972, 'Some Problems in the Measurement of Class Voting', *American Journal of Sociology*, 78.

Kraus, C., 1975, 'Learning About Politics: Shearing Gangs as a Social Unit', in S. Levine (ed.), *New Zealand Politics*, Melbourne, Cheshire.

Kuzmicich, S., 1988, 'General Population Trends', in C. Crothers and R. Bedford (eds), *The Business of Population*, Wellington, New Zealand Demographic Society.

Lamare, J., 1984, 'Party Identification and Voting Behaviour in New Zealand', *Political Science* 36(1):1-9.

Lamb, H., 1987, 'A Glimpse Into the Thinking of Young New Zealanders', Paper presented at the Symposium on IEA Study of Written Composition, American Educational Research Association, 20-24 April.

Lambert, C. and Weir, D. (eds), 1975, *Cities in Modern Britain*, London, Fontana.

Lamming, G., 1979, *In the Castle of My Skin*, Harlow, Longman.

Lane, R., 1978, 'The Regulation of Experience: Leisure in a Market Society', *Social Science Information*, 2(17):147-84.

Lange, D., 1986, *The McIntosh Lecture*, Palmerston North, Massey University.

Lange, D., 1988, *Tomorrow's Schools: the Reform of Educational Administration in New Zealand*, Wellington, Government Printer.

Lanternari, V., 1965, *The Religions of the Oppressed*, New York, Mentor Books.

Larkin, R., 1968, 'Mount Roskill Survey of School Children', mimeo.

LaRossa, R., 1977, *Conflict and Power in Marriage: Expecting the First Child*, Beverley Hills, Sage.

Larson, M.S., 1977, *The Rise of Professionalism, A Sociological Analysis*, Berkeley, University of California Press.

Lash, S. and Urry, J., 1981, *The End of Organised Capitalism*, Cambridge, Polity Press.

Laslett, P., 1965, *The World We Have Lost*, London, Methuen.

Lauder, H., 1987, 'The New Right and Education Policy in New Zealand', *New Zealand Journal of Educational Studies*, 22(1):180-200.

Lazonick, W., 1990, *Competitive Advantage on the Shopfloor*, Cambridge, Harvard University Press.

Lea, J. and Young, J., 1984, *What is to be Done About Law and Order?*, London, Penguin Books.

Leadbeater, C., 1988, 'Power To The Person', *Marxism Today*, October:14-23.

Leckie, J., 1985, 'In Defence of Race and Empire. The White New Zealand League at Pukekohe', *New Zealand Journal of History*, 19(2):103-129.

Le Heron, R., 1987, 'Global Processes and Local Adjustments: Understanding Changes in Food and Fibre Production in New Zealand', in J. Fairweather (ed.), *Proceedings of the Rural Economy and Society Study Group Symposium on Rural Research Needs*, Christchurch, Lincoln College Agribusiness and Economics Research Unit, Discussion Paper 113.

Leibrich, J. *et al.* (eds), 1987, *In Search of Well-Being. Exploratory Research into*

Complementary Therapies, Wellington, Health Services and Development Unit, Department of Health.
Levine, H. and Levine, M., 1987, *Stewart Island: Anthropological Perspectives on a New Zealand Fishing Community*, Wellington, Anthropology Department, Victoria University.
Levine, M., 1987, 'Exclusion and Participation: The Role of Women in a New Zealand Fishing Village', in H. Levine and M. Levine (eds), *Stewart Island: Anthropological Perspectives on a New Zealand Fishing Community*, Wellington, Department of Anthropology, Victoria University.
Lewis, P. and Pearlman, C., 1986, *Media and Power: From Marconi to Murdoch*, London, Camden Press.
Lipietz, A., 1987, *Mirages and Miracles: The Crises of Global Fordism*, London, Verso.
Lipset, S.M., 1963, *Political Man*, New York, Anchor Books.
Lipset, S.M., and Rokkan, S., 1967, *Party Systems and Voter Alignments*, New York, Free Press.
Litchtheim, G., 1971, *Imperialism*, Great Britain, Allen Lane.
Littlejohn, J., 1963, *Westrigg: the Sociology of a Cheviot Parish*, London, Routledge and Kegan Paul.
Littler, C.R., 1978, 'Understanding Taylorism', *British Journal of Sociology*, 29(2):185-202.
Littler, C.R., 1982a, 'De-skilling and Structures of Control', in S. Wood (ed.), *The Degradation of Work? Skill, Deskilling and the Labour Process*, London, Hutchinson.
Littler, C.R., 1982b, *The Development of the Labour Process in Capitalist Societies: a Comparative Study of the Transformation of Work Organisation in Britain, Japan and the USA*, London, Heinemann Educational.
Littler, C.R. (ed.), 1985, *The Experience of Work*, New York, St Martins Press.
Littler, C.R., 1987, 'Labour Process Literature – A Review', in K. Hince and A. Williams (eds), *Contemporary Industrial Relations in Australia and New Zealand: Literature Surveys*, Wellington, Industrial Relations Centre, Victoria University.
Littler, C.R. and Salaman, G., 1982, 'Bravermania and Beyond: Recent Theories of the Labour Process', *Sociology*, 16(2):251-269.
Lloyd, A.G., 1987, 'The Australian-New Zealand Farm Problem and the Appropriate Role of Government', *The Australian Economic Review*, Third Quarter:3-20.
Lombroso, C., 1911, *Criminal Man*, New York, Putnam.
Loney, M., Boswell, D. and Clarke, J. (eds), 1983, *Social Policy and Social Welfare*, Milton Keynes, Open University Press.

Lowe, R.J., 1984, 'Comparing 1981 and Earlier Census Data', *New Zealand Population Review,* 10(1):43-46.
Luketina, F., 1986, *The 1984 Southland Floods*, Wellington, Department of Social Welfare, Research Report Series, No.4.
Lumley, B. and O'Shaughnessey, M., 1985, 'Media and Cultural Studies', in Z. Baranaski and J. Short (eds), *Developing Contemporary Marxism*, London, MacMillan.
MacIntyre, A., Allison, N. and Penman, D., 1989, *Pesticides: Issues and Options for New Zealand,* Wellington, Ministry for the Environment.
MacIntyre, S., 1986, 'The Patterning of Health by Social Position in Contemporary Britain: Directions for Sociological Research', *Social Science and Medicine,* 23(4):393-415.
Macionis, J.J., 1987, *Sociology,* Englewood Cliffs, Prentice-Hall.
Mackinnon, C., 1979 *The Sexual Harassment of Working Women*, New Haven, Yale.
Mackintosh, M.M., 1988, 'Domestic Labour and the Household', in R.E. Pahl (ed.), *On Work,* Oxford, Basil Blackwell.
MacRae, T., 1986/87, 'Two Men, Two Different Paths', *Tu Tangata*, Issue 33:34-36.
Maddison, A., 1964, *Economic Growth in the West,* London, Twentieth Century Fund.
Maddison, A., 1982, *Phases of Capitalist Development,* Oxford, Oxford University Press.
Mahar, C., 1985, 'Elite Rural Women', *Sites*, 11:20-26.
Maharey, S., 1987, 'Shaping The Future? Labour Ideology and Socialism', *Race, Gender, Class*, (5):71-85.
Maharey, S., 1989, 'New Times, Privatisation and The Democratic Alternative', Paper given at the 'Say Yes To Public Services' Conference, Wellington, New Zealand Public Service Association.
Maharey, S., 1989, *Fordism and Post-Fordism in New Zealand*, Address to the PSA Conference, Wellington.
Maharey, S., 1990, 'Understanding the Media', in P. Spoonley and W. Hirsh (eds), *Between the Lines: Racism and the New Zealand Media*, Auckland, Heineman Reed.
Mahuta, R., 1978, 'Maori Communities and Industrial Development', in M. King (ed.), *Tihei Mauri Ora,* Auckland, Methuen.
Mann, S.A. and Dickinson, J.H., 1978, 'Obstacles to the Development of a Capitalist Agriculture', *Journal of Peasant Studies,* 5:466-481.
Mars, G., 1982, *Cheats at Work: An Anthropology of Workplace Crime,* London, George Allen and Unwin.

Marshall, G., Newby, H., Rose, D. and Vogler, C., 1988, *Social Class in Modern Britain*, London, Hutchison.
Marshall, T., 1972, 'Value Problems of Welfare Capitalism', *Journal of Social Policy*, Cambridge, Cambridge University Press.
Martin, J., 1981, *State Papers*, Massey University, Department of Sociology.
Martin, J., 1983a, 'Whither the Rural Working Class?' *New Zealand Journal of History*, 17:21-42.
Martin, J., 1983b, *Labour and Kiwifruit: Some Social and Economic Implications of the Expansion of the Kiwifruit Industry in the Bay of Plenty*, Wellington, DSIR.
Martin, J., 1984, 'Rural and Industrial Labour and the State', in C. Wilkes and I. Shirley (eds), *In the Public Interest: Health, Work and Housing in New Zealand*, Auckland, Benton Ross.
Martin, J., 1987, 'Arbitration, the Sheepowners and the Shearers', *New Zealand Journal of Industrial Relations*, 12:175-186.
Martin, J. E., 1990, *The Forgotten Worker: the Rural Wage-Earner in Nineteenth Century New Zealand*, Wellington, Allen and Unwin.
Marx, K., 1867, *Capital*, Volume 1, London, Penguin (1976).
Masterman, L., 1986, *Learning the Media*, London, Comedia.
Mataira, K., 1984, *Maori Artists of the South Pacific*, Raglan, New Zealand Maori Artists and Writers Society Inc.
Maunier, P., 1985, 'Farm Ownership, Farm Work and Farm Decisions: Aspects of Women's Roles on Farms', *Conference Papers of the Women's Studies Association, August 1984*, Auckland, Women's Studies Association.
Maxwell, G., 1989, Family Trends in Australia and New Zealand, Wellington, unpublished paper.
May, (Cook) H., 1988, 'Motherhood in the 1950s', in S. Middleton (ed.), *Women and Education in Aotearoa*, Wellington, Allen and Unwin and Port Nicholson Press.
May, H., 1992, *Minding Children, Managing Men: Conflict and Compromise in the Lives of Postwar Pakeha Women*, Wellington, Bridget Williams Books.
Mayo, E., 1933, *The Human Problems of an Industrial Civilisation*, London, Macmillan.
McAllister, I. and Vowles, J., 'The Rise of New Politics and Market Liberalism in Australia and New Zealand', *British Journal of Political Science*, (forthcoming 1994).
McClintock, W. and Taylor, N., 1983, *Pines, Pulp and People: a Case Study of New Zealand Forestry Towns*, Christchurch, Lincoln College Centre for Resource Management Information Paper 2.
McCulloch, G., 1988, 'From Currie to Picot: History, Ideology and Policy in New Zealand Education', *Access*, 7:1-15.

McGrath, F., 1988, 'Private Medical Insurance – To Have Or Not To Have', *New Zealand Medical Journal,* 101(841):112-115.
McGuire, M.B., 1985, 'Religion and Healing', in P.E. Hammond (ed.), *The Sacred in a Secular Age,* Berkeley, University of California Press.
McIntyre, J., 1981, 'The Structural-functional Approach to Family Study', in F.I. Nye and F.M. Berado (eds), *Emerging Conceptual Frameworks in Family Analysis in the 1980s,* New York, Praeger.
McKeown T., 1979, *The Role of Medicine,* Princeton, Princeton University Press.
McKinlay, P., 1987, 'The Role of The State', Paper prepared for the Royal Commission on Social Policy, Wellington, Royal Commission of Social Policy.
McKinlay, R., 1992, 'Women and Unpaid Work', in C. Briar *et al.* (eds), *Superwoman, Where are You? Social Policy and Women's Experience,* Palmerston North, Dunmore Press.
McLennan, R. and Gilbertson, D. (eds), 1984, *Work in New Zealand,* Wellington, A.H. and A.W. Reed.
McLeod, A.L. (ed.), 1968, *The Pattern of New Zealand Culture,* Ithaca, NY, Cornell University Press.
McLintock, A.H., 1948, *The History of Otago,* Dunedin, Whitcombe and Tombs.
Mead, S.M. (ed.), 1984, *Te Maori: Maori Art from New Zealand Collections,* Auckland, Heinemann.
Meade, A., 1984, 'After School, and in the Holidays', *SET: Research Information for Teachers* No. 1 (item 2).
Mellor, J.R., 1977, *Urban Sociology in an Urbanised Society,* London, Routledge and Kegan Paul.
Merton, R., 1938, 'Social Structure and Anomie', *American Sociological Review,* 3:672-82.
Merton, R., 1969 (1957), *Social Theory and Social Structure,* New York, Free Press.
Metcalfe, A., 1988, *For Freedom and Dignity: Historical Agency and Class Structures in the Coalfields of New South Wales,* Sydney, Allen and Unwin.
Metge, J., 1964, *A New Maori Migration,* London, Athlone Press.
Middleton, S., 1984, 'Sex Role Stereotyping: a Critique', *New Zealand Women's Studies Journal* 1(1):65-74.
Middleton, S., 1985, 'Feminism and Education in Post-War New Zealand: A Sociological Analysis', D.Phil. thesis, University of Waikato.
Middleton, S., 1987, 'Feminism and Education in Post-War New Zealand: An Oral History Perspective', in R. Openshaw and D. McKenzie (eds), *Reinterpreting the Educational Past,* Wellington, NZ Council for Educational Research.
Middleton, S., 1988, 'A Short Adventure Between School and Marriage?: Contradicitions in the Education of the New Zealand Postwar Woman', 'Researching Feminist Life Histories' and 'Towards a Sociology of Women's

Education in Aotearoa', in S. Middleton (ed.), *Women and Education in Aotearoa*, Wellington, Allen and Unwin and Port Nicholson Press.

Middleton, S. (forthcoming), 'Women, Equality and Equity in Liberal Educational Policies 1945-1988: A Feminist Critique', in S. Middleton, A. Jones and J. Codd (eds), *New Directions in New Zealand's Educational Policies*.

Middleton, S., 1993, *Educating Feminists: Life Histories and Feminist Pedagogy*, New York and London, The Teaching College Press, Columbia University.

Mies, M., 1986, *Patriarchy and Accumulation on a World Scale*, London, Zed Books.

Miles, R., 1982, *Racism and Migrant Labour*, London, Routledge and Kegan Paul.

Miles, R., 1989, *Racism*, London, Tavistock.

Miliband, R., 1969, *The State in Capitalist Society*, London, Quartet Books.

Mill, K.M., 1987, 'Gender Differences in Friendship Patterns', M.A. thesis, University of Waikato.

Miller, B.C., 1986, *Family Research Methods*, London, Sage.

Miller, R. and Vowles, J., 1989, 'Delegates Revisited: A Sociology of New Zealand's National and Labour Parties in 1988', Paper presented to the Australasian Political Studies Association Conference, University of New South Wales, Sydney.

Mills, C. W., 1976 (1959), *The Sociological Imagination*, Harmondsworth, Penguin.

Mingione, E., 1988, 'Work and Informal Activities in Urban Southern Italy', in R. Pahl (ed.), *On Work*, Oxford, Basil Blackwell.

Ministerial Advisory Committee on a Maori Perspective the Department of Social Welfare, 1986, *Puao-Te-Atatu*, Wellington, Government Printer.

Ministry of Women's Affairs, 1988, *Deregulation of Broadcasting*, Report and recommendations from a consultative meeting convened by the Ministry of Women's Affairs, June 3.

Misa, T., 1987, 'All the Politician's Men: How the Ad Agencies and Strategists Conspire to Capture your Vote', *North and South*, August:56-71.

Mishra, R., 1977, *Society and Social Policy: Theories and Practice of Welfare*, London, Macmillan.

Mishra, R., 1984, *The Welfare State in Crisis: Social Thought and Social Change*, Great Britain, Wheatsheaf.

Mitchell, H.A. and Mitchell, M.J., 1989, 'Profiles of Maori Pupils with High Marks in School Certificate English and Mathematics, Volume 1', Nelson, Mitchell Research.

Mol, H. (ed.), 1972, *Western Religion: A Country by Country Sociological Inquiry*, The Hague, Mouton.

Mollenkopf, J. and Castells, M., 1991, *Dual City: Restructuring New York*, New York, Russell Sage Foundation.

Moore, J., 1987, 'Japanese Industrial Relations', *Labour & Industry*, 1(1):140-155.

Moran, W., 1988, 'Sectoral and Statutory Planning for Rural New Zealand', in P. Cloke (ed.), *Rural Planning in Western Economies*, London, Allen and Unwin.
Moran, W. and Anderson, A.G., 1988, 'Predicting Enterprise Choice: Exit from Dairying in New Zealand', *Journal of Rural Studies*, 4:203-213.
Morgan, D.H.J., 1985, *The Family, Politics and Social Theory,* London, Routledge and Kegan Paul.
Morgan, P., 1978, *Delinquent Fantasies*, London, Croom Helm.
Morgan, D., 1991, *Discovering Men: Critical Studies on Men and Masculinities*, New York and London, Routledge.
Morley, D., 1980, *The 'Nationwide' Audience*, London, BFI.
Morris, A. and Young, W., 1987, *Juvenile Justice in New Zealand*, Wellington, Victoria University of Wellington, Institute of Criminology.
Mulgan, R., 1984, *Democracy and Power in New Zealand,* Auckland, Oxford University Press.
Munro, R.G., 1989, 'Report to the Executive of the NZPPTA on the Personnel Provisions of Tomorrows Schools', Wellington, PPTA.
Murie, A. and Forrest, R., 1988, *Selling the Welfare State. The Privatisation of Public Housing*, London, Routledge.
Murray, C., 1987, 'The American Experience with the Welfare State', Paper to the NZCIS Conference on the Welfare State, Wellington, 9 November.
Muthumala, D., Scott, W., Westrate, J. and Morris A., 1989, *Health Expenditure Trends in New Zealand,* Wellington, Department of Health.
Myers, V., 1975, 'Housing Classes and Social Structure: A Reappraisal', M.A. thesis, University of Auckland.
Nagel, J., 1988, 'Voter Turnout in New Zealand General Elections, 1928-1988', *Political Science,* 40(2):16-38.
Nash, R., 1989, 'Tomorrow's Schools: State Power and Parent Participation', *New Zealand Journal of Educational Studies,* 24(2).
Nash, W., 1936, *Appendices to the Journals*, New Zealand House of Representatives, Wellington, Government Printer.
National Housing Commission, 1988, *Housing New Zealand,* Wellington, Government Printer.
Navarro, V., 1976, *Medicine Under Capitalism,* New York, Prodist.
Nelson, L., 1969, *Rural Sociology: Its Origin and Growth in the United States*, Minneapolis, University of Minnesota Press.
Neville, R.J.W. and O'Neill, C.J., 1979, *The Population of New Zealand: Interdisciplinary Perspectives,* Auckland, Longman Paul.
New Zealand, 1927, *Population Census, 1926, Volume 1 – Increase and Geographical Distribution,* Wellington, Government Printer.
New Zealand, 1977, *Census of Population and Dwellings. Volume 1B – Location and Increase of Population*, Wellington, Government Printer.

New Zealand Census of Population and Dwellings, several dates, *Religious Professions*, Wellington, Department of Statistics.

New Zealand Council for Educational Research, 1987, 'How Fair is New Zealand Education? Part 1', Wellington, The Royal Commission on Social Policy.

New Zealand Federation of University Women, 1977, *Sydenham, An Informal History,* New Zealand Federation of University Women Canterbury Branch, Christchurch, Pegasus Press.

New Zealand Official Yearbook 1986-87, 1987, Wellington, Department of Statistics.

New Zealand Planning Council, 1982, *Who Makes Social Policy?,* Wellington, New Zealand Planning Council.

New Zealand Planning Council, 1985, *From Birth to Death,* Wellington, New Zealand Planning Council.

New Zealand Planning Council, 1989, *From Birth to Death II,* Wellington, New Zealand Planning Council.

New Zealand Planning Council, 1989, *The Economy in Transition: Restructuring to 1989,* Wellington, New Zealand Planning Council.

Newby, H., 1980, 'Rural Sociology: a Trend Report', *Current Sociology,* 28:1-121.

Newby, H., 1987, 'Emergent Issues in Theories of Agrarian Development', in D. Thorniley (ed.), *The Economy and Society of Rural Communities,* Aldershot, Avebury.

Nichols, T., 1975, 'The Sociology of Accidents and the Social Production of Industrial Accidents', in G. Esland and G. Salaman (eds), *People and Work,* London, Open University Press.

Nichols, T. (ed.), 1980, *Capital and Labour,* Glasgow, Fontana.

Nichols, T. and Beynon, H., 1977, *Living with Capitalism: Class Relations in the Modern Factory,* London, Routledge and Kegan Paul.

Nolan, F. *et al.*, 1986, *The 1976/81 Intercensal Consistency Study,* Christchurch, Mathematical Statistics Division, Department of Statistics.

Novitz, R., 1978, 'Marital and Familial Roles in New Zealand: the Challenge of the Women's Liberation Movement', in P.G. Koopman-Boyden (ed.), *Families in New Zealand Society,* Wellington, Methuen.

Novitz, R., 1982, 'Feminism', in P. Spoonley *et al.* (eds), *New Zealand: Sociological Perspectives,* Palmerston North, Dunmore Press.

Novitz, R., 1987, 'Bridging the Gap: Paid and Unpaid Work', in S. Cox (ed.), *Public and Private Worlds: Women in Contemporary New Zealand,* Wellington, Allen and Unwin.

Novitz, R., 1987, 'Treasury: A Sociological Analysis', Contribution to a Panel Discussion, New Zealand Sociological Association Conference, Palmerston North.

Novitz, R., 1989, 'Women: Weaving an Identity', in D. Novitz and B. Willmott (eds), *Culture and Identity in New Zealand,* Wellington, Government Print.

O'Brien, M., 1988, *Law, Welfare and Social Planning, Study Guide One*, Palmerston North, Department of Social Policy and Social Work, Massey University.
O'Brien, M., and Wilkes, C., 1993, *Tragedy of the Market*, Palmerston North, Dunmore Press.
O'Connor, J., 1973, *Fiscal Crisis of the State*, New York, St. Martin's Press.
O'Meagher, S., 1986, 'The America's Cup Campaign – How the Bankers and Image Makers Manipulated New Zealand Pride', *North and South*, October:24-35.
O'Neill, C.J., 1979, 'Fertility: Past, Present and Future', in R.J.W. Neville and C.J. O'Neill (eds), *The Population of New Zealand: Interdisciplinary Perspectives*, Auckland, Longman Paul.
O'Reagan, P. and O'Connor, T., 1989, *Community. Give It A Go!*, Wellington, Allen and Unwin/Port Nicholson Press.
Oakes, L., 1986, *Inside Centrepoint. The Study of a New Zealand Community*, Auckland, Benton Ross.
Oakley, A., 1972, *Sex, Gender and Society*, London, Temple Smith.
Oakley, A., 1974, *The Sociology of Housework*, London, Martin Robertson.
Oakley, A., 1981, *Subject Women*, Oxford, Robertson.
Oakley, A., 1983, 'Interviewing Women: a Contradiction in Terms', in L. Stanley and S. Wise (eds), *Breaking Out: Feminist Consciousness and Feminist Research*, London, Routledge and Kegan Paul.
Oakley, A., 1986, *The Captured Womb: A History of the Medical Care of Pregnant Women*, London, Basil Blackwell.
OECD, 1978, *Public Expenditure Trends*, Paris, Organisation for Economic Co-operation and Development.
OECD, 1981, *The Welfare State in Crisis*, Paris, Organisation for Economic Co-operation and Development.
OECD, 1985, *The Role of the Public Sector*, Paris, Organisation for Economic Co-operation and Development.
Offe, C., 1984, *Contradictions of the Welfare State*, London, Hutchinson.
Oliver H., 1987, 'The New Zealand Labour Party and the Rise of Rogernomics 1981-84', M.A. thesis, Massey University.
Oliver, W., 1988, 'Social Policy in New Zealand: A Historical Overview', Royal Commission on Social Policy, *The April Report*, Volume I, Wellington, Royal Commission on Social Policy.
Olssen E., 1977, 'Social Class in Nineteenth Century New Zealand', in D.C. Pitt (ed.), *Social Class in New Zealand*, Auckland, Longmans.
Olssen, E., 1987, 'The Origins of the Labour Party: A Reconsideration', *New Zealand Journal of History* 21(2).
Olssen, E., 1988, *The Red Feds: Revolutionary Industrial Unionism and the New Zealand Federation of Labour 1908-1913*, Auckland, Oxford University Press.

Olssen, M. (ed.), 1988, *Mental Testing in New Zealand,* Christchurch, Christchurch University Press.

Oppenheim, R., 1976, 'The Structure of a New Zealand Community', D.Phil. thesis, Waikato University.

Orange, C., 1987, *The Treaty of Waitangi,* Wellington, Allen and Unwin and Port Nicholson Press.

Pahl, R., 1966, 'The Rural-Urban Continuum', *Sociologia Ruralis,* 6; reprinted in R. Pahl (ed.), *Readings in Urban Sociology,* Oxford, Pergamon Press.

Pahl, R. (ed.), 1968, *Readings in Urban Sociology,* Oxford, Pergamon.

Pahl, R., 1969, *Whose City,* London, Longmans.

Pahl, R., 1977, 'Managers, Technical Experts and the State', in M. Harloe (ed.), *Captive Cities,* London, Wiley.

Pahl, R., 1984, *Divisions of Labour,* Oxford, Basil Blackwell.

Pahl, R. (ed.), 1988, *On Work,* Oxford, Basil Blackwell.

Pahl, R., Fynn, R. and Buck N.H., 1983, *Structures and Processes of Urban Life,* London, Longmans.

Palmer, G., 1987, 'Society and Crime', Address given at Manawatu Prison, Linton, 26 June.

Palmer, G., 1987, *Unbridled Power: An Interpretation of New Zealand's Constitution and Government,* (Second Edition), Auckland, Oxford University Press.

Palmer, G., 1989, 'The Treaty of Waitangi-Principles for Crown Action', Paper to Australasian University Law Schools Conference, Wellington.

Palmerston North City Council, 1969, *Trends in Recreation Preference,* Palmerston North, Palmerston North City Council, Report No. 13.

Papps, T.O'H., 1985, 'Growth and Distribution of Population: Historical Trends',in ESCAP, Population Division (eds), *Population of New Zealand,* Country Monograph Series No. 12, New York, United Nations.

Parekowhai, C., 1988, 'Korero ki Taku Tuakana: Merata Mita and Me', *Illusions,* 9:21-26.

Park, R., 1952, *Human Communities,* New York, Free Press.

Parkin, D., 1974, 'Congregational and Interpersonal Ideologies in Political Ethnicity', in A. Cohen (ed.), *Urban Ethnicity,* London, Tavistock.

Parkin, F., 1979, *Marxism and Class Theory. A Bourgeois Critique,* London, Tavistock.

Parsons, T., 1951, *The Social System,* London, Routledge and Kegan Paul.

Parsons, T., 1954, *Essays in Social Theory,* Glencoe, Illnois, Free Press.

Pearce, D., 1987, *Tourism Today. A Geographical Analysis,* London, Longman.

Pearce, F., 1976, *Crimes of the Powerful,* London, Pluto Press.

Pearce, N.E., Davis, P.B., Smith, A.H. and Foster, F.H., 1985, 'Social Class, Ethnic Group and Male Mortality in New Zealand, 1974-8', *Journal of Epidemiology and Community Health,* 39:9-14.

Pearson, B., 1963, *Coal Flat,* Auckland, Paul's Book Arcade.
Pearson, D.G., 1980, *Johnsonville. Continuity and Change in a New Zealand Township,* Auckland, Allen and Unwin.
Pearson, D., 1989, 'Pakeha Ethnicity: Concept or Conundrum?', *Sites,* 18:61-72.
Pearson, D., 1990, *A Dream Deferred. The Origins of Ethnic Conflict in New Zealand,* Wellington, Allen and Unwin.
Pearson, D. and Thorns, D., 1983, *Eclipse of Equality,* Sydney, Allen and Unwin.
Pearson, G., 1984, *Hooligan: A History of Respectable Fears,* London, Macmillan.
Pearson, R., 1988, 'Female Workers in the First and Third Worlds: The Greening of Women's Labour', in R.E. Pahl (ed.), *On Work,* Oxford, Basil Blackwell.
Percy, K., 1982, *Homelessness in the Auckland Region,* Wellington, National Housing Commission.
Perry, N., 1991, Book Review of *New Zealand Society: A Sociological Introduction, Australia and New Zealand Journal of Sociology,* 27 (3): 396-402
Phillips, A. and Taylor, B., 1980, 'Sex and Skill: Notes Towards a Feminist Economics', *Feminist Review,* 6:79-88.
Phillips, J., 1983, *Mothers Matter Too,* Wellington, Reed.
Phillips, J., 1986, *The Mother Manual,* Auckland, Reed Methuen.
Phillips, J., 1987, *A Man's Country? The Image of the Pakeha Male: A History,* Auckland, Penguin Books.
Phillips, R., 1981, *Divorce in New Zealand: A Social History,* Auckland, Oxford University Press.
Phizacklea, A. (ed.), 1983, *One-Way Ticket: Migration and Female Labour,* London, Routledge and Kegan Paul.
Piesse, D., 1978, 'Houses for Homes: The State and Housing Provision in New Zealand', M.A. thesis, University of Auckland.
Piliavin, S. and Briar, S., 1964, 'Police Encounters With Juveniles', *American Journal of Sociology,* 70:206-14.
Pinker, R., 1979, *The Idea of Welfare,* London, Heinemann.
Pitts, J.R., 1964, 'The structural-functional approach', in H.T. Christensen (ed.), *Handbook of Marriage and the Family,* Chicago, McNally.
Pollert, A., 1988, 'Dismantling Flexibility', *Capital and Class,* 34:42-75.
Pomare, E. and de Boer, W., 1988, *Hauhora, Maori Standards of Health, A Study of the Years 1970-1984,* Wellington, Department of Health.
Pomeroy, A., 1985, 'A Sociological Analysis of Structural Change in Pastoral Farming in New Zealand', Ph.D. thesis, Essex University.
Pomeroy, A., 1988, 'The Politics of Inequality: Farming Women', unpublished paper presented to SAANZ Annual Conference, Canberra, December.
Pool, I., 1977, *The Maori Population of New Zealand 1769-1971,* Auckland, Auckland University Press.
Pool, I., 1988, 'Implications of Change in the Cohort/Age Structure of the New

Zealand Population', in C. Crothers and R. Bedford (eds), *The Business of Population*, Wellington, New Zealand Demographic Society.

Pool, I. and Pole, N., 1987, *The Maori Population to 2100: Demographic Change and It's Implications*, Wellington, New Zealand Demographic Society.

Population Monitoring Group, 1985, *The New Zealand Population: Trends and Their Policy Implications*, 1985, Report No. 3, Wellington.

Posner, T., 1985, 'Transcendental Meditation, Perfect Health and the Millennium', in R.K. Jones (ed.), *Sickness and Sectarianism. Exploratory Studies in Medical and Religious Sectarianism*, Aldershot, Gower.

Powell, W., 1987 'Hybrid Organisational Arrangements: New Forms or Transitional Development?', *California Management Review*, Fall: 67–87.

Powell, W. and DiMaggio, P., 1991, *The New Institutionalism in Organisational Analysis*, Chicago, Chicago University Press.

Pratt, J., 1987a, 'Dilemmas of the Alternative to Custody Concept: Implications for New Zealand Penal Policy in the Light of International Evidence and Experience', *Australian and New Zealand Journal of Criminology*, 20:148-62.

Pratt, J., 1987b, 'Taking Crime Seriously: Social Work Strategies for Law and Order Climates', *New Zealand Sociology*, 2:36-50.

Pratt, J., 1988, 'Law and Order Politics in New Zealand 1986: A Comparison with the United Kingdom 1974-9', *International Journal of the Sociology of Law*, 16:103-126.

Pratt, J. and Treacher, P., 1988, 'Law and Order and the 1987 New Zealand Election', *Australian and New Zealand Journal of Criminology*, 21:253-268.

Pringle, A., 1993, 'The Pursuit of Flexibility in the New Zealand Supermarket. The Employment Contracts Act, Continuities and Discontinuities', *New Zealand Journal of Industrial Relations (forthcoming)*.

Pringle, R., 1991, *Secretaries Talk: Sexuality, Power and Work*, London, Verso.

Przeworski, A., 1985, *Capitalism and Social Democracy*, Cambridge, Cambridge University Press.

Pulotu-Endemann, K. and Spoonley, P., 1992. 'Being Samoan', A. D. Trlin and P. Spoonley (eds), *New Zealand and International Migration. A Digest and Bibliography, No. 2*, Palmerston North, Department of Sociology, Massey University.

Purcell, K. et al., 1986, *The Changing Experience of Employment: Restructuring and Recession*, London, Macmillan.

Race Relations Conciliator, 1986, 'Investigation into Allegations of Discrimination in the Application of Immigration Laws in New Zealand', Auckland, Office of the Race Relations Conciliator.

Radford, C., 1983, 'Rural Depopulation and Resettlement', M.A. thesis, Auckland University.

Rainbow, S., 1989, 'New Zealand's Values Party: the Rise and Fall of the World's First National Green Party', in Hay, P. *et al.* (eds), *Environmental Politics in Australia and New Zealand*, Hobart, University of Tasmania.
Rainbow, S., 1993. *Green Politics,* Auckland, Oxford University Press.
Ramsay, P.D.K., Sneddon, D., Grenfell, J. and Ford, I., 1983, 'Successful and Unsuccessful Schools: A Study in Southern Auckland', *Australia and New Zealand Journal of Sociology,* 19(2):272-304.
Ratcliffe, J., Wallack, L., Fagnani, F. and Rodwin, V., 1984, 'Perspectives on Prevention: Health Promotion vs. Health Protection', J. de Kervasdoue, J. Kimberly and V. Rodwin (eds), *The End of an Illusion, The Future of Health Policy in Western Industrialized Nations,* Berkeley, University of California Press.
Redfield, R., 1947, 'The Folk Society', *American Journal of Sociology,* 52:294-308.
Reed, R., 1988, 'From Hot Metal to Cold Type Printing Technology', in E. Willis (ed.), *Technology and the Labour Process: Australasian Case Studies,* Sydney, Allen and Unwin.
Report of the Commission of Inquiry, 1971, *Housing in New Zealand,* Wellington, Government Printer.
Reskin, B.F., 1988, 'Bringing the Men Back In: Sex Differentiation and the Devaluation of Women's Work', *Gender and Society* 2(1):236-245.
Reveley, J., 1993, 'Flexibility and Labour Market Restructuring: The Waterfront Industry', in P.S. Morrison (ed.), *Labour, Employment and Work in New Zealand,* Wellington; Department of Geography.
Rex, J. and Moore, R., 1967, *Race, Community and Conflict,* London, Institute of Race Relations, OUP.
Riessman, C.K., 1983, 'Women and Medicalization: A New Perspective', *Social Policy,* 14:3-18.
Ritchie, J. and Ritchie, J., 1978, 'A Girl For You, A Boy For Me', in J. and J. Ritchie, *Growing Up in New Zealand,* Auckland, Allen and Unwin.
Ritchie, J.E., 1963, *The Making of a Maori,* Wellington, Reed.
Ritchie, J., 1992, *Becoming Bicultural,* Wellington, Huia/Daphne Brasell.
Robb, J. and Carr, M., 1969, *The City of Porirua: the Results of a Social Survey,* Wellington, Victoria University, Department of Sociology.
Robb, J.H., 1987, *The Life and Death of Official Social Research in New Zealand,* Victoria University of Wellington, Department of Sociology, Working Paper 7.
Robb, M. and Howorth, H., 1977, *New Zealand Recreation Survey: Preliminary Report,* Wellington, New Zealand Council for Recreation and Sport.
Roberts, B. *et al.,* 1985, *New Approaches to Economic Life: Economic Restructuring, Unemployment and the Social Division of Labour,* Manchester, Manchester University Press.
Roberts, K., 1978, *Contemporary Society and the Growth of Leisure,* London, Longman.

Roberts, K., 1981, 'Culture, Leisure, Society – the Pluralist Scenario', in T. Bennett et al. (eds), *Culture, Ideology and Social Process,* Milton Keynes, Open University Press.

Roche, M. and Le Heron, R., 1988, *Economic Structural Changes: Their Implications for Planning and Research,* Wellington, SSRFC.

Rochford, M.W. and Robb, M.J., 1981, *People in the Social Services: A New Zealand Survey,* Wellington, New Zealand Social Work Training Council.

Rodgers, R.H., 1973, *Family Interaction and Transaction: The Developmental Approach,* Englewood Cliffs, NJ, Prentice Hall.

Roethlisberger, F.J. and Dickson, W.J., 1939, *Management and the Worker,* Cambridge, Mass., Harvard University Press.

Rojek, C., 1985, *Capitalism and Leisure Theory,* London, Tavistock.

Roper, B., 1991, 'From the Welfare State to the Free Market: Explaining the Transition. Part I: The Existing Accounts', *New Zealand Sociology* 6(1): 38-63.

Roper, B., 1992, 'Business Political Activism and the Emergence of the New Right in New Zealand, 1975 to 1987', *Political Science* 44(2).

Rose, M., 1975, *Industrial Behaviour,* London, Allen Lane.

Rosemergy, M. and Meade, A., 1986, 'Family Networks: Who Cares for the Caregiver While the Caregiver's Caregiving?', *SET: Research Information for Teachers* No 2 (item 2).

Rosenberg, C.E., 1987, *The Care of Strangers: The Rise of America's Hospital System,* New York, Basic Books.

Rosenberg, W., 1993, *New Zealand Can be Different and Better,* London, Routledge.

Roy, D.F., 1954, 'Efficiency and the 'Fix': Informal Intergroup Relations in a Piecework Machine Shop', *American Journal of Sociology,* 60:259-266.

Roy, D.F., 1960, 'Banana Time, Job Satisfaction and Informal Interaction', *Human Organisation,* 18(4):158-168.

Royal Commission on Social Policy, 1988, *The April Report,* Volumes I, II, III(1), III(2), IV, Wellington, Royal Commission on Social Policy.

Rubery, J., 1978, 'Structured Labour Markets, Worker Organisation and Low Pay', *Cambridge Journal of Economics* 2:17-36.

Rubington, E. and Weinberg, M. (eds), 1973, *Deviance: The Interactionist Perspective,* New York, Macmillan.

Ryan, W., 1972, *Blaming the Victim,* New York, Random House.

Sabel, C., 1982, *Work and Politics,* Cambridge, Cambridge University Press.

Sachs, C., 1983, *The Invisible Farmers,* Totowa, Rowman and Allanheld.

Sainsbury, D., 1987, 'Class Voting and Left Voting in Scandinavia', *European Journal of Political Research,* 15.

Salaman, G., 1987, *Working,* London, Tavistock.

Saunders, P., 1981, *Social Theory and the Urban Question,* London, Hutchinson.

Saunders, P., 1984, 'Beyond Housing Classes', *International Journal of Urban and Regional Research,* 8:202-222.

Saunders, P., 1986, *Social Theory and the Urban Question*, (Second Edition), London, Hutchinson.
Saville-Smith, K., 1987, 'Women and the State', in S. Cox (ed.), *Public and Private Worlds: Women in Contemporary New Zealand*, Wellington, Allen and Unwin and Port Nicholson Press.
Scarbrough, E., 1987, 'The British Electorate Twenty Years On: Electoral Change and Election Surveys', *British Journal of Political Science*, 17.
Sceates, J., 1981, 'Family Formation in New Zealand: An Analysis of the Timing and Spacing of Pregnancies', *New Zealand Population Review*, 7(3):29-47.
Schmalenbach, H., 1961, 'The Sociological Category of Communion', in T. Parsons *et al.* (eds), *Theories of Society*, Volume 1, Glencoe, Free Press.
Schmalenbach, H., 1961, 'The Sociological Category of Communion', in T. Parsons *et al.* (eds), *Theories of Society*, Vol.1, Glencoe, Free Press.
Scott C., Fougere, G. and Marwick, J., 1986, *Choices for Health Care*, Wellington, Government Printer.
Select Committee on Women's Rights, 1975, *The Role of Women in New Zealand Society*, New Zealand, Government Printer.
Sellin, T. and Wolfgang, M., 1969, 'Measuring Delinquency', in T. Sellin and M. Wolfgang (eds), *Delinquency: Selected Studies*, New York, Wiley.
Seton, J., 1983, 'We're Taking This Car to Invercargill or The Male Must Get Through', *Alternative Cinema*, Summer 1983-84:11-12.
Shaffer, R.J., 1973, 'Woodville: Genesis of a Bush Frontier Community', M.A. thesis, Massey University.
Shaiken, H., 1984, *Work Transformed: Automation and Labor in the Computer Age*, New York, Holt, Rinehart and Winston.
Shapcott, D., 1988, *The Face of the Rapist: Why Men Rape – The Myths Exposed*, Auckland, Penguin Books.
Sharp, R. and Broomhill, R., 1988, *Short Changed: Women and Economic Policies*, Sydney, Allen and Unwin.
Shirley, I., 1979, *Planning for Community*, Palmerston North, Dunmore Press.
Shirley, I., 1981, 'Social Indicators and Social Planning', Welfare Administrators Conference, Palmerston North, Massey University, 19 February.
Shirley, I. (ed.), 1982, *Development Tracks*, Palmerston North, Dunmore Press.
Shirley, I., 1990, 'New Zealand: The Advance of the New Right', in I. Taylor (ed.), *The Social Effects of Free Market Policies*, England, Wheatsheaf and Harvester Press.
Shirley, I. and Tennant, M., 1990, *The Social Laboratory*, Wellington, Allen and Unwin.
Shuker, R., 1987, *The One Best System*, Palmerston North, Dunmore Press.
Siddiqui, H., 1987, 'Social Policy in the Third World', an unpublished paper, Department of Social Policy and Social Work, Massey University.

Siegfried, A., 1982, *Democracy in New Zealand*, Wellington, Victoria University Press.
Sim, J., 1982, 'Scarman: The Police Counter Attack, *Socialist Register*:57-77.
Simkin, C.G.F. (ed.), 1954, *Statistics of New Zealand, 1840-1852*, Wellington, University of New Zealand.
Simon, R., 1982, *Gramsci's Political Thought: an Introduction*, London, Lawrence and Wishart.
Simpson, T., 1983, *A Vision Betrayed: The Decline of Democracy in New Zealand*, Auckland, Hodder and Stoughton.
Sinclair, K., 1969, *A History of New Zealand*, Harmondsworth, Middlesex., Penguin Books.
Sinclair, K., 1980, *A History of New Zealand*, (Second Edition), London, A. Lane.
Sinclair, K., 1986, *A Destiny Apart. New Zealand's Search for National Identity*, Wellington, Allen and Unwin.
Sissons, J., 1989, 'Ethnic Politics in New Zealand', *Sites*, 18:3-4.
Smith, A., 1776, *Inquiry into the Nature and Causes of the Wealth of Nations*, Books I and II, reprinted in 1937, London, Dent Dutton.
Smith, A.B. and Swain, D.A., 1988, *Childcare in New Zealand: People, Programmes, Politics*, Wellington, Allen and Unwin.
Smith, B., 1981a, 'Forestry and Rural Social Change', *Town Planning Quarterly*, 63:27-29.
Smith, B., 1981b, 'Rural Change and Forestry', *People and Planning*, 20:10-13.
Smith, D., 1987, *The Everyday World As Problematic: A Feminist Sociology*, Boston, Northeastern University Press.
Smith, D., 1988, *The Chicago School: A Liberal Critique of Capitalism*, London, Macmillan.
Smith, M.P., 1980, *The City and Social Theory*, Oxford, Basil Blackwell.
Smith, M.P. (ed.), 1989, *Pacific Rim Cities in the World Economy*, Volume 2, New Jersey, Transactions.
Smith, M.P and Feagin, J.R. (eds), 1987, *The Capitalist City: Global Restructuring and Community Politics*, Oxford, Basil Blackwell.
Smith, P.M., 1986, *Maternity in Dispute, New Zealand 1920-1939*, Wellington, Government Printer.
Social Indicators Survey, 1984, *Report on the Social Indicators Survey 1980-81*, Wellington, Department of Statistics.
Society for Research on Women, 1984, *The Right Time: A Study of Women Expecting their First Child after the Age of Thirty*, Wellington, SROW.
Solomos, J., 1989, *Race and Racism in Contemporary Britain*, London, Macmillan.
Somerset, H.C.D., 1938 (1974), *Littledene: a New Zealand Rural Community*, Wellington, New Zealand Council for Educational Research.
Spoonley, P. *et al.* (eds), 1982, *New Zealand: Sociological Perspectives*, Palmerston North, Dunmore Press.

Spoonley, P., 1982, 'Race Relations', in P. Spoonley, D. Pearson and I. Shirley (eds), *New Zealand: Sociological Perspectives*, Palmerston North, Dunmore Press.

Spoonley, P., 1987, *The Politics of Nostalgia. Racism and the Extreme Right in New Zealand*, Palmerston North, Dunmore Press.

Spoonley, P., 1988, 'Conflict, Co-option and Contradiction. The State's Experiments with Biculturalism in New Zealand', Paper for Sociological Association of Australia and New Zealand Annual Conference, Canberra, A.N.U.

Spoonley, P., 1988 (1993), *Racism and Ethnicity*, Auckland, Oxford University Press.

Spoonley, P. and Hirsh, W. (eds), 1990, *Between the Lines. Racism and the New Zealand Media*, Auckland, Heinemann Reed.

Stacey, M., 1969, 'The Myth of Community Studies', *British Journal of Sociology*, 20:134-47.

Stacey, M., 1988, *Sociology of Health and Healing: A Textbook*, London, Unwin Hyman.

Star, L., 1989a, 'Sports Opera: Television New Zealand's Rugby World Cup and the Symbolic Annihilation of Women', *Women's Studies Conference Papers 1988*, Auckland, Women's Studies Association.

Star, L., 1989b, 'Telerugby Tele90: Tell It Rightly', *Race, Gender, Class*, 9 and 10.

Star, L., 1989c, 'White Man's Faith', Paper presented at the 1989 Women's Studies Association Conference, Christchurch, August 1989.

Stark, R. and Bainbridge, W.S., 1985, *The Future of Religion*, Berkeley, University of California Press.

Starr, P., 1982, *The Social Transformation of American Medicine*, New York, Basic Books.

Stebbins, R., (no date), 'Methodological Notes on the Study of Serious Leisure', Calgary, unpublished.

Stein, M.R., 1960, *The Eclipse of Community*, Princeton, Princeton University Press.

Stokes, E., 1983, *The Impact of Horticultural Expansion in the Tauranga District*, Wellington, Ministry of Works and Development Town and Country Planning Division, Technical Report 14.

Stone, R.C., 1973, *Makers of Fortune*, Auckland, Oxford University Press.

Stothart, R., 1978, 'Hope and Reality: A Consideration of Government Involvement in the Development of Recreation', *Report of Proceedings of International Conference on the History of Sport and Recreation in the Pacific Region*, School of Physical Education, University of Otago.

Stothart, R., 1980, *Recreation Reconsidered Into the Eighties*, Auckland, Auckland Regional Authority and N.Z. Council for Recreation and Sport.

Strauss, A., 1978, *Negotiations*, San Fransisco, Josey Bass.

Streeck, W., 1992 *Social Institutions and Economic Performance*: Studies of *Industrial Relations in Advanced Industrial Capitalist Economies*, London, Sage.
Susser, M.W., Watson, W. and Hopper, K., 1985, *Sociology in Medicine,* (Third Edition), London, Oxford University Press.
Sutch, W.B., 1973, 'Towards a National Design Sense', in S.D. Webb and J. Collette (eds), *New Zealand Society: Contemporary Perspectives,* Sydney, Wiley.
Sutherland, E., 1948, *White Collar Crime*, New York, Dryden.
Sutherland, E. and Cressey, D., 1966, *Principles of Criminology*, Philadelphia, J.P. Lipppincott.
Sutherland, I.L.G. (ed.), 1940, *The Maori People Today*, Wellington, Whitcombe and Tombs.
Swain, D.A., 1978, 'Alternative Families', in P.G. Koopman-Boyden (ed.), *Families in New Zealand Society*, Wellington, Methuen.
Swain, D.A., 1978, 'Parenthood', in P.G. Koopman-Boyden (ed.), *Families in New Zealand Society*, Wellington, Methuen.
Swain, D.A., 1984, 'Nit-picking and Heresy: Current Theories and Research in Family Sociology', in P.D.K. Ramsay (ed.), *Family School and Community*, Sydney, Allen and Unwin.
Swain, D.A., 1985, 'The Transition to Parenthood and a Developmental Conceptual Framework for the Analysis of Family Change', D.Phil. thesis, University of Waikato.
Swain, D.A., 1987, 'Children, Families, Law and Social Policy in Aotearoa/New Zealand', *Journal of Comparative Family Studies,* 18(2): 175-206.
Swain, M. and Swain, D.A., 1982, *Families and Child Care: Report of a Research Project on the Impact of Child Care on the Families Enrolled at a Hamilton Child Care Centre*, Hamilton, University of Waikato and Hamilton Day Care Centres Trust.
Tait, D., 1984, *New Zealand Recreation Survey: 1974-1975,* Wellington, New Zealand Council for Recreation and Sport.
Task Force on Economic and Social Planning, 1976, *New Zealand at the Turning Point,* Wellington, Government Printer.
Task Force to Review Education Administration in New Zealand [Picot Report], 1988, *Administering for Excellence,* Wellington, Government Printer.
Tauroa, H., 1985, *Report of the Advisory Committee on Youth and Law in our Multicultural Society*, Wellington, Department of Justice.
Taylor, A., 1988, *Maori Folk Art*, Auckland, Century Hutchinson.
Taylor, I., 1987, 'Law and Order, Moral Order – the Shifting Rhetorics of the Thatcher Government', *Socialist Register*.
Taylor, I., Walton, P. and Young, J., 1973, *The New Criminology,* London, Routledge and Kegan Paul.

Taylor, L., 1971, *Deviance and Society,* London, Michael Joseph.
Taylor, N. and McClintock, W., 1984, *Rapid Growth and Resource Development: Social Issues and Strategies for Coping,* Wellington, Ministry of Works and Development Town and Country Planning Directorate.
Taylor, N. and Sharp, B., 1983, *Social Impacts of Major Resource Development Projects: Concerns for Research and Planning,* Christchurch, Lincoln College Centre for Resource Management Discussion Paper.
Tennant, M., 1986, "Magdalens and Moral Imbeciles': Women's Homes in Nineteenth-Century New Zealand', *Women's Studies Int. Forum,* 9(5):491-502.
Tennant, M., 1989, *Paupers and Providers: Charitable Aid in New Zealand,* Wellington, Allen and Unwin.
Terkel, S., 1977, *Working,* Harmondsworth, Penguin.
Tesh, S.N., 1988, *Hidden Arguments,* New Brunswick, Rutgers University Press.
Thompson, E.P., 1967, 'Time, Work and Discipline, and Industrial Capitalism', *Past and Present,* 38:56-97.
Thompson, J., 1984, *Studies in the Theory of Ideology,* Cambridge, Polity Press.
Thompson, K., 1985, *Work, Employment and Unemployment: Perspectives on Work and Society,* London, Open University Press.
Thompson, K., 1986, *Beliefs and Ideology,* Chichester and London, Ellis Horwood and Tavistock Publications Limited.
Thompson, P., 1983, *The Nature of Work: An Introduction to Debates on the Labour Process,* London, Macmillan.
Thompson, R., 1969, 'Sport and Politics', in J. Forster (ed.), *Social Process in New Zealand,* Wellington, Longman Paul.
Thompson, R., 1975, *Retreat from Apartheid: New Zealand's Sporting Contacts with South Africa,* London, Oxford University Press.
Thorns, D.C., 1972, *Suburbia,* St. Albans, Paladin.
Thorns, D.C., 1981, 'The Implications of Differential Rates of Capital Gains from Owner Occupation for the Formation and Development of Housing Classes', *International Journal of Urban and Regional Research,* 2(5):205-217.
Thorns, D.C., 1988, 'Regional and Urban Change: The Restructuring of New Zealand's Traditional Social Base', *Economic Structural Changes: Their Implications For Planning and Research,* Palmerston North, SSRFC, November 16, 58-87.
Thorns, D.C., 1989, 'The New International Division of Labour and Urban Change. A New Zealand Case Study', in M. Smith (ed.), *Pacific Rim Cities in the World Economy,* New Jersey, Transactions.
Thorns, D.C., 1989b, 'The Impact of Home Ownership and Capital Gains Upon Class and Consumption Sectors', *Environment and Planning D., Space and Society.*
Thorns, D.C., 1992a, *Fragmenting Societies?,* London, Routledge.

Thorns, D.C., 1992b, 'Post-Modern Cities and Consumption. The Impact of Urban Restructuring upon Australian and New Zealand Cities', *STEPRO Working Papers*, Utrecht, University of Utrecht.

Timms, D., 1972, *The Urban Mosaic*, Cambridge, Cambridge University Press.

Tipples, R., 1987, 'Rural Work Force', in L.T. Wallace and R. Lattimore (eds), *Rural New Zealand: What Next?* Christchurch, Lincoln College Agribusiness and Economics Research Unit, Discussion Paper 109.

Titmuss, R., 1974, *Social Policy: An Introduction*, London, George Allen and Unwin.

Toennies, F., 1887 (1955), *Community and Association*, London, Routledge and Kegan Paul.

Touraine, A., 1974, *The Post Industrial Society*, New York, Random House.

Townsend, P., 1979, *Poverty in the United Kingdom*, London, Penguin.

Toynbee, C., 1979, 'Class and Social Structure in Nineteenth-Century New Zealand', *New Zealand Journal of History*, 13(1):65-80.

Treasury, 1987, *Government Management*, Volume 1, Wellington, Government Printer.

Treasury, 1987, *Government Management: Brief to the Incoming Government, 1987*, Volume II, (Education Issues), Wellington, Treasury.

Trlin, A., 1977, 'State Shelter and Welfare in Suburbia', in A. Trlin (ed.), *Social Welfare in New Zealand*, Wellington, Methuen.

Trlin, A.D. and Ruzicka, L.T., 1977, 'Non-Marital Pregnancies and Ex-Nuptial Births in New Zealand', *Journal of Biosocial Science*, 9(2):163-74.

Trotter, C., 1989, 'The Big Deal', *New Zealand Listener*, September 9: 16-17,40,43.

Turkington, D.J., 1976, *Industrial Conflict: a Study of Three New Zealand Industries*, Wellington, Methuen.

Turner, B., 1987, *Medical Power and Social Knowledge*, London, Sage.

Turner, B.S., 1983, *Religion and Social Theory*, London, Heinemann.

United Nations, 1988, *Demographic Yearbook 1986*, New York, United Nations.

Upton, S., 1987, *The Withering of the State*, Auckland, Allen and Unwin.

Urry, J., 1987, 'Survey 12: Society, Space and Locality', *Environment and Planning D: Society and Space*, 5:435-44.

Van den Haag, E., 1975, *Punishing Criminals*, New York, Basic Books.

Vellekoop, C., 1969, 'Social Strata in New Zealand', in J. Forster (ed.), *Social Processes in New Zealand*, Auckland, Longman Paul, 1969.

Vowles, J., 1985, 'Business and Labour: Major Organised Interests in the Political Economy of New Zealand', in H. Gold (ed.), *New Zealand Politics in Perspective*, Auckland, Longman Paul.

Vowles, J., 1985, 'Delegates Compared: A Sociology of the National, Labour, and Social Credit Conferences 1983', *Political Science*, 37.

Vowles, J., 1987a, 'The Fourth Labour Government: Ends, Means, and For Whom', in J. Boston and M. Holland (eds), *The Fourth Labour Government*, Auckland, Oxford.

Vowles, J., 1987b, 'Social Structure and Political Attitudes: the 1984 Election in Three Auckland Marginals', *Political Science*, 39.

Vowles, J., 1988, 'What About the Workers? Class and the 1987 Election in New Zealand', Paper presented to the Australasian Political Studies Association Conference, University of New England, Armidale, New South Wales.

Vowles, J., 1989a, 'Playing Games With Electorates: New Zealand's Political Ecology in 1987', *Political Science,* 41(1): 18-34.

Vowles, J., 1989b, 'Business, Unions, and the State: Organising Economic Interests in New Zealand', in H. Gold (ed.), *New Zealand Politics in Perspective,* (Second Edition), Auckland, Longman Paul.

Vowles, J., 1989c, 'The New Labour Party: For New Times or Old Times?', *Sites,* 20.

Vowles, J., 1990a, 'Nuclear-Free New Zealand and Rogernomics: the Survival of a Labour Government', *Politics*, 24.

Vowles, J., 1990b, 'Party Strategy and Class Composition: New Zealand's Labour and National Parties', unpublished manuscript, Department of Politics, University of Waikato.

Vowles, J., 1992a 'Business, Unions, and the State: Organising Economic Interests in New Zealand', in H. Gold (ed.), *New Zealand Politics in Perspective*, Auckland, Longman Paul.

Vowles, J., 1992b 'Social Groups and Electoral Behaviour', in M. Holland, (ed.), *Electoral Behaviour in New Zealand,* Auckland, Oxford Univertsity Press.

Vowles, J., 1992c, 'Party Strategies and Class Composition: the New Zealand Labour and National Parties in 1988', *New Zealand Sociology* 7(1):36-61.

Vowles, J., 1993, 'Gender and Electoral Behaviour in New Zealand: Findings From the Present and Past', *Political Science* 45(1).

Vowles, J., 1994, 'Dealignment and Demobilisation: Nonvoting in New Zealand 1938-1990', *Australian Journal of Political Science* 29(1).

Vowles, J., and Aimer, P., 1993, *Voters' Vengeance: the 1990 Election in New Zealand and the Fate of the Fourth Labour Government,* Auckland, Auckland University Press.

Waitzkin, H., 'The Social Origins of Illness: A Neglected History', *International Journal of Health Services*, 11:77-103.

Walby, S., 1986, *Patriarchy at Work,* Cambridge, Polity Press.

Walker, J., 1988, *Louts and Legends,* Sydney, Allen and Unwin.

Walker, R., 1989, 'Balancing Scales', *New Zealand Listener*, 26 August.

Walker, R., 1989, 'The Maori People: Their Political Development', in H. Gold (ed.), *New Zealand Politics in Perspective,* (Second Edition), Auckland, Longman Paul.

Walker, R.J., 1975, 'The Politics of Voluntary Association', in I.H. Kawharu (ed.), *Conflict and Compromise,* Wellington, Reed.

Walsh, P. and Fougere, G., 1987, 'The Unintended Consequences of the Arbitration System', *New Zealand Journal of Industrial Relations* 12(3): 187-198.

Ward, L.E., 1928, *Early Wellington,* Wellington, Whitcombe and Tombs.

Watson, S. and Gibson, K. (eds), 1993, *Post Modern Cities,* Sydney, University of Sydney.

Weber, A.F., 1963, *The Growth of Cities in the Nineteenth Century,* Ithaca, New York, Cornell University Press.

Weber, M., 1921, *The City,* New York, Free Press.

Webster, A.C. and Perry, P.E., 1989, *The Religious Factor in New Zealand Society,* Palmerston North, Alpha Publications.

Webster, P., 1979, *Rua and the Maori Millennium,* Wellington, Price Milburn and Victoria University Press.

West, D. et al., 1974, *The Delinquent Way of Life,* London, Heinemann.

West, J. (ed.), 1982, *Work, Women and the Labour Market,* London, Routledge and Kegan Paul.

Whannel, G., 1983, *Blowing the Whistle: The Politics of Sport,* London, Pluto Press.

Wilensky, H., 1974, *The Welfare State and Equality: Structural and Ideological Roots of Public Expenditures,* Berkeley, University of California Press.

Wilensky, H., 1987, 'Leftism, Catholicism, and Democratic Corporatism: The Role of Political Parties in Recent Welfare State Development', P. Flora and A. Heindenheimer (eds), *The Development of Welfare States in Europe and America,* New Brunswick, Transaction Books.

Wilensky, H. and Lebeaux, C., 1965, *Industrial Society and Social Welfare,* New York, Free Press.

Wilkes, C., 1988, 'The Art of the State: The Jessop Thesis and the Case of Labour Monetarism in New Zealand', Paper given at the 'Say Yes To Public Services' Conference Papers, Wellington, New Zealand Public Service Association.

Wilkes, C. and Shirley, I. (eds), 1984, *In the Public Interest: Health, Work and Housing in New Zealand,* Auckland, Benton Ross.

Wilkes, C.D. et al., 1984, *The New Zealand Class Structure,* Palmerston North, Sociology Department, Massey University.

Wilkes, C.D., 1988, *The Art of the State,* Working Papers on the State, Volume 4, Sociology Department, Massey University.

Wilkes, C.D., (forthcoming), *Social Classes in New Zealand,* Auckland, Oxford University Press.

Williams, J., 1985, 'Redefining Institutional Racism', *Ethnic and Racial Studies*, 8(3):323-348.
Williams, R., 1973, *The Country and the City*, London, Chatto and Windus.
Williamson, B., 1982, *Class, Culture and Community*, London, Routledge and Kegan Paul.
Willis, E., 1983, *Medical Dominance, Division of Labour in Australian Health Care*, Sydney, Allen and Unwin.
Willis, E., 1986, 'RSI as a Social Process', *Community Health Studies*, 10(2):210-218.
Willis, E. (ed.), 1988, *Technology and the Labour Process: Australasian Case Studies*, Sydney, Allen and Unwin.
Willmott, P. and Young, M., 1957, *Family and Kinship in East London*, London, Routledge and Kegan Paul.
Willmott, W.E., 1985, 'Community at Tinui: Hearts and Boundaries', *New Zealand Geographer*, 41(1):15-20.
Wilson, B.R., 1973, *Magic and the Millennium*, London, Heinemann.
Wilson, E., 1983, 'Feminism and Social Policy', in M. Loney, D. Boswell and J. Clarke (eds), *Social Policy and Social Welfare*, Milton Keynes, Open University Press.
Wilson, J., 1975, *Thinking About Crime*, New York, Basic Books.
Wilson, J. and Hernstein, R., 1986, *Crime and Human Nature*, New York, Simon and Schuster.
Wilson, M., 1988, *Labour in Government*, Wellington, Allen and Unwin.
Wirth, L., 1938, 'Urbanism as a Way of Life', *American Journal of Sociology*, 44:1-24.
Wirth, L., 1964, 'Rural-Urban Differences', in A. Reiss (ed.), *Louis Wirth on Cities and Social Life*, London, University of Chicago Press.
Women's Studies Association, 1988, *Submission To The Royal Commission on Social Policy*, Wellington, Women's Studies Association.
Wood, G.A., 1975, 'Church and State in New Zealand in the 1850s', *Journal of Religious History*, 8(3):255-270.
Wood, S. (ed.), 1982, *The Degradation of Work? Skill, Deskilling and the Labour Process*, London, Hutchinson.
Woodfield, A., 1987, 'Public versus Private Provision of Social Welfare Services in New Zealand', Paper presented at The Welfare State Seminar, Wellington, New Zealand Centre for Independent Studies.
Woodward, D., Green, E. and Hebron, S., 1988, 'Research Note: The Sheffield Study of Gender and Leisure: Its Methodological Approach', *Journal of Leisure Studies*, 7:95-101.
Worsley, P., 1968, *The Trumpet Shall Sound*, London, McGibbon and Kee.

Wright, E., 1985, *Classes,* London, Verso.
Wright, E.O., 1978, *Class, Crisis and the State,* New York, Verso.
Young, J., 1973, *The Drugtakers,* London, Paladin.
Young, J. and Matthews, R. (eds), 1987, *Controlling Crime,* London, Sage.
Young, M. and Willmott, P., 1975, *The Symmetrical Family,* Harmondsworth, Penguin.
Young, M.F.D. (ed.), 1971, *Knowledge and Control: New Directions in the Sociology of Education,* London, Collier Macmillan.
Zapf, W., 1972, 'Social Indicators: Prospects for Social Accounting Systems', *Social Science Information,* 11 (3/4), The Hague, Mouton and Co.
Zimbalist, A., 1979, *Case Studies in the Labour Process,* London, Monthly Review Press.
Zodgekar, A.V., 1975, 'Maori Fertility in a Period of Transition', *Journal of Biosocial Science,* 7(3):345-353.
Zodgekar, A.V., 1980a, 'Demography of Ageing', Paper presented to the Third National Conference on Geriatric Medicine and Gerontology, Wellington.
Zodgekar, A.V., 1980b, 'The Fertility Transition in the Non-Maori Population of New Zealand', *Journal of Biosocial Science,* 12(2): 165-178.
Zodgekar, A.V., 1985, 'Demographic Characteristics of The Labour Force', in ESCAP, Population Division (eds), *Population of New Zealand,* Country Monograph Series No. 12, New York, United Nations.
Zodgekar, A.V. and McClellan, V., 1986, 'Fertility of the Babyboom Generation: The New Zealand Experience', *New Zealand Population Review,* 12(3): 205-217.
Zuboff, S., 1988, *In the Age of the Smart Machine,* Oxford, Heinemann.
Zukin, S., 1991, *Landscapes of Power. From Detroit to Disneyworld,* Berkeley, University of California Press.
Zuzanek, J., 1979, *Evaluation of the Instruments Used in Leisure Studies in Canada, 1972, 1975, 1976 and 1978,* Waterloo, University of Waterloo.

Index

A
ageing 22, 301, 302, 305, 309, 313, 314, 315

B
behavioural ecologists 42, 44
bicultural 22, 96, 173
Bourdieu, P. 162, 168, 170, 171, 172, 193, 265
Braverman, H. 238, 239, 240, 241, 242

C
Castells, M. 38, 45, 48, 49, 50, 51
Chicago School 27, 41, 42, 46, 54, 244
Chinese 85, 321
Christian Fundamentalism 293, 302
Christian religion 278
Christian Right 303, 306
citizenship 126, 127, 134, 138, 139, 142, 158
class analysis 57, 63, 68, 74, 75, 76, 77, 78, 79, 80, 240
class relations 50, 73, 76, 99, 140
class-relational model 75, 76
colonisation 55, 68, 82, 99
community 8, 9, 18, 26-38, 42, 44, 46, 59, 90, 92, 127, 144, 251, 257, 275-290
community, definition of 26

conservation 267
crimes 231
cultural capital 171, 172, 265

D
democratic socialism 133
deviance 213, 306
domestic work 75, 76, 77, 103, 104, 108, 250
Durkheim, E. 14, 41, 304, 305

E
economic liberalisation 50, 143
employment 15, 21, 22, 32, 34, 44, 50, 51, 52, 53, 54, 57, 70, 78, 94, 96, 101, 103, 104, 105, 118, 119, 120, 121, 126, 131, 134, 135, 137, 138, 139, 140, 141, 142, 143, 164, 165, 237, 238, 244, 245, 246, 247, 248, 249, 251, 266, 269, 288
Employment Contracts Act 242, 247
Engels, F. 16, 39, 40, 42, 150
ethnic 29, 35, 36, 37, 44, 50, 67, 69, 77, 79, 83, 84, 85, 88, 89, 93, 95, 98, 105, 111, 140, 146, 150, 163, 166, 170, 173, 174, 178, 199, 238, 248, 251, 253, 265, 268, 271, 288, 296, 297, 321, 322
ethnicity 7, 9, 18, 37, 45, 67, 81, 84, 88,

89, 90, 93, 105, 106, 110, 128, 147, 178, 185, 190, 191, 257, 323
ex-nuptial fertility 318, 319

F

families and family life 11, 12, 25, 31, 131, 277
feminist 17, 18, 19, 64, 99, 100, 105, 106, 107, 108, 109, 116, 118, 121, 140, 187, 199, 266, 283, 284, 285, 289
Fordism 78, 93, 141, 239, 240, 242
functionalist 24, 76

G

gender 7, 9, 18, 29, 35, 36, 50, 67, 76, 79, 83, 98, 99, 100, 101, 102, 103, 105, 106, 107, 108, 109, 111, 128, 146, 150, 155, 163, 178, 190, 191, 204, 211, 238, 243, 244, 245, 246, 247, 251, 255, 257, 263, 264, 266, 280, 282, 284
gendered culture 99
Giddens, A. 28, 266

H

health 9, 11, 46, 73, 79, 83, 87, 115, 118, 119, 124, 127, 132, 134, 135, 137, 138, 139, 143, 144, 146-160, 243, 245, 256, 257, 263, 266, 267, 288, 312, 313
health care 100, 123, 134, 146, 150, 151, 155, 156, 157, 158, 159, 313, 314
hegemony 96, 117, 119, 152, 180, 199, 200, 204, 283
household 20, 24, 71, 72, 103, 104, 183, 189, 204, 237, 249, 250, 251, 252
housework 21, 101, 104, 105

I

ideology 9, 27, 28, 29, 30, 31, 37, 95, 105, 110, 122, 124, 155, 171, 179, 188, 199, 201, 267, 271, 274, 284, 296, 306
Indians 85
Irwin, K. 106
iwi 31, 89, 90, 91, 92, 94, 96, 97, 106, 127, 194, 276

J

James, B. 109, 11, 24, 35, 78, 99, 100, 104, 105, 113, 120, 127
Jesson, B. 78, 118, 120, 121, 122, 124, 125, 292

K

Keynes, J. 119, 134

L

labour 67, 68, 86, 131, 133, 136, 141, 168, 171
labour force 21, 22, 57, 75, 320
labour, Maori 86, 87, 88, 94
labour market 96, 140, 150, 164, 240-248, 251
labour, migrant 87, 88, 93, 94, 320, 321
labour movement 134, 135, 139, 142
Labour Party 72, 73, 155, 179, 180, 183, 184, 188, 189, 190
labour process 61
labour, rural 70
labour theory of value 62
labour, women's 71, 72, 76, 77, 120, 124, 125, 127, 249-252, 317
left realism 226
leisure 9, 32, 33, 34, 144, 253, 254, 255, 256, 257, 258, 259, 260, 261, 262, 263, 264, 265, 266, 267, 268, 269, 294
liberalism 122, 133, 180
libertarian right 116, 117, 121, 122, 123, 124, 125, 126, 127
Littledene 33, 34, 35, 55, 60

M

Maori art 272-279
Maori crime 228, 229
Maori families 21, 35
Maori fertility transition 319
marriage 11, 12, 13, 21, 22, 32, 104, 108, 169, 238, 245, 250, 314, 316, 317, 318
Marx 16, 41, 46, 63, 75, 76, 222, 223, 263
Marxist 16, 18, 48, 49, 63, 76, 82, 84, 88, 116, 117, 162, 168, 223, 263, 264, 265, 266
mass media 193
Merton, R. 15, 219, 220
Metge, J. 31, 36
Middleton, S. 23, 106, 107, 108, 109, 163
midwifery 151, 153, 154
migration 36, 44, 85, 86, 88, 93, 219, 294, 299, 308, 309, 310-313, 320-323
Morgan, D.H.J. 19, 20, 100, 224
mortality 146, 147, 148, 150, 151, 152, 153, 154, 156, 311, 312, 313, 315, 323
multicultural 22, 322

N

National Party 180, 182, 184, 187, 188, 214
neo-Marxism 217, 222, 266
new criminology 222, 226
New Labour 179, 182
New Right 82, 93, 95, 96, 123, 124, 136, 142, 143, 144, 162, 163, 167, 175, 217, 224, 225
new technology 241, 243, 244, 247, 248
Novitz, R. 17, 101, 102, 104, 124

O

Old Age Pensions Act 1898 137

P

Pacific Islands 87, 88, 93, 95, 101, 105, 163, 207, 253, 320, 321
Pakeha 12, 22, 23, 24, 30, 31, 36, 69, 82, 83, 84, 85, 86, 89, 91, 95, 96, 106, 109, 171, 190, 229, 230, 253, 272, 273, 274, 276, 277, 278, 279, 280, 284, 290, 312, 320, 321
Park, R. 41, 42, 269
Parsons, Talcott 15, 169
patriarchy 140, 266
Pearson, D.G. 7, 26, 28, 29, 31, 32, 33, 44, 65, 76, 83, 84, 85, 89, 137, 294
Perry, N. 8, 9, 65, 178, 292, 300
phenomenology 14, 17, 18, 20
pluralism 92, 262, 265, 295
pluralist 116, 117, 205, 263
politics 46, 61, 76, 80, 84, 88, 89, 93, 95, 96, 106, 110, 111, 141, 144, 150, 155, 163, 177, 178, 179, 181, 187, 190, 191, 196, 210, 244, 289, 302
population 9, 21, 22, 32, 39, 41, 42, 43, 44, 48, 51, 53, 57, 58, 59, 70, 76, 84, 94, 95, 96, 105, 143, 152, 158, 165, 169, 184, 185, 186, 190, 213, 214, 216, 219, 220, 227, 231, 232, 257, 274, 294, 295, 296, 298, 299, 301, 303, 305, 306, 308-323
post-Fordism 78, 93, 94, 96, 141, 247
post-industrial 53, 54, 135
post-Modernist 50, 53
poverty 39, 74, 130, 131, 132, 133, 135, 136, 143, 218, 224, 226, 287
prejudice 83

R

racism 9, 37, 81, 82, 83, 84, 85, 88, 89, 90, 93, 95, 100, 290
radical deviancy theory 217, 221
recreation 27, 43, 46, 253, 254, 255, 256, 257, 258, 259, 260, 263, 267, 268, 269

religion 9, 27, 111, 178, 259, 264, 273, 278, 279, 287, 292-307
religious 12, 36, 37, 77, 254, 273, 292-307
restructuring 48, 49, 50, 51, 53, 54, 121, 144, 247
Ritchie, J. 30, 35, 36
Royal Commission on Social Policy 113, 129
rural 9, 26, 27, 32, 33, 34, 36, 37, 39, 44, 55-65, 68, 70, 72, 86, 87, 96, 142, 163, 171, 178, 180, 182, 184, 191, 219, 249, 250, 251, 274, 277, 320
rural sociology 9, 27, 55, 56, 59, 60, 61, 62, 63, 64

S

secularisation 292, 293, 294, 295, 300, 303, 306
Shirley, I. 7, 41, 46, 123, 124, 125, 130, 137, 138, 141, 143
social class 67, 147, 163, 166, 173, 262, 264, 265
Social Credit 181, 182
social inequality 147, 174
social organisation 26, 55, 99, 178, 194, 246
social policy 9, 12, 30, 31, 117, 130, 132, 133, 134, 135, 136, 137, 138, 139, 140, 141, 142, 144, 225, 266, 267, 287
Social Security Act 1938 137
socialist feminist 118
sociology of education 166, 168, 170, 172
sports 32, 40, 98, 100, 195, 200, 203, 208, 209, 254, 259, 260, 261, 262, 268, 269
state 154
State Owned Enterprises 116
structural-functionalism 14, 167

Swain, D.A. 11, 13, 14, 16, 19, 20, 22, 23, 24
symbolic interactionism 14, 15

T

te tangata whenua 22
Thorns, D. 39, 47, 48, 49, 50, 52, 76, 137, 142
Toennies, F. 27, 59

U

unemployment 51, 52, 87, 94, 119, 124, 133, 141, 142, 144, 180, 218, 219, 220, 223, 224, 226, 227, 228, 231, 251, 267, 288
urban 9, 12, 16, 27, 31, 34, 36, 37, 38, 39-54, 55-60, 70, 72, 73, 87, 88, 93, 95, 96, 133, 163, 171, 172, 178, 179, 180, 184, 190, 191, 214, 219, 220, 223, 228, 251, 255, 256

V

values 8, 12, 21, 27, 42, 45, 46, 47, 52, 89, 110, 122, 130, 133, 166, 169, 182, 188, 198, 203, 205, 220, 224, 233, 261, 262, 263, 264, 267, 268, 273, 276, 277, 282, 292, 300, 303, 317, 318

W

Waitangi Tribunal 91, 92, 95, 96, 116
Walker, R.J. 92, 140, 174, 274, 276
Weber, A.F. 39, 41, 46, 75, 76
welfare state 96, 119, 123, 125, 126, 127, 131, 132, 133, 134, 135, 136, 138, 141, 142, 143, 146, 156, 177, 180, 181, 224, 225
white-collar crime 220, 227, 231
Wilkes, C.D. 66, 76, 77, 78, 93, 123, 124, 125, 126, 141, 143
women's art 280, 283, 284, 285

women's sport 211, 255, 262
working class 40, 47, 54, 68, 71, 72, 73, 75, 76, 77, 79, 87, 127, 132, 133, 142, 163, 164, 169, 170, 179, 180, 189, 190, 223, 254, 255, 264, 265, 272
Wright, E. 75, 76

Z
zonal model 42